Nuclear Energy
and
Insurance

NUCLEAR ENERGY AND INSURANCE

by
James C. Dow, M.A.

LONDON
WITHERBY & CO LTD
32-36 Aylesbury Street
London EC1R 0ET

Published 1989

ISBN 0948692 58 1

Printed in Great Britain by
Witherby & Co. Ltd.
32-36 Aylesbury Street
London EC1R 0ET
Telephone: 01-251 5341
Fax: 01-251 1296

FOREWORD

The thought of writing a book on "Nuclear Energy and Insurance" would fill most people with horror and the average insurance practitioner would have difficulty in completing more than a few pages on the subject. The extent of James Dow's knowledge and his command of the English language is such that he has managed to produce an authoritative chronicle covering the entire history of nuclear energy insurance. James has been involved with his subject on a day-to-day basis almost from the beginning and not only has he personally recorded much of this history, he has from time to time been instrumental in creating it.

This book stands not only as a tribute to the working life of the author but also represents a fine textbook for the student as well as an outstanding work of reference for the insurance industry.

Murray Lawrence *Chairman of Lloyd's*

PREFACE

New areas of insurance have, historically, tended to arise from a demand for financial protection following a series of disasters like the fires which culminated in the Great Fire of London in 1666, or recognition of new dangers in our daily lives like the railway accidents of the nineteenth century or the risks to the public of growing road traffic in the twentieth century.

Atomic risks were different, perhaps unique, in precipitating an awareness in both Government circles and industry of a need for insurance before the peaceful uses of nuclear energy had developed to the stage of confronting the State and the public with the hazards of radioactivity; still less before any significant accidents had occurred; so the insurance response to nuclear energy was an anticipative prophylaxis rather than a posterior analgesic.

It did not require an atomic reactor accident to alert people to the dangers because the world had at the end of the 1939-45 War already seen the horrifying consequences of nuclear explosions which disclosed not only the destructive force of the nucleus of the atom but also the life-threatening hazards of radiation and the long-term after effects of radioactive fallout.

Indeed, it was the risk of contamination of ships from the Pacific atmospheric atomic bomb tests in the 1940's that seems first to have set insurers thinking, the risks associated with nuclear explosions being the dominant fear overshadowing the more sober appraisal of the characteristics of controlled nuclear fission that came later and which satisfied insurers, despite strong reservations, that a limited amount of cover would be a practical possibility if not a commercially-attractive proposition.

The sixth Chapter of this book traces the early, hesitant steps towards the evolution of "nuclear insurance", as it is usually called; a term of convenience rather than exactitude because it seems to suggest an entirely new branch of insurance with a status of its own like that of Marine, Life or Motor insurance.

Insurance in the field of nuclear energy is more correctly regarded as the application of some of the usual, well-established forms of cover to unusual kinds of industrial plant, materials and liabilities, characterised by the peculiar dangers of radioactivity which have no parallel among the common hazards of industry and commerce. It had, and still has, the feature that individual insurance underwriters are none too keen to look upon nuclear risks as a potential source of good business and profit — certainly not to the extent of competing with their fellow insurers for the limited amount of business obtainable.

Only by joining together in Syndicates or Pools have the members of the national insurance markets been able to make proper provision for nuclear risks; only by close international collaboration among the national Pools have the insurers of the world been able to assemble adequate capacity — though still, even after thirty years, not sufficient to provide complete coverage for a large nuclear installation.

It is the co-operation among the insurers of many often very different countries and economies that has been, in effect, the saviour of much of the commercial nuclear industry all over the western world so far as its need for insurance protection is concerned. A large part of my working life has been associated with helping to develop and sustain this international effort and it has taken me to many parts of the world in pursuit of mutual support amongst the insurers. It has involved viewing many of those very installations that are the focus of this remarkable combined operation. Countries as different as Korea and Switzerland, Brazil and Belgium, the USA and Yugoslavia, France and the Philippines are among the many where I visited nuclear installations. Some of the journeys were adventures in themselves like the helicopter flight from Quezon City in the Philippines to Napot Point on the Bataan Peninsula; 150 mph journeys on the Japanese Bullet trains en route to the beautiful and remote coastal sites of nuclear power stations in Honshu, Kyushu and Shikoku Islands — often seeing the ancient temples of Kyoto, Nara and elsewhere en route; rising at 4.30 on a frosty June morning to fly from Buenos Aires to Argentina's western province of Cordoba; and in general the interminable inter-continental flights, pausing only to put down for an hour at Anchorage, Moscow, Bangkok, Dubai, Kota Kinabalu; ... and the first visit to Beijing — or Peking as we call it in the West.

However, much of the work undertaken by the Pool officials and some of their Committee members involves meetings, working parties, attending — and sometimes speaking at — seminars, symposia and IAEA training courses in places as different as Karlsruhe and Kuala Lumpur. Everywhere one meets with first class professional work and the utmost friendliness from people of various races, cultures and ideologies, bound by the aim of finding common ground to ease the way to providing the nuclear industries of all countries with financially strong, technically sound and reliable insurance programmes for what is, by any standard of judgement, a problematic area of risk.

I should be surprised if any section of the international insurance business has achieved a stronger working relationship on such a world-wide scale. I wonder, too, whether insurers and the international, inter-Governmental bodies like the International Atomic Energy Agency and the Organisation for Economic Co-operation and Development's Nuclear Energy Agency have ever achieved a better and more harmonious modus operandi in pursuing their common aim to assure the provision of the financial security required by nuclear operators to cover their liabilities and provide compensation for the victims of any escape of radioactivity from their installations.

There are those who say that after some 30 years of living with nuclear energy insurers should treat it as "normal". This view is rarely found amongst those who actually assume the financial risk. They are bound to say to those who think they make too much fuss about hazards — "Remember TMI: remember Chernobyl". Yet, to be fair, one must also say to those who look upon nuclear energy as a disaster for mankind that the industry as a whole has had a superb safety record, although insurers must always be wary of the assertions of the protagonists of nuclear power that a serious accident is highly improbable if not virtually impossible. Every insurer knows that, however confident the predictions may be, accidents do happen and they usually result from a combination of improbable events. In judging the issue, insurers have to steer a middle path between Chernobylism and nombrilism and continue to have confidence in the sober, objective assessments undertaken on their behalf by their own engineering and other technical specialists. And yet, although a number of compensation payments have been made to former employees suffering illnesses which were or could have been caused by radiation, I have still to hear of any claims from members of the public for bodily harm or disease (as distinct from psychological damage and financial loss) due to radioactivity emitted from a nuclear site — not even in those areas, near places like Sellafield, with a reportedly high incidence of leukaemia.

Those who have understandable fears about the risks associated with nuclear energy should take comfort from the fact that most of the world's insurers are not irresponsible gamblers or ill-informed speculators. They do not consciously and consistently accept bad business. It is significant that they are willing to expose the funds of their shareholders and policyholders to the risks of controlled nuclear fission — and to do it at prices which are highly reasonable. It may not be generally realised that to insure £1,000-worth of nuclear plant or materials against loss or damage from a wide range of perils costs a competent, experienced and large-scale nuclear operator appreciably less than £5 a year.

When I was approached with a request to write this book, on the strength of my having been involved in this specialised area of the insurance business for nearly 30 years — that is almost from the beginning — I had no ambition to be an author of any kind. However, I was persuaded that there were relatively few people who could have acquired the knowledge and experience to set down the record and to explain some of the factors that go into the assessment and underwriting of nuclear risks, and into understanding the physical hazards and the legal liabilities involved. Because of the pooling system, and in spite of their involvement in the management of the Pools of the leading insurers in most countries, very few of those who participate in the risks and expose their funds to the possibility of a heavy nuclear loss can be in a position to gain very much insight into this narrow area of the insurance business. Therefore, I have sought to give not only a little of the scientific and technological background and to explain some of the features of the complex legal framework, but also to provide a glimpse of what goes on in the back rooms of those who are striving to provide reliable insurance on terms which are fair and reasonable and to give a good service to the many hundreds of insurance companies all over the world who are prepared to commit some of their resources, often to a significant degree, to the financial protection required by the nuclear industry. Much of what might be told, particularly concerning the insurances of individual electrical utilities and other concerns, cannot be because of the restraints of commercial confidentiality; and respect for the privacy of individuals deters one from disclosing even whether they have insurance cover at all.

Much of the work undertaken internationally by those who manage the Pools or provide expertise in other ways has been unrecorded, partly for those reasons. However, I feel that the tremendous practical achievements of the International Conferences, Working Parties, other group meetings and the work of individual experts should be more widely recognised. For this reason I have given some account of the joint studies that have been undertaken in several extremely important areas of nuclear insurance.

This book is essentially a retrospective review of the insurance field as it relates to nuclear energy. It is certainly not a text-book but may help newcomers to the business to understand why certain methods and procedures were adopted in the first place and the reasons for later changes. I have sought to pay tribute to the many who pioneered the first steps towards the provision of insurance cover, but I have stopped short at the contemporary scene, because it is a moving picture. Developments are still in progress; innovative practices are being evolved and tried out. The co-operation and harmonisation which has characterised this business internationally for so long will certainly continue to be practised for the common good, but new ideas emerge from time to time and must be examined and tested.

As for the future, it is difficult to make predictions other than to say that so long as insurers have to work in such a difficult field with such a very small spread of risks, nuclear insurance is not likely to become undistinguishable from normal insurance underwriting. This business does not lend itself to the kind of strategic planning, marketing and other processes of management that would be normal in the affairs of a large modern insurance company. One cannot apply, in assessing the insurance prospects on a commercial basis, the criteria available to the very broad fields of conventional insurance business.

It seems likely that nuclear hazards will continue to be well controlled and that the installations will be safely operated with a relatively low incidence of claims due to day-to-day accidents and mishaps. In spite of the constant and effective steps being taken to improve safety, however, human behaviour will continue to be unpredictable, and grave errors will occur from time to time, though perhaps at very long intervals. We must therefore expect occasional severe and extremely costly nuclear incidents, but little growth in premium income in real terms.

James C. Dow, M. A. July 1988

ACKNOWLEDGEMENTS

My grateful thanks are due to:

Mr. Geoffrey Kellett, Chairman of the British Insurance (Atomic Energy) Committee for encouraging me to make the attempt to write this book and for authorising me to use the Committee's extensive records and the other archives and technical material held by the Secretariat;

Mr. Alf Nunn, General Manager, and other Secretariat colleagues for granting me various facilities;

Dr. Tony McCabe of the National Vulcan Engineering Insurance Group, the Committee's principal Technical Specialist, for checking much of the material used in the first three Chapters and Appendix A (any remaining deficiencies are entirely my responsibility);

Mr. Robin French of the Association of British Insurers for allowing me to consult the early British Insurance Association archives deposited with the Guildhall Library in the City of London; and to his colleague Mr. Vic Went for identifying and listing those relating to atomic energy;

Mr. Peter Worsfold of the Institute of London Underwriters for reading through the section in Chapter 4 dealing with the Transport Conventions; and his colleague Mr. Bob Jones for supplying information about them;

Mr. Ron Hazell of the ABI for enabling me to consult early records of the Fire Offices' Committee covering matters relating to atomic energy;

Mrs. Pam Bayley, the senior secretary on the staff of the BI(AE)C's Secretariat for finding time among her other duties to type out numerous tapes and manuscripts and keeping me up to the mark when production flagged; and to her colleagues, Mrs. Pauline Carter and Mrs. Audrey Whitfield who also helped with the typing.

Miss Natasha Podro, without whose patient help there might have been no index.

The author and publisher would like to thank the United Kingdom Atomic Energy Authority for allowing illustrations to be reproduced in this book.

The opinions expressed in this book are entirely my own and do not necessarily represent the views of the British Insurance (Atomic Energy) Committee or any other body of Insurers. J.C.D.

CONTENTS

I

Some Science and Technology

CHAPTER I

THE NATURE OF NUCLEAR ENERGY

Since at least the time of the ancient Greek philosophers the nature of matter has been a source of curiosity and theory. It was Empedocles who in the 5th Century BC believed that everything was composed of one or more of 4 elements, these being earth, fire, air and water. The nature of matter and the behaviour of substances like amber (which attracted feathers when rubbed) fascinated and troubled thinkers and scientists from time to time throughout the centuries, but did not perhaps achieve any truly scientific progress until the 18th Century when chemists began to identify different substances and to distinguish the simple elements, which could not be decomposed chemically, from the compounds which could. This led to methods of measuring and weighing chemical compounds and to the pursuit of the ancient hypothesis that matter is made up from atoms (a word derived from the Greek "atomos", meaning indivisible). The nature of "electricity" (from the Greek word for amber), first so-called in Elizabethan times, was also investigated in the 18th Century — notably by Benjamin Franklin.

Atoms and Electrons

In 1803, the English Chemist John Dalton presented a paper to a learned Society explaining his ideas about atomic theory in which he introduced the concept of atoms having a weight, and that they were the extremely small particles from which matter was made up. His theory was that every chemical element is made up of a particular type of atom and that the weight of that atom determines the weight of the element in which it is comprised.

As for the nature of the atom itself it was considered that this must be made up of smaller electrically-charged particles.

Later scientific work, by Faraday for example in 1833, led to the concept of atoms being inside negatively-charged particles which, much later (in 1874) was further explored by G.J. Stoney, the Irish physicist, in a paper presented to a meeting of the British Association in Belfast. In 1891 he coined the term "electron" in a paper given in Dublin to a meeting of the Royal Society.

Experiments were performed involving passing electrons through

1

a rarified gas in a tube attached to a source of electric current. When the current flowed between the anode (positive pole) and cathode (negative pole), with the two poles properly lined-up, a small fluorescent patch appeared. The phenomenon giving rise to this became known as "cathode rays". The nature of these rays was the subject of much observation and experiment. Sir William Crookes, in 1879, suspected that they were negatively charged particles. J.J. Thomson was able to confirm this in 1897. This dispelled any doubts as to the existence of such particles (i.e. electrons) inside atoms, as originally conceived by Faraday.

Further experiments were carried out to try to determine the weight of an electron and the value of its negative electric charge, and these led to the discovery that the electron had a mass which was 1,800 times less than that of hydrogen which itself is the lightest-known atom.

It was discovered that electrons could also be produced by heating metal or irradiating it with ultra-violet light and that they were emitted spontaneously by radioactive substances and the cosmic radiation from the sun and stars.

This extremely simple outline of the steps on the way to the scientific discovery and evaluation of the energy that comes from the atom conceals an immense amount of theoretical and experimental work. This is well-documented in many studies of the history of science and scientific manuals but it is not the purpose of this chapter to attempt to do more than to sketch in the scientific background to the release of power from the atom.

Further, highly-important studies took place. For example, in 1895, the German scientist, Roentgen, discovered X-rays in the course of experiments with fluorescent substances. These enabled him to demonstrate, with the use of photographic plates, that cathode rays could penetrate most materials but were stopped by others and would produce photographic images of the interior. This even worked with the bones in the hand.

In 1896, as a result of experiments on the emission of X-rays by phosphorescent substances, the French physicist Henri Becquerel decided to investigate the behaviour of uranium salts, when sheets made up of these were brought into contact with photographic plates. These experiments showed that even when concealed from the light a cross-shaped piece of copper placed between one of the sheets of uranium salts and the photographic plate produced a clear impression of the cross.

This phenomenon was further investigated as the subject for a thesis by Marie Curie and her husband who discovered as a result of working with certain uranium minerals or pitchblendes, that they

2

had a radioactive power greater than that of uranium. In 1898 they separated out a new radioactive substance which they called polonium, and shortly afterwards another element — radium — which was several million times more radioactive than uranium itself. These studies led other scientists to discover yet more radioactive substances, totalling 9 altogether, at this time.

Alpha, Beta and Gamma Radiation

During this period a great deal of experimental activity was going on, notably at Cambridge University where, in particular, the young New Zealander, Ernest Rutherford carried out some extremely important investigations into the nature of radioactivity in the Cavendish Laboratory under its Director, J.J. Thomson. He discovered that radioactive substances emit different kinds of rays by observing the way in which such radiation was absorbed by different materials or different thicknesses of the same material. Using aluminium plates he found that one type of radiation was absorbed by a thickness of only 0.01 mm, whereas other types of radiation could pass through this thickness. On the other hand, some of the rays could not go through a thickness greater than about 1 mm. There was a third, much more penetrative, type of radiation which required a thickness of about 10 cm to absorb it, a discovery with which the French scientist, Paul Villard, is usually credited. The three types of ray are distinguished by their penetrative power and are called, respectively, Alpha, Beta and Gamma. It was found that they could also be distinguished by differences of behaviour in an electric field, and by this means Rutherford discovered that those with the smallest penetrative power (Alpha rays) were positively charged, and the Beta rays were negatively charged. The Gamma rays were not affected because they did not carry an electric charge. This meant that Gamma radiation was similar to light and to X-rays because it was electrically neutral, a fact recognised in 1900 by Villard whose experiments showed that it was undeflected in a magnetic field. The previous year, Becquerel and others were able to demonstrate that Beta rays were in fact extremely fast electrons emitted from radioactive substances.

Alpha rays proved to be rather more difficult to understand, and Rutherford (who by now was working at McGill University in Canada) did not complete his research until 1909 after conducting many experiments with various other physicists. Apart from the low penetrative power of Alpha particles, it was found by using a very simple apparatus involving radon in a vacuum in a thin glass tube that they were very much heavier than Beta particles and carried a

3

positive charge. This produced helium in another tube which was interpreted as meaning that in the course of being emitted and passing through the glass of the thin tube into the thick one they lost their positive charge by acquiring electrons, thus demonstrating that each of them was originally an atom of helium which had lost electrons.

The Nucleus of the Atom

This enabled Rutherford to find a means of using Alpha particles as "projectiles" to be fired at atoms which deflected them. This led to the discovery that atoms consist almost entirely of empty space and are not, as previously thought, solid. Thus was formed the concept of the atom consisting of an extremely small but relatively extremely heavy nucleus containing practically the whole of the mass of the atom and carrying a positive electric charge. The nucleus is surrounded by electrons which protect it against everything from outside except very high energy particles. Since the atom is electrically neutral the electrons are negative. This means that in order to maintain the neutrality of the atom as a whole, the greater the electrical charge of the nucleus the greater must be the number of negative electrons revolving round it, rather like the planets round the sun.

Further discoveries arose from the fact that in some circumstances an atom may lose one or other of its electrons and therefore become positively charged because the previous balance is destroyed. However, an electron cannot be drawn away from its atom unless it is overcome by some external force in the form of radiation or collision with a very fast particle. Indeed, if the energy from these sources is high enough it could remove even the whole of the electrons which form the "satellites" of the nucleus. Conversely, an atom could acquire additional electrons causing it to become negatively charged. Atoms which are altered by these means are known as positive or negative "ions" and the phenomenon is known as ionisation.

Apart from continuing to work with uranium salts, Rutherford also investigated another radioactive substance, thorium, which an American colleague of his at McGill University, R.B. Owens, had been working on for some years. The object of the experiment was to discover the ions produced by thorium. These were collected in a special device, and it was noted at the end of the experiment that the walls of the collector continued to give out ionising radiation which emanated from something on the surface although it died away, in fact losing half of its power every minute.

4

Radioisotopes

All this led to a great deal of new research and discovery in the early years of the present century and one aspect of this should be mentioned as a matter of interest in relation to the development of nuclear energy as a source of power and for industrial purposes. This concerns radioisotopes. When chemical methods were used to ascertain the properties of elements formed when various radioactive atoms disintegrated, it was found that the properties of two elements in certain cases were so close that if they were mixed they could not be chemically separated. This meant that the elements must have different atomic weights. Such almost identical elements were called isotopes because they occupied the "same place" — the approximate meaning of the original Greek words "iso topos". Further experiments using mass spectrography disclosed the fact that most chemical elements are really a mixture of isotopes. The number of distinct natural chemical elements is 92. Over 300 stable isotopes of the elements are known and, by 1965 more than 1100 unstable (radioactive) isotopes had been identified.

Transformation of Elements

Many new radioactive substances were found, some of which lost their radioactivity within a very short time, and were thus regarded as unstable, whereas others did not seem to vary at all, although Rutherford and the English chemist, Frederick Soddy, explained that radioactive elements must all be undergoing change, or as they came to call it, transformation or a succession of transformations characterised by the emission of an Alpha or a Beta particle. If an Alpha particle, i.e. a helium nucleus with an atomic weight of 4, were to be emitted, the weight of the atom would be reduced by 4 units. The emission of a Beta particle had hardly any effect owing to the exceedingly small mass of an electron compared with even the lightest atom, i.e. that of hydrogen. The nucleus of hydrogen, with a charge of + 1, being the lightest, was called a "proton" (Greek for "first"). The emission of an Alpha particle also changed the electrical charge because it has a positive charge of 2, thus reducing the charge of the nucleus by 2 units. Taking the case of the disintegration of radium, the atoms of which are not all stable, it meant that on the basis of this theory the loss of a single Alpha particle would mean a reduction in atomic weight from 226 to 222. In fact, an atom of radium is transformed into an atom of radon gas (atomic weight 222) which, by the same process, is further transformed into an element with an atomic weight of 218 (Polonium 218) formerly known as radium A.

The Curies found that the disintegration of radium salts produced heat. In fact, 1 gramme produced 140 gram-calories of heat per hour. On the other hand, in order to produce the same amount of heat from, for example, radioactive potassium, one would require 40 kilogrammes and it would take a whole year. Radium was therefore significantly more powerful.

It was by now becoming quite clear that the energy of Alpha particles, and more particularly, the Beta particles, was in fact very large, and there was also some energy in Gamma particles. Many means of detecting particles were developed, including such devices as ionising chambers, bubble chambers, spark chambers, scintillation counters and, of course, photographic plates.

The structure of atomic nuclei: protons and neutrons

Hitherto, attention had been focussed on the structure of the atom but it had become clear that the nucleus of the atom must also have a structure because, particularly in the case of heavy elements, it was capable of spontaneous disintegration. Mass spectrography provided a means of investigating the make-up of nuclei, but it became necessary to find an artificial means of breaking them up rather than merely observing natural disintegrations. Various experiments were undertaken by the daughter of Marie Curie and her husband, Joliot, which presented certain difficulties of interpretation until they were repeated by the English scientist, Chadwick, in the Cavendish Laboratory in 1932. This persuaded him that there was a new radiation other than electro-magnetic radiation which imparted momentum and kinetic energy to light atoms and which must therefore be part of the structure of the atomic nucleus. As this new radiation was electrically neutral the particles in it were called neutrons. Neutrons, through not being electrically-charged, are able to cross considerable thicknesses of matter, as they are not slowed down by electrical forces. In fact, only a collision with another nucleus would slow them down.

The work on neutrons in the 1930's quickly led to the discovery by the American C.D. Anderson of a fourth elementary particle: the "positron". This is, in effect, the opposite or "anti-particle" of the electron, since it has a positive charge.

Binding energy; nuclear force

The protons and neutrons ("nucleons") which make up the nucleus of an atom are bound up together by a force which must be different from gravity because the weights are too small for this to be adequate. The energy binding an atomic nucleus has therefore to be far higher than gravity and, in fact, even in the case of the helium nucleus, has a value of 28.18 million electron volts (MeV). The higher the atomic number the higher the energy: thus Uranium 238 has an energy equal to 1782 MeV. However, there is more to it than that: if only gravity and electrostatic forces were acting on the constituents of a nucleus then for every one containing more than one proton (i.e. all except hydrogen) the repulsive electrostatic force would be such that the protons and neutrons would be dispersed and the nucleus could not exist. Therefore there is another force, which has to prevail over the electrostatic forces: this is the nuclear force. It is distinguished from gravitational and electrostatic forces by reason of its acting over very short distances.

Photons and other particles

A nucleus in an excited state emits a definite quantum or "photon", moving at the speed of light, when it passes to a lower state of energy. This interpretation of known photoelectric phenomena was proved by equations derived in 1905 by Albert Einstein. The term photon (from the Greek for "light") was apparently not generally used in this sense until it was introduced in 1928 to describe the quantum of radiation, as it had been conceived by Einstein in 1905 and reinforced in 1912 by the discoveries of K.T. Compton and others. In 1923, A.H. Compton showed by experiment that photons must be considered as corpuscular.

Einstein's theory of relativity says that mass and energy are interchangeable. Those whose physics are rusty may like to be reminded of his formula, highly relevant to nuclear energy:

$$E = M c^2$$

when

E = energy
M = mass
c = velocity of light (c^2 is 9×10^{20})

Any atomic or molecular action — chemical, electronic or nuclear — giving out more energy than is required to promote the action results in the conversion of the corresponding amount of mass into energy. In chemical reactions, the loss of mass is so small as to be virtually undetectable. The complete conversion of mass into energy would release very large amounts of energy. Such energy, as mentioned earlier, is measured in electron volts in the nuclear field.

High energy photons constitute the Gamma rays emitted by radio-active substances. The emission of Gamma rays is secondary to the emission of Alpha or Beta particles. Alpha particles exist inside the nucleus. The probability of their escaping by spontaneous emission depends upon its energy level. Theories developed by the Russian-born scientist G. Gamow showed in 1928 how such escapes may be achieved and accounted for the huge variation in the lives of radio-active materials, ranging from milliseconds to thousands of millions of years.

Beta particles — i.e. electrons — are also emitted from the nucleus of an atom and yet the nucleus contains only neutrons and protons. This peculiarity was explained by a hypothesis advanced in 1927 by the Austrian-born German mathematical physicist, W. Pauli. This suggested that when a neutron spontaneously converted into a proton and an electron it was accompanied by another particle, called a "neutrino" by the Italian-born Enrico Fermi, who elaborated the theory. This strange particle has no mass or electrical charge but it pairs with electrons although extremely difficult to detect. In 1934 Fermi constructed a theory to prove this although 20 years later, the existence of the neutrino was still hypothetical.

Artificial Radioactivity

In the meantime, experiments in the production of artificial radio-activity were being conducted by, among others, the Joliot-Curies involving the bombardment of the nuclei of various types of light elements with Alpha particles in apparatus known as the Wilson chamber. They found that the radioactive nuclei formed by this mass had a half-life which was always the same for the same nucleus and could therefore be used to identify it.

Bombardment could be carried out using not only Alpha particles, but also other material particles such as protons and electro-magnetic radiation — Gamma rays. Enrico Fermi working in Rome used neutrons for this type of experiment, finding that various nuclei sometimes disintegrated in different ways. In some cases the neutrons were slowed down and exhibited very different properties. These were called thermal neutrons and were found to be more efficient in producing radioactive elements by means of neutron capture than fast neutrons.

By 1939 it had been discovered that when a uranium nucleus is hit by a neutron it splits into 2 usually non-identical fragments, comprising two atoms. In fact it not only undergoes fission but can form new elements, known as trans-uranic elements, with different (higher) atomic numbers, such as plutonium, which do not exist naturally.

8

Fission

The natural behaviour of unstable atoms is to change into something stable. As mentioned previously, this is usually achieved by radio-active disintegration or decay but in the case of the atoms of heavy elements the process involves the nucleus splitting into nuclei of lighter elements — i.e. nuclear fission. When free neutrons produced in this way collide with the nucleus of another neutron they produce still more.

This is known as a "chain reaction" and it is the exploitation of this that has enabled man to create enormous amounts of controlled nuclear energy. The only naturally occurring material which can be used for this is Uranium 235. A specific amount of fissionable material is required to start a chain reaction: this is known as the "critical mass".

Acceleration and Fusion

The study of the fission process required the use of devices which could speed up the various elementary particles used in the bombardment of nuclei. These were known as accelerating machines or particle accelerators and they are essential tools of nuclear physics research even to this day. They may be either linear accelerators (such as the constant voltage linear accelerator used by J.W. Cockcroft and E.T.S. Walton in the 1930's in the Rutherford Laboratory at Cambridge) or similar accelerators, including the betatron, the cyclotron and the synchrotron. Although conceived earlier, some of these machines which can generate thousands of millions of electron volts were not built until the 1940's or even after the end of the 1939-45 war. Accelerators, which are devices for producing high energy particles, should not be confused with fusion devices. These function at enormously high temperatures, at which matter takes on a special gaseous form known as plasma. Because it has low density it can be contained within a magnetic field. The aim of this work is to achieve the production of energy by fusing together two light nuclei to produce a heavier one as distinct from nuclear fission. While the latter process is the basis of the production of usable power from the atom in what are known as nuclear reactors, the practical use of nuclear fusion and fusion reactors seems likely to require very many more years of research and development.

Nuclear Reactors

To be useful as a continuous source of substantial energy for industrial use, the fission chain reaction had to be controlled.

Machines or devices to achieve this were developed at the beginning of the 1940's, notably in the U.S.A. It was essential that they should be capable of producing a controlled self-sustaining chain reaction from a critical mass of fissile material (i.e. uranium) such that nuclear energy could in time become an economically practicable source of industrial power, so it had to produce usable heat. Thermal reactors require "slowed-down" neutrons in sufficient quantity to produce a chain reaction. This requires the introduction of a "moderator".

The best fissionable material was considered at the time to be Uranium 238. Water could be used as a moderator. However, the hydrogen in water would capture so many of its slow neutrons that if this form of uranium were to be used a different moderator would have to be adopted. More suitable moderators were found to be deuterium oxide ("heavy water") and carbon. Successful results were obtained in the U.S.A. using graphite. The objective was to produce a net gain of neutrons after taking into account those lost by leakage; by capture through reaction with Uranium 238 (the natural uranium isotope which makes up 99.279% of an atom of uranium); capture by the moderator or magnetics; and through capture of slow neutrons by Uranium 235 or fast neutrons by both this and Uranium 238.

To produce the most efficient results in terms of thermal power, the physicists have to get the balance right. Various factors enter into the process, including the manner in which the uranium is arranged, i.e. the geometry of the system as well as the relative proportions of uranium and moderator and the balance between the escape of neutrons and the take-up of thermal neutrons by uranium nuclei. The latter could be increased by "enriching" the uranium in the isotope 235 instead of using a larger amount of uranium.

By 1941, nuclear physicists had acquired sufficient knowledge to be able to construct a device (which was 'sub-critical' — i.e. small enough not to start a spontaneous chain reaction) for research purposes. It consisted of a lattice of uranium metal and graphite and the intention was to calculate from this device what the critical size would have to be to obtain a self-sustaining reaction. One development was the concept of reducing the prospective size for criticality by surrounding the system (or "core" as it came to be known) with a neutron reflector to minimize neutron loss. The same materials as for the moderator could be used as a reflector.

Experiments were conducted in 1941 at Columbia University in the U.S.A. The experiments demonstrated the great importance of purity in the materials used. There was insufficient uranium to build a reactor but a very pure form of uranium dioxide (UO_2) produced good results so the University of Chicago decided to construct a self-sustaining chain-reacting system, consisting of layers of graphite bricks with uranium dioxide and pieces of uranium metal — described as a "pile" — inside a graphite oblated sphere flattened on the top. As a safety measure strips of cadmium were inserted as neutron absorbers to prevent an instantaneous chain reaction occurring when the critical size was reached, as a result of spontaneous action or the influence of cosmic rays. In fact, when the new atomic pile was put together for the first time, criticality was achieved sooner than expected. The quantities required were 40 tons of uranium and 385 tons of graphite. The approach to criticality could be observed by carefully withdrawing the cadmium strips and measuring the intensity of the neutrons inside the pile with special counters. The first controlled self-sustaining chain reaction was initiated on 2nd December, 1942.

Controlled Nuclear Fission

The ability to control the approach to criticality and the chain reaction was clearly a crucial safety requirement if the experimental atomic pile was to be developed into a nuclear reactor for the production of industrial power. Failure to do so would result in so much energy being produced that the core could become excessively overheated and might break up, although in doing so it would be reduced to smaller pieces, too small to be critical. Thus, particularly if the reactor consisted of ordinary uranium and a moderator, a nuclear explosion was simply not possible. The main damage would come from radiation.

Instead of the cadmium strips of the first American pile, nuclear reactors are now controlled by movable control rods made of cadmium or another efficient neutron absorber, boron. When these are inserted into the core, they stop the reaction. Moved in or out by varying amounts, they enable the operator to start up, and to control the nuclear reaction with some precision.

The development of larger experimental reactors called for increasing attention to the problem of cooling. The first coolants considered were air and helium gas but there is no record of the latter being used in the early years. Later, for the larger experimental reactors, built in the U.S.A., water was found to be more suitable.

However, water caused problems because it corroded the uranium and a great deal of work had to be put into the development of a suitable jacket or "can" to protect the uranium used to fuel the reactor but, more importantly, to retain the fission products. This was eventually brought to a successful conclusion and more information will be given later on nuclear fuel and the fuel cycle and the development of different types of reactors leading to large power reactors for the commercial production of electricity.

Hazards of nuclear energy

Mention has been made of the very high temperatures obtainable from a chain reaction as a result of the enormous amounts of energy that can be created in an atomic pile or nuclear reactor.

This is both a virtue and a vice. Without the economical production of great heat from relatively small amounts of material, nuclear energy would have no industrial value as a source of heat. But if the reaction can lead to extremely high temperatures and levels of radioactivity effective means of controlling the reaction and of cooling the reactor are essential if the core is not to become very dangerous indeed.

Excessive temperature, "runaway" and meltdown

The first danger in the event of failure of the control system or loss of coolant is spontaneous overheating, or excessive temperature leading to a reactivity accident (what used to be called "reactor runaway") and damage to or possible melting of the uranium fuel in the core.

Reference has already been made to the importance of being able to adjust or stop the nuclear reaction by the use of control rods and of cooling the reactor core. If either or both of these fails, usually as a result of an accident or some natural external cause, but possible also as a result of bad design, mechanical or structural defect or human error, the resulting damage can be severe. Obviously the uranium is highly radioactive and therefore difficult if not impossible to approach. Parts of the core, probably the canning or cladding material round the uranium, can be reduced to rubble. But worse, the uranium itself can melt and fall to the bottom of the structure or vessel containing the core. This is known as a melt-down and if the molten mass cannot be contained or cooled down it may get out of the container and even penetrate the ground below — this being the ultimate possibility, though fortunately very remote.

This therefore is one of the special hazards associated with the exploitation of nuclear energy in nuclear reactors. Needless to say the cost of such an accident and its consequences are enormous, and may involve danger to the reactor-operators and the public, so the most stringent and far-reaching safety measures are taken to try to ensure that it will not happen, or that its effects can be reduced to tolerable levels. More will be said of controls and safety in a later Chapter.

RADIATION AND RADIOACTIVE CONTAMINATION

Nature of radiation

The common term, radiation, covers a variety of electro-magnetic waves and particles which as normally employed are harmless, indeed beneficial: the light radiated from a reading lamp and the warmth radiated from a domestic heater for example. In the context of nuclear energy, the radiation which concerns us is that which is capable of ionisation, that is, converting an atom into an ion by causing it either to gain or to lose one or more electrons thus becoming electrically charged, positively or negatively.

Ionising radiation may be caused either directly by charged particles, particularly Alpha and Beta particles; or indirectly by way of neutrons and X-rays, for example, which are not electrically charged. Its effect is to bring about chemical changes in the materials which are irradiated. It may also cause physical alterations through displacing atoms which results in a change of shape. Exposure to radiation may also cause individual flashes of light or "scintillations" in certain solids or liquids. In man and animals it may cause harmful biological changes. It can even kill.

Natural or background radioactivity and radiation

Radioactivity arising from the disintegration and transformation of the nuclei of certain atoms, and the radiation to which that gives rise, has existed since before the creation of our planet. Indeed it is universal and mankind has evolved, survived and multiplied in a radioactive environment and continues to do so. Man has been one of the most conspicuously successful of the living species. And yet, radioactivity can be shewn to be not merely harmful but lethal.

The point is that all living things, man, beast or plant, tolerate radioactivity if the level is low enough to be compatible with a healthy life. Indeed the human body is itself slightly radioactive because all living tissue contains radioactive substances. Most of the external natural radiation comes from terrestrial sources but nearly half originates in the cosmos.

(i) Cosmic rays

Cosmic rays originate mainly in deep space; some come from solar flares. They react with earth's atmosphere producing different sorts of radiation or radioactive matter. They irradiate the earth directly, though not uniformly. Places at high altitude are affected more. The North and South Poles also. If the "normal" dose of cosmic radiation is that received at sea-level, people living in

13

mountainous regions will receive more. Those who travel by sea and land receive less than those who fly at 10,000 metres. Those who fly at much greater heights, perhaps in the supersonic Concorde, receive still higher levels of cosmic radiation though for a shorter time. The period of exposure is obviously an important factor as well as the intensity of it.

(ii) Terrestrial radiation

On earth natural radioactivity is emitted from rocks bearing one of the potassium isotopes (Potassium-40) or one less familiar to the layman, Rubidium-87; also from the more familiar uranium which, as explained earlier, produces Uranium 238, thorium which produces Thorium-232 and Actinium-227 and 228. Radioactive elements, as mentioned earlier, arise from the decay of these substances which have always been in the ground. Primordial radionuclides (radioactive nuclei which have been on earth since it was formed) are also found, notably in coal.

However, by far the most important source of natural radio-activity on earth is radon, a heavier-than-air gas which has two radioisotopes, formed from the decay of Uranium-238 and Thorium-232. It seeps out of the soil in varying quantities. It gets into buildings by coming through the ground floor and from some of the construction materials, notably granite. It concentrates in unventilated or ill-vented or heavily-insulated homes and offices. As well as granite, materials made with pumice, blast furnace slag and fly ash from coal-burning, and concrete containing alum shales or calcium silicate slag (a by-product of potassium-processing) are also significantly radioactive. Radon can also be emitted from natural gas and even from water although levels in water would be very low except when the source is a deep well. However, the radon gas is released by boiling and, when ingested in cold water, it is quickly eliminated from the body. If radon enters a building, good ventilation may allow it to disperse harmlessly but a high level of insulation may lead to concentrations harmful to the lungs. Another common natural radioactive gas found in the atmosphere is argon which comes from one of the isotopes of potassium.

Since life continues to thrive and multiply in a radioactive environment, one may ask why there is so much concern about the dangers of nuclear energy. Putting it simply, it is largely a matter of degree, of relative hazards. Radioactivity can, fortunately, be easily detected and precisely measured by various devices — and even qualitatively evaluated by means of various types of measurement.

Units of radioactivity

It is very important, especially for those having to make an objective assessment of risk, such as safety experts, Government authorities and insurance underwriters, to see the hazards of nuclear energy in a proper perspective by recognising what levels and types of radiation are more or less harmful than others. Before investigating artificially-created radioactivity and the injury or damage that can be caused by the radiation and radioactive contamination arising from it, it is necessary to pause in order to consider the various measurements used to evaluate radiation and its effects.

The need for scientific precision has led the experts to develop a series of units of measurement which are, to say the least, confusing to the layman. A brief and simplified description of the units in use follows — not in any particular order of importance or logic:

curie (Ci)
— a unit of radioactivity, being the activity of 1 gram of Radium-226, corresponding to the quantity of radioactive material in which 3.7×10^{10} nuclei disintegrate per second. Named after Marie Curie discoverer of radium. (This was the more generally used unit until superseded by the Becquerel, qv)

*becquerel (Bq)
— a unit of radioactivity, equivalent to 1 disintegration of a nucleus per second (approximately 2.7×10^{-11} curie). Named after Henri Becquerel, discoverer of radioactivity.

roentgen (R)
— a unit of exposure to radiation (originally related only to X-rays and to Gamma rays) based on the capacity to cause ionisation in dry air producing 1 electrostatic unit of electricity equivalent to 2.58×10^{-4} coulomb per kilogram in air. Tissue exposed to 1 roentgen absorbs a dose of about 1 rad. (qv). Named after W.C. Roentgen, discoverer of X-rays.

rad
— a unit to measure the absorbed dose of radiation (rad = radiation absorbed dose) corresponding to 0.01 joules per kilogram of material. (See "gray")

rem
— a unit to measure the effective dose of radiation absorbed by tissue coupled with a Quality Factor, (qv) the biological changes caused by the absorbed radiation (stands for "roentgen equivalent man").
Being replaced by the sievert (qv).

*sievert (Sv)
— the unit of radiation dose equivalent which is the product of an absorbed dose in "grays" (qv) and the Quality Factor (qv) (1Sv = 100 rem). Named after a Swedish scientist.

*gray (Gy)
— the unit of absorbed radiation dose, one joule per kilogram, i.e. 100 rads. Named after the British radiologist, L.H. Gray.

(*These terms are used in what is known as the S.I. System (Système International) intended to replace the older terms such as rad, rem and roentgen).

The following are also useful:

half-life
— the time taken for the atoms in a radioactive substance to disintegrate to half their original value. The period may be measured in milliseconds to thousands of millions of years (Since the process is one of fading radioactivity which is never totally extinguished it is not possible to measure the whole life which is of course much more than 2 x half-life).

quality factor
— a measure of the differing harmful biological effects of different types of radiation. Alpha particles emitted by ingested matter have a factor of 20 compared with 10 for X-rays and neutrons, for example (c.f. linear energy transfer).

linear energy transfer (let)
— the rate at which charged particles lose energy when passing through matter (c.f. Quality Factor).

coulomb
— the quantity of electricity conveyed in one second by 1 amp.

joule
— the unit of work or energy represented by a force of 1 newton (qv) acting over a distance of 1 metre; or, 1 watt acting for 1 second.

newton
— the force producing an acceleration of 1 metre per sec. on a mass of 1 Kg. Named after Sir Isaac Newton.

Prefixes denoting scale

Tera (T)	=	$\times\ 10^{12}$
Giga (G)	=	$\times\ 10^{9}$
Mega (M)	=	$\times\ 10^{6}$
Kilo (K)	=	$\times\ 10^{3}$

pico (p)	=	$\times\ 10^{-12}$
nano (n)	=	$\times\ 10^{-9}$
micro (μ)	=	$\times\ 10^{-6}$
milli (m)	=	$\times\ 10^{-3}$

Detection and measurement

Even though all forms of radiation involve oscillations or vibrations, only visible light (at 1.75×10^{14} Herz or cycles per second) is detectable by the human senses (Should exposure to radiation cause injury and pain then obviously its consequences can then be detected by humans). The discovery of X-rays by Roentgen was facilitated by their visible effect on photographic plates. Film badges worn by workers and others are still a universal means of detecting exposure to radiation.

Mention has been made earlier of devices used to measure the rate of disintegration of atoms and to detect and count particles. These included ionising, bubble and spark chambers and scintillation counters. The ionisation chamber as an instrument for measuring Alpha and Beta particles, Gamma and X-rays and (with suitable adaptations) neutrons was in use in simple forms even just before the turn of the century. It had certain practical drawbacks and other ionisation instruments were developed enabling the proportions of the pulses produced by a single particle to be greatly amplified by the use of certain gases.

Perhaps the best known instrument is the Geiger counter or Geiger-Müller tube (first used in 1908 by Rutherford & Geiger to count Alpha particles) which is employed to determine the rate at which radiation is being received at a given point. The Geiger-counter can be made in various convenient sizes and, like similar ionisation instruments would be either to detect radiation or to measure it with a rate meter.

It is perhaps sufficient for present purposes to say that there are various other types of counters, without going into details. It is, however, important to know that instruments such as these are used to detect and measure nuclear radiation for the purpose of ensuring the health and safety of nuclear workers and the public at large by monitoring exposure to keep it within what are regarded as tolerable and safe levels and to record the dose actually received. Film badges, which are very widely used, in hospitals to nuclear power stations, have been mentioned. Those more closely engaged with installations or nuclear materials associated with high levels of radioactivity would be equipped also with a small type of electrostatic ionisation chamber, looking something like a fountain-pen, which they would carry at all times in the vicinity of, say, a reactor. These would be checked daily or weekly for any dose of radiation (mainly Gamma rays) that may be received. Detectors of this type are called dosimeters and will record the cumulative dose received over the chosen period which can then be checked against the recognised "safe" limits for exposure to ionising radiations originating from artificial sources. Of course, natural background radiation is detected and measured by similar means and the quantities and qualities thus determined provide yardsticks with which to compare man-made radioactivity.

Ionising radiation from man-made sources

To be economically and industrially useful, the radioactivity in natural sources such as uranium and thorium has, as we have seen, to be subjected to various processes to release the vast amounts of energy locked in the nucleus of the atom. These processes, using reactors, create new radioactive elements like plutonium which are far more powerful sources of energy than those occurring naturally. Because natural sources are part of man's world and are tolerated by man they are in principle safe. Probably few humans or animals, if any, acquire radiogenic diseases from their daily exposure to natural background radiation.

To enable people to work with higher radioactivity than occurs naturally it became clear at a very early stage that safety levels must be determined. The dangers were not at first perceived although the early pioneers like the Curies and Roentgen soon learned that radiation can cause injury and disease. Roentgen suffered burns to one of his hands after working with X-rays, for example. Although it was not realised in the 1890's, working with radium and uranium could induce diseases like leukaemia from which some later died. Only as recently as the 1920's was it learned that other types of cancer such as bone sarcoma could result from the ingestion of radioactivity when this was found in women workers who, while painting luminous numbers on watch dials, habitually applied the brushes to their lips to put a point on them. The paint contained radium.

The use of radium and X-rays for diagnostic and curative purposes brought undoubted medical benefits but the risks became increasingly obvious. With the means of detection and measurement available it was possible to ascertain to some extent the levels of exposure which, sooner or later, damaged human tissues, and therefore to determine the safe doses. This being an international problem, radiologists set up the 1st International Congress of Radiology in 1925. They established an organisation called the International Commission on Radiation Units and Measurements (ICU). A second Congress was held in 1928 at which the still very active and highly respected International Commission for Radiological Protection was set up (although its original name was the International X-ray and Radium Protection Committee). The work of the ICU and ICRP has enabled standard units to be introduced on an international scale and recommendations on safety levels for medical uses, for radiation workers and for the public at large to be worked out and regularly reviewed and refined in the light of experience.

Man had discovered how to produce radiation at far higher levels than occur in the natural environment and the development of reactors and other nuclear installations meant that nuclear energy could, by artificial means, be still further boosted to the enormous levels necessary for industrial use. These vastly increased energy levels were accompanied by extremely high levels of radiation from the Alpha and Beta emitters and Gamma rays. These could be contained and made biologically safe (or safer) by shielding the source with materials which could either stop or greatly reduce the escape of radiation. According to the type of particles involved, suitable shielding materials could be placed between the radioactive matter and the operators or scientists concerned. We have seen that Alpha particles travel only a short distance even in the air. They are stopped by a very thin barrier — even paper. Beta particles need a somewhat thicker shielding, but the very heavy shielding provided by lead or very thick concrete, for example, is required only in the case of Gamma-rays and neutrons. Ingested Alpha particles are, however, very dangerous inside the body.

Apart from reactor cores, radioactive materials have to be handled or worked upon in many ways. The major activity is the "fuel cycle" — covering the mining, refinement and enrichment of uranium, the manufacture of fuel, its transportation and its "combustion" in reactors, the safe storage and cooling of used or "spent" irradiated fuel elements in water (another extremely effective shield) and subsequent reprocessing for the extraction of plutonium and other useful radio elements, leading finally to the treatment and possible disposal of radioactive wastes. However, radioactive isotopes are also used in the manufacture of radioactive chemicals and neutron sources for medical, agricultural and industrial purposes. Nuclear matter is used in laboratories for research, and for teaching purposes — and in the manufacture of nuclear explosives. The levels of such radioactivity are so much higher than the natural background radiation (including radon) that if it is not properly handled, and if those handling the materials and devices involved and also the public are not shielded against the biological hazards, great physical harm and loss of life could occur.

In fact, since man started producing unnatural radioactivity, much of this has got into the atmosphere. Because some of the radio-isotopes concerned have extremely long half-lives, their effects persist long after they were first released. For example, the half-life of Uranium 235 is 700 million years, that of Thorium 232 14,000 million years and that of Plutonium 239 (as produced in reactors) 24,000 years. Radio-iodine (Iodine 131 — the most significant nuclide produced in a reactor core) — has a half-life of about 8 days. Broadly speaking, the most rapidly decaying substances (and some last only for minutes or even milliseconds) are the most potent because their activity is so high, but they also have the shortest lives. That does not mean slow-decaying radio-active substances cannot be very dangerous. Obviously they are and this why it is so vitally necessary to have a precise knowledge of the dangers, and how much radiation is "safe".

Safe levels of radioactivity

Normal sources of radioactivity such as outer space, radioactive rocks in the earth and certain gases emanating from them have been referred to. This means that mankind is surrounded by radioactivity. Measurements of these sources show that the average individual dose received is about 300 micro-Sieverts a year from cosmic rays at sea level; from sources on earth — rocks in the ground, the sea, gases in the air, radioisotopes in food and water — and building materials — 750 - 900 micro-Sieverts per annum. The amounts actually received by each person vary somewhat according to where they live and what they do, as explained earlier. Air crews, for example, would receive in addition about 40 - 50 micro-Sieverts per journey on an average 7 hour flight. The variation in terrestrial radiation is on average from 300 to 600 micro-Sieverts a year but in some places the natural dose (received by about 3% of the population) may be as much as 1000 micro-Sieverts and for another 1½%, some 1,400 micro-Sieverts. There are places where the natural background radiation is even higher — in the granite areas of Sri Lanka 30,000 - 70,000 micro-Sieverts, for example. On the beach at a holiday resort in Brazil, as much as 17,000 micro-Sieverts (17 milli-Sieverts) has been measured. Radiation in the town (Guarapari) is only about 5% - 10% of this level but still many times above the worldwide average. The source is thorium, and sources similarly rich in this element are found also in India. In one of these areas people have been found who absorb anything up to 50 times the average dose from normal terrestrial radiation. Other naturally high areas are found in Iran, France, Nigeria and Madagascar. London has about 800 micro-Sieverts and Aberdeen twice that.

These figures, which have been assessed by UNSCEAR (United Nations Scientific Committee on the Effects of Atomic Radiation), illustrate the fact that man seems to be able to tolerate a certain amount of radioactivity without coming to much harm although it is not certain whether some individuals may be unusually sensitive even to normal radiation. A well known example of this is the risk of skin cancer for those who are highly exposed to sunlight — i.e. cosmic radiation.

One of the questions that had to be faced as scientists learned more about the harmful effects of ionising radiation was the extent to which natural background radioactivity could be safely increased by releasing into the atmosphere additional amounts from man-made sources. Although radiation can damage or change many substances exposed to it (apart from making them radioactive) the first consideration has always, and properly, been the safety of radiation workers and the general public.

The international body principally concerned with establishing and publishing figures for what are regarded as safe levels is the ICRP, previously mentioned. Most countries follow their guidelines although some national Governments insist upon even lower dose rates than those advised by the ICRP — who review and if necessary revise their figures from time to time in the light of experience.

For the general public the principal risk to human tissue comes from diagnostic X-rays. It is usual to consider the extent to which X-rays may be given without a risk of genetic damage — the Genetically Significant Dose. Another source of harmful man-made radiation is the fall-out from nuclear explosions — usually for military purposes in the course of weapons-testing. This reached a peak between 1954 and 1958; and 1961 and 1962.

The debris from atmospheric tests of nuclear bombs is very widely dispersed, most of it going into the stratosphere — circling the earth, into which the radioactive particles fall slowly over a long period. Several hundred different radionuclides are involved, mostly in very small quantities or comprising rapid-decay isotopes. Three of these constitute a danger to man, Caesium-137, Zirconium-95 and

21

Strontium-90. Experts have reckoned that of the total amounts of these elements arising from all the nuclear explosions in the atmosphere only these, and Carbon-14, contribute more than 1% of the world-wide dose equivalent received by mankind. However, the effects of such radioactive fall-out will persist for very many years and the total dose equivalent commitment from such tests so far has been calculated at 30 million man-Sieverts (the amount in Sieverts times the world population). The effects will last for millions of years even if no more atmospheric testing were to be undertaken.

It is important to keep these amounts in proportion because the normal effective dose from this source is no more that 10 micro-Ssieverts on average although some parts of the world are more exposed than others.

As for exposure to other sources of man-made radioactivity, such as the nuclear fuel cycle and nuclear reactors (particularly those in power stations) two standards are employed. Nuclear operators, scientists and others who choose to work with radioactive substances are subject to close monitoring and regular health checks. Consequently it is considered appropriate for them to take higher doses (within the internationally established safe limits) than the general public. They are much less likely to have contact with radiation from such sources but, on the other hand, are not under constant scrutiny.

What actually constitutes a safe dose of radiation over a given period is a subject of endless study and debate. Broadly speaking, it is any dose below the threshold at which biological or genetic harm can be caused. For practical purposes, various levels are more or less generally agreed, although responsible independent bodies like the ICRP and, in Britain, the independent National Radiological Protection Board, assume that there is no totally safe threshold because some individuals may be exceptionally sensitive to even *very* low doses, particularly if these may be repeated over a period of years, as in the case of radiation workers. However, for these people it is, in view of the special safeguards, the level below which malignant conditions would not be induced: for adult occupational workers, 50 mSv/year; for individual members of the general public, 5 mSv/year. Compare this with the national average annual background from the cosmos and from earth of, say 1.2 mSv. Most people, particularly in the developed countries are X-rayed for various reasons: this source is estimated to be responsible for an additional dose equivalent to about 20% of natural background.

The contribution of nuclear power and associated activities is of particular interest to insurers since they are likely to be concerned in the financial compensation of members of the public on behalf of the responsible nuclear operators. Much controversy has been aroused concerning the safety of nuclear power in recent years and it is highly important for those who have to make soundly based, technically realistic and objective assessments of the risks to be aware of the facts. The principal fact in relation to the release of radioactivity in the course of normal operation of reactors is that the doses they deliver to atmosphere are extremely low. Considerably less comes from the nuclear fuel cycle than from the world's nuclear power stations. Of course, people living near any nuclear installation (which are permitted to release small amounts of low level radioactivity in liquid or gaseous form) receive more than those beyond a radius of a few kilometres.

The maximum permitted dose to the public coming from nuclear installations through all pathways (i.e. including the food-chain for example) is, as previously mentioned 5 mSv (500 m/rem) per annum, or one-tenth of that permitted to radiation workers. In the U.K., the actual average dose per person per annum from all civil nuclear installations including research establishments is less than 3 *micro*-Sieverts, i.e. a minute fraction of natural background radiation.

It should be stressed that these figures relate to radioactivity released from nuclear establishments operating safely and normally and refer to releases off site into the environment. On-site levels are higher; and the amount released in consequence of an accident, particularly if containment is breached, are obviously an entirely different matter.

The purpose of this book is to examine all aspects of non-military nuclear energy as they must concern insurers and their clients. The more profound technical elements are the province of specialists employed by the insurance industry and ancillary services and can be studied in depth in the many books and publications dealing with the chemistry and physics of nuclear energy. This opening Chapter has therefore been limited to giving an account, in broad and simplified terms, of the scientific background and the main stepping stones in the development of nuclear energy as a useable, modern and arguably safe resource, and a review of some of the hazards with which it nevertheless confronts mankind.

More specific areas of interest and concern relating to the risks and liabilities which insurers are called upon to shoulder on behalf of others and their approach to this challenge will be examined in succeeding Chapters.

Chapter II

PEACEFUL USES: RESEARCH & DEVELOPMENT

The principal object of developing nuclear energy was the provision of a new — very substantial — source of useable power for industry and other needs, primarily as a source of heat for the generation of electricity. During and since the 1939-45 War, and in the uneasy peace that folowed, considerable effort and resources were diverted to research and development leading to the production of atomic or hydrogen bombs and other weapons using nuclear explosives. While work on developing weapons of war continues in several countries it is, and always has been, paralleled by the constructive activities of those concerned with the peaceful use of nuclear energy as an alternative to the exploitation of finite sources of energy material such as fossil fuels, and the very limited though attractive applications of the winds, the tides and the rivers.

Nuclear materials and radioactive substances of all kinds are to be found in many different types of establishments. Whatever the levels of radiation emitted, such materials are subject to varying degrees of control, inspection and licensing, and more will be said about this in Chapters 4 and 5. The establishments concerned may range from a large nuclear power plant generating several thousand megawatts of heat from enriched nuclear fuel to a dentist's surgery equipped with an X-ray machine. The nuclear matter may range from the faintly radioactive tritium in the luminous dial of a telephone to lethal quantities of highly irradiated nuclear fuel extracted from inside a reactor core.

All radioactivity presents some kind of risk even though at the lowest levels the risk may be tolerable to most, if not all of us. Where there are actual or potential dangers to living creatures, the environment and to the property therein it is necessary to identify the major sources of radiation and risk by law. The installations and materials so identified may need special insurance arrangements. Consequently, it is useful in considering what types of activities and materials to focus on in this Chapter, to examine some authoritative definitions which are widely accepted internationally as well as nationally.

Definitions

As will be explained in Chapter 4, the control of nuclear energy and the safeguarding of the public interest, is the subject not only of national laws but also some highly important International Conventions, such as the 1960 Paris Convention (adopted by the Organisation for Economic Co-operation and Development) and the 1963 Vienna Convention (adopted by the International Atomic Energy Agency — one of the agencies of the United Nations Organisation). The definitions applied to the more significant civil nuclear facilities and materials, regarded particularly from the legal and insurance angles, relate to "nuclear installations", "nuclear reactors", "nuclear material", "nuclear fuel", "radioactive products or waste" and "nuclear substances". While most of the OECD countries have ratified the Paris Convention, very few signatories have formally ratified the Vienna Convention. However, many countries have special legislation relating to the control of radioactive substances and to the liabilities of nuclear operators and Governments in the field of nuclear energy. The general practice is to classify nuclear installations and materials along Paris or Vienna lines, so in most countries nuclear industry, the State and the Insurers are more or less agreed on terms.

It is interesting to consider what is generally meant by a "nuclear installation", or "reactor", for example, by examining and comparing the definition in the Conventions. (Note: "PC" = Paris Convention. "VC" = Vienna Convention.)

Installations and Reactors

"Nuclear Installation" means reactors other than those comprised in any means of transport; factories for the manufacture or processing of nuclear substances; factories for the separation of isotopes of nuclear fuel; factories for the reprocessing of irradiated nuclear fuel; facilities for the storage of nuclear substances other than storage incidental to the carriage of such substances; and such other installations in which there are nuclear fuel or radioactive products or waste as the Steering Committee of the European Nuclear Energy Agency (hereinafter referred to as the "Steering Committee") shall from time to time determine.

(PC Art. 1(a) (ii))

"Nuclear Installation" means —
  (i) any nuclear reactor other than one with which a means of sea or air transport is equipped for use as a source of power, whether for propulsion thereof or for any other purpose;

(ii) any factory using nuclear fuel for the production of nuclear material or any factory for the processing of nuclear material, including any factory for the reprocessing of irradiated nuclear fuel; and

(iii) any facility where nuclear material is stored, other than storage incidental to the carriage of such material;

provided that the Installation State may determine that several nuclear installations of one operator which are located at the same site shall be considered as a single nuclear installation.

(VC Art. I 1(j))

"Nuclear reactor" means any structure containing nuclear fuel in such an arrangement that a self-sustaining chain process of nuclear fission can occur therein without an additional source of neutrons. (VC Art. I 1(i))

The Paris Convention does not define "nuclear reactor" separately.

The relevant United Kingdom Law (Nuclear Installations Act, 1965, as amended) contains the following interpretations in Section 26:

"Nuclear Installation" means a nuclear reactor or an installation such as is mentioned in Section 1(1)(b) of this Act.

(Section 1(1)(b) refers to

"… an installation designed or adapted for —

(i) the production or use of atomic energy; or

(ii) the carrying out of any process which is preparatory or ancillary to the production or use of atomic energy and which involves or is capable of causing the emission of ionising radiations; or

(iii) the storage, processing or disposal of nuclear fuel or of bulk quantities of other radioactive matter, being matter as is produced or irradiated in the course of the production or use of nuclear fuel.")

"Nuclear reactor" means any plant (including any machinery, equipment or appliance, whether affixed to land or not) designed or adapted for the production of atomic energy by a fission process in which a controlled chain reaction can be maintained without an additional source of neutrons.

(U.K. Nuclear Installations Act 1965)

Materials

Turning to the radioactive materials used or stored in nuclear installations, in transit between them or possibly disposed of below ground or under or into the deep oceans, we find the following:

"Nuclear substances" means nuclear fuel (other than natural uranium and other than depleted uranium) and radioactive products or waste. (PC Art. 1(a)(v))

"Nuclear material" means —
(i) nuclear fuel, other than natural uranium and depleted uranium, capable of producing energy by a self-sustaining chain process of nuclear fission outside a nuclear reactor, either alone or in combination with some other material; and
(ii) radioactive products or waste. (VC Art. 1(1)(h))

"Nuclear fuel" means fissionable material in the form of uranium metal, alloy, or chemical compound (including natural uranium), plutonium metal, alloy or chemical compound, and such other fissionable material as the Steering Committee shall from time to time determine. (PC Art. 1(a)(iii))

"Nuclear fuel" means any material which is capable of producing energy by a self-sustaining chain process of nuclear fission. (VC Art. 1(1)(f))

The U.K. 1965 Act contains the following related interpretations in Section 26:

"nuclear matter" means, subject to any exceptions which may be prescribed —
(a) any fissile material in the form of uranium metal, alloy or chemical compound (including natural uranium) or of plutonium metal, alloy or chemical compound or any other fissile material which may be prescribed; and
(b) any radioactive material produced in, or made radioactive by exposure to the radiation incidental to the process of producing or utilising any such fissile material as aforesaid.

"Excepted matter" means nuclear matter consisting only of one or more of the following, that is to say —
(a) isotopes prepared for use for industrial commercial, agricultural, medical, scientific or educational purposes;
(b) natural uranium;
(c) any uranium of which Isotope 235 forms not more than 0.72%;
(d) nuclear matter of such other description, if any, in such circumstances as may be prescribed (or for the purposes of the

application of this Act to a relevant foreign operator, as may be excluded from the operation of the relevant International Agreement by the relevant foreign law).

This description under U.K. Law was later extended (in the Excepted Matters Regulations, 1978) and now covers uranium in which the mass of the fissile isotope 235 does not exceed 1% of the total uranium mass. It includes uranium recovered from spent nuclear fuel. This (unlike natural uranium) contains small amounts of material which are radioactive contaminants.

"Radioactive products or waste" means any radioactive material produced in or made radioactive by exposure to the radiation incidental to the process of producing or utilising nuclear fuel but does not include
(i) nuclear fuel, or
(ii) radioisotopes outside a nuclear installation which are used or intended to be used for any industrial, commercial, agricultural, medical or scientific purpose.
(PC Art. 1(a)(iv))

"Radioactive products or waste" means any radioactive material produced in, or any radioactive material made radioactive by exposure to the radiation incidental to, the production or utilisation of nuclear fuel, but does not include radioisotopes which have reached the final stage of fabrication so as to be useful for any scientific, medical, agricultural, commercial or industrial purpose. (VC Art. 1(1)(g))

The significance of "excepted matter" will be dealt with later. This term is not employed in either Convention, but it is of interest that in 1977 the Steering Committee of the OECD's Nuclear Energy Agency decided (being empowered to do so) that uranium with a very low specified level of radioactivity or containing no more than 1% Uranium 235 was not a "nuclear substance" within the meaning of the Paris Convention. (In consequence of this they excepted from the definition of "nuclear installation", factories or storage places concerned only with the excluded substances.)

It will be seen that there is broad agreement as to what constitutes a nuclear facility or nuclear matter. This is important not only to Governmental authorities deciding to whom they must apply the special legal régimes relating to the exploitation of civil nuclear energy, but also to those who must provide the various forms of insurance. The nature of the materials in use or in the course of carriage and the classification of the installations involved may affect the manner in which cover will be provided.

Practices vary from one country to another according to national nuclear laws and the response of the country's insurance industry. But there is a broad measure of agreement, inspired by one or other of the Conventions, as to what we are dealing with when referring to nuclear installations and nuclear or radioactive matter.

Nuclear Installations

So far as nuclear installations are concerned, for practical purposes they include:
— Research and prototype reactors
— Materials testing reactors
— Teaching and demonstration reactors
— Electricity generating stations equipped with nuclear power reactors
— Uranium processing and enrichment factories
— Fuel manufacturing plants
— Factories for reprocessing irradiated fuel elements and plutonium extraction
— Stores for new or irradiated fuel elements
— Radioactive waste treatment plants and disposal sites
— Factories for the separation of isotopes and manufacture of radiochemicals
— Nuclear laboratories
— Any other premises or sites designated "nuclear" by law or the controlling authorities (commonly called licensed sites).

Nuclear Matter

Nuclear or radioactive matter, substances or materials would normally be classified according to the category of site or premises where located. However, when elsewhere — normally in the course of carriage by land, sea, river or air — the classification for legal and insurance purposes would normally be determined according to the type and content of the nuclear matter, the level of radioactivity, and the quantity in terms of the mass of particular radioisotopes such as Uranium 235, Plutonium 239 and so on. Irradiated machinery parts and radioactive waste may also be concerned as well as radioactively contaminated clothing, footwear and equipment (from nuclear plants or radiography departments of hospitals or possibly naval submarines, for example, although reactors installed in naval ships are completely outside the scope of the present account). The substances to be taken into consideration include the following:

— Natural uranium, i.e. mainly Uranium 238, containing no more
than 1% of Uranium 235, or less (when on a licensed site)
— Thorium
— Enriched uranium
— Irradiated uranium or plutonium nuclear fuel
— Depleted uranium
— Nuclear waste from the combustion of nuclear fuel
— Other nuclear waste in the form of solids, and liquid or gaseous
effluents (if above permitted safe levels for release into the
environment)
and, if on a licensed site or in course of carriage with nuclear matter
or radiochemicals
— Any quantity of radioisotopes or radiochemicals
— X-ray equipment and sealed neutron sources used for measure-
ments, weld-testing and the like
    It will be noted that even what is, under the U.K. Law, Excepted
Matter (and is excluded by OECD/NEA from the scope of a "nuclear
substance") may nevertheless be classified as "nuclear" when it
forms part of a stock of materials including specifically nuclear
matter in use or in store at a nuclear installation so designated by law.

Nuclear Reactors

In Chapter 1 there was a reference to the very first of the nuclear
reactors (initially called atomic piles because of the way they were
constructed). These devices were the means by which the powerful
energy of the atom could be harnessed and made useful because they
provided a means of slowing neutrons down to a relatively low speed,
so that they had about the same thermal energy as the molecules
of the medium in which the neutrons were being scattered. Such
energy is "thermal" because it depends on temperature. These slowed
down neutrons are called thermal neutrons and are a significant
element in the nuclear fission process carried out in a reactor.
    Various media, called moderators, are efficient in slowing down
neutrons to speeds at which they can be captured by fissile material
so as to cause nuclear reactions. Thus a reactor operating on this
basis must always incorporate a moderator as well as a source of
neutrons and a material such as Uranium 235 the nucleus of which
is able to capture slow neutrons. The only exception is a type of
reactor known as the Fast Reactor because it is able to work with
fast neutrons and does not require a moderator. It has to be fuelled
with a material consisting of, or enriched with, Plutonium 239
capable of capturing fast neutrons.
    In the case of some moderated reactors, an extra layer of the

31

moderator or some other material may be included to increase efficiency by scattering back some of the neutrons, which might otherwise escape capture. This material is called a reflector.

Whatever their purpose, all nuclear reactors have to be shielded to protect operators and the environment from the biological hazards of ionising radiation; and, because nuclear reactors produce great heat, they must be cooled by an efficient heat transfer or removal medium which may be water, gas (including air) or liquid metal. Finally they must be capable of being controlled and, if need be, rapidly and safely shut down so that, even when not operating, any residual radioactivity inside the shielded vessel containing the core and other internal parts and equipment will be totally contained and will not heat up.

Research and Prototype reactors

It was not until such requirements were satisfactorily met that the very first nuclear reactor as briefly described in Chapter 1 could be safely put into operation at America's University of Chicago on 2nd December 1942.

The Chicago pile was handled with caution because of the known dangers. It was initially operated at the very low power of 0.5 watt, shortly to be raised to a maximum of 200 watts, because of the radiation risks to the operators (even though it was shielded) and there was no engineered cooling system, only ambient air. The primary purpose of this experimental pile was to demonstrate that a controlled chain reaction could be produced. It was dismantled early in the following year and rebuilt at another site near Chicago with certain modifications, including more shielding, enabling it to be operated at 2 kW, with occasional short burst of up to 100 kW.

The first objective of the wartime research was to apply nuclear technology to weapons. The scientists and the military needed something that would be of small size but capable of producing an enormous release of energy. This ruled out natural uranium because of the quantity required to provide enough Uranium 235 to form a critical mass. However, it was known that the exposure of the 99.3% non-fissile content of uranium — U238 — to neutrons converted it into a material — Plutonium 239 — which was fissile. Above all, a small quantity would produce a chain reaction and it did not require a moderator because it was capable of capturing fast neutrons.

Thus, reactor research in wartime and immediately post-war was focussed primarily on the best means of manufacturing plutonium for military purposes and the first of the large, regular reactors in the U.S.A. and countries like the United Kingdom were created initially for this purpose.

Although the main thrust of reactor research in the 1940's was directed towards producing artificial fissile material for weapons, accompanied by the development of a source of heat for power production, other experimental reactors were constructed for varied peaceful purposes, such as the production of radioisotopes for medical, industrial and other purposes and as a source of neutrons or Gamma rays for irradiating various materials; for the development of different forms of solid and even liquid nuclear fuel; and for teaching and demonstration purposes.

Various types of research reactors are likely to be encountered by insurers although in the 1940's and early 50's the majority of nuclear research was carried out, often in great secrecy, in centres owned or controlled by Government departments or agencies.

Because of the use of natural uranium fuel and a graphite moderator, these early research reactors tended to be large and heavy. Being air-cooled they could not be operated at very high temperatures. Nevertheless, particularly in the United States, it was desired to have a compact form of reactor which could be installed in a submarine. It was this requirement which spurred the development of reactors using water (instead of graphite) as a moderator — which doubled up as a coolant either in association with a suitable system for the circulation of cooling water or as a boiler. Fuel quantities and weights were reduced by using the more efficient enriched uranium (i.e. natural uranium which was processed to increase the U235 content by removing some of the U238).

Apart from the weight and bulk of graphite, another reason for using alternatives was the fact that it captures some of the neutrons released in a chain reaction without undergoing fission. At the relatively low operating temperatures of the first reactors, this built up energy in the graphite — a phenomenon not well understood in the early days although the American scientist E. P. Wigner predicted in 1942 that materials subjected to bombardment by high energy particles would have their structure altered to an extent that could be damaging: hence the term "radiation damage". Irradiation of graphite causes dimensional and property changes. However, experimental work on graphite-moderated reactors continued, particularly in the United Kingdom where it was carried forward to such effect that all the commercial nuclear power reactors currently operated in this country are, to this day, graphite-moderated types.

Among the more important of the research and prototype reactors, some of which have been in use since the pioneering days, are the following:

33

Graphite-moderated

Apart from the first American atomic piles, in 1947 the British Government agency, the Atomic Energy Authority, developed at their Harwell establishment (as their first research reactor) an air-cooled, graphite moderated low energy pile known from its initials as GLEEP, followed the next year by the British Experimental Pile — BEPO (nuclear physicists all over the world have a passion for acronyms).

BEPO had a larger cooling system; it could therefore run at higher power and had a higher flow of neutrons (neutron flow). It was used for experiments on the effects of radiation on various metals.

The first large-scale prototype reactors of this type, Windscale No. 1 and No. 2 Piles, were built at the U.K. Atomic Energy Authority's site at Windscale in Cumberland in 1950 for the purpose of producing plutonium for defence. Cooling was achieved by blowing through air at atmospheric pressure. (Water would have been preferred, as used in the USA, but finding sites with sufficient pure water was said at the time to be one of the reasons for ruling it out.) There was no intention then to try to make use of the heat generated to produce power although the feasibility of this had been considered as early as 1947, and some work was done by the boiler-making industry on the steam aspects of such plant.

Both Windscale Piles were shut down and permanently sealed in 1957 following a serious accident when No. 1 Pile caught fire while undergoing treatment to remove Wigner energy from the graphite moderator (so called after the E. P. Wigner mentioned earlier in this chapter as the scientist who predicted this phenomenon). More information about this accident will be given in Appendix A.

Great Britain and the USA were not alone in this early field of reactor research although little attention was paid elsewhere to natural uranium graphite-moderated designs, particularly those which were cooled by air. However, there was one at the important Belgian nuclear research centre at Mol, the BR-1 ("Belgian Reactor 1") which went into operation in 1958. This was an air-cooled, graphite-moderated, natural uranium reactor of similar character to those in France, the United Kingdom and the U.S.A.

A more advanced experimental model, the G.1 Reactor, at the French Atomic Energy Commission's famous nuclear research centre at Marcoule achieved criticality in 1956 and was successfully operated at a thermal power of up to 38 MW. In common with all reactors it produced plutonium but, more interestingly, used its heat to make steam to drive a generator rated at 5750 kW of electricity although only 2 MW(e) was produced when it operated.

Consequently the French G.1 is to be regarded as one of the first experimental prototype power-producing reactors rather than just a research reactor. At this same centre, in 1960, they started up an uncooled natural uranium graphite-moderated reactor of negligible power, called MARIUS, the main purpose of which was to undertake neutron physics experiments for graphite-moderated systems.

Similar research was in progress in Italy, another country noted for its nuclear research and the calibre of its scientists in this field since the earliest days. The National Committee for Nuclear Energy (CNEN) developed a 10 W (thermal) uncooled graphite-moderated enriched uranium reactor, the RB-1, at Montecuccolino, near Bologna, which went critical in 1962.

Hitherto, we have examined the early graphite-moderated reactors which were uncooled and led to the first large scale plutonium producing piles. Before the accident which brought this development to an end in the United Kingdom, the Atomic Energy Authority were working on a design which would use carbon dioxide gas for cooling and heat transfer. This was considered a very suitable medium for the conversion of the considerable heat produced in the reactor into steam by means of heat exchangers which would make large-scale electricity generation possible. At the same time it did not affect the capacity of this reactor to produce plutonium.

The lack of enriched uranium in the U.K. meant that natural uranium had to be used to fuel the power reactors. Therefore, the nature and efficiency of the nuclear fuel was a most important factor in the search for a commercially and economically viable large scale reactor for the electricity supply industry. It had also to be graphite-moderated because heavy water was not available.

Apart from the uranium content, the construction of the fuel rods or elements, particularly the cladding or "canning" material, was extremely important and this was also a subject of research. This led to the development of a new magnesium alloy, magnesium oxide, later called Magnox, which gave its name to the first of the British gas-graphite commercial power stations.

Much of this research was carried out at Harwell in a period of some two or three years after the start-up of the air-cooled Windscale piles in 1951. It involved constructing a reactor core in a mild steel pressure vessel, the core consisting of magnox-clad fuel rods in vertical channels in blocks of graphite. Carbon dioxide gas was blown through the fuel channels under pressure and led through shielded pipes to a heat exchanger which heated water circulating in separate tubes to make steam which could drive a turbine. This research reactor demonstrated the feasibility of producing both useful quantities of plutonium and electricity on an industrial scale. With the assistance of various industrial concerns, it led to the design by the Atomic Energy Authority of what was called the PIPPA reactor (Pressurised Pile for producing Power and Plutonium). This was the prototype for the British electricity supply industry's gas-graphite reactors (still called a "pile" in those days) which initiated the world's first industrial-scale nuclear power station.

The majority of research and prototype reactors moderated by graphite were, at this time, cooled by air or gas, or were operated at sufficiently low temperatures to be uncooled. However experimental reactors cooled by light water, heavy water and organic material were also under development, mainly in the USA, but also in various other countries including the USSR, France, Germany and Canada. They are mentioned at this point because they still incorporated graphite as a moderator and, sometimes, also as a reflector.

The first Soviet graphite moderated reactor cooled by light water was the R.P.T. (Reactor for Physical and Technical Research) which started operating in 1952 at the Atomic Energy Institute of the Moscow Academy of Sciences. Fuelled with fully enriched uranium the core was contained in a steel tank surrounded by the usual thick concrete biological shield. It had a nominal thermal power of 20 MW, its main purpose being to test the fuel elements and to irradiate various materials. As well as being classified as a graphite-moderated reactor, this could also be allocated to other recognised classifications, viz Tank Type or Light-Water Reactor (L.W.R.).

Other experimental reactors using graphite as a moderator were under development. One of the most interesting ventures was an international project jointly owned and operated by the OECD's Nuclear Energy Agency, Euratom (the European Atomic Energy Community) and UKAEA. This was located at Winfrith Heath in the county of Dorset, and consisted of a High Temperature Reactor, known as Dragon. This was fuelled with 93% enriched uranium and thorium clad in graphite, cooled by helium gas and moderated and reflected by graphite. It achieved first criticality in 1964, its nominal power being 20 MW. Its purpose was to demonstrate the principles and possibilities of high temperature facilities. The basic research for this project had been initiated by the UKAEA in 1959 using a facility called the Zero Energy Nitrogen Heated Thermal Reactor (ZENITH), fuelled with either fully enriched uranium or plutonium and heated with nitrogen. After a very successful run the Dragon Project ceased to operate in 1976, upon the lapsing of the original international Agreement to operate it.

The Hot Enriched Carbon Moderated Thermal Oscillator Reactor (HECTOR) was developed at the UKAEA's Harwell establishment.

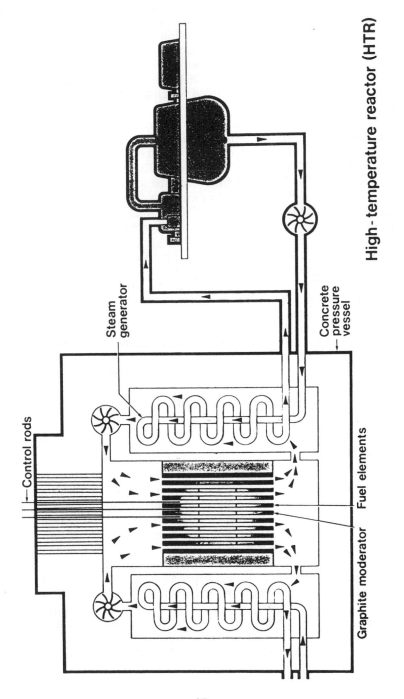

High-temperature reactor (HTR)

Steam generator

Concrete pressure vessel

Control rods

Fuel elements

Graphite moderator

Graphite served both as a moderator and reflector and the fuel was 80% enriched uranium. The outer region of the core was cooled by carbon dioxide. This gas was also used to heat the inner region. Its nominal power was 100 W (thermal). The purpose of HECTOR, which went into operation in 1963, was to test materials and reproduce the conditions associated with different designs of power reactors.

Two interesting American projects belonging to the early 1960's, both graphite-moderated, were the Oak Ridge National Laboratory's "Molten Salt Reactor Experiment" and the U.S. Atomic Energy Commission's "Ultra High Temperature Reactor Experiment" at Los Alamos. The first used fully enriched uranium cooled by salt and part of the fuel was in the core and part dissolved in liquid salts. Its purpose was to study the uses of liquid nuclear fuel. The second used graphite as a reflector as well as a moderator and was cooled by helium gas.

Graphite moderation continued to be utilised for research reactors developed in the 1960's as in, for example, Poland's Zero Energy Reactor, ANNA, at the Polish Institute for Nuclear Research; the Swiss Proteus Reactor at the Wuerenlingen Research Institute; and the nitrogen-cooled High Temperature Lattice Test Reactor at the Richland, Wash. establishment of the U.S. Atomic Energy Commission (as it was then called: now the Nuclear Regulatory Commission).

However, many more research and prototype reactors and demonstrators were designed to use water as a moderator (and reflector) and some with other materials such as sodium and beryllium.

Water-moderated

In the early days the principal attraction of light water as a moderator was its superiority over gas as a heat transfer medium which made it more suitable for the reactors with compact, high density cores required for military purposes. On the other hand, because water captures comparatively large numbers of neutrons the uranium fuel must be enriched by the isotope U235. Furthermore, the boiling point of water being only 100°, it has to be pressurised to allow reactors to operate at useful temperatures to prevent it boiling. The maximum coolant temperature in the primary circuit and the need to pressurise it are associated with arguments on obtaining the best steam cycle efficiently, i.e. the secondary steam side and the generation of electrical power. Heavy water (D_2O) shares the drawback of having to be pressurised if required for use at temperatures above its boiling point, but it is good material for neutron moderation. This is because it is very efficient at slowing down neutrons while having a very small cross-section for neutron capture. Thus it can be used with natural uranium. Like light water (H_2O) it can double up as a coolant. It has to be specially manufactured and is not very abundant. It is expensive, a consideration which not everybody regards as justifying its use in commercial reactors.

As there are more than 200 water-moderated research reactors world-wide it is not possible to describe more than a representative sample. The possession and operation of such facilities has, since the 1950's, spread to many countries, far beyond those in Europe and North America who originated the early research and development. Some 60 nations, including those in the category of developing countries, operate all types of research and testing reactors, the majority being water-moderated, this being the system adopted for a high proportion of the power reactors with which the world's nuclear electricity generating stations are equipped. It is not possible to do justice to the work of so many dedicated nuclear scientists and engineers, academic and Government research institutes without examining all the various facilities — a task which would take up a disproportionate share of this book. Therefore, it is necessary to take a few examples mainly to illustrate the different types of water moderated research reactors.

One of these is generally known as the *Swimming Pool Reactor*. The first went into operation at the Oak Ridge National Laboratory (ORNL) Tennessee in the USA in 1951 although it was used mainly for testing materials by exposing them to the radiation from the high neutron flux produced by this reactor. A similar American reactor went critical in 1952 at the National Reactor Testing Station at Arco, Idaho. The Pool-type research reactor is so called because its core, consisting usually of rods of enriched uranium, is suspended in a pool of water in a thick concrete tank which also serves as a biological shield. The core is encased in a suitable reflecting material such as beryllium or graphite, or both. The water is also an effective shield and does not become radioactive provided fission products do not leak from the core. This does not happen unless a fuel element becomes defective, a fault that would be immediately detected by safety devices.

The Americans have designed, built and operated many Swimming Pool Reactors, a number of which have been purchased by other countries. Perhaps the first to operate outside N. America was the American-designed German research reactor at Garching, near Munich, a 1 MW reactor fuelled by 20% enriched uranium which went critical in 1957 and reached its full power 2 years later. Shortly after, a similar facility designed by the same American firm, AMF Atomics, started operating at the Israel Atomic Energy Commission's Centre at Rehovath in 1959; as did another at the Italian Nuclear Plant Research Company (SORIN) at Saluggia, near Milan in 1960. AMF also sold such a reactor to the Greek Atomic Energy Commission who installed it in a research centre near Athens which, according to the London "Financial Times" (20th February, 1958), was to be built at an estimated cost of US$1.25M, with a contribution of US$350,000 from the U.S. Atomic Energy Commission. This AMF reactor went critical in 1961 as did a similar one owned and operated near Lisbon by the Portuguese Junta de Energia Nuclear (JEN). Around this period the University of Teheran in Iran installed an AMF Swimming Pool Reactor.

Various other manufacturers and designers were concerned in this field. Even as early as 1957 a reactor designed by Canadair as a Pool test reactor was operated by Atomic Energy of Canada Ltd at Chalk River, Ontario; Indatom of France built one called Melusine, operated at Grenoble by the French A.E.C. and another, Triton, which was constructed at the Fontenay-aux-Roses Centre; the Spanish J.E.N. operated a 3 MW Swimming Pool Reactor (JEN-1) built by General Electric Co. of America and themselves, near Madrid; the same G.E. model was installed and operated in Venezuela by the Instituto Venezolana de Investigaciones Cientificas; and at Quezon City in the Philippines by the Philippine Atomic Energy Commission in 1961. The British firm, Associated Electrical Industries (now part of G.E.C.) put a British made Swimming Pool Reactor (Merlin) into operation at Aldermaston in 1960. The USSR also had an important programme of building and operating their series of IRT research reactors of this type, from 1957 onwards. Over the following years, other countries such as Turkey, Brazil, Colombia, Bulgaria, Thailand, Poland and Japan started working with Swimming Pool reactors. Still more were constructed in the U.S.A. Many of these reactors are in operation to this day.

A very similar design of water-moderated research reactors, known as the *Tank Type*, was developed alongside the Swimming Pool. The first were, not surprisingly, constructed in the U.S.A. for materials testing. They differed a little from Swimming Pools in that the fuel core, consisting of flat plates of enriched uranium, was suspended in water contained in a steel tank surrounded by a thick concrete biological shield. The water provided cooling by means of forced convection. The first of these operated at low power as early as 1950 at the O.R.N.L. gradually building up to 3 MW (thermal) by 1953. It used beryllium as a reflector. USAEC also owned a 40 MW version which was operated at Idaho Falls in 1953 by the Phillips Petroleum

Company. It incorporated numerous research facilities permitting the introduction of materials for testing contained in what were called "rabbits" which could be passed pneumatically or hydraulically through shielded penetrations into the reactor, to be exposed to radiation. The same company operated the SPERT-2 (Special Power Excursion Reactor) which could also be moderated by heavy water, but it is not certain whether it ever was.

A Tank type was also operating at 3 MW in 1957 at the Atomic Energy Institute of the Moscow Academy of Sciences. This was the WWR-2 Research Reactor, based upon the WWR-C, which went critical as early as 1954. Similar reactors were started up in the late 1950's in Romania, Czechoslovakia, Poland, Hungary and Egypt.

In 1959, the Swedish A.B. Atomenergi commissioned their R-2 Tank type at Studsvik; at the Mol centre in Belgium CEN built their 50 MW BR-2 (designed in association with the Nuclear Development Corporation of America). The Netherlands also were to enter this particular field with the High Flux Reactor, designed and built by the American firm Allis-Chalmers, which went critical at the Petten Reactor Centre in 1961. Westinghouse, world-famous for their electrical signal and brake equipment and soon to be known for their widely used Pressurised Water Reactors for nuclear power stations, developed a 60 MW Tank type reactor moderated, cooled and reflected by light water which operated at Waltz Mill, Pennsylvania between 1959 and 1962 when it was eventually shut down as the result of core damage and radioactive contamination sustained in a nuclear accident in April 1960.

To prepare for the intended development of nuclear power by many countries, it was clearly necessary for research reactors suitable for *teaching* purposes to be made available. A number of the early light water-moderated reactors graphite-reflected were designed for this purpose. One of the earliest was developed in the 1950's at the Argonne National Laboratory in Illinois, U.S.A. It was named Argonaut (Argonne Nuclear Assembly for University Training). The first went critical at this laboratory in 1956. Argonaut-type reactors were soon to be set up in other countries, usually designed and built by local firms. Examples were the Siemens-Schuckertwerke Argonauts at Garching and at the Karlsruhe Reactor Research Centre in Germany; the British Hawker Siddeley "Jason" Reactor at the UKAEA's Winfrith Establishment (redesigned and called "NESTOR" — used also as a neutron source); and similar ones at the Royal Naval College, Greenwich and Queen Mary College in the University of London; the Dutch Low Flux Reactor (L.F.R.) at the Petten Research Centre; the Kinki University Research and Training Reactor at Osaka, Japan (built by Advanced Technology Labs —

a division of American Radiator and Standard Sanitary Corporation); and several more, including one built for Liverpool and Manchester Universities at Risley in England, and one for the Scottish Universities at East Kilbride.

As mentioned earlier, heavy water (D_2O) could be used as a moderator for this group of research reactors. The *Heavy Water Moderated* group prepared the way for some very important designs of power reactors, fuelled with natural uranium which could be used in relatively modest quantities (and therefore with smaller reactor units), to produce substantial power levels because of the neutron-capturing qualities of D_2O. Natural uranium is obviously far more abundant than that which has to be enriched with U235. More will be said about heavy water later.

Although the first research reactor with heavy water moderation was set up at the Argonne National Laboratory as early as 1944, it had to be dismantled after a few years because of suspected corrosion of the aluminium cladding of the fuel rods. It was the Canadians who, in collaboration with the UK and USA, at that time made the running with this type of experimental reactor. They operated 3 at the Atomic Energy of Canada Ltd's Chalk River establishment, notably the 40 MW NRX-Reactor which reached full power in 1948, the same year as the similar French experimental isotope producer ZOE (Zéro Oxyde d'Urane Eau Lourde or EL-1) at Fontenay-aux-Roses. The French also developed a second small Heavy Water Reactor (EL-2) at Saclay which reached criticality in 1952. Cooling, in this case, was effected by CO_2. In the United Kingdom, the first Heavy Water moderated research reactor was a Tank Type which was also reflected and cooled by D_2O. DIDO, as it was called, was operated at 10 MW at Harwell from 1956 by the UKAEA, who set up a Materials Testing Reactor of similar power at Dounreay in Scotland. The Australian Atomic Energy Commission had a similar facility in operation soon after at their Lucas Heights establishment in New South Wales. In 1959, a 12 MW Tank Type, FR-2, became critical at Karlsruhe in Germany. In the same year Ispra-1 started up in Italy, and the following year the Swiss Reactor Company, Ltd., put their 20 MW DIORIT into operation at Wuerenlingen; and, at their Trombay Establishment near Bombay, the Indian Atomic Energy Commission set up their Canadian built NRX-type reactor.

Japan joined the countries researching into Heavy Water reactors in 1960 with their 10 MW JRR-2 at the Japan Atomic Energy Research Institute at Tokai Mura in Ibaraki-Ken, which was followed by the similar JRR-3 2 years later.

One of the most important developments of the Experimental

Heavy Water reactors in Europe was the Halden HBWR installed at the Norwegian Institutt for Atomenergi's site at that location in 1959, which they have operated ever since as a research facility for the Organisation for Economic Cooperation and Development (OECD — formerly O.E.E.C.). This has a thermal capacity of 20 MW and uses slightly enriched uranium.

The Halden project was also a *Boiling Water Reactor*, which represents another type of water-moderated facility under development in those early years. As part of the power producing family of reactors, BWR's (using light water) have become one of the most important of the designs employed in this field, although considerably less in number than Pressurised Water Reactors.

The BWR's were always associated with the production of electricity and were therefore considered as power stations with turbo-generators driven by steam extracted from the reactor which in this form is, of course, a boiler. Normally the steam goes straight to the turbine, thus eliminating the need for a heat exchanger although this system does mean that the water droplets in steam may be slightly radioactive, requiring a degree of shielding of the circuit. Another advantage of the BWR system is that it may be operated at lower pressures than pressurised reactors.

The first experimental Boiling Water Reactor was the U.S. Atomic Energy Commission's EBWR operated by the Argonne National Laboratory which became critical in 1956. Originally designed for about 60 megawatts of heat — 60 MW(th) — it used only 20 MW(th) for the turbine which generated 5 megawatts of electricity (5 MW(e)). (The additional output was dissipated in heat exchange equipment as process steam.) The researchers and designers developed new models such as the General Electric BWR at Vallecitos used for power production and components testing which reached its full power of 50 MW(th) in 1957. Another early small BWR designed by the Argonne Nuclear Laboratory was the 3 MW(th) Stationary Low Power Plant (SL-1) at Idaho Falls. This went into operation in 1959 and was partly destroyed by an accident in 1961. In 1960 a similar experimental power reactor of this type was put into operation in Germany by the Atomic Power Station Research Company at Kahl. This was owned by the electricity company, RWE, and Bayernwerk and designed jointly by AEG and the American G.E. It produced 60 MW(th) and 16 MW(e) gross. Similar developments with BWR's took place in the USSR at this time.

Reactors of this size were not economical for commercial production and thermal efficiency was rather low but in this same year (1960), at Dresden, the Americans started to operate a much larger power reactor, producing 626 MW(th). A smaller but more efficient

BWR was the Elk River Reactor which went into power production at the U.S.A.E.C.'s plant in Minnesota.

Even more important, because the prototype of what was to become by far the most widely adopted commercial power reactor system, was the light water moderated *Pressurised Water Reactor*. The first of these to go into operation (in 1957) for power production was the Westinghouse design at the Shippingport Atomic Power Station in Pennsylvania USA (now shut down for decommissioning). This achieved its full power of 225 MW(th). The design pressure of the reactor vessel was 2500 p.s.i.a. at 600°F. As a matter of interest the steel cylindrical vessel was 32.5 feet high, with a diameter of 9 feet. Including the thick concrete shielding, the height and diameter were, respectively, 20 feet (with an 18 foot dome) and 38 feet.

Although they provided a valuable means of gaining experience and testing various components and operating procedures, the first of the Pressurised Water Reactors (mainly located in the USA and USSR) were producers of electricity rather than research reactors as such. However, a small Westinghouse light water moderated pressurised water reactor was installed in 1960 at the Belgian CEN research centre at Mol. Designated the Belgian Thermal Reactor (BR-3) it had a gross thermal capacity of 40.9 MW and a net electrical output of 10.5 MW. Its primary purpose was for operator training although the electrical output (surplus to on-site requirements) was fed to the public grid. BR-3 was used for testing the fuel assembly to be used in the "Vulcan" power project developed from it a few years later described in the British Government White Paper "Nuclear Power for Ship Propulsion" in May 1964 (Cmnd 2358). This project was a joint venture shared with the U.K.A.E.A. The moderator was initially composed of a mixture of light and heavy water the proportions of which could be varied to control the level of the nuclear reaction ("reactivity") in the core, which consisted of narrow stainless steel tubes containing bundles of uranium oxide pellets (about 7% enriched). This type of fuel element is known as a "pin" and these were just over 1200 mm in length. The tubes were filled with helium before being finally sealed. The moderator was contained in zircaloy tubes. BR-3/Vulcan is still operating at Mol.

The decade from 1958-68 was notable for the development of a number of prototype pressurised power reactors which were moderated with Heavy Water, either water or gas-cooled. The more important in this group as prospective new designs for use in power stations were the so-called *Pressure Tube* reactors. The first significant experimental plant was built by Atomic Energy of Canada, Ltd. at Rolphton, Ontario, and became critical in 1962. Instead of a large pressure vessel containing core, moderator and coolant, it was made up of 132 Zircaloy tubes, containing slugs of natural uranium fuel. The tubes were held in a horizontal calandria containing the heavy water moderator inside a tank. This tank was contained in another containing light water which served as a reflector. Control of the activity of the reactor was managed by regulating the volume or density of the D_2O moderator and by a "booster" control rod. For a period betwen 1968 and 1971 the reactor was operated with light water (H_2O) as moderator. This design, which operated at about 83 MW(th), (19 MW(e)) led to the extremely successful full scale CANDU reactor system (first operated in 1964 as Ontario Hydro's Douglas Point Nuclear Power Station) with which all Canada's nuclear electricity generating stations are equipped and which have been installed and successfully operated in a number of other countries.

The Americans constructed a similar type of small Heavy Water moderated Pressure Tube reactor in South Carolina (operated by Carolinas Virginia Nuclear Power Associates). In Switzerland, at Lucens in the Vaud, the S.N.A. (National Atomic Company) constructed an experimental power station equipped with their own design of Pressure Tube reactors. This produced about 30 MW of heat (net electrical output 7.6 MW) and was cooled with CO_2 gas. Unfortunately, this project had an unhappy outcome because, after less than 3 years operation, there was a serious accident involving major damage to one of the pressure tubes and the fuel inside it. As a result the reactor had to be permanently shut down, decommissioned and eventually dismantled. (This accident is fully written up in the American technical journal "Nuclear Safety", Vol. 22 No. 1.)

In the United Kingdom, the AEA constructed a Pressure Tube Heavy Water moderated reactor at their Winfrith establishment. Known as the Steam Generating Heavy Water Reactor (SGHWR) — although it used boiling light water as coolant — it produced 100 MW of electricity. It is a valuable source of data and operational experience in the fields of water reactions, coolant chemistry and radiological protection. At one time, in the mid-70's, it was considered to be a suitable successor to the gas-cooled reactors used in the British commercial electricity supply industry — the Central Electricity Generating Board (CEGB) — and other countries showed interest. Although the first is still in operation in Winfrith, a plan to build SGHWR power stations for the CEGB or their Scottish counterparts, the South of Scotland Electricity Board, was abandoned by the then Secretary of State in 1978 on economic grounds. (Detailed accounts of this design were published in the August 1974 issue of "Nuclear Engineering International"; and the

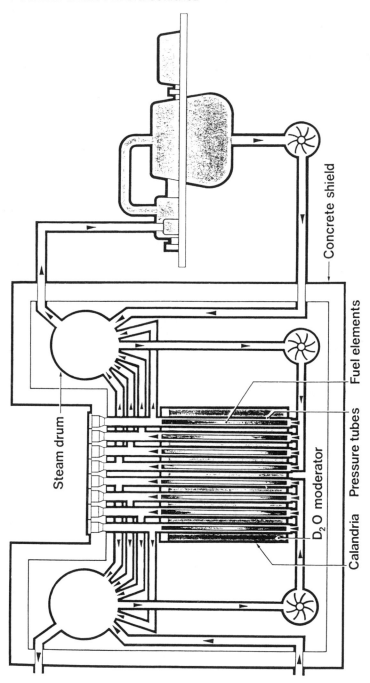

Steam generating heavy water reactor (SGHWR)

Concrete shield

Fuel elements

Pressure tubes

D_2O moderator

Calandria

Steam drum

UKAEA's publication "Atom" in November 1974 at pp, 200-214.)

Solid elements were the most commonly used form of fuel in water-moderated reactors but, from the earliest days, in the 1940's, liquid fuels were also employed. This was in the form of uranyl sulphate dissolved in water which served also as the moderator. Such reactors are assigned to the general description of *Aqueous Homogeneous*. One of the first of these was the American AE-6, owned by the USAEC and operated by Atomic International at Los Angeles from 1952 (reconstructed in 1956). A heavy water-moderated version, the HRE-1, was operated about the same time at the Oak Ridge National Laboratory and the Americans had several other Aqueous Homogeneous research reactors in operation during the 50's and 60's, one of them being located at the University of Puerto Rico. The Dutch developed their own version, the Suspension Test Reactor (SUSPOP) at Arnhem in 1955 although as this was not intended to reach criticality it was a Sub-Critical Assembly rather than a reactor. The Japan Atomic Energy Research Institute (at Tokai Mura) had an American Atomic International L-54 Reactor in operation by 1957; another of these was installed at the Enrico Fermi Nuclear Study Centre in Milan and was operating by 1960.

The *Solid Homogeneous* was another and more popular type of water-moderated reactor, used mainly for training and isotope production. The TRIGA (designed and built by the General Atomic Division of the American General Dynamics Corporation) must rank first among these.

These small facilities had a number of practical uses, the main ones being summed up in the meaning of the acronym **T**raining **R**esearch and **I**sotope production reactor **G**eneral **A**tomics. The reactor operated at low power — 10 kW — yet was capable of serving as a useful training facility. It had a sufficiently high neutron flux for the performance of worthwhile experiments and its irradiation equipment enabled it to be used for radioisotope production. It was safe to operate and one of its favourable features (shared with some other types) was what is known as a negative coefficient of reactivity. In simple terms this means that the reactor is so designed that in the event of an excessive rise in temperature the rate of change of reactivity (i.e. the nuclear reaction going on inside the core) falls away as the temperature rises. This, and other safety concepts, were basic to the design of the TRIGA when it was first planned by the manufacturers in about 1956. Inherent safety is the objective of all reactor designs and was particularly important in systems intended for use in countries new to nuclear technology including the developing countries of the Third World who were enouraged to build up the know-how and experience of their research and academic installations with the help of financial grants from the U.S.A.E.C. for the purchase and installation of reactors like the TRIGA series. Other safety considerations included a fuel that was practically inert chemically so it would not react with the coolant (also used in other similar types); a coolant that could become minimally radioactive, if fission products escaped from a leaky fuel cladding, to enable radioactivity to be quickly detected (— requirements met by water or CO_2); solid fuel so that in the normal way fission products would remain inside the fuel elements. Obviously safety is also provided by means of controls such as the safety rods which must be capable of being introduced between the fuel rods or plates very rapidly ("scrammed" is the technical term). Since all reactors must have some excess reactivity rapid power surges (lasting only a few milliseconds) are possible and even automatic control rods may not act quickly enough.

Taking these various features into account, the designers of TRIGA decided to use zirconium hydride as a moderator mixed in with solid highly enriched uranium fuel (therefore "solid homogeneous"), and light water as a coolant (natural convection of refrigerated water). Graphite was chosen as the reflector and the water also acted as a biological shield. The first was built for the John Jay Hopkins Laboratory in San Diego, California and achieved criticality in 1957. Within two years this version, the Mark I, was being exhibited in and, in some cases, sold to various other countries. For example, there was an exhibition in Geneva in 1958 at which a Triga Mark I was demonstrated, later to be installed at Lovanium University in what was then the Belgian Congo (now Zaire). At this time TRIGA's were also installed in the University of Minas Gerais in Brazil and in the American Veterans' Administration Hospital in Nebraska. A more advanced version, producing 30 MW(th), went to the Italian CNEN's establishment in Casaccia in 1959 (also known as RC-1). Another of these went to Seoul University to be operated by the Office of Atomic Energy of the Republic of Korea. A 100 KW(th) version went to the Atominstitut der Österreichischen Hochschulen in Vienna; others to Rikkyo University at Yokosuka and the Musashi College of Technology at Kawasaki, both in Japan. The Vietnam Atomic Energy Commission installed one at the Dalat Nuclear Research Centre, with a nominal power of 250 kw. The Mark II version was well adapted for such functions as the irradiation of specimens in neutron beams and the rapid transfer of short-lived radioisotopes from reactor to laboratory through a pneumatic (or "rabbit") tube. Its many practical applications included activation analysis (detection of trace elements by means of short-lived radioisotopes); chemical research into the structure of molecules, solids and liquids; highly controlled preparation of isotopes; engineering research into hydrodynamics and corrosion; agricultural research including the study of the concentration of materials in plants and the induction of mutations to develop new strains; medical research including diagnosis and treatment with isotopes.

The first British TRIGA to be installed by private industry, as announced in "The Times" of 19.6.70, was set up in the Billingham Laboratories of I.C.I. Imperial Chemical Industries Ltd. in 1971. Another version (Mark III) was also developed at San Diego. This was able to incorporate what was known as a pulsing facility, capable of boosting the power for a period measured in milliseconds only, up to 15,000 megawatts of heat. A TRIGA with a pulsing facility was installed in 1975 by the Japan Atomic Energy Research Institute at their large Tokai Mura establishment 130 km north of Tokyo for various testing and study purposes. The models without this facility are known as steady state reactors.

The manufacture and supply of TRIGA's was taken over during the 1960's by Gulf Energy and Environment Systems, Inc., usually referred to as Gulf Atomics.

In 1978 a pair of TRIGA's — steady state and pulsing — sharing the same pool, were installed by Gulf Atomics at Pitesti, in Romania, for the Pentra Institute of Nuclear Technology. The pulsing version was known as the ACPR (Annular Core Pulsing Reactor). Numerous other TRIGA's of various types are in operation in many countries and have played — and are playing — a highly important role in the world of nuclear research, the preparation of radioisotopes and the training of nuclear physicists and technicians. It has in many countries been associated with the beginning of their entry into the nuclear energy field and ultimately the production of electricity by this means — even, and perhaps, more particularly, the developing countries. It has, for this reason, been the subject of a rather fuller account than other research and teaching reactors.

Polyethylene-moderated

Of the solid homogeneous types there were others, of course, one of the most widely used by research institutes and Universities being the AGN-201 developed in 1957 by Aerojet General Nucleonics of the USA. Instead of water, carbon or zirconium hydride, they used polyethylene. The 20% enriched uranium was mixed with this and the reflector was graphite. They were uncooled since they operated at very low power — the majority as low as 0.1 watt. Some versions had a higher capacity up to, say, 75 watts, but not higher until the AGN-211 P installed in 1961 at Basle University in Switzerland which operated at 2 kW. This company also developed the more powerful AGNIR (Aerojet-General Nuclear Industrial Reactor) in 1965 at their San Ramon Nuclear Division in California where they had built the first of the AGN's some 8 years before.

The German firm, Siemens, developed a similar small solid homogeneous reactor, the S.U.R. (Siemens Unterrichts-reaktor) for educational purposes and these were installed in various locations throughout the Federal Republic of Germany in the 1960's. All were rated at 0.1 watt.

Organic-moderated

From the 1960's onwards a small amount of experimental work was done with organic moderators — essentially composed of hydrocarbons, the hydrogen in which was considered to be likely to be just as effective as the hydrogen in water. The first of the organically moderated experimental reactors was the USAEC's O.M.R.E., operated for a time at Idaho Falls by Atomics International. Difficulties were encountered in this field of research because such compounds decomposed under irradiation. Subsequently, improved results were obtained with certain polyphenols, as at the zero-power ROSPO facility at Cassacia which used liquid terphenyl ("Santowax") as moderator and coolant. This reactor operated for some 20 years after first achieving criticality in 1963.

In general there seems to have been little progress towards the practical use of organic moderators.

Fast reactors

The various types of research reactors described so far, some of which are now little more than curiosities, have all been thermal reactors in which in order to maintain a chain reaction the neutrons have to be slowed down by incorporating a moderator. Much of the early experimental work was focussed on finding the most suitable moderators for use with the different fuels — hence the division of the different designs of thermal reactors described by reference to the type of moderator, following the classification adopted in the I.A.E.A.'s authoritative Directories of research reactors.

The energy in reactors using natural or enriched uranium comes almost entirely from the small U235 content which will fission easily whereas the bulk of the uranium (U238) will not, although being a "fertile" material it absorbs neutrons and when irradiated it produces plutonium (Pu239) most of which is unconsumed when the fuel has to be removed and replaced. Pu239 can undergo fission and therefore can be used as a reactor fuel.

The fissionable atoms in plutonium are sufficiently abundant not to require slowing down to produce a chain reaction. So no moderator is needed and the reaction can be maintained with "fast" neutrons. This led to the term "fast" reactor.

The fuel used (known as mixed oxide or MOX) is mixed with the depleted uranium (containing almost 100% U238) which is extracted along with the plutonium when irradiated natural uranium or enriched uranium is reprocessed (see Chapter 3). These materials (which might otherwise go to waste, unless the plutonium is preserved for military use) can thus be put to productive use in a fast reactor.

More than that, early experiments demonstrated that if the reactor core (which need only be quite small) is surrounded by a "blanket" of depleted uranium this captures the spent neutrons available in consequence of the efficiency of plutonium as a fuel, to make more plutonium. Since a fast reactor of this type produces more plutonium than it uses it is known as a "breeder" or *Fast Breeder Reactor*.

The first of these reactor types was installed at Los Alamos by the United States AEC. Fuelled with Plutonium 239 in vertical rods, assembled in a very small core, 6 inches by 6 inches, and producing 25 kW of heat, this device was called "Clementine", apparently because at the time "49" was used as a code number for plutonium, and it recalled the popular song about the lady of this name and her association with a "forty-niner" — one of the miners in the 1849 gold rush. (Anyhow, whether true or not, this explanation is solemnly rolled out repeatedly in the technical literature.) "Clementine" was cooled with mercury, the reflector was uranium and steel (because these materials would not slow the reaction by reflecting back too many neutrons) and it operated from 1946-53. It was then shut down partly because of contamination of the mercury by a failed fuel element.

Shortly after, in 1954, the United Kingdom A.E.A. built their first Zero Energy Fast Reactor (ZEPHYR) at Harwell, following four years of experimental work on the reactor physics of fast neutrons. This reactor, which was uncooled, was dismantled in 1958. In the meantime, another, ZEUS (Zero Energy Uranium System), with a capacity of 100 W was built at Harwell for the purpose of evaluating a design for a comparatively large-scale Fast Breeder Reactor (to be erected at Dounreay in Scotland). Although uncooled, it used magnesium and aluminium to simulate cooling of the core (details of this facility were written up in the British technical journal, "Nuclear Engineering" — now entitled "Nuclear Engineering International" — in 1956 — Vol. 1. 72 and 234). The DFR (Dounreay Fast Reactor) was specifically intended to provide heat for the generation of electricity and to gain the necessary experience

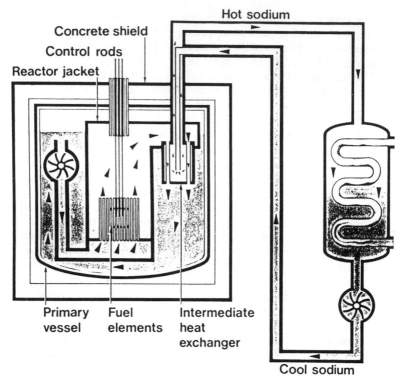

Prototype Fast Reactor

to construct a sufficiently large Fast Reactor to be capable of economic production of electricity on an industrial scale. Criticality was achieved in 1959 and the DFR was run at low power for some time. Electricity was first produced in 1962 (output being 15 MW(e)) and this reactor reached its full power of 60 MW(th) in 1963, being in use until 1977. The next stage in the UKAEA's work on Fast Reactor technology was the construction of the intended larger prototype for industrial power production. The PFR (Prototype Fast Reactor) as it was called achieved criticality at Dounreay in 1974 producing 600 MW of heat and a net electrical output of 250 MW(e). This reactor is equipped with the type and size of enriched uranium or plutonium that could be used in a commercial power reactor, with uranium as a reflector and liquid sodium as coolant — a far more efficient medium than water or CO_2. With a net electrical efficiency of some 40% it holds out obvious promise as a source of power for electricity generation on a commercial scale and on the basis of experience with the PFR the UKAEA has designed a Commercial Demonstration Fast Reactor.

The French Commissariat à l'Energie Atomique also undertook extensive experimentation and development work on Fast Reactor systems, culminating in the Super-Phénix at Creys-Malville, a full-scale sodium-cooled fast breeder power reactor built and operated by an international consortium in association with Electricité de France (E.d.F.) the French national electricity supply company. The first experimental Fast Reactor in France was the air-cooled 2 kW Harmonie at the Cadarache research centre of the CEA who owned this facility jointly with EURATOM (the European Atomic Energy Community established on 1st January 1958 by Belgium, France, Federal Republic of Germany, Italy, Luxembourg and the Netherlands). It was designed and built by the Belgian company, Belgonucléaire. Harmonie started up in 1965 and was followed by MASURCA ("Maquette Surgénératrice Cadarache" or "Cadarache Fast Reactor Model") air-cooled and with a thermal capacity of 1 kW, also jointly owned. A more powerful experimental Fast Reactor, the sodium-cooled 20 MW(th) Rapsodie was also brought into operation at this time at Cadarache. In 1968, construction work started on Phénix, a relatively large prototype for a Fast Reactor to be operated at the CEA's Marcoule establishment by EdF for electricity production on a commercial scale. This was comparable with the British PFR; it was fuelled by plutonium and depleted uranium, reflected by steel and depleted uranium and cooled by sodium. It became critical in 1973 and had a thermal capacity of 653 MW(th) achieving a net electrical efficiency of over 40%.

While France and the United Kingdom have been at the forefront of Fast and Fast Breeder reactor developments, they have not been alone. Indeed, the first experimental work, as already stated, was undertaken with the American "Clementine" as long ago as 1946. This was followed by the Argonne Fast Source reactor, air-cooled and operating at 1 kW(th) in 1959; and the Los Alamos 1 MW Molten Plutonium Reactor ("LAMPRE") which was in use between 1961 and 1964. Its fuel consisted of 90% plutonium and 10% iron alloy which had a melting point of 410°C, so at operating temperatures it was molten — hence its name. Cooling was provided by sodium. This unusual assembly had the primary purpose of testing the possibility of using molten metallic plutonium as a fuel. It was shut down permanently after what was considered to be a successful run of tests, these being transferred to a new test facility soon after.

Related research was pursued in the course of the U.S.A.'s Liquid Metal Fast Breeder Reactor (LMFBR) programme, using facilities such as the USAEC Fast Flux Test Facility at Richland, Washington, which started up in 1977.

The U.S.S.R. was also involved in Fast Reactor research, their first breeder reactor being set up in 1953. By 1969 they had started up their fourth: a sodium-cooled enriched uranium fuelled reactor, depleted uranium and steel reflected with a thermal power of 60 MW(th) and gross electrical output of 12 MW(e). This was set up at Melekess in the Ulyanovsk region, owned and operated by the Scientific Research Institute for Atomic Reactors.

These were the main initial research activities in the fast breeder field and, with the coming into operation in France in 1986 of Super-Phénix (see Chapter 3), the first commercial power station with this type of reactor, it seems likely that further practical developments will follow. In other countries similar protracted and sophisticated research has been undertaken, such as Canada, Germany and Japan (with the Joyo facility); and in India, where the prospect of using their extensive supplies of thorium in LMFBRs has attractions.

Nuclear Fusion

Chapter 1 contains a brief reference to an alternative method of deriving power from the atom by means of fusing nuclei instead of splitting atoms. Because the practical exploitation of fusion seems to be some way in the future, this review of research and development has been concerned with nuclear fission which has been capable of practical applications for many years. However, the prospects for power production in the future opened up by *fusion* research are exciting and of such enormous significance that the research and experimentation going on in this field in several countries cannot be ignored.

Fusion, which involves the merging of the nuclei of atoms, can be achieved with a substance as common as hydrogen in the form of deuterium or tritium. So, if difficult technical problems can be solved, nuclear power could be derived from water; and it would not involve radioactivity as we know it in connection with the fissioning of uranium or plutonium.

The techniques required to produce fusion are difficult because normally nuclei repel each other and must therefore be forced together by creating plasma at extremely high temperatures which is held in a magnetic field. There are several techniques which require special apparatus. The "main-line" approach involves the use of a torus — which has been likened to a ring doughnut in shape. This is also known as a "Tokamak" a word derived from the Russian acronym TO-KA-MAK, variously said to stand for "toroidal-magnetic chamber", "toroidal-chamber-current" or "toroidal chamber with magnetic coils".

The United Kingdom Atomic Energy Authority has always been a leader in this field at their research establishment at Culham in Oxfordshire. This is now the site of the highly prestigious international research project known as JET (Joint European Torus). This is intended to establish the scientific feasibility of fusion devices and to produce the conditions necessary to develop a fusion reactor which, in turn, would enable electricity to be generated out of gases derived from water.

JET is a joint venture of the 12 countries of the European Economic Community. But similar research has been undertaken for many years in Japan (with the JT-60 device at Naka-Machi), the U.S.A. (with the TFTR — Tokamak Fusion Test Reactor in Princeton) and the U.S.S.R. (with the T.15) among others. Under the auspices of the International Atomic Energy Agency, it is hoped that an international conventional design for a nuclear fusion reactor can be produced by 1990. This will be an essential preparation for the development of controlled thermonuclear fusion as a source of energy for the generation of electricity.

A Note on Heavy Water

Having given some account of reactors which are moderated by heavy water it may be useful to say something about this odd-sounding material, D_2O as distinct from H_2O ("light water") which is the form of water more familiar to the layman.

Hydrogen, H_2, combined with oxygen, makes water. Hydrogen was discovered to be one of the stable isotopes in 1931. Scientists, notably E. Rutherford in England and W.D. Hawkins in the USA had, some 10 years previously, considered there might be a form of hydrogen with a greater atomic weight than ordinary hydrogen. Various leading scientists carried out experiments involving evaporating liquid hydrogen which led to the separation of a heavier hydrogen isotope. Much of the credit for this is due to an American scientist, H. C. Urey. It was later found that the electrolysis of water evolved the lighter isotope, leaving the heavier as a residue. This discovery was made in 1933 at the University of California by G.N. Lewis and others. Because the atomic weight of the heavier isotope was about twice that of the lighter it was decided that it should have its own name: "deuterium" (D).

Heavy water is slightly denser than light water (about 10:9); it has a freezing point of 3.82°C and a boiling point of 101.42°C.

The large-scale manufacture of heavy water became a military necessity during the 1939-45 War because of its use as a moderator in plutonium-producing reactors. Subsequently the development of heavy water-moderated commercial power reactors required industrially and cost efficient methods of production to be developed.

Heavy water can be produced by various methods from hydrogen or ordinary water. Electrolysis of water has been mentioned. Evaporation or distillation is another; chemical exchange yet another: for large-scale production hydrogen gas and steam are passed up a tower containing a catalyst, with water flowing downwards. An exchange of isotopes occurs between the hydrogen and the water molecules in the steam, resulting in a concentration of D_2O in the steam which is condensed and carried down to the bottom of the tower in an enriched form. The use of hydrogen sulphide in this process speeds up the production of deuterium.

Heavy water is expensive to produce, relatively scarce and therefore costly. It can easily be lost by spillage, evaporation or degradation by ordinary water. But it is an excellent moderator enabling the cheaper and more plentiful natural uranium to be used most efficiently as a reactor fuel.

CHAPTER III

INDUSTRIAL APPLICATIONS

Power Reactors

Much of the experimentation with small reactor systems already described was aimed at discovering and developing large reactors for economic and safe production of sufficient heat for the industrial production of electricity. As a result, the nuclear energy industry has settled for a limited number of different reactor types to be used in power stations. There are nearly 400 individual reactor units in operation all over the world. Most power stations have at least 2 reactor units — some 4, 6 or even 8 — so the number of nuclear power stations throughout the world is about 200 with a combined electrical output of some 250,000 MW(e). Of the total number of reactor units in operation by the end of 1986, 100 were in the USA (with another 17 under construction); 50 in the USSR (with 25 under construction); 38 in the United Kingdom (with 4 under construction); 35 in Japan (with 10 under construction); 21 in the Federal Republic of Germany (with 4 under construction); 18 in Canada (with 5 under construction); 12 in Sweden (with none under construction); 8 in Belgium (with none under construction); 8 in Spain (with 2 under construction); 7 in Korea (with 2 under construction); 7 in Czechoslavakia (with 9 under construction); 6 in Taiwan (with none under construction); 5 in Switzerland (with none under construction); 5 in the German Democratic Republic (with 6 under construction). About 14 other countries had 4 or less nuclear power reactor units in operation or operable at the end of 1986. Numerous others are planned for countries in most parts of the world, including those new to the use of nuclear energy for the production of electricity.

There has been an extremely small incidence of nuclear or radiation-related accidents in nuclear power stations, and this, together with an experience of 30 years' successful technical operation, and over 40 years of careful reactor research and experimentation on an international as well as national scale, should reassure those who are apprehensive about the spread of nuclear electricity generating stations.

With so many plants to consider, it is not practicable to review them all. It is sufficient for insurers to know the main commercial reactor systems — all somewhat different — adopted by Governments or other bodies responsible for the authorisation and operation of nuclear installations such as are insured or likely to be insured. They are:

Gas-cooled reactors (GCR)

Pressurised Water reactors (PWR)

Boiling Water reactors (BWR)

Pressurised Heavy Water reactors (PHWR or CANDU)

Small numbers of other types installed in nuclear power stations include:

Advanced Gas-Cooled reactors (AGR — in U.K. only)

Fast Breeder reactors (FBR)

High Temperature Gas-Cooled reactors (HTGCR)

The power reactor types used in the USSR are not likely to be encountered by insurers but they should be mentioned as including two types the use of which is more or less confined to that country as follows:

Boiling Water Graphite-Moderated reactors ("RBMK")

Light Water Gas-Cooled reactors (LWGCR)

The world's first nuclear power station at Calder Hall in Cumbria operated by the U.K. Atomic Energy Authority was equipped with the British *carbon dioxide-cooled, graphite-moderated reactors (GCR)* based on the PIPPA reactor design they had developed at Harwell. Four such reactors, capable of each generating 50 MW of electricity, were constructed at Calder Hall, alongside the Authority's Windscale establishment.

Calder Hall nuclear power station, or Calder Works as it is also called, was commissioned in 1956 and officially opened by Her Majesty Queen Elizabeth II as the world's first commercial power station to use nuclear energy. A second four-reactor station was commissioned at Chapelcross in Ayrshire, Scotland, 2 years later. Thirty years on, both are fully operational and supplying electricity to the national grid although no longer operated by the UKAEA, who divested themselves of most of their commercial activities in 1971. A limited company, British Nuclear Fuels, was then set up and took over the ownership and operation of the eight *Magnox* reactors at these two nuclear power stations, together with various installations concerned in the nuclear fuel cycle.

The successful debut of nuclear power generation at these locations

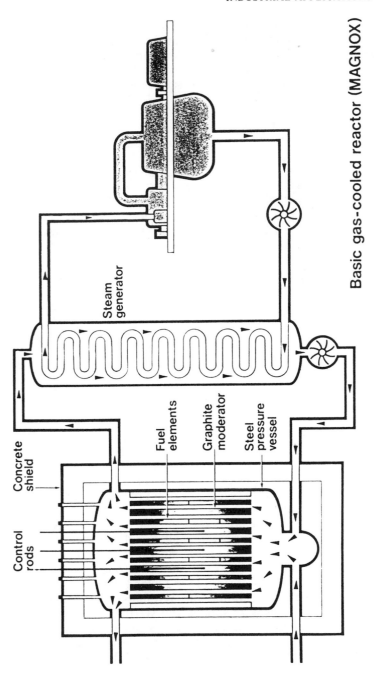

Basic gas-cooled reactor (MAGNOX)

led to a decision being quickly taken to adopt this system for the first phase of an ambitious programme of nuclear power stations to be operated in England, Scotland and Wales by the Central Electricity Generating Board. The first of these at Berkeley (Gloucestershire) and Bradwell (Essex) started operation in 1962 and the third at Hunterston (Scotland) in 1964, producing about 150 MW(e) of electricity per reactor unit. Another 12 Magnox reactors of increasing size and electrical output came into operation over the next 10 years at various locations in England and Wales.

This design was abandoned by the British after the completion of the last of the Magnox power stations at Wylfa on the Isle of Anglesey. This was when the *Advanced Gas-Cooled Reactors (AGR)* were constructed and brought into operation. They were based upon a design developed by UKAEA who operated the first (the prototype, WAGR) at their Windscale establishment from 1962 onwards until it was finally shut down in 1981.

Gas-cooled graphite moderated power reactors of various types operate elsewhere — several in France, with one each in Italy, Japan and Spain, and some of the other types of power reactors are cooled by gas. However, gas-cooled reactors account for less than 20% of the systems installed in the world's power stations.

The most widely-used type is the *Pressurised Light Water Reactor (PWR)* which accounts for more than 50% of those in industrial operation. When the new stations under construction are completed, that percentage will be even higher, a fact well illustrated by reference to the reliable directories of nuclear power stations such as those published by the International Atomic Energy Agency or the Annual World Nuclear Industry Handbook published by the British journal, "Nuclear Engineering International". These also demonstrate the dominance of the American Westinghouse Corporation in the supply and/or design of reactor systems installed not only in the USA but in numerous other countries worldwide. (France has become another supplier of the PWR in recent years, not only for their own power stations but to a number of other countries).

The USSR is also a major constructor and user of the PWR system, having some 20 units in operation all over the Soviet Union. They have supplied their system to a number of other countries among a group known as the Centrally Planned Economies as well as to one of the nuclear power stations in Finland. However, the United States have the largest number of PWR units in operation — 63 — of which two thirds were supplied by Westinghouse. Combustion Engineering supplied another 13 and 8 came from Babcock and Wilcox, whose reactors are installed at the Three Mile Island (TMI) nuclear power station in Pennsylvania. TMI 2 was involved in the

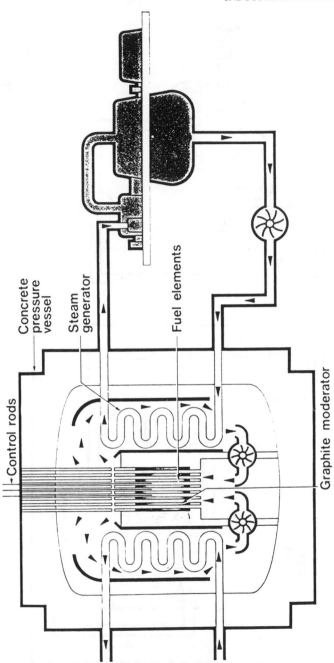

Advanced gas-cooled reactor (AGR)

Concrete pressure vessel

Steam generator

Fuel elements

Control rods

Graphite moderator

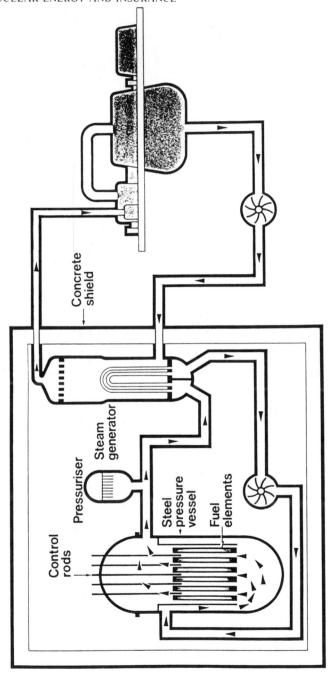

Pressurised water reactor (PWR)

Concrete shield

Steam generator

Pressuriser

Steel pressure vessel

Fuel elements

Control rods

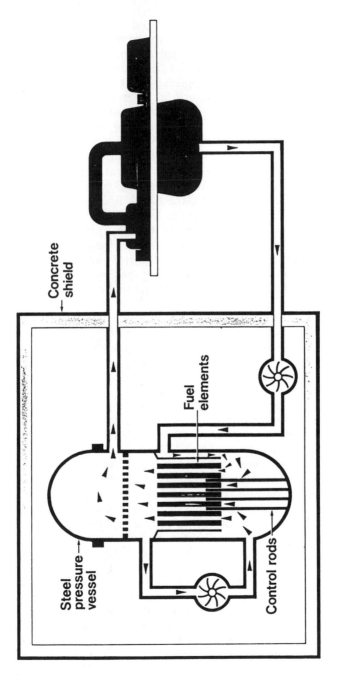

Boiling water reactor (BWR)

Concrete shield

Fuel elements

Steel pressure vessel

Control rods

major nuclear accident which occurred in 1979.

The next most frequently used type of nuclear reactor and steam supply system after the PWR is the *Boiling Water Reactor (BWR)*. The majority of these are in the USA, some 30 being installed in various States, all of them supplied by the General Electric Company (GE) who have supplied several to other countries.

Apart from the USA, Japan is the most important user of the BWR system in terms of the number of units. Nowadays it is Japanese designed and constructed BWRs that are installed in nuclear power stations in various regions of Japan. However, this system has considerable support also in the Federal Republic of Germany supplied by the German Companies AEG or KWU. There is also an important Swedish design, the ASEA Boiling Water Reactor of which 9 units are in operation in Sweden and 2 in Finland.

Commercial power reactors of the *Pressurised Heavy Water* moderated type (PHWR) using natural uranium fuel are almost exclusively of the pressure tube type designed and supplied by Atomic Energy of Canada Limited (AECL) — the CANDU, as it is known, which is used in all the Canadian nuclear power stations. Several other countries have the CANDU reactors, among them Argentina, India, Korea and Pakistan.

As mentioned previously, there is a number of other types of reactors which are used in very small numbers in commercial power stations.

The only other major nuclear power reactor system is the *RBMK* which is unique to the USSR. It is somewhat of a hybrid and might be described as a Boiling Light Water Pressure Tube Graphite-moderated, reactor. It is also known as the *Leningrad Thermal Reactor* and at least 25 units are operating in various parts of the Soviet Union, producing some 15,000 MW(e) of electricity. It was one of these that was destroyed in the Chernobyl disaster in 1986.

A potentially very important type of reactor system which is beginning to come into commercial use, is the *Fast Reactor* referred to in the description of early research work where it was explained that, having no moderator, they can use natural uranium, and can be so designed that they will breed from that uranium more re-usable plutonium than they consume in the reactor core. Thus they are often known as Fast Breeder Reactors (FBR).

Nowadays the fuel in the core of a fast reactor is a mixture of uranium and plutonium oxide, sometimes called Mixed Oxide, abbreviated MOX. The "breeding" process is achieved by surrounding the core with a "blanket" of Uranium 238 which is a by-product of the enrichment process and, unless used in this way, would be treated as waste. The ability to use this material as a

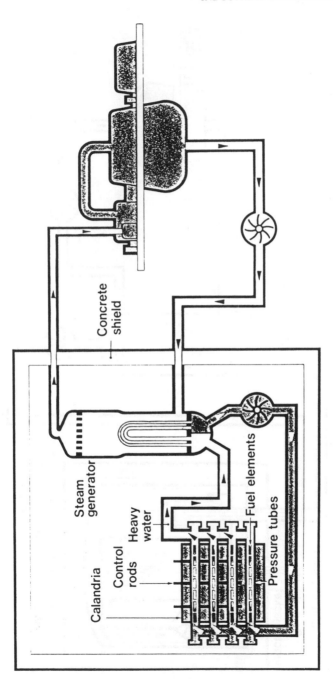

Pressurised heavy water reactor (CANDU)

Concrete shield

Steam generator

Control rods

Calandria

Heavy water

Fuel elements

Pressure tubes

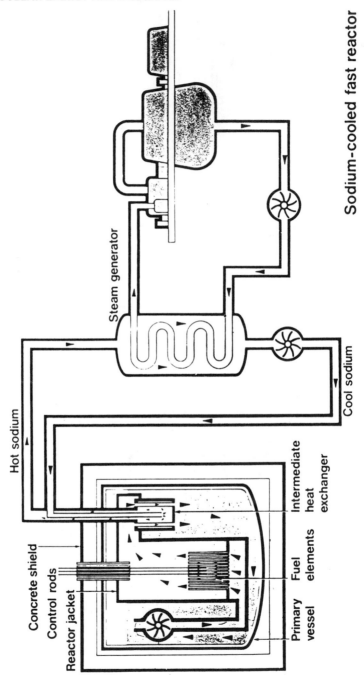

Sodium-cooled fast reactor

Steam generator

Cool sodium

Hot sodium

Intermediate heat exchanger

Concrete shield

Control rods

Reactor jacket

Fuel elements

Primary vessel

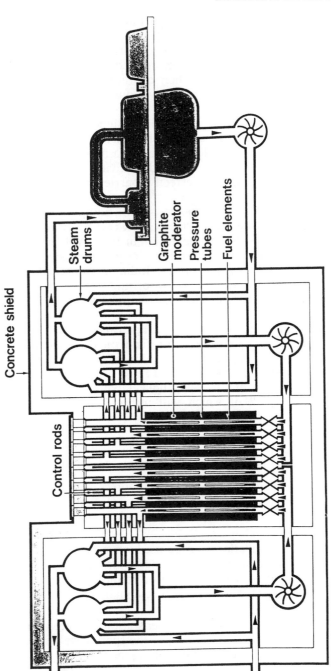

Concrete shield

Steam drums

Control rods

Graphite moderator

Pressure tubes

Fuel elements

Boiling light water, graphite moderated reactor (LENINGRAD)   USSR

productive nuclear fuel is most important because it is a means of reducing demands on the supply of natural uranium which is not inexhaustible, giving the Fast Reactor a rôle in the fuel cycle.

Fast reactors use liquid sodium as a coolant and heat transfer medium, but apart from that their operation is similar to that of the other type, the Thermal Reactor, various examples of which have been described above.

Fast reactors require to be carefully designed from the point of view of safety because the core of the reactor has what is known as a high volumetric power density, necessitating a more than usually effective barrier to the release of radioactivity. In fact the current designs have no less than four effective barriers and other first-class safety features.

The first full-scale nuclear power station equipped with the Fast Reactor system is the Super-Phénix, at Creys-Malville in France, which entered into industrial operation in 1987. Although operated by the French nationalised electricity concern, Electricité de France, they are working in concert with the Italian nationalised electricity industry (ENEL) and a German Consortium — SBK, in which with Belgian, British and Dutch electricity supply industries have small shares.

Other countries, notably Germany, Japan and the United Kingdom are entering into the Fast Reactor field on a commercial scale, although experimentally at this stage. Future large commercial power stations equipped with high-powered FBRs are planned for France, the Federal Republic of Germany, India, Japan, the United Kingdom and the USSR, all of which will utilise U238 and breed new plutonium.

Other industrial applications of power reactors

Nuclear reactors are little used as power sources outside the electricity supply industry except for the propulsion of mainly naval vessels, particularly submarines and also ice-breakers in countries such as the USSR and Canada.

Land-based installations can be used when there is a need for a substantial amount of process heat and/or steam. There are possible applications in metal-smelting and iron foundries. Nuclear reactors have been designed for use in coastal desalination plants for countries short of fresh water.

Where a reactor at a nuclear power station produces more steam than is needed to drive the turbines, the spare heat can be, to use the technical term, "decoupled". This is being done, for example, at the Stade nuclear power station near Hamburg in West Germany, which also supplies steam to a salt refinery, and for space-heating and pre-heating of steam and fuel lines at an adjoining oil-fired power station. In Canada, the Bruce nuclear power station supplies bulk steam to the nearby Heavy Water plant. Steam has also been supplied by a Swiss nuclear power station to a nearby paperboard mill.

In Canada, a specially designed AECL swimming pool reactor, known as the "Slowpoke" is already in use for the space-heating of buildings.

The Nuclear Fuel Cycle

This term relates to the various operations necessary for the manufacture of nuclear fuel and reprocessing or other treatment following irradiation in a reactor. Reactors produce irradiated uranium and plutonium, the latter product being an essential part of the fuel cycle as related to Fast Reactors. The fuel cycle is generally considered to encompass the following:

Mining and milling of uranium (or thorium)

Refining and Conversion

Enrichment (except for natural uranium fuel)

Fabrication (into fuel rods or pellets)

Irradiation

Storage (of spent fuel)

Reprocessing (including plutonium extraction)

Waste management

Disposal

The world's largest suppliers of uranium are Australia, Canada, and the U.S.A. There are mines in several other parts of the world including Latin America, Namibia, South Africa (as a by-product of gold ores) and the U.S.S.R. Some of France's supplies come from Gabon and Niger. The crude ore is processed in the mining areas and from it is produced a yellow substance, uranium oxide, consisting of U238 with 0.7% U235. Because of its colour, it is known as "yellow cake". Natural uranium is slightly radioactive and toxic but cannot form a critical mass unless it is interspaced in suitable geometric form and placed with a moderator. It can be safely transported and is sent to countries which have fuel fabricating facilities of which there are about 15.

69

Thorium also occurs naturally and more extensively than uranium but is so widely dispersed in the earth's crust that only a limited number of deposits is sufficiently concentrated to be economically workable. It is extracted mainly in parts of India, Brazil and the U.S.A.

Refining, Conversion and Fabrication

These operations are carried out in large factories in several countries, the United Kingdom being one of the leaders. They may be carried out separately or all concentrated in one manufacturing complex.

At the first stage uranium ore concentrate (UOC) is dissolved in nitric acid to produce uranyl nitrate, which has to be filtered and purified. This is necessary to remove water, silicon and trace metal impurities to ensure acceptable neutron cross-sections.

The purified uranyl nitrate is evaporated to concentrate it and then denitrated to form uranium trioxide (UO3). This is converted by further chemical processes into uranium dioxide (UO2) and then into a green salt, uranium tetrafluoride (UF4) by hydrofluorination. This then follows two separate paths, either

1) it passes to a fluidised bed where it is mixed with fluorine to produce uranium hexafluoride (UF6), commonly known as "Hex" — a salt which is solid at low or "room" temperatures, but which if heated to above 56°C sublimates into a corrosive gaseous form. This then goes on to the enrichment stage; or

2) the UF4 is reduced to uranium metal for casting into natural uranium fuel rods.

Enrichment of Uranium

Most nuclear reactor systems utilise enriched fuels and therefore uranium enrichment is a very important part of the fuel cycle. Its place in the manufacturing sequence is between the conversion of natural uranium to UF6 and the reconversion of enriched UF6 to UO2 and pelletising.

There are several enrichment technologies, all of which have the purpose of increasing the U235 content of natural uranium by separating out the U238. The amount of U235 required for reactors using enriched uranium is usually up to 3% (For weapons grade material it is very much higher).

Because of the restraining effects of the Non-Proliferation Treaty and the Treaty of Tlatelolco (see Chapter 4) the number of countries with industrial enrichment capabilities is relatively small. The main producers and suppliers are in Brazil, France, Germany, the

Netherlands, Japan, the United Kingdom, the USSR and the USA. Argentina (where uranium ore is mined) is developing a small plant, complementing a conversion and fuel fabricating plant. India also plans to enter the uranium enrichment field and other countries may be involved in a small way in enrichment for peaceful purposes. The principal technologies in industrial use are:

1. Gaseous diffusion
Uranium hexafluoride or "HEX" (UF6) is used, being in gaseous form, because this system exploits the different rates of diffusion of gases through a porous barrier or "sieve". The molecules of U235 pass through more quickly than the heavier U238 so they can be separated. The amount of U235 separated out is extremely small so the process has to be repeated many times, using what is known as the cascade principle. The proportion of U235 is thus gradually increased until the desired level of enrichment.

2. Gaseous centrifuge
The other principal enrichment process used on a large commercial scale also has the purpose of separating U238 from U235, using UF6 gas.
   The molecular weight difference between U235 and U238 is exploited by rotating the gas at a very high speed in a high vacuum. The centrifuges are quite small units, can run virtually without maintenance and consume only a small amount of electricity compared with gaseous diffusion plants. The cascade system is also central to this process and in a large factory there may be many of thousands of units in a cascade.

3. Jet nozzle separation
This method ("Trenndüse") involves passing gaseous UF6, mixed with hydrogen, helium etc., through an air nozzle. The lighter molecules concentrate on the outside of the stream of gas and the heavier on the inside. The stream enters a slit in a tube (a "paring" tube) located opposited the centre of the nozzle and this receives most of the heavier molecules from the inner part of the stream, thus achieving a partial separation. This can be repeated as necessary on the cascade principal.

4. Laser Separation
Another separation technique, nowadays known as AVLIS (Atomic Vapour Laser Isotope Separation), involves isotope laser photo-chemistry, a process for which the experts have high hopes. The technical language for the system is "isotopically selective photoionisation of uranium atoms induced by lasers". It works on the differences of atomic or molecular structure instead of the difference in weight.

71

This process has not yet reached the stage of large-scale industrial exploitation.

Reprocessing of Spent Fuel

After a period of irradiation in a reactor the nuclear fuel loses its efficiency and is then regarded as spent. It is not only hot but highly radioactive and dangerous. When removed it must, before it can be transported elsewhere, be stored safely for some months. Irradiated spent fuel cannot therefore be simply discarded.

The option of keeping it in safe storage more of less indefinitely when nothing is to be done with it (the once-through cycle) is one that many countries, notably the U.S.A., have chosen. However, irradiated fuel contains very valuable nuclear materials which can be extracted and reprocessed such as plutonium and depleted uranium. These can be recycled as fuel for power reactors — plutonium oxide may be mixed with uranium oxide to produce the mixed oxide fuels (Mox) (previously mentioned as the fuel for fast reactors); depleted uranium may be re-enriched for example. There are also other useful residues. About 3% of the spent fuel is highly radioactive waste which has to be dealt with in such a way that it cannot present an unacceptable hazard to mankind and the environment.

A number of countries has for many years favoured the reprocessing option rather than "once-through" in what is known in the industry as the "backend" of the fuel cycle. While the economies of the backend are open to argument (and have been studied by the OECD who found little to choose between the options) it seems from the standpoint of risk to the environment that it may be better not to put large quantities of radioactive material, however carefully packaged or vitrified, into more or less permanent storage or even to bury them deeply underground or under the sea, when they can be reprocessed in reasonable safety, reinserted into reactors and "burned up" in the fission process.

A typical sequence of reprocessing operations is that irradiated spent fuel in heavily shielded flasks arrives from the power stations. The fuel elements are transferred under water into storage ponds where they are kept until they have cooled down and the radioactivity decays to the required levels. They are then removed to a feed pond and by remote control transferred to shielded "caves" in which, still remotely controlled, "decanning" takes place, i.e. the cladding is sheared off by a multi-ram hydraulic powered machine accurately controlled from outside the shear cave. The fuel from inside the element is cut up and dropped into dissolvers containing heated nitric

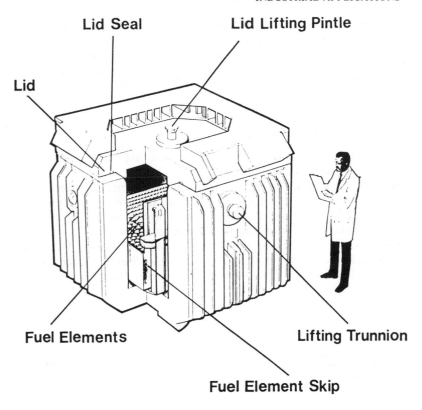

Lid Seal

Lid Lifting Pintle

Lid

Fuel Elements

Lifting Trunnion

Fuel Element Skip

Transport Container for Magnox Irradiated Fuel

acid. For enriched material a neutron poison is added to guard against accidental criticality.

The dissolved fuel then passes through chemical processes enabling the uranium and plutonium to be separated from the fission products. The result is separate solutions of uranyl nitrate and plutonium nitrate which are purified, evaporated and then converted respectively to uranium trioxide (UO_3) powder and plutonium dioxide (PUO_2) powder.

The plutonium dioxide powder is packed in stainless steel drums and stored. The uranium trioxide powder is also packed in sealed drums and either stored, recycled into new fuel or returned to the customer. The plutonium may not be returnable because of restrictions on the transfer of this material under the international Non-Proliferation Treaty aimed at controlling the supply and movement of material which could be used in the manufacture of nuclear weapons (see Chapter 4). The quantity of plutonium compared with the uranium is relatively small because far less is extracted from the spent fuel.

Radioactive Waste Disposal

Radioactive waste is the final product of the fuel cycle. At the fuel processing plants high and intermediate level waste would be handled and probably retained by the operators. Where spent fuel arises from nuclear power stations and other reactor establishments in countries where it is not to be reprocessed it would be classified as high level waste. It may be held on site for a long period in either a storage pool or a dry store. It may be removed to spent storage facilities deep underground as in the USA, Canada, West Germany and Sweden, for example. The Swedish practice involves deep disposal in a granite tomb under the Baltic Sea where it can be safely kept permanently.

"**High**" level waste comprises either irradiated fuel elements or the more highly radioactive waste products from the reprocessing of spent fuel.

"**Intermediate**" level waste, mostly short-lived solids, arises from reprocessing and would include the discarded fuel cladding; it also arises from power stations and would most likely consist of irradiated plant components.

"**Low**" level waste is mildly radioactive: it may be solid, liquid or gaseous and can arise from not only the nuclear industry, but also from hospitals, research centres, laboratories and the like. Solid materials would include untreated slightly contaminated clothing, metal scraps, containers, paper, plastics, glass, instruments and cleaning materials.

As long ago as 1958 the IAEA decided that low and intermediate level solid wastes could, if properly packaged, be safely disposed of into the sea. By 1967 the OECD's Nuclear Energy Agency was able to organise internationally supervised dumping of packaged low level waste into the deep Atlantic ocean. This was taken over in 1967 by the countries wishing to avail themselves of this facility: Belgium, France, Switzerland and the United Kingdom. The site selected by an international panel of marine scientists was 500 miles south west of Land's End, the area some 1,600 square miles and the depth of the sea-bed about 2½ miles. Previously to this, under the authority of the Atomic Energy Act of 1954 British waste was disposed of into the Hurd Deep in the English Channel. In the later years, up to 1982 when sea dumping was stopped, the operation was carried out annually on behalf of the 4 countries by the UKAEA at Harwell, using a specially equipped ship, the "Atlantic Fisher". The operation was halted in 1982 as a result of objections from the British Seamen's Union and from some European countries: the termination of sea-dumping was supported by the signatories of the London Dumping Convention (see next Chapter) at a Conference in February 1983. The U.S. Congress banned the ocean dumping of nuclear waste in 1972.

The low level wastes immersed in the sea were packed in concrete inside steel drums designed and constructed in accordance with NEA criteria. The system allowed for the slow discharge of contents from the sea-bed, to be dispersed in an extremely diluted form into the sea. The amounts of radioactivity were so small that the addition to the sea's natural radioactivity has not been detectable by the careful monitoring carried out under international control, of the dumping area. (The sea is believed, by the scientific experts to contain 500,000 million curies of natural radioactivity, including 1,000 million curies of radium — more toxic than plutonium — and millions of tonnes of uranium). Deep ocean disposal of low, and even intermediate, level wastes has always been regarded by the experts as very safe if properly done and closely controlled. It is unfortunate that public and political pressures have put an end to it, but perhaps in time the method will be re-established as being, at the least, less undesirable than retention or disposal on land. Disposal into the sea of low level liquid waste from coastal nuclear sites is, however, still permitted in various countries. These releases have to be within the permitted safe levels laid down by the ICRP and national authorities such as, in the United Kingdom, the Department of the Environment and the Ministry of Agriculture, Fisheries and Food (MAFF). The individual installation's site licences would also specify the permitted levels which could well be even less than the international standards, one criterion being known in the technical jargon as ALARA ("as low as reasonably achievable"). In any event, such authorised emissions are scarcely likely to have a measurable effect on the natural radioactivity of sea-water.

Low level waste is, otherwise, packaged in concrete and steel drums and buried in fairly shallow trenches (about 8 metres deep) either on the nuclear site or in a special disposal site.

Nuclear waste, as distinct from spent fuel for reprocessing, is normally handled within the country of origin. Transportation to special disposal sites in usually undertaken by road or rail. In the case of all but low level waste special shielded containers or "coffins" complying with stringent international safety standards, are employed. In the U.K. irradiated fuel is carried by rail in massive and immensely strong 14 inch thick steel boxes or "flasks". They are approved by the Department of Transport and comply with British Rail's requirements for dangerous goods. The handling, treatment, transportation, storage and disposal of radioactive wastes of all types have had an impressive safety record worldwide.

Radiochemicals and Irradiation

The radioactive isotopes of many elements, commonly called radioisotopes, are put to a large variety of uses in industry, medicine, agriculture, educational establishments and elsewhere.

Uses

1. They may be used as small power sources in isotopic generators installed in orbiting satellites or in navigational warning lights. An example of the latter was installed off the Kent Coast by Trinity House, the British lighthouse authority, as long ago as 1967. The generator known as RIPPLE (Radioisotope Powered Prolonged Life Equipment) was powered by heat from the decay of Strontium 90, converted to produce 1 watt by thermocouples. This same prepared isotope, or alternatively Plutonium 239 would be used to generate electricity in an American satellite. The generation of up to 100W is said to be possible although power will gradually drop as the decay of the radioactivity providing the heat progresses. This may take from months to many years according to the radioactive substance used and its half-life. Very low-powered isotope batteries for cardiac pacemakers are another of the many applications of radioisotopes in the generation of small amounts of electricity. All such devices have to be sealed in order to contain the radiation within safe levels.

2. Apart from generating power, radioisotopes have been used for decades in industry for such purposes as testing welds; tracing the flow or leakage of gases or liquids which have had small amounts of radioactive materials incorporated in them; measuring wear in moving parts; and in ionisation smoke detectors. In agriculture radioactive tracers are used to study nutrition in plants and animals, animal health, absorption in soil of fertilisers, pest-control and even food preservation.

3. Irradiation techniques can be used, within strict limits laid down by international bodies such as the United Nations Food and

Agriculture Organisation and the World Health Organisation, to inhibit the sprouting of harvested vegetables, to prolong shelf-life, to control organisms and parasites in food, deinfestation and disinfection. A joint FAO/IAEA/WHO Committee recommended in 1980 that an average dose of ionising radiation of 10 kilogray (KGy) was acceptable from a toxicological view-point. Irradiated food is subject to national regulatory controls in many countries which insist upon clearance by Governmental authorities before it may be consumed. However, not all countries approve of irradiated foodstuffs for human consumption. The U.K. prohibits foodstuffs irradiated with 50 rads and above and an energy level of 5 MeV and above except for patients requiring a sterile diet.

The radiation sources for food irradiation are commonly the following:

Gamma rays from the nuclides Cobalt 60 or Caesium 137

X-rays from machines operating at or below 5 MeV

Electron beams generated in machines operating at or below 10 MeV

These machines may be installed in special radiation centres which are not necessarily "nuclear installations" in law because of the small quantities and/or low levels of radioactivity involved.

4. Another more important area for the practical application of radioisotopes is medicine. They are used in the treatment of certain cancers and other diseases by penetrating radiation and for various diagnostic purposes. Injection or ingestion of very small doses of suitable radioisotopes allow the absorption of certain vitamins or blood flow to be measured by means of instruments for the detection and measurement of radiation. Radioisotopes of cobalt, iodine, gold, phosphorous, calcium or strontium, among others, are in common use medically.

Radioisotopes are produced initially by irradiating the appropriate stable isotope in a particle accelerator, research reactor or even power reactor. Concerns such as Government Departments, Atomic Energy Authorities or research centres, universities and power stations in many countries supply radioisotopes to the manufacturers. These may consist of safely encapsulated or sealed radiation sources containing perhaps a small sintered pellet of the substance. The manufacture and supply of the finished product, whether it be an isotopic battery, a diagnostic "label" for medical use or a neutron source for testing the quality of welds or casts in industry, is undertaken by specialist firms, many in the private sector. They usually fall outside the categories of nuclear installations subject to the international nuclear liability Conventions because the quantities and/or radiation levels are too low. The others are normally subject to tight controls under stringent regulations concerning radiation and radiactive substances. However, some are on such a large scale that they do not qualify for exemption.

The field for radioisotopes is enormous and growing. Research, much of it on an international scale, is ceaseless; new ideas and new products arise frequently.

Nuclear Explosives

Nuclear explosive devices, sometimes called explosive nuclear assemblies, are normally associated with atomic bombs or hydrogen bombs. But such explosives are no more limited to military uses than are the many conventional explosives and can be applied to peaceful uses where massive civil engineering excavations are required for, say, the construction of harbours or long distance canals.

This field of development has its difficulties, not the least being the severe restraints on the manufacture, testing and supply of nuclear explosives imposed by international treaties (see Chapter 4) covering the testing and proliferation of nuclear weapons which could be open to abuse if there were to be an uninhibited development of such explosives in all countries. Thus, an important element is provision for international observation of peaceful nuclear explosions ("PNE") under the auspices of the International Atomic Energy Agency.

Nevertheless, international studies have confirmed that there are practical applications in the civil use of such explosives. Apart from the examples mentioned above, mining is one possibility because the vast power of such explosions underground is able to change the stress distribution of rocks over a large area.

By far the most important work on nuclear explosives has been carried out under the United States Plowshare programme which was initiated as long ago as 1957 by the Atomic Energy Commission (now called the Nuclear Regulatory Commission). Apart from earthmoving or excavation, the recovery of gas and oil and underground gas-storage were seen as realistic prospects. One actual project, devised in the early 60's, was Operation "Gasbuggy". This was to involve a deep underground explosion to stimulate a gas deposit for extraction through a "chimney" created above the point of the explosion which is equivalent to a well bore in orthodox oil or gas extraction. The extraction of oil from oil shale is another application in suitable locations providing the broken up shale can be burned or retorted on site to produce economic oil, which may

then be pumped to the surface from the bottom of the cavity.
Operation "Gasbuggy" was successfully carried out in December 1976 in the San Juan Basin of New Mexico by the El Paso Gas Company, the USAEC and the Department of Mines. The 26 Kiloton device was exploded at a depth of 280 feet. In 1969, Project Rulison took place in Colorado when a 40 Kiloton thermonuclear device was exploded at a depth of 1.5 miles to stimulate a natural gas deposit. Project Ketch, however, designed by the Columbia Gas System to create a vast underground cavern for gas storage under a forest in Pennsylvania had to be abandoned in 1968 in the face of strong public opposition. The Financial Times of 13.9.69 reported that the British Gas Council was investigating this method as a possible means of storing natural gas under the North Sea, but nothing more was heard of it subsequently.

A very different use of a peaceful nuclear explosion occured in the USSR in 1970 when it was reported that explosions were set off to extinguish two uncontrolled gas well fires.

Ore-leaching is yet another operation in which nuclear explosives can be utilised, particularly for diffusely distributed minerals such as low grade copper oxide, for which other methods would be uneconomic. Once the ore is broken up the copper can be leached out with acid which is then pumped to the surface where conventional separation techniques would be used.

The use of nuclear explosives to build a new harbour in Australia or a second Panama Canal are among ideas that have been discussed but never pursued and it seems unlikely that much progress will be achieved outside the USSR and USA (where experience in underground weapons testing and the availability of large uninhabited areas provide great advantages): but even there, progress has been slow.

II

Legal Frameworks

Chapter IV

INTERNATIONAL LEGAL OBLIGATIONS AND REGULATORY CONTROLS

We have already seen that as early as 1895 when Roentgen discovered X-rays it was realised that exposure to radiation could cause damage to the skin. Efforts were made in 1916 by the Roentgen Society to promote safety standards in relation to radiation and in the United Kingdom in the 1920's the X-ray and Radium Protection Committee began to consider the need for establishing what were the maximum safe dosages to which workers in this field could be exposed. The International Commission on Radiological Protection, the ICRP, which is still in existence, was set up in 1928 and they have done a great deal of work over nearly 60 years in determining acceptable levels of radiation for workers in the field and for the public in general. However, the development of, and research into, nuclear energy was limited to a large extent to laboratory work until the early days of the second World War when the focus of attention was mainly on plutonium production and nuclear explosives for use in weapons. This sort of development work was either in the hands of the Government or military services or under controlled conditions carried out by academic and other research institutes. The ending of the War in 1945 meant a great increase in the development and research on reactors of various kinds, for the production of electricity. It was no longer possible for this work to be concentrated in the hands of Government Departments or kept under extremely strict restraints and subject to secrecy. However, if it was to be released to the public domain, development of nuclear energy must obviously still be subject to Governmental regulation of work involving the use of fissile matter and the handling of radioactive substances. Even though it was possible for much of this work to be maintained by Government organisations or public bodies under Government control, the involvement of large numbers of privately employed scientists and other technical people was necessary and likewise, with a view to developing nuclear energy for industrial purposes, commercial concerns would be needed to assist in the design and manufacture of plant.

However, initially in the United Kingdom development of nuclear energy was in the hands of the State, as set out in the Atomic Energy Act of 1946. Under this Act, the Secretary of State was permitted to prohibit anybody from manufacturing atomic energy except under licence. In 1954, an Act was introduced setting up the Atomic Energy Authority in the United Kingdom. This was a statutory corporation, the intention of which was to take out of Government hands the production and use of atomic energy and to carry out research. It was within the framework of this legislation that the first of the commercial-size nuclear power stations were designed and constructed in the United Kingdom, starting with that at Calder Hall in 1957. These were the fore-runners of the large-scale commercial power stations subsequently to be developed and operated by the Central Electricity Generating Board in England and Wales and the South of Scotland Electricity Board in Scotland. It was in preparation for developments like this in the field of power production and in other areas of nuclear energy that the Nuclear Installations (Licensing and Insurance) Act of 1959 was brought into force. This legislation, like that in a number of other countries, including the United States, was in many respects a precursor of the international Conventions in the field of civil liability.

The 1959 Act provided, for example, that the liability of the operator towards the public should be absolute, that is to say, in the event of any ionising radiation released from his premises causing hurt or damage to third parties, and this included employees, the operator would be strictly liable without need for proof of fault or negligence. It also introduced the concept of channelling of all liability to the operator so that in the event of damage arising in consequence of a nuclear incident or arising from any nuclear matter on the site of the licensed premises claims would be directed solely to the licensed operator and no other person. This meant that in the event, for example, of the accident being due to a defect in the plant or to the acts of, say, a contractor working on the site, the operator would nevertheless be alone responsible for the payment of compensation. While imposing on the operator a very heavy burden of legal responsibility, the 1959 Act in the United Kingdom also provided certain safeguards in the sense that he was not to be subject to unlimited financial responsibilities and there was to be some limitation in time with respect to the period during which the victim of any release of ionising radiation could bring a claim against the operator. It was recognised that the consequences of exposure to ionising radiation in human beings could take very many years to appear and it was clearly inappropriate that the operator of a nuclear installation should never be sure when, if ever, he was going to be subject to a claim for compensation. Consequently a limit of 10 years was imposed on the bringing of claims counted from the date of the incident which gave rise to the injury. Another very important aspect of this legislation was a limitation in the amount of compensation that the operator himself would be liable to pay to the victims of an incident. This amount was fixed in 1959 at £5M. This figure was not keyed to just one incident but was the maximum that he could be called upon to pay out regardless of the number of years the plant was in operation and the number of successive incidents.

These limitations were designed largely to respond to the representations made by insurers who were consulted by the Government. Another reason for imposing limitations as well as very strict legal requirements with respect to the operator's responsibilities was the desire of the U.K. Government, and indeed the Governments of Western Europe in general, not to risk stifling this new industry at birth by imposing impossibly heavy financial responsibilities on the operators and others who would be concerned in the industrial and commercial development of nuclear energy. The compensation limits were balanced, however, by the assumption of Government of a commitment to meet claims in excess of the £5M limit imposed on the operator and for which he was required to obtain commercial insurance or other financial security. The Government also undertook to meet claims arising after the expiry of the 10 year period up to a maximum of 30 years.

Mention has been made of the development of similar legislation in other countries. Examples of pre-Convention legislation, such as the British 1959 Act, adopted in other countries include the Price Anderson Act of 1957 amending the United States Atomic Energy Act of 1954, the German Atomic Energy Act of 1959 and the Swiss Federal Law on the Exploitation of Nuclear Energy for Peaceful Purposes and Protection from Irradiation of 1959. These, like the British legislation, introduced the concept of channelling legal liability onto the owner and operator of a nuclear installation, strict liability and limitation of financial responsibility in amount and in time.

At the same time, the Organisation for European Economic Co-operation, as it was then called (now OECD), was studying the need for an international Convention to ensure the introduction of harmonised liability legislation concerning nuclear energy in the member States. In view of the influence on the development of national legislation of the OECD's Convention on Third Party Liability in the Field of Nuclear Energy, or the Paris Convention as it came to be called, and of its sister Convention, that introduced by the International Atomic Energy Agency a few years later, known as the Vienna Convention, it is appropriate at this point to review these Conventions, particularly from the point of view of their importance to insurers and those requiring insurance or other financial security, before examining the national legislation of the United Kingdom and a number of other countries.

The Paris Convention

This important international Convention was the outcome of some years of discussion and negotiation between the Governments of the OEEC. The countries concerned were the following:

Austria	Netherlands
Belgium	Norway
Denmark	Portugal
France	Spain
Federal Republic of Germany	Sweden
Greece	Switzerland
Italy	Turkey
Luxembourg	United Kingdom

This work was carried out under the auspices of an arm of the OEEC, the European Nuclear Energy Agency. (The name of this Agency was altered to Nuclear Energy Agency when, some years later, the membership of this Organisation was widened to include a number of non-European countries and its name was changed to Organisation for Economic Co-operation and Development.) The completion of an agreed wording for this quite complex Convention was a considerable achievement because every part of it required to be approved unanimously by all the countries involved. The Convention was signed on 29th July 1960 by the 16 countries mentioned above. It did not, however, come into force until 1968, because, in order to be effective, the Convention had to be ratified by a minimum of 5 of the signatories. Ratification involved introducing legislation which, in effect, enacted the compulsory provisions of the Convention. The countries who had ratified the Convention by 1968 were the following:

Belgium	Sweden
France	Turkey
Spain	United Kingdom

Except for Austria, Luxembourg and Switzerland, the other original signatories ratified subsequently (Finland also became a party by way of accession).

The preamble to the Convention stated that the European Nuclear Energy Agency was charged with "encouraging the elaboration and harmonisation of legislation relating to nuclear energy in participating countries, in particular with regard to Third Party Liability and Insurance against atomic risks". Their desire was to ensure "adequate and equitable compensation for persons who suffer damage caused by nuclear incidents whilst taking the necessary steps to ensure the development and production of uses of nuclear energy for peaceful purposes is not thereby hindered". The preamble also stated the conviction of the member countries of the "need for unifying the basic rules applying in the various countries to the liability incurred for such damage, whilst leaving these countries free to take, on a national basis, any additional measures which they deem appropriate, including the application of the provisions of this Convention to damage caused by incidents due to ionising radiations not covered therein".

In our consideration of various types of nuclear installations and nuclear materials in Chapter 2, we have already encountered a number of the definitions appearing in the Paris Convention. There are two more which are of importance, as follows:

Nuclear Incident
"A nuclear incident" means any occurrence or succession of occurrences having the same origin which causes damage, provided that such occurrence or succession of occurrences or any of the damage caused arises out of or results from the radioactive properties, or a combination of radioactive properties with toxic, explosive, or other hazardous properties of nuclear fuel or radioactive products or waste or with any of them.

Operator
"Operator" in relation to a nuclear installation means the person designated or recognised by the competent public authority as the operator of that installation.

The Convention allows what was described as the Steering Committee of the Nuclear Energy Agency to make certain variations or interpretations of the Convention without referring back to the full body of the OECD. The Steering Committee is a Committee of Governmental Experts appoints by the member States. In connection with the definitions the opening section, i.e. Article 1, of the Convention specifies that if in its view the small extent of the risks involved so warrants, the Steering Committee may exclude any nuclear installation, nuclear fuel or nuclear substances from the application of this Convention and they indeed did so subsequently in the shape of a decision taken in 1964 which will be described later.

The purpose of this review of the Paris Convention is mainly to look at such aspects of it as are of particular concern to those who may be called upon to provide the Liability insurance cover required by nuclear installation operators in order that they may be licensed to operate and may continue to operate their nuclear installations or to handle or to carry certain radioactive substances under the authority of their national Governments. Those aspects of the Convention which are considered to be of particular interest and importance are as follows:

Territorial limitation

Because the Paris Convention is a regional agreement there are certain limitations as to the extent of its application and the manner in which victims of a nuclear incident causing trans-frontier damage living in a country which is not a party to the Convention or, to use the language of the Convention, is a "non-contracting State", may benefit from the provisions of the Convention and any national legislation thereunder. Consequently it is made plain in Article 2 that the Convention does not apply to nuclear incidents occurring in the territory of non-contracting States or to damage suffered in such territory unless otherwise provided by the legislation of the Contracting Party (meaning the OECD member Government which has ratified the Convention) in whose territory the nuclear installation of the operator liable is situated. There is an exception to this in relation to certain rights conferred under Article 6 (e) of the Convention which states that

"any person who has his principal place of business in the territory of a contracting party or who is the servant of such a person and who has paid compensation in respect of damage caused by a nuclear incident occurring in the territory of a non-contracting State or in respect of damage suffered in such territory shall, up to the amount which he has paid, acquire the rights which the person so compensated would have had against the operator but for the provisions of Article 2".

In considering Article 2, it should be recognised that the Convention does give an option to contracting States to extend the operation of the Paris Convention to incidents occurring in their territory even if the damage is suffered on the territory of a non-contracting State; or, conversely, to damage suffered in the contracting State which arose from an incident in a non-contracting State; or even to incidents occurring in and damage suffered in the territory of a non-contracting State.

While the Steering Committee and the OECD would obviously like to see as much harmonisation of national legislation as possible it had to be recognised that the position of different countries was not the same because of their geographical situation. This became particularly evident when it was realised that a nuclear incident might, if it was serious enough, cause trans-frontier damage. The consideration was even more relevant in relation to the international transportation of nuclear matter. This, if involved in an accident, could release radiation and cause injury and damage in the countries which were crossed during the course of transit even though some of them might not be contracting States. Another consideration was the position that might arise in the event of the carriage of nuclear matter on the high seas on board ship, when the ship might be registered in the territory of a contracting State although the nuclear incident causing the damage occurred on the territorial waters of a non-contracting State. The Steering Committee made a recommendation in 1971 suggesting that the scope of the application of the Paris Convention should be optionally extended by national legislation to any damage suffered in a contracting State or on the high seas on board a ship registered in a contracting State even though it originated in a non-contracting State. This would mean that the victims of nuclear injury or damage in a country which was party to the Paris Convention would have equal rights of compensation even if their injury or loss was the consequence of an accident occurring outside the territory of the contracting State and not in another contracting State. It is necessary for insurers to appreciate this concept and be aware of the position under national legislation exercising the option to extend territorial scope because it could affect the scope of the liabilities of the nuclear operator when it comes to considering the potential cost in terms of claims from Third Parties arising from a nuclear incident at an insured installation or from an occurrence in another country or from the carriage of nuclear material such as, say, irradiated fuel on the high seas.

This is a point of particular interest to the insurers of Transport risks. It is possible that a British ship registered in the United Kingdom might carry a cargo of irradiated nuclear fuel to the U.K. from a country like Japan which, although a member of the OECD, is not a party to the Paris Convention. The voyage would very likely pass close to or through the territorial waters of countries which are not contracting States, one of these being the United States of America. It could make a considerable difference to the insurers' exposure to risk if it were possible for claims to be brought against the operator for whom the material is being carried back to the United Kingdom, as well as the consignee if he accepts legal responsibility, by people in States which but for an alteration in the territorial scope as allowed under the Convention would not otherwise have been subject to the restrictions of the Paris Convention.

This aspect of the Convention emphasises the international value of such an agreement and its significance to insurers particularly those concerned with the international aspects of nuclear risks. Other points arising in connection with the Transport risk will be looked at subsequently.

However, the most important provisions of the Paris Convention from the point of view of the extent of an operator's liabilities such as would require insurance and which were intended to be enshrined in national legislation are the following:

Legal liability of the operator

The Convention is very positive; it states in Article 3 (a) that the "operator of a nuclear installation shall be liable, in accordance with this Convention, for:

(i) damage to or loss of life of any person; and

(ii) damage to or loss of any property"

However, liability for damage to property does not extend to the nuclear installation itself and any property on the site of that installation which is used or is to be used in connection with that installation. With respect to nuclear substances in the course of transit for which the operator has a legal liability it was recognised by the Steering Committee in 1981, that the operator should not be liable for damage to such nuclear substances, this being considered to be in the spirit of the Convention regarding damage to property on the site of a nuclear installation. Also in relation to nuclear matter in transit, the Convention in this part provides that the operator shall not be liable for damage to the means of transport upon which nuclear substances involved in an incident were located at the time of an incident. In the event of what is sometimes called mixed damage, when a nuclear incident is accompanied by a "non-nuclear" incident Article 3 (b) specifies that in those circumstances the damage which is not reasonably separable from nuclear damage shall be regarded as being nuclear. In general, it is necessary for there to be proof that any damage or loss was caused by a nuclear incident and that it involved either nuclear fuel or radioactive products or wastes in a nuclear installation, or nuclear substances coming from such an installation. The Convention also allows Contracting Parties to provide by national legislation that the liability of the operator of a nuclear installation shall include liability for damage arising out of or resulting from ionising radiation emitted by any other source of radiation. This could include, for example, radioisotopes which might not fall within the definition of radioactive substances and would therefore be outside the terms of the Paris Convention.

The Convention makes it clear that in certain circumstances the operator of an installation from which or in which nuclear damage arises may be exonerated from liability. One of the circumstances in which this situation may be met is in the case of nuclear substances stored at a nuclear installation incidentally to their carriage. In this case the person liable would be the owner of the nuclear materials, usually the operator of the installation from which they came, but not the operator of the installation where they are temporarily stored in the course of carriage. It is possible for more than one operator to be liable if, for example, there are several concerns operating nuclear reactors on the site of, say, a research establishment, or there may be several operators involved in the transportation of nuclear matter on the same means of transport. In these circumstances the Convention provides that the liability of such operators shall be joint and several. However, as to the financial liability of such operators, the Convention provides that the total amount for which they shall be liable shall be the highest amount established with respect to any one of them in accordance with the provisions of the national nuclear law dealing with financial limits.

Operator solely liable for compensation

The Paris Convention provides, in Article 6, that a claimant may exercise his right to compensation only against an operator who is liable in accordance with the Convention unless national law gives a right of direct action against the person providing financial security such as an insurer or other financial guarantor. Article 6(b) of the Convention provides that subject to any exceptions otherwise provided in the Convention "no other person shall be liable for damage caused by a nuclear incident" than the operator. What this means in practice is that the operator is the only person (other than his insurer or financial guarantor, if national legislation so provides), who may be called upon to pay compensation. This applies even if the nuclear incident is not due to any negligence or act of omission or commission by the licensed operator himself. Consequently, if a nuclear incident arises as a result of a defect in the nuclear plant or the materials used in it which would otherwise be the fault of the manufacturer or the supplier, or if it is due to some act on the part of contractors carrying out certain maintenance or repairs, the operator nevertheless is the one who is legally liable to pay the compensation. This provision is known as *channelling of liability* and is to be found in virtually all nuclear legislation ratifying the Convention or otherwise based upon the general provisions of the Paris or Vienna Conventions. It means, for example, that a supplier to a nuclear installation would not normally require to cover his liability with respect to any damage arising from a nuclear incident for which he may otherwise have a legal liability. However, his contract may require him to indemnify the operator for claims arising from the supplier's fault. Liabilities of this nature assumed by agreement are not to be encouraged and most insurers would hope that, particularly with respect to the duty to compensate the public, contractors and suppliers would avoid such agreements. The operator would have a right of recourse otherwise only in the event of the damage caused by a nuclear incident resulting from an act or omission of another party done with intent to cause damage. He may also be able to avoid payment of compensation to a third party who is the author of his own misfortune if there is evidence of criminal act or gross negligence by such claimant. In the event of any other person paying out compensation to a third party who is not himself liable under legislation enacted in accordance with the Convention, that person has a right to recover the amounts he has paid from the liable operator in the absence of any formal agreement to the contrary. It may also be the case in individual countries that where the victim of a nuclear incident receives compensation under social security, workmen's compensation or occupational disease compensation systems, the right of beneficiaries of such systems and the rights of recourse by virtue of such systems can be so arranged that the organisations concerned may reclaim from the licensed operator the amounts they have paid out in consequence of the nuclear incident for damage or injury which is caused to the victim.

Operator's liability — financial limits

In accordance with the stated intentions of the authors of the Paris Convention, provision is made to limit the financial responsibility of the operator to pay compensation to third parties. Under the Convention as it was fixed in 1960 the maximum liability of an operator in respect of damage caused by a nuclear incident was 15 million European Monetary Area units of account, or EMA units. The Convention did, however, allow contracting parties taking into account the availability of insurance or other financial security to establish a greater or lesser amount but fixed an absolute minimum of 5 million units of account. The intention was that these units of account may be converted into national currency and rounded off. One unit of account was linked to the official price of 0.88867088 grammes of fine gold in American Dollars and these figures were in effect therefore equivalent at that time to 15 million and 5 million Dollars, respectively. Subsequently this unit of account became quite inappropriate because of changes in the way in which the international monetary system was organised. Consequently, in 1982, under the terms of a Protocol which will be mentioned later, it was decided to adopt another artificial currency known as the Special Drawing Right or SDR. The value of this unit varies according to the average value of a basket of 16 different currencies and is determined annually by the OECD. The revision of the recommended minimum and maximum limits in terms of Special Drawing Rights did not, however, alter the right of national Governments to fix higher or lower amounts having regard to the availability of insurance or other financial security. When this change was made in 1982, the relevant Article 7(b) was also amended to make provision for any contracting party having regard to the nature of the nuclear installation or the nuclear substances involved, and to the likely consequences of an incident originating therefrom, to establish a lower amount. However, it was intended that in no event should such lower amounts be less than 5 million SDRs. When adopting this revision, the Steering Committee of the Nuclear Energy Agency recommended, and the OECD Council adopted the recommendation, that any contracting party establishing the liability of certain nuclear operators at an amount lower than that established for nuclear operators generally, should take steps to make available public funds to satisfy any claim for compensation in excess of the lower amounts so established up to the amount generally established for nuclear operators.

The amounts fixed in terms of the maximum compensation payable to victims by the operator in consequence of a nuclear incident are clearly very low in relation to the potential cost of a major accident from the point of view of damage and injury to third parties. This has always been recognised and reference will be made subsequently to a Supplementary Convention, known as the Brussels Convention, which fixes two layers of additional compensation which shall be payable after the exhaustion of the amount for which the operator is liable, such additional compensation to be payable, firstly by the national Government concerned up to a fixed limit, and thereafter by joint contribution of all the parties to the Brussels Supplementary Convention.

Limitation in time

As mentioned in the opening paragraphs of this Chapter, in reference to the British 1959 legislation, the time scale for the occurrence of disease or death consequent upon exposure to certain types of ionising radiation may be very long indeed. When the Convention was being prepared, representations were made on behalf of insurers, pointing out that it was not practicable for them to keep their books open indefinitely after the occurrence of an incident which may or may not give rise to claims in the relatively distant future. The practical problems of this are fairly obvious, not the least in the event of a dispute when records may be incomplete, recollections faulty, the original installation operator might no longer be in charge and the insurers may not even be in business although there may be successors who may have inherited their financial obligations to future claimants. Consequently, as in the U.K. and certain other legislations which pre-dated the Paris Convention, a limit of 10 years is placed on the period during which the operator or his insurers or other financial guarantors will be liable to meet claims. The 10 years start from the date of the nuclear incident alleged to have caused the injury or damage. Where there has been a series of nuclear incidents originating from the same cause, then the date to be taken for the calculation of the 10-year period, the *"period of prescription"*, is the date of the last known incident. In order to bring a claim the victim must first of all identify the nuclear installation operator said to be liable. Secondly, he must be able to demonstrate that a nuclear incident giving rise to a release of ionising radiation did indeed take place. Thirdly, he has to be able to show that his illness was due to that incident or in the event of his death his successors must be able to show the cause. Consequently, the Paris Convention in Article 8(a) provides that "the right of compensation under this Convention shall be extinguished if an action is not brought within 10 years from the date of the nuclear incident". However, it does allow contracting parties to establish a longer period than 10 years if measures have been taken to cover the liability of the operator for such longer period. To meet the position in the event of damage arising from nuclear substances which have been stolen, lost, jettisoned or abandoned and not been recovered, the Convention provides that the maximum time during which a claim may be brought shall be 20 years from the date of the loss, etc. *not* from the date of the nuclear incident. The period allowed from the date of the nuclear incident is computed in accordance with Article 8(a), i.e. 10 years, but it is subject to a ceiling of 20 years. This limitation is not always clearly understood. However, it is quite certain, and this has been confirmed by both the OECD experts and, in the case of the United Kingdom, the responsible Government department, that the 20 years is an upper limit. Any incident occurring more than 10 years after the loss of the substances concerned means that the 10 year period during which claims may be brought against the operator is reduced by one year for every year after 10 years have elapsed following the *loss* of the nuclear matter. This variation is necessary because it is possible for nuclear materials to be lost perhaps in the course of transit during a voyage in which either the vessel is sunk or the cargo including the nuclear fuel or radioactive waste or whatever it may be has to be jettisoned or abandoned. The theft of radioactive matter is possible although the security and other precautions surrounding nuclear installations and the transportation of nuclear matter are so stringent that it would perhaps take a very determined act, possibly the act of terrorists, to secure such material. However, if stolen matter were stored away and ultimately caused an incident the possibility of persons being injured and making claims as a result of that event cannot be ruled out.

Therefore, we have an almost invariable limit of 10 years from the date of the incident during which the potential victim is able to become aware of his injury and he or his successors in the event of his death can notify the licensed operator concerned of such injury, illness or death. The preparation and quantification of such a claim could be a difficult and lengthy business and it is therefore also provided in the Convention that a claimant may have a period of not less than 2 years in addition to the 10 years, or during the 10 years, in which to actually bring the claim having once identified and notified the operator allegedly responsible. The terms in which this is expressed in the Paris Convention are as follows: "National legislation may establish a period of not less than 2 years for the extinction of the right or as a period of limitation either from the date at which the person suffering damage has knowledge or from the date at which he ought reasonably have to have known of both the damage and the operator liable". However, this does not permit the 10 and 20 year periods to be exceeded insofar as they relate to the maximum time allowed for the claimant to become aware of the loss or injury.

A useful additional right which may be granted under national legislation, although is not obligatory under the Convention, is that any person suffering damage caused by a nuclear incident who has brought an action for compensation within the period provided for, i.e. the 10 year or 20 year limit, may amend his claim in respect of any aggravation of the damage, which of course includes injury, after the expiry of such period provided final judgement has not been entered into by a competent Court.

Insurance Cover

The Paris Convention provides that to cover his liability under the Convention the operator shall be required to have and to maintain insurance or other financial security of the amount established in Article 7 under such type and terms as the competent public authority in the State concerned shall specify. This same Article (10) also provides that the insurer or financial guarantor may not suspend or cancel the insurance or other financial security without giving notice in writing of at least two months to the competent public authority, or in the case of the carriage of nuclear substances during the period of the carriage in question. Finally, this same Article lays down that "the sums provided as insurance, reinsurance or other financial security may be drawn upon only for compensation for damage caused by a nuclear incident".

Another important provision in relation to insurance, particularly having regard to the international aspects, is in Article 12 which requires that compensation payable, insurance and reinsurance premiums, sums provided as insurance, reinsurance or other financial security, and interest and costs shall be freely transferable betwen the monetary areas of the contracting parties.

Article 15 makes it clear that any contracting party may take any necessary measures to provide for an increase in the amount of compensation specified in the Convention. In fact, many of the contracting States have increased the compensation for which the operator is liable under their national legislation considerably beyond the amounts originally laid down in the Paris Convention, so much so that there is now a serious imbalance as between one country and another as to the amount of compensation that the operator is required to pay subject to the availability of insurance cover or other financial security.

Although all the then 16 members of the OECD signed the Paris Convention some have still not ratified, notably Switzerland. Furthermore, a number of Governments entered important reservations when they became signatories. For example, the Governments of the Federal Republic of Germany, of Austria and of Greece reserved the right with respect to Article 6 to provide that persons other than the operator may continue to be liable for damage caused by a nuclear incident, providing they were fully covered in respect of their liability (including defence against unjustified actions) by insurance or other financial security obtained by the operator or out of State funds. The effect of this would seem to be that whereas it is a derogation from the principle of channelling of legal liability solely to the operator it preserves the concept of the operator being solely responsible for the payment of compensation ("economic liability") providing his insurance covers that in respect of damage which is due to the actions of other parties. Also, in respect of Article 8(a) Germany and Austria reserved the right to fix a period longer than 10 years during which the victim could bring a claim providing measures had been taken to cover the liability of the operator for actions begun after the expiry of the 10 year period. These two countries also reserved the right to provide for the operator to be made liable for damage caused by a nuclear incident directly due to an act of armed conflict, hostilities, civil war or insurrection. From an insurance point of view this would be a most unusual responsibility to place upon an insured. The reservation also applied to the right to make provision for the operator to be liable for damage caused by a grave natural disaster of an exceptional character. Since Article 9 allows for Governments to make such provision if they wish the point of the reservation is not altogether clear.

The Brussels Supplementary Convention

Even before the Paris Convention was signed the 6 original member countries of the European Economic Community — Belgium, France, Federal Republic of Germany, Italy, Luxembourg and the Netherlands — were giving thought to the best way of implementing the provision in the Paris Convention for the State to supplement the amount of compensation which the operator would be obliged to pay in the event of a nuclear incident. It will be recalled that the Paris Convention provided that the amount of compensation payable per incident should be 15 million EMA units of account and in no event should the Government concerned fix a figure below 5 million units of account except possibly when dealing with nuclear installations or nuclear materials presenting a very low degree of hazard. Working under the auspices of EURATOM, that is to say, the European Atomic Energy Community, with the assistance also of the British Government, these 6 countries formulated some proposals for what was to have been a "EURATOM Convention" laying down certain provisions whereby the amount of extra compensation, provided by the State in excess of that which was the responsibility of the operator, should itself be subject to certain limitations in amount. It was also considered that further provision above that limit should be made available by the member countries jointly, up to a second upper limit. By 1962 this new Convention had been drafted but the matter was then taken up by the OECD and, in particular, the Nuclear Energy Agency of that organisation.

As a result of an international meeting of Governmental Experts held in Brussels towards the end of 1962 the terms of the new Convention, which had the official title of the "Convention supplementary to the Paris Convention of 29th July 1960 on third party liability in the field of nuclear energy'' were agreed and it was signed by the Governments of

Austria
Belgium
Denmark
France
Federal Republic of Germany
Italy
Luxembourg
Norway
Netherlands
Spain
Sweden
Switzerland
United Kingdom

The main provisions of this Supplementary Convention concern insurers, although the compensation payable relates only to amounts in excess of those for which insurance would have to be provided. They are as follows:

Territorial Scope

The Convention applies to damage caused by nuclear incidents other than those occurring entirely in the territory of a State which is not a party to the Brussels Convention. The incident must be one for which the operator would be liable under the terms of the Paris Convention and the protection of this additional Supplementary Convention would apply to damage suffered:

1. In the territory of a contracting party; or
2. On or over the high seas on board a ship or aircraft registered in the territory of a contracting party; or
3. On or over the high seas by a national of a contracting party provided that, in the case of damage to a ship or an aircraft, the ship or aircraft is registered in the territory of a contracting party.

It is also necessary that the Courts of a contracting party have jurisdiction pursuant to the Paris Convention.

Compensation and financial limits

Compensation to be provided up to a maximum originally of 120 million units of account per incident. This figure represented the totality of compensation to be provided and included that which must be contributed in the first instance by the operator i.e. a minimum of at least 5 million units of account under the Paris Convention. Where higher amounts were fixed by national law the obligation of the State to meet the excess between that amount and the 120 million units would not arise until the amount of compensation payable by the operator was exhausted. The excess compensation to be provided by the State was divided into two layers. The first layer, up to 70 million units of account, was to be the responsibility of the contracting party in whose territory the nuclear installation was situated and the payment was to be made out of public funds. Between 70 million and 120 million units of account the public funds to be made available to meet this sum were to be provided collectively by all the contracting parties according to a formula for contributions specified in the Brussels Convention.

Section (c) of the relevant Article (3) of the Brussels Convention makes the following provisions regarding the manner in which the additional funds will be handled; each contracting party shall either:

(i) establish the maximum liability of the operator, pursuant to Article 7 of the Paris Convention, at 120 million units of account, and provide that such liability shall be covered by all the funds referred to in paragraph (d) of this article; or

(ii) establish the maximum liability of the operator at an amount at least equal to that established pursuant to paragraph (b)(i) (i.e. 5 million units of account) and provide that in excess of such amount and up to 120 million units of account, the public funds referred to in this article shall be made available by some means other than as cover for the liability of the operator, provided that the rules of substance and procedure laid down in this Convention are not thereby affected.

This Article (section (d)) also makes the important provision that the obligation of the operator to pay compensation, interest or costs out of public funds shall only be enforceable against the operator as and when such funds are in fact made available.

The formula whereby the totality of the compensation to be paid by (a) the national Government concerned, and (b) the other contracting parties is of interest. Article 12(a) reads as follows:

(i) as to 50%, on the basis of the ratio between the gross national product at current prices of each contracting party and the total of the gross national products at current prices of all contracting parties as shown by the official statistics published by the Organisation for Economic Co-operation and Development for the year preceding the year in which the nuclear incident occurs;

(ii) as to 50% on the basis of the ratio between the thermal power of the reactors situated in the territory of each contracting party and the total thermal power of the reactors situated in the territories of all the contracting parties. This calculation shall be made on the basis of the thermal power of the reactors shown at the date of the nuclear incident in the list referred to in Article 2(a) (i): provided that a reactor shall only be taken into consideration for the purposes of this calculation as from the date when it first reaches criticality.

It should be explained, at this point, that in Article 2(a) (i) reference is made to a list which is to be established and kept up to date in accordance with Article 13. This requires each contracting party to communicate full particulars of their nuclear installations to the Belgian Government the repository of such information on behalf of the OECD. The Article sets out fairly detailed requirements which include an obligation to give a list of all installations not yet completed and the expected date on which the risk of a nuclear incident will exist. This obviously means the date at which the installation becomes "nuclear" in the sense that there would be on the site of the installation materials or activities which could give rise to a nuclear incident. The list would also have to give, in the case of reactors, the expected date of first criticality and the thermal power. The Belgian Government is given the responsibility of supplying to any contracting party on demand an up to date statement of the nuclear installations concerned and the details that have been supplied in respect of them.

Article 12(b) explains that "thermal power" means (i) before the issue of a final operating licence, the planned thermal power; (ii) after the issue of such licence, the thermal power authorised by the competent national authorities.

Reverting to the provisions of the Brussels Convention relative to the amounts of compensation to be provided by the contracting parties, Article 4(a) says the aggregate liability to be provided for under the *Paris* Convention shall not, to the extent that public funds have to be made available, exceed 120 million units of account. Section (b) of this Article explains the position in the event of an incident involving the responsibility of more than one contracting party in relation to the 70 million units of account slice of the extra compensation. It provides that such funds shall be made available by the contracting parties in proportion to the number of nuclear installations situated in their respective territories which are involved in the nuclear incident and of which the operators are liable. (It is difficult to envisage the real-life circumstances in which more than one installation, in different countries, could be involved in the same incident.) Article 5 allows for the recovery of public funds which have been made available under these provisions from the operator if the damage results from fault on his part. This would be a matter for national legislation, and in considering the insurance of the operators' liabilities those concerned would be well advised to check whether it allows for such rights of recourse to be exercised with regard to the recovery of public funds paid out in excess of the operator's own financial obligation.

Limitation in Time

As in the Paris Convention, the period during which the right to compensation can be exercised by a claimant is 10 years from the date of the nuclear incident or, in an incident involving nuclear fuel or radioactive products or waste which, at the time of the incident, have been stolen, lost, jettisoned or abandoned and not yet been recovered, not exceeding 20 years from the date of the theft, loss, jettison or abandonment. The extensions allowed in the Paris Convention are also allowed under the Brussels Convention.

Reciprocal Agreements with non-contracting States

Article 15 provides that any Contracting Party may conclude an agreement with a State which is not a party to this Convention concerning compensation out of public funds for damage caused by a nuclear incident. Contracting Parties concluding such agreements are required to notify the other Contracting Parties of their intention and agreements actually concluded have to be notified to the Belgian Government. This provision for reciprocal arrangements with countries which do not adhere to the Brussels Convention are of interest although they relate to amounts exceeding those which would be the responsibility of a policy of insurance covering a nuclear operator and are not likely to affect the interests of insurers unless they also cover the amounts that the operator would be obliged to pay in accordance with national legislation based on the Paris Convention. In that event, when insurers come to consider the degree of the risk they are dealing with it is worth bearing in mind that the possible source of claims could go beyond not only the country in which the installation is situated but the countries beyond those which are Contracting Parties.

Disputes

Disputes between two or more Contracting Parties must on request of a Contracting Party concerned be submitted to the European Nuclear Energy Tribunal. This, as a matter of interest, was set up by way of a Convention on the "Establishment of a Security Control in the Field of Nuclear Energy'' adopted in December 1957. It should be noted that no State which ceases to be a party to the Paris Convention can continue to be a Contracting Party to the Brussels Convention. As in the case of the Paris Convention, any State wishing to become a party after the signing of the Convention may do so by way of accession. The only State to have acceded (as in the case of the Paris Convention) subsequent to signature by the parties, was Finland in January 1977.

The Brussels Supplementary Convention entered into force in December 1974 after the necessary 6 ratifications had been obtained. As a matter of interest, 3 countries, the United Kingdom, France and Spain, ratified the Brussels Convention by introducing the necessary legislation which, in the case of the United Kingdom, was incorporated in the Nuclear Installations Act of 1965. The first 6 countries to ratify, including the U.K., were France, Spain, Sweden, Norway and Denmark. Germany, Italy, the Netherlands and Belgium have all ratified since then. The other signatories, i.e. Austria, Luxembourg and Switzerland have not, as yet, ratified.

In a subsequent annex to this Convention, the Governments of the Contracting Parties declared that, for damage caused by a nuclear incident not covered by the Supplementary Convention solely by reason of the fact that the relevant nuclear installation, on account of its utilisation, is not on the list referred to in Article 2, including the case where such installation is considered by one or more, but not all, of the Governments to be outside the Paris Convention, compensation shall be provided without discrimination among the nationals of the Contracting Parties and shall not be limited to less than 120 million units of account. Governments that had not already done so were also required to endeavour to make rules for compensation of victims as similar as possible to those established in respect of nuclear incidents occurring in connection with nuclear installations which *are* covered by the Supplementary Convention.

The Additional Protocol of January 1964

The full title of this Agreement is as follows: ''Decision of the Steering Committee of the European Nuclear Energy Agency on the exclusion of small quantities of nuclear substances from the application of the Convention on Third Party Liability in the field of Nuclear Energy''. This is the Decision referred to briefly in our review of the Paris Convention. It applies also to the Brussels Supplementary Convention. The purpose of this Decision by the Steering Committee with the full authority of the Contracting Parties, was essentially to bring the situation under the Paris and Brussels Supplementary Conventions into line with that established in the Convention introduced by the International Atomic Energy Agency which will be referred to later in this Chapter. The Decision relates to nuclear substances which are consigned by an operator to a recipient for use. They are excluded from the application of the Paris Convention (and also the Brussels Convention) for the period during which they are outside a nuclear installation provided that the consignment, when leaving a nuclear installation, complies with certain provisions set forth in an annex to the Decision and with relevant requirements concerning the safe transport of radioactive materials laid down by regulations issued by the International Atomic Energy Agency. The annex sets out the levels in terms of radioactivity of the nuclear matter and the amounts in terms of the mass of the radioactive matter that allow the nuclear substances, when not on a nuclear installation, to be excluded from the provisions of the Conventions.

The 1964 Decision is regarded as an integral part of both the Paris and the Brussels Supplementary Conventions and for this reason it has been taken slightly out of its chronological order.

It was in the year preceding the 1964 OECD Decision that the members of the United Nations brought to a conclusion their own Convention which was established under the aegis of the International Atomic Energy Agency.

The Vienna Convention

The International Atomic Energy Agency, an agency of UNO, decided in 1959 that it would be appropriate to develop a Convention dealing with civil liabilities in the field of nuclear energy. The desire was that this should have universal application unlike the regional Paris Convention.

When the International Atomic Energy Agency began to approach this question in 1959, a panel of experts was set up, including two nuclear insurance specialists, A.G.M. Batten from the United Kingdom and Dr. W.E. Belser from Switzerland (invited by the late Sterling Cole, IAEA's first Director) as well as the Government representatives from the countries concerned. They met in Vienna at diplomatic level and at expert level. Batten was later succeeded by R.L. Hervey who, with the support of A.C. Miles, participated in an IAEA Working Party on the Convention. A draft Convention very similar in many, though not all, respects to the Paris Convention was eventually devised. An inter-Governmental Committee on Civil Liability (comprising Argentina, Canada, the Czechoslovak Socialist

Republic, Finland, France, Federal Republic of Germany, India, Japan, USSR, United Arab Republic, U.K. and U.S.A.) reported in May 1961 in favour of the proposed new Convention. The full title of this Convention was the "Vienna Convention on Civil Liability for Nuclear Damage". It was finally concluded in May 1963. Before it could enter into force it required to be ratified by not less than ten member States. This was not achieved until 1977. The countries which ratified by that date were the following:

Argentina	Bolivia	Cameroon
Cuba	Egypt	Niger
Peru	Philippines	Trinidad & Tobago
		Yugoslavia

It is noteworthy that, although most of the leading nuclear energy countries have either adopted the Paris and the Brussels Conventions, or introduced convention-type laws, none of the countries ratifying "Vienna" could be counted amongst the leaders in the industrial exploitation of nuclear energy. In fact, only 2 of them have nuclear power stations in operation: Argentina and Yugoslavia.

The Philippines have a fully completed and operational nuclear power station but this has been mothballed and may not be put into operation. Egypt is building a nuclear power station and Cuba plans to build one. The lack of support for the Vienna Convention is a matter of great concern to the International Atomic Energy Agency and it seems likely that considerable efforts will be put into obtaining many more ratifications, particularly in the wake of the Chernobyl accident which demonstrated so dramatically the widespread international scope of the risk of nuclear damage and injury possible following a catastrophic nuclear incident.

In the preamble to the Vienna Convention the contracting parties declared their recognition of the "desirability of establishing some minimum standards to provide financial protection against damage resulting from certain peaceful uses of nuclear energy" and they stated their belief that "a Convention on Civil Liability for Nuclear Damage would also contribute to the development of friendly relations among nations irrespective of their differing constitutional and social systems". As in the case of the Paris Convention, there is a number of important definitions in the first Article of the Vienna Convention. We have met some of these in Chapter 2 when considering the meaning of such terms as nuclear fuel, nuclear material, nuclear reactor, nuclear installation and radioactive products or waste. Several other useful definitions are worth quoting and these are as follows:

"person" means any individual, partnership, any private or public body whether corporate or not, any international organisation enjoying legal personality under the law of the Installation State, and any State or any of its constituent sub-divisions.

"national of a contracting party" includes a contracting party or any of its constituent sub-divisions, a partnership, or any private or public body whether corporate or not established within the territory of a contracting party.

"Installation State" in relation to a nuclear installation means the contracting party within whose territory that installation is situated,or, if it is not situated within the territory of any State, the contracting party by which or under the authority of which the nuclear installation is operated.

Perhaps the most important definition in the Vienna Convention is that for "nuclear damage" which is a serious omission from the Paris Convention. This is a concept which subsequent studies of nuclear liability law and the Conventions have uncovered as a source of difficulty. While the Vienna Convention definition does not answer all the questions it is certainly helpful and is therefore worth quoting in full as follows:

"Nuclear damage means—
(i) loss of life, any personal injury or any loss of, or damage to, property which arises out of or results from the radioactive properties or a combination of radioactive properties with toxic, explosive or other hazardous properties of nuclear fuel or radioactive products or waste in, or of, nuclear material coming from, originating in, or sent to, a nuclear installation;
(ii) any other loss or damage so arising or resulting if and to the extent that the law of the competent Court so provides; and
(iii) if the law of the Installation State so provides, loss of life, any personal injury, or any loss of, or damage to, property which arises out of or results from other ionising radiation emitted by any other source of radiation inside a nuclear installation."

The Vienna Convention embodies in all essential respects the basic principles already found in the Paris Convention with respect to the concept of absolute or strict liability; the limitation of liability in amount and in time; the channelling of all liability to the operator of the nuclear installation, save in circumstances where the damage may be attributable to the direct and criminal act of the perpetrator; unity of jurisdiction in that normally the jurisdiction would lie within the installation state where an installation or materials responsible for the nuclear accident were located. The Vienna Convention also provides that the financial liabilities of the nuclear operator shall be covered either by way of compulsory insurance or some other acceptable form of financial guarantee, approved by the authorities in the country concerned, and provided for under national legislation.

Scope of Operator's Liability

However, the Vienna Convention is rather better expressed in some ways and, in particular, it is more specific as to the "absolute" nature of the liability attaching to an operator. This is covered in Article IV. The first two paragraphs read as follows:

"1. The liability of the operator for nuclear damage under this Convention shall be absolute.

2. If the operator proves the nuclear damage resulted wholly or partly either from the gross negligence of the person suffering the damage or from an act or omission of such person done with intent to cause damage, the competent Court may, if its law so provides, relieve the operator wholly or partly from his obligation to pay compensation in respect of the damage suffered by such person".

Sub-paragraph 3 provides that the operator shall be exempted from liability for damage caused by a nuclear incident directly due to an act of armed conflict, hostilities, civil war or insurrection. He is also relieved of liability for an incident directly due to a grave natural disaster of an exceptional character if the law of the Installation State so provides. As in the Paris Convention, the operator is not liable for damage to the nuclear installation itself or to any property on the site of that installation which is used or can be used in connection with it. He is also absolved from liability for damage to the means of transport upon which nuclear material involved in an incident may have been at the time. However, an Installation State may set this provision aside under its own laws if it desires. In that case, the legislation must, however, be so drafted that the minimum limit of compensation which under the Vienna Convention is US$5M will not be reduced by any payment made as a result of compensating damage to the means of transport.

Limitation in amount

Referring to the financial limits, the figure of US$5M is laid down in Article V. It applies with respect to any one nuclear incident. It may not include any interest or costs awarded by a Court in Actions for compensation. Incidentally, the value given to the U.S. Dollar as applied in the Vienna Convention, is the value in terms of gold on 29th April, 1963 which was US$35 for one troy ounce of fine gold: a financial limit now totally out of date. On the other hand, any country introducing legislation at or soon after the adoption of the Vienna Convention would have converted the US$5M into their national currency at the rate of exchange ruling at that time and it is to be assumed that the current equivalent in national currency would be somewhat higher than the value at that time of the US$5M. (Taking into account the quantity of gold obtainable for that sum at the 1963 price, the equivalent monetary value in 1987 might well be close to $60M.)

Limitation in time

As in the Paris Convention, the rights of claimants to claim compensation will be extinguished ten years after the date of the incident. However, if the cover provided by insurance or other financial guarantee extends for a longer period then the rights of the victims will be so extended but only for the length of time during which cover is available. That aspect is covered by Article VI, Paragraph 1. Paragraph 2 makes similar provision to that in the Paris Convention regarding the absolute overriding ceiling of 20 years from the date of loss, etc., allowed to bring claims for compensation in a case where damage is caused by a nuclear incident involving material which at the time was stolen, lost, jettisoned or abandoned. The victim is allowed up to three years in which to bring an action from the date at which he knew or should have known of the damage and the operator liable, but the 10-year and 20-year periods are not allowed to be exceeded on this account. Once an action has been started, provided final judgement has not been entered, any subsequent aggravation of damage or injury may be taken into account and the amount of the claim amended.

Financial Security

Article VII provides

"1. The operator shall be required to maintain insurance or other financial security covering his liability for nuclear damage in such amount of such type and in such terms as the Installation State shall specify. The Installation State shall ensure the payment of claims for compensation for nuclear damage which have been established against the operator by providing the necessary funds to the extent that the yield of insurance or other financial security is inadequate to satisfy such claims but not in excess of the limit, if any, established pursuant to Article V.

2. Nothing in Paragraph 1 of this Article shall require a contracting party or any of its constituent sub-divisions, such as States or Republics, to maintain insurance or other financial security to cover their liability as operators.
3. The funds provided by insurance, or other financial security or by the Installation State pursuant to Paragraph 1 of this Article shall be exclusively available for compensation under this Convention.
4. No insurer or other financial guarantor shall suspend or cancel the insurance or other financial security provided pursuant to Paragraph 1 of this Article without giving notice in writing of at least 2 months to the competent public authority or, insofar as such insurance or other financial security relates to the carriage of nuclear material, during the period of the carriage in question."

So far as concerns the effect on compensation of provisions under national or public health insurance, social insurance, social security, workmen's compensation or occupational disease compensation system, which include provision for compensating for nuclear damage, the rights of beneficiaries and the rights of recourse that may be available against the operator liable are to be determined by the law of the contracting party or by the regulations of any inter-Governmental organisation which has established such systems.

Operator's Rights of Recourse

Article X provides that an operator shall have a right of recourse only

"(a) if this is expressly provided for by a contract in writing; or
(b) if the nuclear incident results from an act or omission done with intent to cause damage, against the individual who has acted or omitted to act with such intent".

Jurisdiction

Jurisdiction lies only with the Courts of the contracting party within whose territory the nuclear incident has occurred or, if it occurs outside the territory of any contracting party or the place of the incident cannot be determined with certainty, then it is the Courts of the Installation State of the operator liable which have jurisdiction over any actions. This feature is dealt with under Article XI which like the Paris Convention also seeks to cover the position in the case of an incident which occurs partly in one State and partly in another, presumably in the event of nuclear material in the course of carriage crossing the frontiers or territorial waters of more than one state.

Optional Protocol concerning the compulsory settlement of disputes

At the same time as the adoption of the Vienna Convention during the Conference held in Vienna from 29th April to 19th May 1963, which was signed on 21st May 1963, the States also adopted an optional Protocol which laid down provisions for settling disputes between States with regard to interpretation or application of the Convention. In this matter, the jurisdiction of the International Court of Justice is compulsory.

Resolution concerning exclusion of small quantities

Article I (2) of the Vienna Convention empowers the Board of Governors of the Agency to establish maximum limits for the exclusion of small quantities of nuclear material from the application of the Convention. The Agency's Standing Committee on Civil Liability for Nuclear Damage had previously determined that such limits should be established in respect of nuclear material in transit for use outside a nuclear installation but that small quantities of nuclear material inside a nuclear installation, or being disposed of as waste (or having been removed from the nuclear installation by theft, loss, jettison or abandonment) should not be excluded from the application of the Convention. The Board of Governors decided that nuclear material which is consigned by an operator to a recipient for use may be excluded for the period it is outside a nuclear installation provided that the consignment when leaving a nuclear installation complies with the provision set forth in an annex to the Resolution and with other relevant requirements in the current edition of the Agency's own Regulations for the Safe Transport of Radioactive Materials.

This Resolution was the reason for the Decision adopted by the OECD and already referred to in connection with the Paris and Brussels Conventions concerning the exclusion of small quantities. This was the Decision of November 1964 which is also described as the Additional Protocol to the Paris and Brussels Conventions.

Revision of the Conventions

Both the Paris and Vienna Conventions contain provisions enabling them to be revised by a Conference of Members. In the case of the Paris Convention, Article 22(c) provides that a Conference shall be convened by the Secretary-General after a period of five years as from the date of the Convention's coming into force, or at any other time at the request of a contracting party within six months from the date of such request. The Vienna Convention is less specific. Article XXVI(c) states that a Conference shall be convened by the Director-General of the IAEA at any time after the expiry of a period of 5 years from the date of the entry into force of the Convention in order to consider a revision if one-third of the contracting parties express the desire to that effect. There has not, in fact, been any call for a reviewing Conference for the Vienna Convention although from time to time there are discussions at expert level and meetings between the OECD/NEA and Vienna officials and Committee Members who consider certain aspects of the two Conventions. There has been a considerable effort in recent years to progress towards a greater degree of harmonisation between the two Conventions. The likelihood is that the lack of desire to undertake any significant revision at formal level of the Vienna Convention is due to the fact that unfortunately, it has achieved so very little practical support internationally.

The Paris Convention and, incidentally, the Brussels Convention which is so closely related to it, have, however, been kept under review by the Steering Committee of the Nuclear Energy Agency, and apart from any question of revision they have set forth a number of Recommendations and Interpretations. As mentioned in the discussion earlier in this Chapter of the Paris Convention, certain Decisions which the Steering Committee were empowered to take have been implemented.

The 1982 Protocols

When the first review of the Paris Convention became necessary following the expiry of five years after it came into force, i.e. in 1973, no specific changes were desired by the Members. However, at about this time, very important studies were being undertaken into the possibilities of achieving greater harmonisation between the Paris and Vienna Conventions. In 1972, the OECD Nuclear Energy Group of Governmental Experts set up a study which was carried out both within the Group and through co-operation between the Nuclear Energy Agency and the International Atomic Energy Agency Secretariats. This led to the preparation of a proposed Joint Protocol which went to the IAEA Standing Committee on Civil Liability for Nuclear Damage to be considered by a restricted Working Group in May 1974. The OECD Nuclear Energy Agency decided that from a legal point of view a Joint Protocol would be the best method of achieving the harmonisation required, although there were certain reservations concerning questions of transit and the application of the Brussels Supplementary Convention. The IAEA Standing

Committee also considered the draft Joint Protocol but took no action at the time because the Vienna Convention had not by then entered into force and did not achieve sufficient ratifications until 1977. Although no action could be taken at the time with regard to the possible implementation of a Joint Protocol, were it to prove acceptable to the Members of the International Atomic Energy Agency and of the OECD, it was not lost to view.

When the Paris Convention next came up for review, in 1978 i.e. on this occasion ten years after its coming into force, the OECD decided that it should be subject to a full review with certain revisions in mind. The Brussels Supplementary Convention was also reviewed in the same exercise. The Group of Governmental Experts of the Nuclear Energy Agency reached agreement on amendments to be made to both these Conventions at a meeting held in June 1979. They duly reported to the Steering Committee for Nuclear Energy who were invited to approve the Report and the proposed amendments to the two Conventions and to recommend to the Council of the OECD that they should note the Report and adopt the necessary Instruments of revision of the Conventions for signature by the contracting parties.

The most important recommendations which were embodied in the draft Protocol, particularly from the point of view of Third Party Liability and Insurance, related to the amounts of compensation and the limits of financial liability to be borne by the operators in the first place and by the Governments in the second place. Since the Paris Convention was initiated in 1960 and the Brussels Convention in 1964 there had been considerable changes in the area of monetary policy and also there had been a considerable amount of inflation in countries of the OECD and elsewhere. Therefore, as has been mentioned earlier in connection with the two Conventions, it was decided to abandon the Gold Standard as a means of determining the value of the Unit of Account and to adopt instead another artificial currency unit, the Special Drawing Right of the International Monetary Fund. This was considered to be of particular relevance in relation to the provisions of the Brussels Supplementary Convention where the amounts of compensation in excess of that due from the operator were to be paid by Governments; in the first instance by the State in which the installation was located, and in the second instance by the States parties to the Brussels Convention. Since the latter could involve contributions from countries with varying types of currency, the need for an up-to-date Unit was absolutely essential. In the first instance, it was decided that one of the old EMA Units should be equivalent to one Unit of the Special Drawing Right. This would not give any weight to the effects of inflation since 1960, which had rendered the old limits quite inappropriate, particularly the limits of not less than 5 million Units of Account not more than 15 million in the Paris Convention; so it was agreed also to apply a multiple of $2\frac{1}{2}$ to the new figures to account for the degree of inflation which had taken place and could be anticipated by the time the new Protocols could be brought into force. Unfortunately, so far as an increase in the Paris amounts was concerned, the Members of the Group of Experts were unable to achieve unanimity on increasing the range of indemnity limits in the Paris Convention although the conversion from EMA Units of Account to IMF SDRs was unopposed. However, the amounts of the two tiers of Brussels compensation were agreed to require a substantial increase.

Regarding the first tier of extra compensation to be paid by the State in which the installation concerned was located, it was decided to increase this from 70 million to 175 million units. The second tier, which had been 50 million units, increased to 125 million units so that the ceiling of the joint contribution by contracting parties would then become 300 million units expressed in Special Drawing Rights. This was unanimously agreed by the Members of the Group of Experts. Their other proposals related mainly to bringing into effect as amendments of the Convention the various recommendations previously put forward by the Steering Committee, a number of which had been adopted in national legislation by some of the member States. Among the more important ones, from the point of those requiring or providing insurance for nuclear installations, were amendments to the definitions in the Paris Convention of a nuclear incident and of a nuclear installation. The principal effect of the amendment of the definition of nuclear incident was to add to the sources of damage arising out of nuclear incidents "ionising radiations emitted by any other source of radiation inside a nuclear installation". The significant addition to the definition of "nuclear installation" was the following:

> "Any Contracting Party may determine that two or more nuclear installations of one operator which are located on the same site shall, together with any other premises on that site where radioactive material is held, be treated as a single nuclear installation".

This change is of significance particularly in relation to the amount of the operator's financial liability because it means that if two or more installations can be treated as one when they are on the same site, his obligation to compensate third parties is or may be limited to one amount and therefore his insurance requirement is that much less than would be the case if he has to have a separate limit and insurance policy for each of the installations on one and the same site. With respect to the definition of radioactive products or waste, a change was made in this. The reference to radioisotopes outside a nuclear installation was qualified by adding the words "which have reached the final stage of fabrication so as to be usable for any industrial, commercial, agricultural, medical, scientific or educational purpose". The original versions of these definitions are set out in Chapter 2 of this book.

Article 3 of the Paris Convention, which defines the liability of the operator, as quoted earlier in this Chapter, was amended with respect to the Exceptions. These now show that the operator is not liable for damage to property other than

1. The Nuclear Installation itself and any other nuclear installation, including a nuclear installation under construction, on the site where the installation is located; and
2. Any property on that same site which is used or to be used in connection with any such installation.

This alteration brings the Paris Convention into line with the Vienna Convention in making it clear that damage to any property on the site used or to be used in connection with the installation cannot be covered under the Operator's Liability to Third Parties. The previous exclusion of damage to the means of transport is dropped. This amendment also deletes sub-paragraph (c) of Article 3 which is the one enabling contracting parties to provide, under their own legislation, that the liability of the operator includes liability for damage arising out of or resulting from ionising radiations emitted by any source of radiation inside that installation. That aspect is now dealt with under the revised definition of a nuclear incident which is in itself in accordance with the Vienna Convention. It means in effect that any nuclear material which would normally be exempted from the operation of the Convention is not so exempt if it is on the site of what is a defined nuclear installation.

Another amendment which is of interest to those concerned with the provision of liability insurance for the transportation of nuclear materials relates to the need for the operator to supply the carrier with a certificate of financial security. This was laid down in Article 4(c) of the Paris Convention although that did not propose any particular form of certificate at the time. In June 1967 the Steering Committee of the OECD Nuclear Energy Agency devised a model Certificate, the form of which it was recommended should be adopted or closely followed by the States concerned. The question of whether such a Certificate was absolutely essential for the carriage of nuclear material within the territory of the contracting State was also discussed that year, and it led in October 1967 to an Interpretation of the intentions of the Paris Convention. The Steering Committee agreed that it was open to individual countries to decide whether or not the Certificate of Financial Security should be required for transport entirely *within* the national boundaries of a single State. To bring the Paris Convention more into line with what had become international practice, the 1979 recommendations proposed that the supply of such a Certificate should only be compulsory where the transportation of nuclear matter was *international*. The Group of Governmental Experts saw no objection to individual countries requiring a Certificate of Financial Security for domestic movements but they wished this to be an optional provision in the future as far as national legislation was concerned.

These amendments were eventually adopted and incorporated in what became known as the *1982 Protocols* to amend the Paris Convention and the Brussels Supplementary Convention.

In accordance with the usual experience actual ratifications of these Protocols have been slow in coming since 1982. Up to 1986 the following countries introduced legislation ratifying the 1982 Protocol in relation to the Paris Convention — Belgium, Federal Republic of Germany, Italy, Norway, Portugal, Sweden, Turkey, United Kingdom. The Protocol relating to the Brussels Convention had by 1986 been ratified by — Belgium, Federal Republic of Germany, Italy, Norway, Sweden, United Kingdom.

SOME OTHER CONVENTIONS AND TREATIES

The Paris and Brussels Supplementary Conventions of the OECD, together with their amendments and 1982 Protocols, and the IAEA's Vienna Convention are the principal international agreements affecting the compensation of the victims of nuclear incidents and the liabilities of operators and the State to make financial provision for such compensation. Whether they have been ratified by individual countries or not, it is the case that the national nuclear legislation of practically every country which has such laws is very much in line with the provisions of one or other of the international Conventions on liability in the field of nuclear energy.

Because of the fundamental principles related to the channelling of all liability to the operators of nuclear installations on land, there are also specific provisions in parts of the Conventions relating to the carriage of nuclear material on the high seas or overland between different countries which enable certain responsibilities to be assumed under contract by the carriers who for this purpose may have the status of "operator" in relation to the application of the Conventions and the national laws based thereon.

Some other international Conventions have relevance to nuclear materials and waste; and to safety; compensation of the public; and the obligations of nuclear operators, of carriers and of the State. The following, in particular, should be noted:

Convention on the Liability of Operators of Nuclear Ships 1962

This is also known as the "Brussels Nuclear Ships Convention". In spite of its name, it has no relation to the Brussels Supplementary Convention of the OECD. In fact, it is not a Convention of either that body or the International Atomic Energy Agency. It was the result of a Diplomatic Conference on Maritime Law, which adopted the Convention in May 1962. The signatories at the time were: Belgium, Egypt, India, Indonesia, Ireland, Korea, Liberia, Madagascar, Malaysia, Monaco, Panama, Philippines, Portugal, Yugoslavia. Subsequently to the original signature date, Madagascar acceded in 1965 and Zaire in 1967. The Netherlands signed in December 1968. Only two countries have ratified this Convention — Portugal in 1968 and the Netherlands in 1974. It is therefore not in force.

The Convention was obviously aimed at the operators of nuclear merchant ships rather than naval vessels. In fact, as is well-known, although there are large numbers of nuclear-propelled naval submarines and possibly other naval ships, an extremely small number of merchant ships using reactors has been built. This is more likely than any other reason to explain why the Nuclear Ships Convention has not been seriously pursued to the extent of the introduction of national laws relating to it. However, it is of interest and presumably will be the model for such legislation if there are any developments in the future leading to a significant number of nuclear-propelled merchant ships coming into use. Should that happen, then no doubt the Convention will be brought into operation and will have a strong influence on national and international maritime laws relating to this particular type of vessel. It is therefore worth looking at some of the features of the Nuclear Ships Convention.

Among the definitions, for example, the term "nuclear ship" means any ship equipped with a nuclear power plant. In the context of this Convention "operator" means the person authorised by the licensing State to operate a nuclear ship or where a contracting State operates a nuclear ship, that State. "Nuclear power plant" means any power plant in which a nuclear reactor is or is to be used as a source of power, whether for propulsion of the ship or for any other purpose.

It is of interest that a warship is defined in the following terms

"... any ship belonging to the naval forces of a State and bearing the external marks distinguishing warships of its nationality under the command of an officer duly commissioned by the Government of such State and whose name appears in the Navy List, and manned by a crew who are under regular naval discipline".

In other respects, this Convention resembles the others in regard to its provisions regarding the absolute liability for nuclear damage of the operator, the channelling of liability to the operator, and exclusion of damage to the ship itself, its equipment, fuel or stores from the operation of the Convention. In relation to liability for damage, the operator would also be exonerated with respect to any damage resulting wholly or partly from an act or omission done with intent to cause damage by the individual who suffered from the damage.

There is also a limitation of liability in financial terms, the maximum per incident being Gold Fcs.1,500,000 not including any interests or costs awarded by a Court in actions for compensation. Compulsory insurance or other financial security is another requirement up to the extent that insurance is available, beyond which it is the responsibility of the State to provide the necessary funds up to the limit laid down by the Convention.

In view of the use of artificial currency units in the Paris and Brussels Conventions, it is of interest that the Franc mentioned is described as "unit of account constituted by 65 and one half milligrammes of gold of millesimal fineness 900". This amount may be converted into national currency in round figures on the basis of the gold value of those currencies which are not themselves in gold at the date of payment.

The Convention also contains a limitation in time which as in the case of Paris and Vienna is ten years from the date of the incident. Individual States may provide for longer periods of prescription. The 20-year overriding limit in respect of incidents from materials which have been stolen, lost, jettisoned or abandoned also applies. In all other important respects the Brussels Ships Convention is very similar to the Conventions relating to the liability of nuclear operators adopted by the OECD and the IAEA. Article XII is of particular interest and importance to Insurers in this connection since it requires contracting States to adopt the necessary measures to ensure that insurance and reinsurance premiums and sums provided by insurance, reinsurance or other financial security or provided by the States themselves shall be freely transferable into the currency of the contracting State in which the damage was sustained or the contracting State in which the claimant is habitually resident or as regards insurance and reinsurance premiums and payments in the currency specified in the insurance or reinsurance contract.

The Nuclear Ships Convention also obliges the contracting States to take all necessary measures to prevent a nuclear ship flying its flag from being operated without a licence or authority granted by it. Where the ship is not authorised by such contracting State, then the owner of the nuclear ship at the time of the nuclear incident is deemed to be the operator of the nuclear ship for the purposes of the Convention and most importantly his liability shall not be limited in amount. In that event, the contracting State whose flag the nuclear ship flies is deemed to be the licensing State, and in particular would be liable for compensation of victims in accordance with the obligations imposed on the licensing State by this Convention up to the limit laid down therein, i.e. 1,500,000 Gold Francs. Contracting States have to undertake not to grant a licence or other authority to operate a nuclear ship flying the flag of another State.

The application of the Convention dates from the launching of the nuclear ship. Between the launching of the ship and the time she is authorised to fly a flag, the nuclear ship is deemed to be operated by the owner and to be flying the flag of the State in which she was built.

In view of some of the events which have occured in recent years regarding the acceptability of nuclear-propelled ships in the harbours of certain countries, it is of interest that in Article XVII of the Ships Convention it is stated that nothing affects any right which a contracting State may have under international law to deny access to its waters and harbours to nuclear ships licensed by another contracting State even when it has formally complied with all the provisions of this Convention.

General responsibility for the administrative arrangements relating to this Convention, the deposition of ratifications and so forth, was placed upon the Belgian Government.

Convention relating to Civil Liability in the field of Maritime Carriage of Nuclear Material 1971

The existence of a large body of maritime law which related to among other matters to the liability of the carriers of goods by sea resulted in some problems regarding the priority of application of nuclear law over maritime law in relation to the carriage of nuclear materials. Therefore, after the Paris Convention entered into force in 1968 the OECD's Nuclear Energy Agency and the IAEA organised a joint Symposium to try to decide the priorities. The maritime organisations participated in these studies, which led to the setting-up of a diplomatic conference under the auspices of the Inter-Governmental

Maritime Organisation more usually known as IMO. Like the conference which led to the Nuclear Ships Convention nine years earlier, this took place in Brussels and resulted in the adoption of a Convention bearing the title in the heading to this paragraph. It was signed by the following nine countries:

Belgium	Federal Republic of Germany	Sweden
Brazil	Italy	United Kingdom
France	Portugal	Yugoslavia

The general effect of this Convention is that maritime carriers of nuclear substances are exonerated from any liability for nuclear damage caused by a nuclear accident if the operator of a land-based nuclear installation is liable under the Paris Convention, or the Vienna Convention, or under national law. In these circumstances, the national legislation concerned has to be at least as favourable to the victims of a nuclear incident as are the Conventions themselves.

By July 1975 the necessary minimum five countries had ratified the Convention which thereupon entered into force, the contracting parties being Denmark, France, Norway, Spain and Sweden.

Countries which ratified subsequently were Argentina, Germany (Federal Republic), Italy, Liberia and Yemen (Arab Republic). The United Kingdom has not ratified the 1971 Convention.

The International Maritime Committee originally suggested to the Diplomatic Conference in 1971 that the Convention should consist of only one Article in the following terms:

"Any person who, by virtue of an international Convention or a national law applying in the field of maritime transport, is likely to become responsible for damage caused by a nuclear accident, is exonerated from his responsibility, if the operator of a nuclear installation is responsible for this damage by application of the Paris Convention of 29th July 1960 on Liability in the field of Nuclear Energy and its additional Protocol of 28th January 1964, or the Vienna Convention of 21st May 1963 on Civil Liability for Nuclear Damage".

This was not considered to be acceptable by the Diplomatic Conference and they therefore set up a full Committee to draft a complete text. The single Article favoured by the IMC was adopted as Article 1 of the full Convention but it was extended to include a reference also to any national law placing liability on the nuclear operator of a nuclear installation, subject to the sole condition that the latter should in all respects be at least as favourable to potential victims as the Conventions themselves. This latter provision provoked a lot of discussion because some of the participants considered that

116

it was impossible to say exactly whether a law was as favourable to the victims as the Conventions or not.

Various other Articles were added to deal with the particular case of damage caused to the nuclear installation concerned by the means of transport and to the means of transport itself and an Article dealing with the responsibility of the operators of nuclear ships. With the addition of other clauses the final text was approved and signed in December 1971.

Since the sole Article originally proposed to the Diplomatic Conference that was not accepted has been quoted in full, it is worth noting the final version of Article 1 as ultimately approved. This reads as follows:

"Any person who by virtue of an international Convention or national law applicable in the field of maritime transport might be held liable for damage caused by a nuclear incident shall be exonerated from such liability:

(a) if the operator of a nuclear installation is liable for such damage under either the Paris or Vienna Convention, or

(b) if the operator of a nuclear installation is liable for such damage by virtue of a national law governing the liability for damage provided that such law is in all respects as favourable to the persons who may suffer damage as either the Paris or the Vienna Conventions".

Article 2 is also relevant in this connection and it reads as follows:
"1. The exoneration provided for in Article 1 shall also apply in respect of damage caused by a nuclear incident

(a) to the nuclear installation itself or to any property on the site of that installation which is used or to be used in connection with that installation, or

(b) to a means of transport on which the nuclear material involved was at the time of the nuclear incident,

for which the operator of a nuclear installation is not liable because his liability for such damage has been excluded pursuant to the provisions of either the Paris or the Vienna Convention, or, in cases referred to in Article 1(b), by equivalent provisions of the national law referred to therein.

2. The provisions of Paragraph 1, shall not, however, affect the liability of any individual who has caused the damage by an act or omission done with intent to cause damage."

The Convention runs to a total of 12 Articles. As stated earlier, the Convention was signed originally in Brussels in December 1971 but it was allowed to remain open for signature up until 31st December 1972 at the Headquarters of the Inter-Governmental

Maritime Consultative Organisation in London. As with the other Conventions, a State wishing to adopt the Convention after the closing of the signing date, could of course do so by way of accession.

Conventions relating to Dumping of Wastes in the Sea

Although these Conventions relate to the pollution of the sea by the dumping of any objectionable material they do not exclude nuclear waste or other nuclear material that may be dumped in the sea. Therefore, they are of interest to the operators of nuclear installations, to those who are responsible for the carriage of nuclear matter to and the dumping of it into the sea and to those who provide for the compensation of the victims of a nuclear incident arising from the dumping of such material. The relevant Conventions are the following:

Convention on the Prevention of Marine Pollution by Dumping from Ships and Aircraft (This was adopted at Oslo in February 1972)

Convention on the Prevention of Marine Pollution by Dumping of Waste and other Matter (This was adopted in London in November 1972)

Known, respectively, as the Oslo Convention and the London Convention, they make provision for international control in relation to pollution of the sea by the dumping of harmful substances including radioactive matter.

United Nations Convention on Long-Range Transboundary Air Pollution 1979

This Convention, while relating generally to the need for co-operation in the field of environmental protection, does not exclude pollution from radioactive sources although it tends to concentrate on pollution by sulphur compounds. It was prompted by a report which arose from a Conference on Security and Co-operation in Europe which called for international co-operation in the control of air pollution and its effects. The report also referred to the need to develop international co-operation with an extensive programme of monitoring and evaluating long-range transportation of air pollutants starting with sulphur dioxide and possibly extending to other pollutants. The Convention was also inspired by certain provisions of the declaration of the United Nations Conference on the Human Environment. One of the principles contained in this declaration refers to the common conviction that, in accordance with the Charter of the United Nations, and the principles of international law, States have the sovereign right to exploit their own resources in accordance with their own environmental policies and also the responsibility to ensure that activities within their jurisdiction or control do not cause damage to the environment of other States or of areas beyond the limits of international jurisdiction.

The object of this Convention was to reinforce active international co-operation to develop appropriate national policies by means of exchange of information, consultation and research and monitoring to co-ordinate national action for combating air pollution, including long-range transboundary air pollution.

The Convention, in its first Article, defines these as follows:

"Air pollution" means the introduction by man, directly or indirectly, of substances or energy into the air resulting in deleterious effects of such a nature as to endanger human health, harm living resources and ecosystems and material property and impair or interfere with amenities and other legitimate uses of the environment and "air pollutants" shall be construed accordingly.

"Long-range transboundary air pollution" means air pollution whose physical origin is situated wholly or in part within the area under the national jurisdiction of one State and which has adverse effects in the area under the jurisdiction of another State at such a distance that it is not generally possible to distinguish the contribution of individual emission sources or groups of sources.

The Convention goes on to set out certain fundamental principles, the need for consultation and research and exchange of information, the management of air quality, and methods of determining and measuring fluxes of pollutants. The administration of the Convention is vested in the Executive Secretary of the Economic Commission for Europe (ECE).

This Convention was signed at Geneva on 13th November 1979. The contracting parties, within the framework of the United Nations Economic Commission for Europe, are the following:

Austria, Belgium, Bulgaria, Byelorussia, Canada, Denmark, European Economic Community, Finland, France, German Democratic Republic, Federal Republic of Germany, Hungary, Ireland, Italy, Luxembourg, Netherlands, Norway, Portugal, Spain, Sweden, Ukraine, USSR, United Kingdom, United States.

It entered into force, having secured the required number of ratifications, on 16th March 1983.

This Convention makes no provisions as to the liability of the contracting States or individuals for the damaging consequences of an escape of polluting material. However, if the escape is due to the fault of some party, then it would be customary under international law for such fault to be regarded as creating a liability. Thereafter, presumably any actions to recover compensation would have to be pursued in accordance with private or public international law in the absence of any reciprocal or specific agreements as between individual States.

Vienna Convention on the Physical Protection of Nuclear Material — 1980

This was the outcome of many years of work undertaken by the International Atomic Energy Agency in the field of physical protection of nuclear material. Recommendations were produced originally in 1972 and they were revised by a Group of Experts working with the International Atomic Energy Agency's Secretariat in 1975. Further modifications were proposed by the Advisory Group on the specific protection of nuclear material, convened by the Director-General of the Agency in 1977. Those taking part were representatives from the following countries:

Austria, Australia, Canada, Egypt, France, Federal Republic of Germany, German Democratic Republic, India, Iran, Japan, Pakistan, Sweden, USSR, United Kingdom, U.S.A.

This Convention was signed by 47 countries. It required to be ratified by 21 in order to come into force. This was achieved in February 1987 with the ratification by Switzerland.

The other ratifying States were:

Brazil, Bulgaria, Canada, Czechoslovakia, German Democratic Republic, Guatemala, Hungary, Indonesia, Korea, Liechtenstein Mongolia, Norway, Paraguay, Philippines, Poland, Sweden, Turkey, U.S.A., U.S.S.R., Yugoslavia.

The Convention is largely concerned with security measures which the signatories undertake to apply for the purpose of deterring or defeating theft, sabotage, unlawful removal or use of nuclear materials and other deliberate acts of that nature. It also requires States to agree not to export or import nuclear matter or to allow it to pass through their countries without obtaining prior assurance of its physical protection up to specified safety levels.

It is not concerned with any matters relating to liability, compensation or insurance.

IAEA Convention on Early Notification of a Nuclear Accident — 1986

This is one of two new Conventions which were very rapidly drafted and adopted by the International Atomic Energy Agency following the very serious accident at the Chernobyl Nuclear Power Station in the Soviet Republic of the Ukraine. It was wisely decided that it would require no more than three ratifications to bring this Convention into force and that was achieved in a matter of months — a remarkable contrast with the enormous delay in the ratification of the Vienna Convention on Nuclear Liability and certain other Conventions as mentioned above. The first two countries to ratify this new Convention were the USSR and Finland who did so in December 1986. It was possible to bring it into force then because upon signing the Convention in October 1986 3 States — Czechoslovakia, Denmark and Norway — had agreed then to be immediately bound by it. The number of signatories later increased to about 70, of which about 14 have ratified.

The preamble to this Convention refers to the measures that have been taken and are being taken to ensure a high level of safety in relation to nuclear activities to prevent accidents and to minimise the consequences of an accident should it occur and expresses the desire to strengthen international co-operation in relation to the safe development and use of nuclear energy. It records a conviction that the States must provide relevant information about nuclear accidents as early as possible so that the radiological consequences of transboundary movements of radioactivity can be minimised.

The sort of facilities and activities to which this Convention applies are specified in Article 1(2) as follows:

(a) any nuclear reactor wherever located;
(b) any nuclear fuel cycle facility;
(c) any radioactive waste management facility;
(d) the transport and storage of nuclear fuels or radioactive wastes;
(e) the manufacture, use, storage, disposal and transport of radio-isotopes for agricultural, industrial, medical, and related scientific research purposes; and
(f) the use of radioisotopes for power generation in space objects.

The States who are parties to this Convention are obliged to give immediate notification either directly or through the IAEA to any States which may be or are physically affected by a nuclear accident and they are obliged to advise of its nature, the time of its occurrence and its exact location. Incidentally, the type of accident to which this is intended to apply is described in Article 1(1) as being any accident involving facilities or activities of a State, party or persons or legal entities under its jurisdictional control, from which a release of radioactive material occurs or is likely to occur and has resulted or may result in an international transboundary release that could be of radiological safety significance for another State. (One detects certain echoes of the Transboundary Pollution Convention in this type of wording.) Article 3 of the Convention also provides that any other type of nuclear accident which is not defined in Article 1(1) may also be notified.

Amongst the information that must be provided as set out in Article 5, are the general characteristics of the radioactive release, including, if possible, the nature, probable physical and chemical form and quantity, composition and effective height of the radioactive release.

Information must also be given on current and forecast meteorological and hydrological conditions necessary for forecasting the transboundary release of the radioactive materials and the results of environmental monitoring relevant to this. Details of off-site protective measures taken on land must be given as well as the predicted behaviour over time of the radioactive release.

The Convention also provides for the International Atomic Energy Agency to assist States which request it, with the provision of the means of monitoring radiation in order to achieve the objectives of the Convention. Certain provisions are made regarding the signing of the Convention by member States and also by the United Nations Council for Namibia. There are the usual provisions regarding amendments of the Convention, denunciation by a State which is party to it, and the administrative responsibilities of the Director-General of the International Atomic Energy Agency as the Depository of this Convention.

It does not contain any provisions as regarding legal liabilities or compensation and the provision of insurance.

IAEA Convention on Assistance in the case of a Nuclear Accident or Radiological Emergency — 1987

This new Convention was adopted in parallel with the previous one for much the same reasons. It was signed by 57 States in January 1987. Norway agreed to be bound by it without reservation as to ratification when they signed and the USSR have deposited their Instrument of Ratification. About 10 more States signed later and of the total number of signatories some 9 have ratified.

The preamble to this Convention mentions a number of the same points as those referred to in the preamble to the Convention on Early Notification.

It also declares the conviction of the States parties to the Convention of the need for an international framework which will facilitate the prompt provision of assistance in the event of a nuclear accident or radiological emergency to mitigate its consequences. This, indeed, is made the subject of a general provision in Article 1 of the Convention. This also requires the States who are parties to the Convention to facilitate such co-operation as may be agreed in regard to bilateral and multilateral arrangements, or a combination of these, for the purpose of preventing or minimising injury and damage resulting from a nuclear accident or radiological emergency, a matter of great interest to insurers.

Any State needing assistance, whether or not the accident or emergency originates within its own territory, jurisdiction or control, may call for such assistance as it may need from any other State which is a party to the Convention, either directly or through the Agency, or from the Agency or, indeed, from any other international or inter-Governmental organisation. The State requiring assistance is required to specify the scope and type of assistance it requires and provide the assisting party with the information needed so that that party can determine the extent to which it can help. Other points covered in Article 2 include the very practical requirement that the States concerned shall identify the experts who may be able to assist together with the equipment and materials which could be made available and shall notify these to the Agency, as well as the terms, especially financial, under which such assistance could be provided. States are also permitted to request assistance in treating or temporarily re-locating in the territory of another State people involved in a nuclear accident. An obligation is placed on the International Atomic Energy Agency to respond to any request for assistance by

(a) making available appropriate resources allocated for this purpose;

(b) transmitting promptly the request to other States and international organisations which according to the Agency's information may possess the necessary resources; and

(c) if so requested by the requesting State, co-ordinating the assistance at the international level which may thus become available.

The Convention goes on to make provisions regarding the direction and control of assistance; competent authorities and points of contact; a detailed definition of the functions of the Agency regarding the collection and dissemination of information; the giving of assistance in such respects as the preparation of emergency plans, developing training programmes, transmitting requests for assistance, developing radiation monitoring programmes, conducting investigations into the feasibility of establishing monitoring systems, and so on. There is a requirement that the requesting State and the assisting party shall protect the confidentiality of any information that becomes available to them.

Regarding cost, an assisting party may offer assistance without cost to the requesting State. When considering whether to do this or not, they are required to take into account such matters as the nature of the accident, the place of origin, the needs of developing countries, particularly the needs of countries without nuclear facilities and any other relevant factors. When the assistance is provided on the basis of complete or partial reimbursement, then the requesting State is required to reimburse the assisting party promptly. However, assisting parties, particularly in dealing with developing countries, may postpone the receipt of such reimbursement.

Under Article 8, the requesting State is required to afford to the personnel of the assisting party, or personnel acting on its behalf, all the necessary privileges, immunities and facilities that they require to perform their functions. This, in particular, includes immunity from arrest, detention and legal process, including criminal, civil and administrative jurisdiction of the requesting State in respect of acts or omissions in the performance of their duties, and also exemption from taxation, duties and other charges, except those normally incorporated in the price of goods or payment for services rendered in respect of the performance of their assistance functions. Various other protections are afforded to the assisting State, including the return of equipment and property and the decontamination of recovered equipment involved before it is returned.

The transit of the personnel of the assisting party must be facilitated by the requesting State as well as their equipment and property.

Article 10 of the Assistance Convention makes certain provisions regarding the settlement of legal proceedings and claims. Unless otherwise agreed, the requesting State must, in respect of death or injury to persons, damage to or loss of property, or damage to the environment caused within its territory or other area under its jurisdiction in the course of providing the assistance requested, agree

(a) not to bring any legal proceedings against the assisting party, etc.;

(b) to accept responsibility for dealing with legal proceedings and any claims brought by third parties against the assisting party;

(c) to hold the assisting party harmless in respect of legal proceedings;

(d) to compensate the assisting party for (i) death of or injury to personnel, (ii) loss of or damage to non-consumable equipment or materials related to the assistance, except in the case of wilful misconduct by the individuals causing injury, death, loss or damage.

States signing, ratifying, accepting or acceding to the Convention, may declare that they do not consider themselves bound in whole or in part by the paragraph regarding compensation, etc. and that they will not apply Paragraph 2 in cases of gross negligence by the individuals who cause the death, injury, loss or damage.

A requesting State, or the assisting party, are permitted to terminate the assistance at any time after appropriate consultations and by notification in writing.

Article 12 makes it clear that the Convention is not intended to affect reciprocal rights and obligations of the parties under existing international agreements relating to matters covered by this Convention or under future international agreements concluded in accordance with the object and purpose of the Convention.

The Convention also provides the usual arrangements regarding entry into force or signature and amendments and denunciation. As in the case of the Notification Convention, this one is also deposited with the Director-General of the International Atomic Energy Agency who is responsible for the administrative arrangements.

This review of International Agreements in the field of nuclear energy would not be complete without some reference to the Treaty on the Non-Proliferation of Nuclear Weapons, more commonly known as the *Non-Proliferation Treaty (NPT)*. This Treaty, and the *Treaty of Tlatelolco* which applies specifically to the Latin-American and Caribbean States, are of some relevance even in regard to the peaceful uses of nuclear energy because they have the effect of restricting the activities of member States of the International Atomic Energy Agency who are engaged in the manufacture and handling of materials which could be of use in the production of nuclear weapons or explosives.

The Tlatelolco Treaty, called after the place where it was signed in Mexico City (official title is the Treaty for the Prohibition of Nuclear Weapons in the Latin American States) is aimed at the military denuclearisation of the whole zone. It has been signed by 23 of the 33 States concerned — a notable exception being Cuba.

The NPT was probably inspired by the Test Ban Treaty concluded by members of the United Nations in 1963 for the purpose of banning nuclear weapon tests in the atmosphere, in outer space and under water. While it has not been successful in its objective of achieving the discontinuance of all test explosions of nuclear weapons for all time, it has certainly had a restraining effect. The object of the Non-Proliferation Treaty was to secure the agreement of all those nations which were designated "Non-Nuclear Weapons States" (NNWS), who may or may not be involved in the production and exploitation of nuclear materials for energy purposes, from using or misusing those materials or supplying them to Non-Nuclear Weapons States for the purpose of making nuclear bombs and missiles. An essential element of the Non-Proliferation Treaty is that it expects the Non-Nuclear Weapons States to enter into Inspection Agreements with the International Atomic Energy Agency in order to promote the safeguards necessary to ensure that nuclear materials are not being misused but that their movement internationally is under control and also that their whereabouts and quantities are known to the IAEA.

The Treaty was signed in 1967 after two of the Nuclear Weapons States, United States and the United Kingdom, had made voluntary offers to accept Agency safeguards on their peaceful nuclear activities, an offer made subsequently by France also. Another of the Nuclear Weapons States, the USSR, made a similar offer in 1985. (A Nuclear Weapons State is defined as being one which had exploded nuclear weapons before 1967.) The distinction between these States and the Non-Nuclear Weapons States is that they are not prohibited from the manufacture or acquisition of nuclear weapons or other nuclear explosive devices as are the Non-Nuclear Weapons States or NNWS. The full text set out in Article I of the Treaty of the undertaking by the 5 signatory Nuclear Weapons States (NWS) (China, France, UK, USA and USSR) is as follows:

"Each Nuclear-Weapons State Party to the Treaty undertakes not to transfer to any recipient whatsoever nuclear weapons or other nuclear explosive devices or control over such weapons or explosive devices directly, or indirectly; and not in any way to assist, encourage, or induce any Non-Nuclear Weapons State to manufacture or otherwise acquire nuclear weapons or other nuclear explosive devices, or control over such weapons or explosive devices".

The equivalent undertaking by the signatory NNWS is set out in Article II as follows:

"Each Non-Nuclear Weapons State Party to the Treaty undertakes not to receive the transfer from any transferer whatsoever of nuclear weapons or other nuclear explosive devices or of control over such weapons or explosive devices directly or indirectly; not to manufacture or otherwise acquire nuclear weapons or other nuclear explosive devices; and not to seek or receive any assistance in the manufacture of nuclear weapons or other nuclear explosive devices".

The position regarding Safeguards Agreements with the IAEA is set out in Article III and it is obligatory on the NWS. Under formal agreements to be negotiated with the IAEA in accordance with the latter's Statutes and their safeguards system, they are obliged to accept verification of the fact that they are fulfilling their obligations with a view to preventing diversion of nuclear energy from peaceful uses. Such safeguards apply to source or special fissionable material whether it is being produced, processed or used in any principal nuclear facility or is outside any such facility. The undertakings involve an obligation not to provide such material or equipment for the preparation or processing or production of such material to any Non-Nuclear Weapons State, even for peaceful purposes unless the source or special fissionable material has been subject to the safeguards required under this Treaty.

The Treaty is not, however, allowed to affect the right of all parties to develop research, production and use of nuclear energy for peaceful purposes. It does not seek to prevent the exchange of equipment, materials and scientific technological information for the peaceful uses of nuclear energy.

Its provisions regarding peaceful nuclear explosions are of note. It requires each party to the Treaty to ensure that under appropriate international observation and appropriate international procedures any potential benefits from peaceful applications of nuclear explosions will be made available to Non-Nuclear Weapons States and the charges made for such devices will be as low as possible and will exclude any charge for research and development.

There are other provisions regarding nuclear disarmament and nuclear-weapon-free zones which do not really affect the question of the peaceful uses of nuclear energy which is the principal topic of this book.

The NPT was open to all States for signature and subject to ratification by a signatory State. The United Kingdom, the USA and the USSR were designated as the Governments with which Instruments of Ratification and Instruments of Accession shall be deposited. It was laid down that the Treaty was to enter into force after its ratification by the States and the Governments of the depository countries and 40 other States. The Non-Proliferation Treaty came into force in 1970, 135 States are now parties to it.

Its interest to all concerned with ordinary nuclear installations, fuel factories and the transportation of nuclear materials is that they may be subject to scrutiny and actual physical inspection by an independent body, the International Atomic Energy Agency, which has a very large team of highly-qualified inspectors undertaking this work. Consequently, in the case of any country which has concluded

Safeguards Agreements with the IAEA under the terms of the NPT, no activities which could involve the manufacture or supply of materials usable for the production of nuclear weapons could be carried on without detection and control. Thus insurers could be reasonably confident that in the case of these countries there is no likelihood of their unwittingly providing insurance cover for plants which, while engaged in peaceful activities such as the manufacturing or reprocessing of nuclear fuel or the production of electricity by nuclear means, could be clandestinely engaged in work with military application. Unfortunately, a number of important countries which do have nuclear installations have not ratified or acceded to the Non-Proliferation Treaty or, if they have, have not concluded Safeguards Agreements with the International Atomic Energy Agency. Eighteen of the Tlatelolco Treaty States have, however, concluded such Agreements.

As mentioned earlier, the Nuclear Weapons States, i.e. those which have manufactured and exploded a nuclear weapon or other nuclear explosive device prior to 1st January 1967, are not obliged to accept Safeguards Inspections, although France, Great Britain, the USSR and the USA have agreed to do so voluntarily. These voluntary agreements also provide the IAEA with information concerning any transaction in which they are involved as the consignors or consignees of nuclear materials being transferred between different countries. One of the methods adopted to try to ensure that the sending and receiving countries are reporting on the same materials in the same way is to compare the information they lodge with the IAEA with regard to each batch of materials in transit. In practice, it is understood that this has produced some difficulties because the method used to identify individual batches of nuclear matter in transit by the sender and by the receiver do not always match, leading to anomalies in the computer checks carried out by the Agency.

THE IMPACT OF VARIOUS CONVENTIONS ON THE TRANSPORTATION OF NUCLEAR MATERIALS

The Nuclear Liability aspects of the carriage of nuclear matter by land, sea or air, particularly the last two, tend to be somewhat complex because the Vienna and Paris Conventions differ in some respects in the way they deal with the carriage of nuclear materials. The 1971 Maritime Carriage Convention has also to be taken into account, not to speak of some extremely important and very long-standing Marine and other Conventions relevant to the transportation of materials and liabilities of ship owners and the like.

Generally speaking, when we speak of nuclear transport liability we are referring to the transportation of "nuclear materials" (as in the Paris Convention) or "nuclear substances" (as in the Vienna Convention). Because of the channelling principle, the liability referred to is normally that of the nuclear installation operator, although under both Conventions the carrier may, by agreement, assume the responsibilities of the nuclear operator if approved by the Authorities. In that case the carrier becomes the "operator" of an installation for the purposes of the application of the liabilities imposed by both Conventions. The principal Articles in the two Conventions dealing with the transport question are, respectively, Article 4 in "Paris" and Article II in "Vienna". With respect to the possibility of a carrier being regarded as the "operator" for the purposes of determining liability for the transportation of nuclear material or nuclear substances, the Paris Convention (Article 4(d)) contains the following provision:

"A Contracting Party may provide by legislation that, under such terms as may be contained therein and upon fulfilment of the requirements of Article 10(a), a carrier may (at his request and with the consent of an operator of a nucler installation situated in that territory, by decision of the competent public authority), be liable in accordance with this Convention in the place of that operator. In such case, for all the purposes of this Convention a carrier shall be considered, in respect of nuclear incidents occurring in the course of carriage of nuclear substances, as an operator of a nuclear installation on the territory of the contracting party whose legislation so provides." (Article 10(a) is that which refers to the necessity for an operator to have and maintain insurance or other financial security.)

The equivalent provisions of the Vienna Convention are contained in Article II 2 in the following terms:

"The Installation State may provide by legislation that, in accordance with such terms as may be specified therein, a carrier of nuclear material or a person handling radioactive waste may, at his request and with the consent of the operator concerned, be designated or recognised as operator in the place of that operator in respect of such nuclear material or radioactive waste respectively. In this case such carrier or such person shall be considered, for all the purposes of this Convention, as an operator of a nuclear installation situated within the territory of that State."

Thus, in all material respects the two Conventions deal with this matter in the same way. The reason for provisions of this nature appearing in the two Nuclear Liability Conventions is that in the normal way a carrier, whether the carriage be by land, sea or air, would be regarded as the person liable for any injury or damage caused to third parties from anything which he is carrying. It is, of course, a cardinal principle of both Conventions that the operator of the nuclear installation is alone liable for the consequences of a nuclear incident occurring in his nuclear installation or as a result of anything coming from and, possibly, going to his nuclear installation which would be regarded as nuclear matter. This provides a means whereby national laws can preserve the concept of the channelling of all liability to a nuclear operator while also respecting the concept usual in international transport conventions that it is the carrier who must be liable for damage or injury caused to third parties from anything which he is carrying. However, because of the possibility of a clash between the obligations of States and carriers with respect to long-standing international transport conventions and the requirements of "Paris" or "Vienna", both of these Conventions also contain escape clauses:

Article 6(b) of the Paris Convention states:
"This provision shall not affect the application of any International Agreement in the field of Transport in force or open for signature, ratification or accession at the date of this Convention".

Article II.5 of the Vienna Convention contains an identical wording.

Both Conventions, as we have already seen, allow for the possibility of a person paying compensation to an injured third party exercising a right of recourse against the operator liable with respect to such payments. If the carrier has paid compensation and has not been designated an "operator" as provided for under both Conventions if national legislation so decides, then he presumably could exercise his right of recovery against the operator of the land-based installation from which or to which the nuclear matter is being transported. However, where the carrier has by agreement been designated "operator" it would seem to be self-evident that he thereupon becomes the person solely liable to pay compensation to third parties. He would not be able to exercise any right of recovery for such payments under the provisions of the Paris and Vienna Conventions whereby a person paying compensation to a third party acquires by subrogation the rights of that third party to claim against the responsible operator. (Article 6(d) of the Paris Convention and Article XI.2 of the Vienna Convention.) Incidentally, this right of subrogation applies, in the case of the Vienna Convention, only to nationals of Contracting Parties. Whether the carrier can be designated by national law as the "operator" for the purposes of channelling of liability and the payment of compensation presumably depends in the last analysis on whether or not the State concerned is bound by overriding provisions under one or other of the International Transport Conventions. In this connection, it will be recalled that under the 1971 Convention Relating to Civil Liability in the Field of Maritime Carriage of Nuclear Material any carrier who, under an International Convention or national law applicable in the field of maritime carriage, might be held liable for damage caused by a nuclear incident shall be exonerated from such liability.

Regarding damage to the means of transport, the Vienna Convention in Article IV.5 states:

"The operator shall not be liable under this Convention for nuclear damage ....
(b) to the means of transport upon which the nuclear material was at the time of the nuclear incident"

Sub-paragraph 6 allows Installation States by legislation to set this aside provided that "in no case shall the liability of the operator in respect of nuclear damage, other than nuclear damage to the means of transport, be reduced to less than US$5M for any one nuclear incident". The equivalent provision in the Paris Convention (Article 3(a)(ii).2) originally laid down that the nuclear installation operator shall be liable for damage to or loss of any property *other than* to "the means of transport upon which the nuclear substances involved were at the time of the nuclear incident ...". The Paris Convention, of course, also allows the Contracting Parties to have an option (under Article 6(c)) to include amongst the liabilities of the nuclear operator damage to the means of transport. Since most of the Contracting States exercised this option it was decided that the 1982 Protocol should therefore make liability for such damage mandatory by repealing the sub-paragraph 2 of Article 3(a)(ii) quoted above. A further consequential amentment was that the option provided under Article 6(c) was discontinued. The reference, in the prohibition against compensation paid for such damage, to the minimum amount of compensation under the Convention payable to third parties, was altered to 5 million Special Drawing Rights to bring it into line with the changes in that respect made elsewhere in the 1982 Protocol.

Regarding the obligation of a nuclear installation operator to provide the carrier with a Certificate of Financial Security, we have already seen in our review of the 1982 Protocol that the necessity for Contracting States to make this obligatory for international transits was withdrawn and the facility to make it optional for inland transits no longer applied because they were no longer required for inland transits. (Article 4(c) of the Paris Convention.) Under the Vienna Convention, since this has not been amended, it is still required under Article III that the operator liable shall provide the carrier with a Certificate issued by or on behalf of the Insurer or other financial guarantor furnishing the financial security.

The 1971 Maritime Carriage Convention succeeds in enabling a maritime carrier to avoid dual liability where he might otherwise have been liable under a Transport Convention and one or other of the Nuclear Liability Conventions and/or national law. If the carrier has not himself been designated an "operator", this clarifies his position where the appropriate Conventions and/or legislation apply but not, for example, when the nuclear installation operator is not liable for damage to the means of transport. The Paris and Vienna Conventions do not cover the question of damage to cargo on the means of transport whether this be a ship, an aircraft or a rail or road vehicle, to take one example of the uncertainties which still persist in the Transportation field.

This is not the place for detailed examination of the various and in some cases very long-standing international Conventions and other Agreements relating to the liabilities of carriers or shippers. Most of these pre-dated the development of nuclear energy and understandably did not make any specific reference to nuclear damage, but they are worth a mention because they do throw some light on the uncertainties facing those who may incur liability or may have to insure it. The following Conventions should be noted:

The International Convention for the Unification of Certain Rules of Law relating to Bills of Lading, August 1924 (the "Hague Rules")

This Convention has the support of a large number of countries, most of whom are active in the development of nuclear energy. As far as liability is concerned, the basic principle of the Hague Rules is that the carrier is liable for loss of or damage to goods only if such loss or damage was caused by his fault or by the fault of his agents or servants, but there is a reversed onus of proof. However, the carrier may avoid liability if loss or damage is a result of any act, neglect or default of the master, mariner, pilot, or other servants of the carrier, in the navigation or management of the ship. He is also able to avoid liability if the damage resulted from any act or omission on the part of the shipper or owner of the goods, his agent or representative. In the case of dangerous goods which have been carried without the knowledge or consent of the carrier or his agent, the shipper of the goods would be liable for any damage or expenses directly or indirectly arising out of or resulting from such shipment.

If nuclear damage is caused to non-nuclear cargo the owner of the non-nuclear cargo could claim against the carrier under the Hague

Convention and bring an action in a Court of a country which ratified that Convention, or he could claim compensation under the Paris or Vienna Convention if the installation operator responsible comes from a country which has ratified either or both of those Conventions. Another difference between the Hague Rules and the Nuclear Liability Conventions is in the period of prescription allowed for the bringing of claims after the date of the incident. The Paris and Vienna Conventions and most laws based upon them allow up to ten years. Under the Hague Rules, actions for compensation have to be brought against the carrier within one year after the delivery of the goods or the date when they should have been delivered. Another example of this type of inconsistency relates to the question of fault. Under the Nuclear Conventions the responsible operator has an absolute or strict liability. Under the Hague Rules the shipper may be responsible only if the loss or damage is specifically due to act, fault or neglect on the part of himself, his agent or his servant. These are just a few examples of the type of conflicts that may arise, and the situation is still further complicated where the operator or the shipper concerned comes from a country which is not a party to either of the Nuclear Liability Conventions even though there may be appropriate *national* legislation in that country.

Hague-Visby Rules

The position with respect to liability for nuclear damage, among other features, was tackled by the "Protocol to Amend the International Convention for the Unification of Certain Rules of Law Relating to Bills of Lading" which has become known as the Hague-Visby Rules. This new international Convention was concluded in 1968. It makes certain changes in the monetary amount of the liability of the carrier per package or per unit of gross weight of the goods carried but it specifies that the carrier is not entitled to benefit from any limitation of liability if it can be shown that the damage resulted from an act or omission done with intent to cause damage or recklessly and with knowledge that damage would probably result from his act or omission. However, the point of particular importance in the context of the nuclear liability problem is a provision concerning nuclear damage reading "This Convention shall not affect the provisions of any international Convention or national law governing liability for nuclear damage" (Article 4) — in other words the Hague-Visby Rules are intended to exclude any liability for nuclear damage covered by the Paris or Vienna Conventions. Thus, a shipper of goods carried in the ship in which the nuclear damage occurs would have to bring any claim for damage against the operator liable under the Paris or Vienna Convention if that Convention or legislation based upon it applies to the particular case. The 1971 Maritime Carriage Convention goes further, making it clear that if, by virtue of the Vienna or Paris Conventions or any national law based upon these, any carrier might be held liable for damage caused by a nuclear incident, he should be exonerated from such liability on condition that the operator of the nuclear installation is made liable by this instrument. Thus is the channelling principle extended; but as in all these matters everything depends upon whether or not the parties are subject to the relevant Conventions and/or national law.

The Hague-Visby Rules have, since 1968, been ratified by Belgium, Denmark, Ecuador, Egypt, Finland, France, German Democratic Republic, Great Britain (including the Isle of Man, Bermuda and Hong Kong), Italy, Lebanon, Netherlands, Norway, Poland, Singapore, Spain, Sweden, Switzerland, Syria and Tonga.

Carriage of Passengers by Sea

Two other Conventions relevant to carriage by sea, namely the "International Convention for the Unification of Certain Rules Relating to the Carriage of Passengers by Sea", of April 1961; and the "International Convention for the Unification of Certain Rules Relating to Carriage of Passenger Luggage by Sea", of May 1967, govern the liability of a carrier with respect to personal injury suffered by passengers on a ship or damage to their luggage. These two Conventions contain a provision relating to liability for nuclear damage, the wording of which is the same as that adopted in the Hague-Visby Rules. Thus, with regard to injury to passengers and damage to their luggage, if the carrier comes from a State which is a party either to the Paris or the Vienna Convention or, not being a party, has relevant legislation which includes channelling of liability, whether or not that State is a party to the 1961 or 1967 Convention, he would be exonerated from liability for such damage if it is due to nuclear causes. Similarly, in a case where the country of the carrier is not a party to any of these Conventions, then the carrier would under "Paris" or "Vienna" have a right of recovery against an operator liable for the damage although in the case of the Vienna Convention the carrier would have to be a national of a State party to it.

Once again, however, the point has to be made that all this only applies where the parties concerned are subject to the relevant Conventions. Very few States are parties to either the 1961 Convention relating to Passengers or the 1967 Convention which has had few ratifications.

Collisions at Sea

There is yet another international Transport Convention in the maritime field which could become involved. That is the "International Convention for the Unification of Certain Rules of Law with respect to Collisions between Vessels (The Collision Convention)" of September 1910. Understandably this makes no reference to nuclear damage. Thus, it would seem that if a ship carrying nuclear material collided with another ship and there was a nuclear incident which caused nuclear damage to goods carried on board the other ship, those suffering damage could, under the Collision Convention, bring an action for compensation against the owner of the ship carrying the nuclear material. The ship owner concerned would have the same rights of recovery against a responsible nuclear operator as in any other case under the terms of the Paris and Vienna Conventions where they apply. If the Collision Convention did not apply, then actions for compensation would have to be handled in accordance with the Paris or Vienna Conventions providing, again, that these are applicable.

Shipowner's Liability

Finally, there is another Convention preceding the 1971 Convention on Civil Liability in the field of Maritime Carriage of Nuclear Material which should be mentioned although it does not have any particular relevance to the carriage of nuclear material. This is the "International Convention relating to the Limitation of the Liability of Owners of Sea-Going Ships", of October 1957. This allows a shipowner in certain circumstances to limit his financial liability. It is worth mentioning, however, because in a case where a carrier or shipowner is designated "nuclear installation operator" under the Paris or Vienna Conventions, he could not benefit from the limitation rules and the provisions of maritime law.

Carriage by Air

The principal international agreement governing the liability of an air carrier for damage to goods carried on board an aircraft or to persons or to luggage is established by the "Convention for the Unification of Certain Rules relating to International Carriage by Air", 1929 (The "Warsaw Convention") — as amended by the 1955 Hague Protocol. Although more recent than the Hague Convention regarding the liability of shipowners, it is likewise understandable that the original Warsaw Convention makes no specific provision regarding nuclear materials or nuclear damage, which are not expressly excluded. Steps were taken in the 1970's by the International Civil Aviation Organisation to amend certain of the provisions of the Warsaw Convention regarding liability for damage to goods carried by air and to take some account of the need to exclude nuclear damage where there is a liability under Nuclear Conventions or national nuclear legislation, as in the Maritime Conventions. Liability for death or personal injury suffered by a passenger and for damage to his luggage also allows for the possibility of conflict between the Warsaw Convention and the Nuclear Liability Conventions. An opportunity to put this right arose when certain other amendments to this part of the Warsaw Convention were agreed under what is known as the 1971 Guatemala Protocol but that opportunity was not taken.

The Guatemala Protocol makes the carrier absolutely liable for death or personal injury to a passenger except when this is the result of his state of health. There is also an absolute liability for damage to his luggage unless that is due to inherent defect, quality or vice in the baggage. There are specific limits of financial liability per person in the case of death or personal injury and per passenger in the case of damage to luggage, but there is no overall limit of liability for the consequences of an incident involving more than one passenger. There is therefore still a conflict with the Paris and Vienna Conventions in relation to channelling of liability to the operator unless the air carrier opts to become an "installation operator" by agreement and with the approval of the supervising authorities under either of the two Conventions or national law based on them. Whether an aircraft would carry nuclear material as well as passengers is uncertain although it is quite possible that small packages of radioisotopes might be carried with other freight on a passenger aircraft. These, however, might not be liable to the provisions of the Conventions because of the small quantity that would be involved.

Regarding the damage caused by aircraft, the relevant international Agreement is the "Convention on Damage Caused by Foreign Aircraft to Third Parties on the Surface", 1952 (The "Rome Convention"). This makes the aircraft operator absolutely liable for damage to property, death or personal injury to any person caused by an aircraft in flight or any person or thing falling from an aircraft. It is limited to a financial amount determined by reference to the weight of the aircraft. There is a specific limitation in amount per person in the event of death or injury. This Convention contains no reference to nuclear damage or nuclear materials and is not yet in force.

Carriage by Rail

The relevant international agreement regarding damage to goods carried by rail is the International Convention on the Carriage of Goods by Rail, 1961. This is more commonly known by the initials CIM. It contains financial limits and a provision concerning the liability of the sender towards the rail company for damage which may be caused by defective packaging. However, more importantly, CIM has a specific exclusion of nuclear damage which states "The Railway is relieved of its liability under this Convention if the damage was caused by a nuclear incident and if, pursuant to special provisions governing the liability in the field of nuclear energy in force in a contracting State, the operator of a nuclear installation or any other person who has replaced the operator is liable for damage" (Article 64). This exclusion is notably more extensive than that in the 1961 and 1967 Conventions in relation to the Maritime Carriage of Passengers and Luggage.

Regarding damage caused to persons or luggage carried by rail in the same vehicle as nuclear materials, there are two international Conventions which concern the liability of the railway towards passengers for damage to their luggage and for death or personal injury. These are the Convention on the Carriage of Passengers and Luggage by Rail 1961 (known as CIV), and the Supplementary Convention to the CIV of 1966, known as the "Supplementary CIV". Liability under this Convention is very similar to that under the CIM mentioned above, although the financial amounts are different. Both contain a nuclear exclusion in the same terms as that in the CIM.

These Conventions are in force and are applied by practically all the European countries.

Carriage by Road

The relevant international agreement is the "Convention on the Contract for the International Carriage of Goods by Road" 1956, which is known by the initials CMR. In much the same way as the other Transport Conventions, this makes the carrier absolutely liable for damage to or loss of goods occurring during the carriage unless such damage or loss was caused by the wrongful act or neglect of the claimant or by instructions given by him or by the inherent vice of the goods. The carrier may be exonerated from liability if loss or damage can be attributed to certain specific risks such as defective packing in the case of goods which if not properly packed are likely to be damaged. There is a financial limit but this does not apply in a case where the damage was caused by the wilful misconduct of the carrier or his servants or agents. Any damage suffered by the carrier on account of defective packing of goods or because of the dangerous nature of the goods which has not been made known to the carrier is the liability of the sender. In some respects the legal position under this Convention is very similar to that under the Hague Rules although, under CMR, if there is liability under the Paris or Vienna Convention an action may be brought before a Court in one of the contracting States even though that State is not a party to the CMR. There is no express exclusion of nuclear damage or nuclear materials.

It will be seen from this brief review of certain aspects of the various Transport Conventions that there are areas of conflict with the Paris and Vienna Conventions and other areas of uncertainty as to what would apply and whether there would or would not be a dual liability on the carrier and/or operator. The situation is further complicated when one takes into account that not all States, by any means, have ratified or acceded to the various Conventions although those that have the most support would be the Hague Rules and the Warsaw Convention in the non-nuclear field and the Paris Convention with the Brussels Supplementary Convention in the nuclear liability field.

All international Conventions are subject to periodic review and various changes are agreed from time to time in the form of Protocols, Supplementary Conventions or new Conventions. These do not always come into force rapidly, or even at all, because that cannot be achieved unless the minimum number of States as laid down in the various Conventions choose to ratify the Convention by introducing appropriate national legislation.

These areas of conflict or, at any rate, disharmony, are in nobody's interest. Where the carriage of nuclear materials is involved, the position of the operator or the carrier and of the potential victim of any nuclear incident arising from such materials in the course of carriage, can in some cases be quite confusing even to the legal experts. The Paris and the Vienna Conventions shed some light on the position by enabling the carrier to seek recovery from the installation operator for any claims he may be obliged to pay under whatever legal regime he is subject to. In these situations the *installation operator* would have an absolute or strict liability and all liability would be channelled to him. There would, however, be a financial limit, and a limitation in time, which would be in line with the provisions of either Convention according to the way in which national law deals with these features. While the limitation in time is almost invariably ten years, the amount of financial liability varies greatly and may be considerably out of line with the limits imposed on the carrier who is exercising a right of recovery against the operator, by whatever Transport Convention he is subject to. So far as the claimant is concerned, if he brings an action under a Transport Convention his claim may be out of time in a relatively short period even though, were he able to claim against the nuclear installation operator, he would have a much longer period (i.e. up to 10 years). The introduction of new Conventions or International Treaties, and even the amendment of existing ones, can be a lengthy and difficult process. Accession to existing agreements and ratification by all who have signed or acceded to these ought to be much speedier. Were this objective to be achieved, particularly with respect to the Vienna Convention which covers a much wider range of countries than the OECD Paris Convention, and if all Transport Conventions were to be amended by a Protocol excluding all liability for nuclear damage, the position of the operator, the carrier and the Third Party victim could then be made much clearer. All forms of nuclear damage wherever it may occur — whether on land, in the air, or the high seas — would then be subject to the same type of national legislation and international law. Everybody, not the least nuclear operators and their insurers, would know where they stood.

International Safety Regulations and Codes

Before the establishment of inter-Governmental organisations like the United Nations' International Atomic Energy Agency, and the OECD's Nuclear Energy Agency, international safety codes regarding the handling of nuclear materials, radioactive substances and their transportation, were largely the responsibility of private, i.e. non-Governmental, organisations such as the ICRP (International Commission on Radiological Protection) and the ICU (International Commission on Radiation Units and Measurements). Both of these International Commissions were founded by the International Society of Radiology (ISR), another international non-Governmental body which was set up in 1925. They both publish recommendations and guidelines on various aspects of radiological protection and safety which carry considerable weight, although they do not have any legally binding force. The ICU was originally founded in 1925 as the "International X-Ray Unit Committee". Its modern name was adopted in 1965. Their objectives are to develop internationally-acceptable recommendations regarding quantities and units of radiation and radioactivity and the formulation of such recommendations in the field of radiation protection.

Although of non-Government status, both these organisations are official consultants to the United Nations' Economic and Social Council, to the World Health Organisation and to the IAEA. ICRP has special relationships with the European Communities, the ILO, OECD's Nuclear Energy Agency and, among others, the United Nations' Scientific Committee on the Effects of Atomic Radiation (UNSCEAR). Both organisations have published numerous recommendations and papers, those issued by the former being mainly concerned with radiological protection, particularly of radiation workers and of hospital patients, as well as the general public, whereas the ICU are more concerned with the methods of evaluating radiation and measuring doses.

The ICRP have had a considerable influence in the determination of what are safe levels of exposure to radiation for workers on the sites of nuclear installations. They also specify what might be an acceptable exposure for individual members of the public, the norm being one tenth of the dose for those who work at nuclear installations or with nuclear materials. They also have recommended exposure limits for transport workers who may be exposed to radioactive materials carried in the means of transport. In this connection, great importance is attached to the packaging of radioactive materials, and, in the event of the radiation being such as to produce an unacceptably high dose rate, the proper measures for the segregation and shielding of such packages. Apart from the risk of injury to persons, another important consideration relating to the transportation of nuclear materials which may be being carried with other goods, is the possibility of their causing damage to film. The recommendations of the ICRP in all these fields are highly respected and are often absorbed into national regulations.

The International Labour Organisation was founded in 1919 to protect workers against illness and injury arising out of their employment as well as children and young persons and women. They are equally concerned to protect such people against the consequences of ionising radiations and in 1960 they published their Recommendation (which carries the number 114) concerning the protection of workers against ionising radiation. This is backed by an international Convention which has been ratified by at least 39 States who, because the Convention is legally binding, are obliged to fulfil the requirements of the regulations concerning radiation protection in relation to workers at their places of work. The ILO has also produced various manuals and guidelines with respect to radiation protection, including for example a model code of safety regulations, advice on radiation protection in the mining and milling of radioactive ores and so on, all of these being published in Geneva.

The World Health Organisation which, like the ILO, is now a

specialised Agency of the United Nations, is concerned more specifically with the protection of the public against radiation hazards especially in relation to medical uses. They have not, as yet, introduced any legally-binding Conventions or Agreements but have published a series of important recommendations concerning radiation hazards in general and, in particular, such topics as the effects of radiation on human heredity; the medical use of ionising radiation; radiation protection in hospitals and general practice; quality assurance in diagnostic radiology and in nuclear medicine; the management of high-level radioactive waste in the nuclear power field; and others of considerable importance.

The United Nations itself set up in 1955 a special Radiation Protection Committee (UNSCEAR) consisting of nuclear scientists contributed by 20 members. It is located in Vienna and has close contacts with the International Atomic Energy Agency although it is a separate body. It reports annually to the General Assembly of the United Nations and its more recent reports have covered such topics as the levels, sources and effects of ionising radiation, including biological effects.

Another extremely important source of safety recommendations is the International Atomic Energy Agency. They have issued a whole range of recommendations and advice in their Safety Series publications. These recommendations have had a considerable influence in determining standards and in harmonisation of national legislation in the field of radiation protection. They do not, of themselves, have legally binding force but they can be incorporated by the Member States in bilateral or multi-lateral agreements with the IAEA when these declare that the safety standards will apply. Where the IAEA recommendations have been adopted in this way, they have, in practice, the effect of law. Among the most important are the following:

Regulations for the Safe Transport of Radioactive Materials 1985 Edition (No. 6 in the Safety Series);

The Management of Radioactive Waste produced by Radioisotope Users (No. 12);

Basic Factors for the Treatment and Disposal of Radioactive Wastes — 1967 (No. 35)

Management of Radioactive Wastes at Nuclear Power Plants — 1968 (No. 28)

Safe Operation of Nuclear Power Plants — 1969 (No. 31)

Principles for Establishing Limits for the Release of Radioactive Materials into the Environment — 1978 (No. 45)

Manual on Decontamination of Surfaces — 1979 (No. 48)

Fire Protection in Nuclear Power Plants — 1979 (No. 59)

Development of Regulatory Procedures for the Disposal of Radioactive Waste in Deep Continental Formations — 1980 (No. 51)

Criteria for Underground Disposal of Solid Radioactive Wastes — 1983 (No. 60)

There are many others — obtainable from the IAEA in Vienna or their Agents in most countries.

Some of these publications incorporate very detailed guidelines with respect, for example, to acceptable dose levels and methods of packaging materials to be transported. The Safe Transport Regulations set out the limits which should be applied in determining what are small quantities of radioactive materials under the Annex to the Vienna Convention concerning the exclusion of small quantities of nuclear material. These figures are of added importance because they are also incorporated in the Paris Convention. Since they may be changed from time to time, it may be necessary for those who are concerned with this matter to consult the IAEA Transport Regulations although alterations in the figures in the Conventions should be reproduced in national nuclear legislation based upon them.

Equally important are the recommendations issued by the Nuclear Energy Agency of the OECD who have been publishing rules and recommendations on radiation protection since their early days as the European Nuclear Energy Agency of the OEEC. Their Council adopted a Decision in 1959 on the basis of the report of their Steering Committee for Nuclear Energy declaring that member countries should take all necessary measures to ensure adequate protection against the hazards of ionising radiations, both with respect to persons occupationally exposed and for the population at large. This Decision, which has binding authority as far as the Member States are concerned, recommended that radiation protection measures should be in accordance with suggestions published in an Annex of that Decision. This Annex, entitled Radiation Protection Norms, was revised in 1968 as a result of a decision taken by the OECD Council in 1962. In 1981, the Steering Committee for Nuclear Energy decided to adopt various standards prepared by a Joint Advisory Group comprising IAEA, ILO, WHO and the OECD's own Nuclear Energy Agency. These new standards were described as the "Revision of the Radiation Protection Norms" and they were published by the IAEA in 1982 as a revised edition of their "basic" standards for radiation protection. These recommendations are in line with the

ICRP recommendations No. 26, published in 1977.

Among NEA recommendations are protection standards relating to radioluminous timepieces and to gaseous tritium light devices. They have also issued protection standards relating to radioisotopic cardiac pacemakers, and ionisation chamber smoke detectors. In other fields they have issued Decisions concerning sea dumping of radioactive waste, with regard to consultation and surveillance and operational procedures. Apart from these binding Decisions, the Nuclear Energy Agency have published material concerning the safety analysis and control of products containing radionuclides which are available to the general public (1970). Other recommendations of a non-binding character published by the NEA include the following:

Nuclear Legislation — Analytical Studies.

Regulations Governing Nuclear Installations and Radiation Protection (1972)

Radiation Protection Considerations in the Design and Operation of Particle Accelerators (1974)

Objectives, Concepts and Strategies for the Management of Radioactive Waste arising from Nuclear Power Programmes (1977) (This is also known as the Polvani Report)

Regulations Governing the Transport of Radioactive Materials (1980)

Technical Appraisal of the Current Situation in the field of Radioactive Waste Management (1985)

The last of the international bodies specifically concerned with atomic energy to be mentioned in connection with the issue of recommendations in the field of nuclear safety is the European Atomic Energy Community, commonly known as EURATOM. This was founded in 1957 at the time of the European Economic Community set up under the Treaty of Rome and is therefore of regional application. The EURATOM Treaty contains special rules regarding protection against radiation and sets out basic standards in relation to maximum safe doses and the maximum permissible degree of exposure, as well as fundamental principles concerning the medical supervision of workers. EURATOM have issued various Directives concerning radiation protection since the first Council Directives issued in 1959. Like the OECD's Nuclear Energy Agency, they have paid particular attention to recommendations emerging from the ICRP in their Basic Safety Standards which, being Directives and not Regulations, have legal force: under the terms of the EURATOM Treaty member States are required to enact the necessary legislative and administrative provisions to secure compliance with these Standards. They do not have legal force within member countries until they have been ratified by national laws. In addition to the Directives under the EURATOM Treaty, the Commission of the European Communities have published special recommendations in relation to radiation protection.

In the Socialist countries, the body concerned with Radiation Safety operates under the aegis of the 10-member Council for Mutual Economic Assistance (CMEA).

Another international body which includes radiation protection amongst its activities is the United Nations' Food & Agriculture Organisation (FAO) although it is less concerned in this field than the specialised nuclear institutions. The FAO produces reports and recommendations concerning radiation protection, usually in co-operation with the international nuclear bodies, particularly the IAEA. One of its special concerns has been in regard to the irradiation of food.

CHAPTER V

NATIONAL NUCLEAR LAWS

More than 50 countries throughout the western world have laws which relate in some way to nuclear energy whether this be in the field of liability, safety, radiation protection, licensing and controls and so on. It would be impossible to refer to all of these, or even to all the nuclear *liability* aspects. Indeed, such a study would provide ample material for a separate book.

Therefore, this section will be confined firstly, to a review of the United Kingdom legislation, where it is of particular interest to Liability insurers, and secondly, to the nuclear laws of four other countries which are of particular interest.

United Kingdom Legislation

1. The Nuclear Installations Act, 1965

This law was not the first piece of nuclear legislation to be introduced in the United Kingdom but it is, with respect to liabilities, the current and main legislative instrument together with its 1969 and 1983 Amendments.

Mention was made in the previous Chapter of the pre-Convention legislation in certain countries. The U.K. law was the 1959 Nuclear Installations (Licensing and Insurance) Act which set out many of the basic concepts widely observed in nuclear laws in other countries and, indeed, enshrined in the Paris and the Vienna Conventions, notably with regard to the four essentials: absolute or strict liability; the principle of channelling of liability to the operator; the fixing of a financial limit to his obligation to compensate third parties, together with provision for public funds to be made available to supplement this amount; and a limitation in time for the presentation of claims.

In the United Kingdom, insurers have always maintained close co-operation with the relevant Government Departments in the formulation of laws and other rules and regulations relating to the field of nuclear energy. Thus, when the replacement of the 1959 Act was under consideration by the Board of Trade and the Ministry of Power (the Departments of Government then responsible) following British ratification of the Paris Convention, insurers were consulted at all points as they had been in the 50's when the original law was being formulated. British nuclear law is closely in line with the provisions of the Paris and the Brussels Conventions. In particular, it lays great stress upon the overall financial limits placed upon the obligations of a nuclear operator to an extent that goes beyond the concept in the Paris Convention.

When that Convention was being discussed between the Governments concerned, it was recognised that there could not be an unlimited financial commitment and if there were, insurance cover could not be unlimited. With the full backing of the British Government, insurers in the United Kingdom sought to achieve an absolute limit for the financial commitment they would be required to provide for under nuclear liability insurance policies, not only in relation to the total amount to be paid in consequence of each nuclear incident but also in relation to a particular nuclear installation throughout its insured lifetime. This concept has not achieved international recognition either under the Paris of the Vienna Conventions although they both accept the need for a limit to the maximum amount that would be payable by a nuclear operator in consequence of one incident regardless of the number of claimants.

Financial limits and cover

The British concept of overall financial liability is as follows:

Liability, as under any legislation ratifying the Paris Convention, is on a per incident basis but the maximum amount that the licensee is required to pay is fixed in relation to the whole period of his responsibility for the installation. This is known under the British legislation as the "Cover Period" which is defined in Section 5(3) of the Act. The beginning of this period is the date of the granting of the licence or, if that does not coincide with the requirement for financial security, then the date when that obligation starts. It would not end until the nuclear installation ceases to be a nuclear installation, probably when it is decommissioned and dismantled. That date would be determined by the Government Department responsible for health and safety which would state that there was no longer any danger of ionising radiation from anything on the site. The Cover Period as far as a particular operator is concerned might, however, end before the site ceases to be a nuclear installation. For example, when a new site licence is issued for some reason to the same licensee, or there is a change of ownership and a new licence is issued to another licensee. The ending of a Cover Period or the starting of a new Cover Period for one of these reasons would be determined by a direction from the responsible

Government Minister. An existing Cover Period may also be brought to an end if there is a change in the operator's liability, for example, following a statutory increase in the financial limits, (as occurred in 1983); or following a serious accident.

The current maximum liability in amount imposed on the operators of nuclear installations in the United Kingdom is £20M per Cover Period, except in the case of what are described as "small operators" for whom the limit is £5M. These changes were brought about by the Energy Act of 1983, which amended Section 16 of the 1965 Act to increase the previous limit of £5M per Cover Period which applied regardless of the size of the installation.

This change meant that all the existing Cover Periods under the 1965 Act up to the date of the amendment were automatically terminated and for the purposes of insurance or financial security new Cover Periods commenced on 1st September 1983. One of the practical consequences of this change was that the licensee or his insurers would continue to be liable for up to £5M for any claims arising out of an incident occurring before 1st September 1983 and notified within the statutory ten-year prescription period. Thus, so long as that period continued beyond the 1st September 1983, he would be in effect liable not only for the £5M under the old Act with respect to any claims arising within the 10-year prescription period from incidents occuring before that date but, until the possibility of these being brought expires, also for an overlapping amount of £20M. Therefore, with the starting of a new Cover Period, new insurance policies had to be issued from the 1st September 1983, although any liabilities incurred up to the end of August 1983, insured under previous policies, were still covered during the 10-year prescription period. This is because each annual insurance policy covers the liabilities of the nuclear operator which arise from any nuclear incident occurring during the period of that particular policy. Therefore, any claim which is properly brought against the operator during the ten years discovery period would be met under the policy applying to the year in which the incident occurred. This period is known under the Act as the "relevant period". So far as the claimant is concerned, he is able to bring a claim under the Act for a period of up to 30 years after the incident but the liability to meet such a claim beyond 10 years falls upon the Government.

In accordance with the Paris Convention, this Act requires a licensee to make provision either by insurance, or some other means such as may be approved by the Minister with the consent of the British Treasury, for sufficient funds to be available *at all times* to ensure that any claims which have been or may be duly established against the licensee under the Act or any relevant foreign law are satisfied up to the statutory limits of either £20M or £5M per cover period (Section 19(1)). An interesting further provision in this Section of the Act may apply in the case of an operator who selects some form of financial guarantee other than commercial insurance and who has more than two other nuclear sites which require to be covered. Instead of providing £20M (or £5M) for each site, the Act allows him to make funds available for all his sites collectively in such sum as would represent twice the limit of financial guarantee required by the Authorities for two of those sites. These have to be the two most highly-rated in terms of the limit of liability to be covered where there are sites carrying different limits. Therefore, in the case of an operator of, say, several nuclear power stations, it is apparent under this Section of the Act that, if he has funds available to the extent of £40M (i.e. 2 × £20M) however many sites he has in excess of two, that sum of money will meet his financial obligations under the Act. This is compatible with the Paris Convention.

Another unusual provision, which is not generally found in the nuclear liability laws of other countries, is the possibility for the financial guarantee to be reduced by the payment of claims and to remain a valid financial guarantee, without reinstatement, until such time as the amount of claims paid shall reach 60% of the statutory limit. That is to say, in a case where the cover provided by insurance or other financial security is £20M, that cover will remain valid until such time as it has been reduced to £8M. When this point is reached, or about to be reached, then the licensee and his insurers must notify the licensing authority and no further claims may be paid without the authorisation of the responsible Minister. The justification for this provision is derived from the fact that the financial liability of the licensed operator is related not to each incident nor even to each year of cover but to what has been earlier described as the cover period, the period of his responsibility. It is, in other words, what the insurers call a "per installation" limit. It is compatible with "Paris" because under that Convention the *minimum* financial security is 5M.SDR's.

In considering the means by which financial security shall be provided it is important to note that this may either be by way of commercial insurance policies or by such other means as the Minister may approve. The essential requirement is that whatever means is adopted, there will be available at all times sufficient funds to meet claims for compensation from third parties up to the financial limits laid down. It will be obvious that if the operator elects not to buy insurance, then he must have sufficient liquid funds or readily realisable assets available for up to £20M per site or £40M if he has more than two sites. The Government Department concerned with the administration of the Nuclear Installations Act has advised that it would not meet the requirements of the Act if the funds were to be drawn from the licensee's revenues or from the disposal of assets which could not be quickly realised. To set aside a special fund for the purpose of meeting claim payments, to have a line of credit to a bank or, worst of all, to have to borrow the money for the purpose of gaining access to such funds at short notice, would obviously be uneconomic. This is why the preferred method in all countries is to provide the necessary financial security by way of commercial insurance which means that the licensee and the claimants have ready access to the very substantial funds and claims handling expertise of the insurance industry. It came as something of a surprise, therefore, when U.K. insurers learned in 1983 that the Minister concerned and the British Treasury were prepared to approve as an alternative financial security, an arrangement described as "fronting" — a form of "self-insurance". By this means they would allow a licensee to obtain a policy from an insurer, but in practice to pay the claims himself out of his own funds. In other words, the insurance policy would be no more than a "front". Claims met on behalf of the operator by the insurance company would either be reimbursed by the licensee or, very probably, funded in advance.

Most insurers in the United Kingdom do not regard this as a satisfactory alternative form of financial security, since it appears to cut across the intention that the funds required to meet claims for compensation, which must be available at all times, should not be drawn from the licensee's own revenue or fixed assets. In the form of fronting arrangement referred to the licensee's own funds or assets would *in practice* be at risk and be drawn upon to pay claims, whatever role the chosen insurance company might play. It is difficult to see how such an arrangement can be regarded as meeting the aims of the Paris Convention since the obligation to pay compensation must be financially secure and not be an undue burden on the installation operator's finances. This is not to say that the licensee under one of these fronting arrangements would necessarily fail to meet claims. But as payments could be up to £20M, even £40M, it is considered that no prudent insurer, however large, should undertake such a commitment without the certainty of being reimbursed or funded by the licensee he is covering, especially as he could not protect himself under the normal reinsurance arrangements. Even the largest insurance Company could not retain more than, say, £3 million net on a nuclear liability risk, a small one perhaps no more than £100,000. Legal opinions vary as to the validity of "fronted" self-insurance as a proper alternative financial security.

Additional compensation

The U.K. legislation complies with the Brussels Supplementary Convention with regard to the additional compensation which must be provided when the licensee's cover is exhausted. Following the adoption of the 1982 Protocol, the relevant amounts were brought into British legislation by amendment through the medium of Section 2 of the 1983 Energy Act. Consequently, the British Government will meet claims in excess of £20M (or £5M) up to the equivalent of 175 million SDR's out of their own resources and, beyond that, up to 300 million SDR's in association with the other Contracting Parties to the Brussels Convention. Incidentally, it was as a result of the increases required following the amendment of the Brussels Convention that the limits of liability imposed on the operator in the United Kingdom were increased, in the case of other than "small operators", to £20M — 4 times the amount than had been in force since 1959. The thinking behind this increase was that the Brussels amounts had been increased by the OECD by 150%. This, together with the conversion of the SDR's into Sterling at the appropriate rate ruling in 1983, produced the approximation of a four-fold increase.

Meaning of "damage" or "injury"

With regard to such issues as the meaning of damage or of injury the 1965 Act is not of very much assistance. It does not define damage, and so far as injury is concerned the definitions or interpretations in Section 26 of the Act simply state that "injury means personal injury and includes loss of life". Guidance given by the relevant Government Department states that "to be injured for the purposes of the Act" a person must have been killed or have suffered a disease or some impairment to his physical or *mental* condition. In the event of injury or disease arising within the ten years after exposure to radiation in connection with the relevant incident, damages would also be payable with respect to pecuniary loss such as loss of earnings, or loss of support in the case of a dependant, in consequence of the accident.

The term "damage" is usually interpreted widely under English law and the same would appear to hold true with respect to damage to property suffered by third parties in consequence of an escape of ionising radiation from a licensed nuclear site. Providing there was direct radioactive contamination of premises owned by a third party then he could claim not only for the damage or the decontamination expenses but also for loss of use of property, loss of income, loss of profit if business premises, the wages of employees who may still have to be paid when denied access to their place of work, and so on. Expenses incurred as a result of evacuation from a contaminated area would also appear to be an acceptable claim under the heading of economic loss directly caused by radiation damage. However, the official view is that an individual or firm suffering economic loss because they have to be evacuated from an area or cannot gain access to an area which is under threat, but do not suffer direct damage to their own property or persons, would not be able to bring a claim in consequence of a nuclear incident or of an official evacuation ordered in connection with an incident or a threatened incident. Somebody suffering such loss might have a claim under the general law, and a nuclear operator could therefore be legally liable to pay compensation outside the provisions of the Nuclear Installations Act. Finally, people voluntarily evacuating their homes or workplaces because of an unsubstantiated fear of a nuclear accident would appear to have no claim.

In view of the interest that is frequently evinced, particularly amongst the environmental lobbyists, concerning the possibilities of an exposure to radiation causing genetic damage to future generations, it should be mentioned that under English law the term "injury" would include anything which would affect a man in his ability to have a normal healthy child, or a woman in that ability which so affects her when she is pregnant that her child is born with disabilities that would not otherwise have been present. Whether exposure to radiation could possibly cause such genetic damage is an open question and there appears to be no evidence that it could from any experience with human beings or with animals. (The quoted authority for the legal position is the Congenital Disabilities (Civil Liability) Act 1976).

Regarding damage to property on the site of the licensed nuclear installation, compensation would not be payable under the Act if this is the property of the operator himself or is present for the purpose of use in connection with the operation or cessation of the operation of the nuclear reactor, or any other property which is there for the purpose of construction of a nuclear installation whether it is owned by the licensee or not. (This is in accordance with Article 4(a) (2) 1 of the Paris Convention). The property of genuine third parties who are not involved in the operation of the plant, etc., would however be covered.

If a nuclear occurrence off the site of a nuclear installation, involves nuclear matter which having at any time been on a nuclear site is now elsewhere which is not another nuclear site, the operator is liable for the consequences of any nuclear occurence arising from that matter. The reference to "elsewhere" would include carriage on behalf of the licensee anywhere, including carriage to that site from a place outside the relevant territories (that is to say, the countries of the contracting parties to the Paris Convention). It would also apply to any place where it may be when it is not in the course of carriage. For instance, nuclear waste which has been taken away and dumped at sea would be the liability of the operator of the site where is was last located, even though it is not in any readily identifiable place or country.

There are special provisions regarding materials which may be sent to defence establishments by licensees.

Territorial limits

Regarding the territorial application of the U.K. Act, compensation is payable if damage is due to an incident which occurs within the territorial limits of the United Kingdom; or arises from nuclear matter *in the course of carriage* on behalf of a United Kingdom operator and the incident takes place on or over the high seas or within the territory of a non-Convention country; or, the incident arises from nuclear matter which has been lost, stolen, jettisoned or abandoned and it came from a U.K. operator's site, or from carriage on his behalf, but which since its loss has not been in a non-Convention country. Compensation is payable in any case if the injury or damage is suffered in a Convention country, or on or over the high seas, or by or on board a British-registered ship or aircraft.

It is noteworthy that the liability does not attach if injury or damage is suffered in a non-Convention country. The relevant sections of the Act covering these aspects are found within Sections 7 - 10, together with Section12(1) (a) and 13(1).

War and natural disasters

With regard to the options available under the Paris Convention concerning the liability of a nuclear operator for nuclear damage in consequence of armed conflict, hostilities, civil war or insurrection on the one hand, or of a natural disaster of an exceptional nature on the other, the British legislation exonerates him in the case of armed conflict but *not* in the case of a natural disaster.

Transport liabilities

With regard to the Transport Conventions referred to in the previous Chapter, a nuclear operator would remain liable to the extent that these were in force at the time of the signing of the Paris Convention and have not been amended by, for example, an exclusion of nuclear liability. Thus, despite a provision in Article 12(1)(b) that "no other liability shall be incurred by any person in respect of injury or damage", a carrier who is not an "operator" would apparently not be exonerated from any liability he might acquire under one of the Transport Conventions in consequence of an incident arising from nuclear matter unless this contains an exclusion of liability for nuclear damage as is the case with the 1971 Maritime Carriage of Nuclear Materials Convention *and* he belongs to a State which has ratified that Convention. He may be able to recover any claims paid from the installation operator responsible for the consignment but only if the latter is located in a State which is a party to the Paris or Vienna Convention. (However the U.K. has not ratified the 1971 Maritime Carriage Convention).

Time limits

With regard to time limits for the bringing of claims for compensation by third parties, the United Kingdom have exercised their discretion to fix a period longer than the ten years provided for under the Paris Convention by allowing up to 30 years for the bringing of claims. However, so far as the liability of the operator is concerned, this is only ten years and the State would be responsible for meeting claims for the excess of 20 years beyond the 10 years during which the operator continues to be responsible. The Act also takes up the time limit relating to claims arising from incidents attributable to nuclear material which has been lost, stolen, jettisoned or abandoned. Thus, there is an overriding limit of 20 years from the date of the loss, jettison, abandonment, etc. Claims must still be brought within 10 years of the date of the *incident*. That period will be foreshortened by the application of the 20-year ceiling if the incident occurs more than 10 years after the loss of the material in question. So far as the bringing of claims against the Government is concerned, these may be brought for a period of up to *20* years after the occurrence giving rise to the claim (not the usual 30, so special payments out of public funds would be arranged for the excess of 10 years).

Incidentally, the occurrence which determines the date of the commencement of the 10 or 30 years prescription period would be, if there is a succession of occurrences having the same cause, the last of this series of occurrences. The occurrence date is known in the law as the "relevant date". It is more fully defined in Section 15(1) of the Act.

Damage to means of transport

So far as concerns damage to the means of transport in the event of a nuclear occurrence during the carriage of nuclear matter, Section 21(1) of the Act gives effect to the provisions of the Paris Convention regarding the limit for compensation payable under this heading. This means that no payment shall be made out of the operator's funds which would have the effect of leaving less that 5 million SDR's to meet other claims. If that should produce a shortfall in the settlement of the claims, then the use of public funds is permitted up to the maximum of 300 million SDR's overall. However, this applies only to occurrences within the territory of the United Kingdom.

The foregoing observations highlight the main elements of the 1965 Act in so far as they relate to rights to compensation, the bringing of and satisfaction of claims, insurance cover or other financial guarantee for compensation, and the nature and limitations both in terms of time and amount of the operator's liabilities. However, like its predecessor, the 1959 Act, this Statute makes provision for the control of nuclear installations and operations, restricting the operation of certain types of establishments to licensed sites, and it also gives details regarding nuclear site licences. The legal duties of a licensee of a licensed site are set out together with the duties of the United Kingdom Atomic Energy Authority; the duties of the Crown, that is to say, in effect Government establishments; the duties laid upon foreign operators; and the duties of persons causing nuclear matter to be carried (Sections 7 - 12). The Act also contains provisions regarding the obligation to report and to enquire into dangerous occurrences and for the registration of persons who were in the area of a nuclear occurrence during the period when it took place. This is to assist in the verification of claims for injuries or disease which may have been caused by exposure to ionising radiation coming from the nuclear site where the incident took place. Provision is made under the miscellaneous sections of the Act for the appointment of inspectors who are authorised at all reasonable times during the period of a licensee's responsibility to enter any premises comprised in any licensed site and to use such equipment and carry out such tests and inspections as the inspector may consider necessary or expedient. He can also demand the provision of information or to be able to inspect documents. Obstruction of the inspector in the exercise of his powers may be a criminal offence, carrying the penalty of a fine or imprisonment. Indeed, any offence under the provisions of the Act may by punishable as a criminal offence.

The 1965 Act is the principal United Kingdom Statute relating to the licensing and control of nuclear installations, the duties of nuclear operators, compensation, legal liabilities, insurance cover and the like. It comprises 30 Articles, some of considerable length and complexity. After it had entered into force it became apparent that provision regarding liability for damage to on-site property, as dealt with in the section of the Act setting out the duties of a licensee (Section 7), was defective in that taking this Section and Section 12(1) together it appeared that a claim for damage to on-site property could be made against a licensee *or anybody else* (in spite of the "channelling" principle) even though, in accordance with the provisions of the Paris Convention, it was intended that none of the funds available for the compensation of third parties should be used for the compensation of on-site damage involving property of the licensee or property deemed to be his which was either part of the installation, or used in connection with it, or was being constructed to be used in connection with it.

Section 12(1) provides for damage to be compensated wherever it has occurred and that no other liability shall be incurred by any person in respect of such damage. The reference to "any person" and not just the licensee created the problem because the duties imposed by Section 7 on the licensee (and by Sections 8, 9 and 10 on the UKAEA, the Government and certain foreign operators) did not extend to the on-site property of the licensee and others. Thus, there was no "duty" in respect of such property so the reference to "no other liability" in Section 12(1) could not apply to such property. Therefore any injured party, whether he be the licensee himself, a contractor, a supplier, etc. could claim under common law for any damage due to this property in spite of the intention of Section 12(1)(b) that "no other liability" could be incurred by any person.

An amendment was necessary and this was brought into effect as part of a further Nuclear Installations Act dated 1969 (see below) which, by adding a new sub-section to Section 12 of the 1965 Act excluded this "other liability" unless, by agreement, a party accepted liability for such damage to on-site property as he may be responsible for. When it was the licensee who accepted such responsibility, he could, of course, cover it under his Material Damage insurance because that could be extended to cover on-site property belonging to third parties such as contractors. When the person responsible who agreed to accept liability was, for example, a supplier of goods and services he should be able to obtain a reasonable amount of insurance cover against this liability.

The wording of the amendment as set out in the 1969 Act is

tortuous and confusing to the non-lawyer (and probably to lawyers as well) but legal experts are satisfied that it achieves the necessary correction of the provisions of Section 7 and Section 12(1) of the principal Act and it is not proposed to quote it verbatim.

Nuclear Installations Act, 1969

Section 1 adds the above mentioned sub-section (3A) to Section 12 of the 1965 Act. It also contains several other amendments, the most important being alterations in the amounts of compensation payable after the satisfaction of claims for damage to the means of transport and also that payable by the Government in excess of the financial obligation imposed on the operator — figures that were later overtaken by a change in the relevant amounts under the 1982 Protocol to the Brussels Convention.

Another amendment affects the extension of compensation to persons who, not having a duty under Sections 7, 8, 9 or 10 of the principal Act, have made a payment in respect of an occurrence in a non-relevant territory.

Energy Act 1983

Further legislation relevant to the 1965 Act is contained in Part 2 of the 1983 Energy Act which has already been referred to in connection with increased limits of financial liability brought into effect on 1st September 1983. This legislation increased the limit of the compensation payable by a licensee (except for one operating a small installation) from £5,000,000 to £20,000,000. It also adopted the amendments to the Brussels Convention whereby the artificial unit of currency was altered from EMA Units of Account to I.M.F. Special Drawing Rights. The amount payable by individual Governments in excess of the compensation payable by operators was increased to 175 million Special Drawing Rights and the further sum payable jointly by the parties to the Brussels Convention was increased to a ceiling of 300 million Special Drawing Rights. It was this enactment also which altered the amount of funds which had to be left after meeting claims for damage to the means of transport to 5 million Special Drawing Rights. (It had previously been £2.1M — i.e. the equivalent of the old 5 million EMA Units).

Section 25 of the 1983 Act inserted an addition to the 1965 Act explaining Special Drawing Rights in the following terms:

"In this Act "Special Drawing Rights" means Special Drawing Rights as defined by the International Monetary Fund; and for the purpose of dertermining the equivalent in Sterling on any day of a sum expressed in Special Drawing Rights, one Special Drawing Right shall be treated as equal to such a sum in Sterling as the International Monetary Fund have fixed as being equivalent of one Special Drawing Right —

(a) for that day, or

(b) if no sum has been fixed for that day, for the last day before that day for which a sum has been so fixed.

A certificate given by or on behalf of the Treasury stating —

(a) that a particular sum in Sterling has been so fixed for a particular day, or

(b) that no sum has been so fixed for a particular day and that a particular sum in Sterling has been so fixed for a day which is the last day for which a sum has been so fixed before the particular day,

shall be conclusive evidence of those matters for the purposes of sub-section (1) of this Section; and a document purporting to be such a certificate shall in any proceedings be received in evidence and, unless the contrary is proved, be deemed to be such a certificate ..." and so on.

One or two other minor amendments were made to the 1965 Act such as extending the definition of "Excepted matter" by including the words "scientific or educational" in place or the words "or scientific".

These are the principal Acts of Parliament of direct concern to those who have to deal with the duties of nuclear installation operators, their legal liabilities, the rights to compensation of third parties, the provision of insurance or other financial security, and so on. However, there are numerous other items of U.K. legislation: some are Acts, some are Statutory Instruments, some are Regulations brought into force under the authority of certain Acts. Along with the United States and, to a lesser extent, Germany and Italy, the United Kingdom is one of the world's most prolific sources of nuclear energy-related legislation and rules and regulations, for the control of radioactive material and safety. They include the following:

Atomic Energy Act 1946

The Atomic Energy (Miscellaneous Provisions) Act 1981

Radioactive Substances Acts 1948, 1960

The Radiological Protection Act 1970
as amended by the Health & Safety At Work, etc. Act 1974

Atomic Energy Authority Acts 1954, 1959, 1971 and 1986

Atomic Energy Authority (Special Constables) Act 1976

The Control of Pollution Act 1974

Dumping at Sea Act 1974

Nuclear Installations Regulations 1971

Radioactive Substances (Carriage by Road) Regulations, 1970, 1974 and 1975

The Merchant Shipping (Dangerous Goods) Regulations 1981 amended 1986

The Ionising Radiations Regulations 1985

Nuclear Installations (Excepted Matter) Regulations 1978

Radioactive Substances (Substances of Low Activity) Exemption Order 1986

Code of Practice for the Storage of Radioactive Materials in Transit 1975

Code of Practice for the Carriage of Radioactive Materials Through Ports 1975

These are just some examples of the multiplicity and complexity of the controls surrounding the nuclear energy industry and the use, handling and disposal of radioactive substances in the United Kingdom.

The overall legal position in the United Kingdom

The Atomic Energy Authority Act of 1946 was the first Statute specifically related to the nuclear energy field, but certain rights and safeguards have always been available to the public in relation to hazardous activities under English Common Law. Those who possess dangerous goods are strictly liable for any harm they may cause, and this would apply to radioactive substances. Notwithstanding the International Conventions and the United Kingdom legislation, an employer would always be liable to any employee for any harm caused by his negligence. He would also be liable vicariously for any actionable wrong or tort committed by his employees. However, that is about as far as the liability of a nuclear installation operator would have gone in the absence of special legislation.

The broad effect of the various U.K. Statutes and Regulations in the nuclear field may be summarised as follows:

1. The Government may promote and control the development of atomic energy and may also prohibit its manufacture except under licence.

2. Nobody other than the Atomic Energy Authority or a Government Department is permitted to install and operate a nuclear plant on an *un*licensed site.

3. A licence may not be granted to any person other than a body corporate. It can be revoked or varied by the responsible Minister. If a second installation is built on a licensed site, the installation may be counted as one for licensing purposes.

4. A licensee has a duty to secure that nuclear occurrences do not cause injury or damage to any other person from the hazardous properties of nuclear matter nor that any ionising radiation from anything on the site or anything that has been on the site can cause injury or damage. (This duty does not extend to damage to the licensee's own property).

5. The person on whom that duty is imposed must compensate those suffering injury or damage and he is solely liable.

6. The import, export, sale and supply of radioactive substances, the use of radioactive apparatus including mobile apparatus, and the accumulation of radioactive wastes are subject to controls. The disposal of radioactive wastes requires Ministerial authorisation.

7. The National Radiological Protection Board are responsible for research into and the provision of information and advice concerning protection against the dangers of radiation.

8. The Secretary of State for Employment is responsible for the protection of persons employed in factories against ionising radiations and for making safety regulations.

9. The Secretary of State for the Environment is responsible for the *safety* of transport by road of radioactive substances, the registration of users and authorisation for the accumulation and disposal of radioactive waste.

10. The transportation of radioactive materials by road is subject also to *regulation* by the Secretary of State for the Environment. (Under these requirements, radioactive material means "any radioactive substance, the specific activity of which exceeds 0.002 of a micro-curie per gramme of substance, including any article or part of an article made wholly or partly from or having on its surface such a substance".)

11. Radioactive materials may be kept only on registered premises unless the user is exempt from registration. (UKAEA are so exempt).

12. Only a consignor of radioactive material can be a carrier unless the carrier has a Certificate signed by the consignor. The carrier, or the driver of the means of transport, has various statutory responsibilities.

13. The carriage of radioactive materials by sea is subject to statutory rules under the Merchant Shipping (Dangerous Goods) Rules 1965 as is carriage by air (Air Navigation Order 1980).

14. Damage or injury caused by a breach of duty under the Nuclear Installations Act must be compensated wherever it occurs unless caused by certain occurrences taking place outside the United Kingdom wholly within the territorial limits of one of the territories subject to the International Conventions (a "relevant territory") or in a country not a relevant territory. This exemption does not apply to injury or damage incurred by, or by persons or property on, a ship or aircraft registered in the United Kingdom.

15. There is no liability for injury or damage caused by an occurrence which constitutes a breach of duty if it is attributable to hostile action in the course of any armed conflict. There *is* a liability for occurrences attributable to a natural disaster even if that disaster is of such an exceptional character that it could not reasonably have been foreseen.

16. No claim for compensation may be entertained if brought more than thirty years after the date of a nuclear occurrence or, in the case of nuclear material which is stolen, lost, jettisoned or abandoned, more than 20 years of the date of such theft, etc. A licensee of a nuclear installation is not responsible for the payment of compensation for claims brought more than 10 years after the occurrence, subject to the overriding 20-year limit relative to theft, loss, jettison or abandonment.

17. A licensee must make funds available at all times sufficient to satisfy claims, by insurance or other means approved by the Secretary of State, to an amount not exceeding £20M (or £5M in the case of designated small installations) for the whole period of his responsibility, known as the "cover period". A new cover period may be established by the Secretary of State by reason of the gravity of an occurrence or having regard to previous occurrences, or for various other reasons.

18. A licensee with three or more separate sites, who is providing funds by means other than insurance, may be permitted to establish a fund equal only to twice the highest amount of

financial liability imposed upon him for any one site, the effect of which is he may not be required to maintain a fund of more than £40M for any number of sites exceeding 2 for the cover period.

19. Contravention of any of the provisions of the Atomic Energy Authority Act, Nuclear Installations Acts, or Radioactive Substances Acts, may constitute an offence punishable on conviction by a fine or imprisonment.

20. Various obligations fall upon the United Kingdom Government by virtue of its membership of the European Atomic Energy Community (EURATOM) in regard to research and information; the grant of licences; security and classification of information; health and safety; investment and joint undertakings; supplies, including materials coming from outside EURATOM; the use of fissile materials; safeguards; operating records; loss of materials; and inspections. (EURATOM Treaty 1957)

It cannot be emphasised too strongly that the various U.K. laws, statutory instruments, orders and regulations are in many respects quite complex and detailed. For an authoritative statement of the law those concerned must have recourse to the actual Statutes themselves and any interpretation of these should be undertaken by a legally qualified expert. Obviously this applies equally to foreign laws, of which there are too many to describe in any sort of detail. However, although most of the nuclear legislation in other countries is in line with the International Conventions whether or not the country concerned is a party to such Conventions, some of them have special features which call for comment. The most important of these laws, particularly from the point of view of insurers, are the following:

United States of America

The Price-Anderson Act. The section of the American legislation of most interest to insurers is Section 170 of the original Atomic Energy Act of 1954, setting out certain provisions regarding the Indemnification and Limitation of Liability. However, the legislation relative to these items (Public Law 85-256, September 2, 1957) is commonly called the Price-Anderson Act, because that was the title of an amending law which was introduced in 1957 by two Congressmen named Price and Anderson. It has to be renewed by

Congress every 10 years. This Act provided that the operator of a nuclear installation must provide funds sufficient to meet compensation of $60M per incident by way of private insurance. The Government would be responsible for $500M in addition.

An extension of this Act was approved in 1965. This provided that the Government's share of the amount of compensation was to be reduced by the amount by which private insurance exceeded $60M. By then, the amount of capacity insurers could provide had grown to $160M.

Government contribution to the amount of compensation to be made available to claimants was further reduced in 1975 by the introduction of an obligation which was placed upon the nuclear industry itself to supplement the insurance available from private sources on an industry-wide pooling basis. This scheme, which is sometimes described as a retrospective premium payment, obliged every nuclear installation operator to contribute $5M for each reactor operated by him in the event of an incident occurring which exhausted the insurance availability of $160M, or whatever higher figure might at the time of the incident be provided by private insurers. It was laid down, however, that no single nuclear installation operator would be obliged to contribute more than $10M in any one year to this fund. To allow for the possibility of an individual operator being unable to meet his obligation, the insurance Pools agreed to provide a back-up protection of a further $30M over and above the then fixed amount of the cover under the Third Party insurance policies issued by them.

The Price Anderson Act covers all the personal liability of those who may have some part in the responsibility for a nuclear incident, that is suppliers of goods and services, etc. There is, therefore, in effect, a channelling of liability to the reactor licensee, although the United States Congress has discretion to extend liability to others, as under legislation based upon the International Conventions (to which the USA is not a party). The liability of the reactor licensee is strict or absolute, although he has certain defences except in the event of what the law describes as an exceptional nuclear occurrence (ENO) (a concept introduced by amendment of the Act in 1966). Whether a particular nuclear accident would fall within this classification is a matter to be determined by the Nuclear Regulatory Commission. It would include an accident which caused substantial off-site radiation and damage. (As a matter of interest, the Three Mile Island accident was not declared to be an ENO because very little radiation escaped to atmosphere although there was very extensive damage within the installation). In the event of an ENO being declared the licensee would be wholly responsible and he would be regarded as having a liability without proof of fault.

Under the original Price Anderson Act, the period during which claims must be brought against the operator was 10 years. In 1975 this was increased to 20 years in the event of an ENO being declared.

The question of whether it was constitutional to impose limits on the amount of compensation that a victim could claim, or the time during which he could claim it, was settled once and for all by the Supreme Court of the United States, which in 1978 declared that such limits were constitutional.

It is of interest that the 1975 amendments, particularly those regarding the provision of a second layer of indemnification to supplement private insurance and the provision of a $30M back-up by private insurance to cover those operators who may not be able to meet their obligation to contribute $5M per reactor, arose out of proposals made by the insurance Pools.

The Price Anderson Act contains, as do most nuclear laws, a large number of definitions which should be referred to, since some of these are different from those to be found in the Paris or Vienna Conventions, and some are new to those familiar with those Conventions or the national laws based upon them.

It should be noted that due to the increase in the insurance capacity available from the American nuclear Pools and their reinsurers worldwide since the 1975 Amendment, the need for the Government to provide an additional layer over and above that obtainable from a combination of private insurance and the contributions of the nuclear industry (i.e. $560M) was eliminated. Proposed amendments on renewal of the Act in 1987, would raise the liability of operators from $5M to $63M per accident, representing in practice nearly $7,000M for the collective secondary financial protection on a post-accident assessment basis. The Pool's primary insurance cover was expected to be increased to $200M.

Japan

Japan is not a contracting party under any of the International Conventions. However, they have had nuclear liability legislation in force since 1961 and this legislation, with subsequent amendments, contains a number of features of interest although it is broadly in conformity with the provisions of the International Conventions. The Statute in question is Law 148 of 1961 as amended by Law 55 of 1968, as amended by Law 53 of 1971, as amended by Law 44 of 1979. Other amendments have been effected by way of Cabinet Orders.

The liability of the nuclear operator is absolute as in other similar

163

legislation although where he has paid compensation for damage caused by the wilful act of a third party, he has a right of recourse against such party. This right can be waived by special agreement with any person. Japanese legislation departs from normal practice in one important respect. This is that the liability of the operator is not limited. Financial security is required and may be provided by way of either private insurance, or a deposit of cash or securities, or some approved equivalent financial security. Although the operator's liability is unlimited, the amount of financial security he is required to provide by insurance or other means is Yen 10,000,000,000 in the case of reactors with a thermal capacity above 10 MW, and reprocessing factories. The sum is Yen 2,000,000,000 for installations below 10 MW and above 100kW and for spent fuel and for transport risks. It is Yen 200,000,000 for installations below 100 KW and for other fuel risks.

The law exonerates the operator from liability for the consequences of grave natural disasters and serious disturbances. If the operator takes out insurance cover which would not extend to serious natural hazards, the operator must conclude an indemnity agreement with the Japanese Government under which he would be indemnified for any compensation he has to pay arising from a nuclear incident caused by an earthquake or volcanic eruption. A similar agreement must be concluded for payment of compensation due to damage caused by the normal operation of a reactor, since that would not be insurable under a policy of insurance. An indemnity must be obtained from the Government also with respect to any claims which have not been brought within ten years of the date of the occurrence.

The Japanese Government would intervene in the payment of compensation if the total cost of damage exceeds the amount of financial security which has been provided. The Government would also accept responsibility for compensating victims of a nuclear incident caused by a grave natural disaster of an exceptional character or a serious social disturbance.

The usual 10-year limit applies to the bringing of claims for compensation against the nuclear operator. Where the operator has an indemnity agreement with the Government with respect, for example, to compensation paid in consequence of a nuclear incident caused by an earthquake, the operator must exercise his claim under the indemnity agreement within two years.

Switzerland

Like Japan, Switzerland is not a contracting party to the International Conventions although a signatory of the Paris and

Brussels Conventions. Until recently, Swiss nuclear law was, nevertheless, very much in line with the provisions of the Conventions. However, under the Act of 19th March 1983 on Nuclear Third Party Liability, some changes were made, the most important of which was the adoption of unlimited liability for nuclear operators. (Previously under Swiss Nuclear Liability law, the financial obligation of the operator was limited to Sw.Fcs. 300M for nuclear power plants, although the Swiss Government were understood always to be doubtful about the rectitude of having such a limit, and this said to be was their reason for never actually ratifying the Paris and Brussels Conventions).

The new law also eliminated the exoneration of nuclear operators from liability for nuclear damage consequent upon an act of war or a grave natural disaster of exceptional character, although it relieved him of liability if he was able to show that damage was caused intentionally by the injured party: he may also be totally or partially relieved of liability if it can be proved that the injured party caused the damage by gross negligence. There is a right of recourse against persons causing damage intentionally or who have stolen or unlawfully received the nuclear substances from which the damage arose. A right of recovery can also be arranged by contract.

The operator is also liable for loss following from measures ordered or recommended by the authorities to avert or mitigate an immediately threatening nuclear danger. The Swiss Law is unusual in being so specific as to the obligation of the operator to meet the costs of such measures, a subject which has been debated to a considerable extent in recent times by the legal experts. However, the obligation of the operator to pay for such forms of economic loss does not extend to loss of profits.

So far as time limits are concerned, any claim arising from the occurrence which caused damage must be brought within thirty years, and the injured party must bring proceedings under the Nuclear Act within three years from the date on which he became aware of the damage and of the identity of the person liable or responsible for the insurance cover. In the case of what is described as deferred damage, i.e. when the injury cannot be determined due to the prolonged effects of, say, exposure to radiation, in under 30 years, the Confederation will meet the cost of compensation for such long delayed injuries.

The law recognises that the provision of insurance cannot be on an unlimited basis. Therefore, the operator is required to take out insurance cover only for such maximum amount as can be provided by the private insurance industry. This was originally set at Sw.Fcs. 300M per nuclear installation, plus at least Sw.Fcs. 30M for interest and costs. (The amount for nuclear substances in the course of transit through Switzerland is at least Sw.Fcs. 50M plus at least Sw.Fcs. 5M for interest and costs). The law provides for the Federal Council to increase these amounts according to the availability of insurance, and by 1987 the figures had in fact been amended to, respectively, Sw.Fcs. 400M and Sw.Fcs. 40M for the insurance of nuclear installations. Insurers were permitted to exclude certain types of damage or liabilities from their policies. The Swiss Confederation is liable for the provision of insurance cover with respect to such excluded risks, together with the excess above the financial limits in the insurance policy up to a maximum of Sw.Fcs. 1,000M per nuclear installation or transport operation, plus Sw.Fcs. 100M for interest and costs. The Confederation, incidentally, charges operators a premium for this cover. The premiums levied by the Confederation for their part of the cover are paid into a special nuclear damage fund.

Beyond these limits, the operator is again liable up to the maximum of his total assets.

The law provides that where the private insurer or the Confederation make payments or set up reserves for an occurrence having caused damage, the cover may be reduced by that amount although when the payments or reserves amount to one tenth of the cover the policy-holder, and the Federal Authorities, must be notified. At that point, additional insurance must be taken out to reinstate the full initial cover. Insurers may suspend or terminate the insurance — but, unless the insurance is replaced by another before hand, the suspension or termination may take effect only six months from the date of notification.

Germany

The German Atomic Energy Act of 1st August 1985 justifies special mention, because it too represents a departure in some respects from the provisions normally applied in accordance with the Paris and Brussels Conventions. Germany now has an unlimited liability regime, and this is more controversial than in the case of, say, Switzerland or Japan because the Federal Republic of Germany is a contracting party to these Conventions. The Law makes a number of specific references to the Paris and Brussels Conventions. For example, it specifies that the provision of the Paris Convention concerning exemption from liability for damage cause by nuclear incidents directly due to armed conflict, hostilities, civil war, insurrection, or a grave natural disaster of an exceptional character, shall not be applicable. This does not apply in the case of damage suffered in another State if at the time of the incident that State has compensation arrangements in relation to the Federal Republic of Germany which are equivalent in nature, extent and amount.

Another important aspect of the German law is that the operator of a nuclear installation is liable without the territorial restrictions provided for in the Paris Convention.

So far as compensation of the public is concerned, and the provision of insurance cover or other financial security, the German law recognises that in practice such financial security cannot be unlimited.

The nuclear operator is permitted to restrict his insurance cover to such amount as is recognised as being reasonable. When the new law was introduced, that limit was fixed at DM200M per incident. Beyond that figure, the German nuclear industry are required collectively to make provision for an additional DM300M to be funded by retrospective premium payments somewhat on the lines of the scheme in the USA. Beyond the DM500M provided by way of private insurance and the financial obligations laid additionally and collectively upon the German nuclear industry, the State provides an additional DM500M, making the total DM1,000M. These amounts include the cost of emergency measures for incidents which are not defined as "nuclear occurrences". There is no provision for financial security above DM1,000M. Liability for damage in another State is limited to the equivalent of 300 million SDR's for those who have ratified the Brussels Supplementary Convention as amended by the 1982 Protocol. This figure is reduced to 120 million SDR's for those who have not ratified that Protocol. For all others, the limit is 15 million SDR's.

Under German law, the victims of a nuclear incident occurring outside Germany, even in a non-contracting State, may be compensated by the Federal Government regardless of the existence or non-existence of nuclear legislation in those countries.

The legislation in the United States, Japan, Switzerland and Germany has been given special attention, not because it ranks any more highly than that in other countries but because the laws contain features of special interest when compared with the more usual provisions found in legislation which conforms more closely with the Paris and Brussels Conventions or Vienna Convention. There are nuclear liability laws in many countries, all of which more or less follow the essential provisions of the Conventions or, where they diverge from these, do not go significantly beyond the discretions allowed to the contracting parties under those Conventions. This, at any rate, can be said of the so-called WOCA countries (World Outside Centrally-Planned-Economy Areas). The legislation of certain other countries has not be examined because the texts are not readily available. So far as is known, there are either effective nuclear liability laws, or other statutes containing sections regarding nuclear liability, in almost 30 countries, as follows:

Austria	Belgium
Brazil	Canada
Chile	Denmark
Federal Republic	Finland
of Germany	German Democratic
France	Republic
Hungary	Italy
Japan	Korea
Malaysia	Mexico
Netherlands	Norway
Philippines	Poland
Romania	South Africa
Spain	Sweden
Switzerland	Taiwan
United Kingdom	United States
Yugoslavia	of America

Greece and Turkey have ratified the Paris Convention. Other countries are drafting appropriate legislation including Egypt, Indonesia and the People's Repulic of China, sometimes in consultation with the Legal Division of the International Atomic Energy Agency.

One of the best sources of information in this field is the twice-yearly Nuclear Law Bulletins published by the OECD's Nuclear Energy Agency in Paris. The quarterly Bulletins of the International Atomic Energy Angency, published by their Vienna Headquarters, provide occasional reports and articles from a very wide international spectrum concerning Treaties, Conventions and Agreements of interest in relation to nuclear energy.

III

The Insurance Dimension

CHAPTER VI

APPROACHES TO INSURANCE

The hazards associated with radioactive matter were known to the Insurance Industry from well before the advent of the 1939/45 war. Although not as a source of power, radioistotopes and X-rays were used in industry and medicine probably from the early 1920's for radiography, as tracers and as radioactive sources in instruments used for the measurement of the thickness of materials, testing the integrity of welds and the like. Radium was used in the treatment of cancer, radioisotopes were used in agricultural research to demonstrate, for example, the absorption of fertilisers in plants. The hazards associated with radioactivity and, in particular, the risks they presented to human beings were reasonably well understood and did not present insurance underwriters with any insuperable problems regarding the provision of cover, with respect to both property damage and, perhaps more importantly, the liability of those handling such substances towards third parties.

Compared with the risks that arise from the exploitation of nuclear energy as a source of power and the equipment, such as nuclear reactors, used, the risks associated with radioisotopes, X-ray machines and the like were of a minor nature. Such materials, provided they are in small quantities, would almost certainly now come within the category of Excepted Matter under UK nuclear legislation and would, for the same reason, be likely to fall outside the scope of the Paris and Vienna Conventions. The development of nuclear energy for both military and civil purposes during the war years was largely of a secret nature. Public awareness of the astonishing and frightening forces that could be released from the nucleus of the atom was not awakened until the explosion of the atomic bombs in 1945, which destroyed Hiroshima and Nagasaki. Although these events are quite unlike the controlled fission that can be achieved in a nuclear reactor, they have unfortunately coloured the public attitude to nuclear energy to a large, although perhaps lessening extent, ever since 1945.

The objective of all Governments after the 1939/45 war, apart from any military requirements, was to develop this source of energy for civil purposes particularly for the generation of electricity. The industrial exploitation of atomic energy and its implications for the

169

insurance industry were very quickly realised in North America and the advanced countries of Europe and elsewhere.

However, the focus of attention of insurers was first of all directed to the possible implications of nuclear explosions primarily from the testing of atomic bombs which was a subject of particular interest to Marine insurers. The insurance risks associated with trials in the Pacific were considered at a meeting in October 1946 of the International Union of Marine Insurers. This led to the Institute of London Underwriters in the Marine insurance field notifying representative organisations of the non-Marine company insurance market that the implications of atomic energy were begining to receive international consideration. The organisation first approached was the Fire Offices' Committee, which handled the technical and other interests of the majority of the Fire insurance companies — those which adhered to the rules, the tariffs and the standard policy conditions laid down by the FOC and its sister organisation, the FOC (Foreign). The credit for bringing this subject to the forefront in international discussion, first among Marine insurers and then more widely, belonged to Mr. Max Nielson, Chairman of the Danish Marine Underwriters Association, and he also contacted the FOC suggesting that, as the subject of atomic energy must be of concern to all branches of insurance, they might take a lead in the matter.

Within a matter of weeks, the Emergency Powers Committee (Foreign), which was a body under the general aegis of the FOC set up to deal with special problems during the war, considered the matter, particularly from the point of view of whether or not cover against damage by atomic bombs would be excluded from insurance policies by the operation of the standard War and Civil War Agreement through which insurers agreed on an international scale not to cover war risks. However, the whole subject was considered to be of sufficient importance to justify the setting up of a special joint Sub-Committee to consider generally the risk of "damage by the release of atomic energy", as they put it. At the same time, the insurance periodicals began to publish articles on the topic based largely upon an item in the Danish insurance periodical "Asurandoren" by T. Leth. The Post Magazine, the Policyholder and The Review were amongst the British insurance journals which addressed this topic between November 1946 and January 1947.

Meanwhile, the various insurance interests were pursuing the subject. Further Sub-Committees comprising the same Company members as that set up by the EPC were established by the FOC(F) and eventually by their opposite numbers in the Accident insurance field, the Accident Offices' Association (Overseas) (A.O.A.(O.)), the latter being set up in March 1947. Insurance representatives also began consulting experts in the field, such as Sir Edward Appleton. Fleet Street started taking notice and the Daily Express of 21.9.47. contained a piece by one Chapman Pincher, describing some of the plans of the Atomic Energy Council under the Chairmanship of Lord Portal with respect to the development of atomic power stations. Soothing noises were coming from the experts regarding the potential hazards of the exploitation of atomic energy. Danish insurers, for example, consulted the highly-eminent Professor Nils Bohr, who was reported as saying that if an atomic explosion were to occur in a nuclear installation, safeguards were such that any damage would be confined to the works. Swedish insurers were also beginning to take an interest, and by February 1947 it was being reported that under the general insurance provisions adopted in Sweden for houseowners' and householders' insurances, losses due to atomic energy were being excluded. The question of excluding such losses from Fire insurance policies and Marine insurance policies was being held over until some sort of lead was obtained from the London Market which might be followed by other countries on a wide international scale. The opinion of French insurers at about this time was also in favour of excluding phenomena due to atomic energy from the explosion cover that was otherwise included in Fire policies. However, by May of 1947 the opinion reached by the London insurance bodies discussing the matter was that there was no pressing need to consider the adoption of a special exclusion clause.

In those days British bodies such as the FOC, FOC(F), AOA, AOA(O), ILU, and so on, had a great influence on the practice and development of insurance in many parts of the world and were often consulted on a variety of practical questions, such as policy wordings, fire protection, insurance rates and the like by equivalent bodies in other countries. It was not, therefore, surprising that a number of those who were interested in the question of what should be done about atomic energy risks looked to the London Market for a lead. However, the joint Sub-Committee set up in 1946, continued to take the view that there was no pressing need for action and persisted in this attitude for a number of years after 1947. Meanwhile, other countries, notably those in the Continent of Europe, began to adopt various wordings to exclude the effects of atomic energy, atomic explosions and the like from their general insurance policies, notably the French, the Belgians and the Dutch. Before the end of 1948, some of the leading British insurance companies were begining to suggest that, pending any agreement on how to deal with injury or damage resulting from the release of atomic energy by providing insurance for such risks, insurers should agree to exclude these risks at least from Personal Accident insurances. The Americans who during this year decided to exclude the "discharge, explosion, existence or use in time of peace or war of any weapon of war employing atomic fission or radioactive force", opened up discussions with their Atomic Energy Commission on the problems of insurance in relation to the peaceful exploitation of atomic energy. By April 1949 the respected French insurance journal, "L'Argus", published an article entitled "A new risk — atomic energy" which referred to the "catastrophic" risks that might be expected from the peaceful uses of atomic energy. In May of 1949, the New York "West East Insurance Monitor" published a letter from the "Skandia", a leading Swedish insurance company, reporting that Swedish insurers had established a Committee which would shortly submit an exclusion clause for application to policies covering industrial and commercial risks. In July of 1949 it was learned that the Canadian Underwriters' Association were considering the adoption of a clause to be applied to Fire and Explosion policies to exclude atomic or nuclear fission or radioactive materials or products or devices or apparatus. Throughout 1949, the British Joint Sub-Committee continued to review the position from time to time and to maintain contact with experts in the field, including Government Departments, in order to obtain their view on possible action to exclude from insurance policies, destruction or damage due to atomic weapons or to the release of atomic energy used for peaceful purposes.

The bulk of the work being done in this field at the time was undertaken by the Joint Sub-Committee, in consultation from time to time with the Institute of London Underwriters, and the British Insurance Association was kept informed. By March 1950, the Chairman of the BIA and the Chairman of the FOC were in contact with the Chairman of Lloyd's, who was fully informed of the actions and discussions being undertaken by the Company market. He expressed an interest in being brought into consultation at such time as the Companies may feel that some definite action should be taken in relation to atomic energy. However, throughout the rest of this year of 1950, there were no significant developments in the United Kingdom. The Joint Sub-Committee continued to keep a watchful eye upon the actions taken by the insurance industries in other countries, particularly the United States of America, from which regular news was obtainable throught the American organisations of leading British Companies.

1951, likewise, saw no particular developments, with British insurers continuing to maintain the view that, at least as far as the United Kingdom was concerned, there was no immediate need for action regarding either the exclusion of atomic energy risks or of weapons explosions and that it would be premature to consider making provision for the insurance of peaceful uses of nuclear energy.

At the beginning of 1952, the United States' Fire Companies' Conference considered that it was time for joint international action to be taken to exclude the risk of atomic fission from insurance policies and sought the support of the FOC(F) and Lloyd's. However, the British point of view was that it was still not necessary to take any action in connection with business in the United Kingdom but the position with regard to insurances in foreign countries should be kept under constant review.

In the summer of 1952, the Joint Sub-Committee had a discussion with the author of a book which had attracted attention entitled "Atomic Energy for the Layman", Sir Arthur Dixon, a former Civil Servant at the Home Office. On the subject of the dangers of atomic energy, he took the view that there was little risk to be associated with an atomic power plant and certainly no possibility of a nuclear explosion as such occurring, although there could be conventional explosions in boilers and heat exchangers. In April of 1953, it was learned that the United States' Fire Companies' Conference had themselves decided to take no further action, at that time, to exclude the risks associated with atomic fission from Fire insurance policies, a decision that was presumably influenced by the attitude of the London Market.

Outside the deliberations of the insurance organisations, increasing attention was being paid to the development of nuclear energy in both the general and the specialised press and, of course, in Government circles. A White Paper was published in 1953 concerning the future control of atomic energy development and envisaging new legislation to amend the Atomic Energy Act of 1946 and possibly the Radioactive Substances Act of 1948. It emphasised that the control of atomic policy would be a matter for Government at the top level for a long time to come. This White Paper was reviewed at length in an article appearing in "The Economist" in November 1953 which referred to steps taken in the United States by the Atomic Energy Commission to provide information enabling private companies to work, in partnership, on projects for privately-owned nuclear reactors including those that could be designed to produce electricity cheaply. "The Economist" suggested that in the United Kingdom it would seem to be unnecessary for the Exchequer to carry the whole cost of developing nuclear energy if private industry were prepared to assume part of the burden.

We have seen that, since at least 1946, the insurance press had also begun to address the topic of the risks, for insurers, associated with atomic energy or at any rate atomic explosions. Experts were beginning to deliver lectures to the insurance educational establishments. Indeed, quite early during this initial phase of interest, Dr. T.E. Allibone, F.R.S. presented a paper in December 1950 to the Chartered Insurance Institute entitled "Atomic Energy and Insurance" (published in Volume 49 of the Journal of the CII) — an interesting commentary, saying nothing about insurance. By the end of 1952, there had been sufficient discussion within their own organisations, among practical insurance men, for A.G.M. Batten, then Accident Manager of the Alliance Assurance Company Limited, to prepare a paper for delivery to the London Insurance Institute on 2nd February 1953. He was very soon to achieve prominence within insurance circles as an internationally recognised expert in the field of nuclear insurance, particularly the Liability side. The subject of his talk was "Public Liability Insurance in Relation to Atomic Energy". He pointed out that for many the term "Atomic Energy" meant nothing more nor less than the atomic bomb and it was generally not realised that there were many more benevolent forms in which atomic energy was already, even then, being used. He made the justifiable comment that no one so far seemed to have ventured to record the effects that this new form of energy would have upon Public Liability insurance. In his lecture he explained the considerable hazards associated with the release of nuclear energy, its sources and the various uses to which it being put. Safety measures, the problems of the storage of radioactive material and above all the disposal of radioactive waste were also described in Batten's paper. With considerable prescience he pointed out that possibly more important than anything else would be the arrangements for the proper disposal of radioactive residues, the safest method being, in his view, dumping in a deep ocean. He also foresaw the development of rockets that could carry substances into space where they would become satellites of Earth. That insurance underwriters would have to be prepared to provide cover for the various uses of nuclear energy was never questioned, although the restraints on the extent to which such cover could be given were well understood.

Before the end of 1954 it was becoming clear, particularly in the United States and United Kingdom, that the insurance industry was going to have to tackle the question of providing cover against Property Damage and perhaps even more importantly Third Party risks if the nascent nuclear industry was to become commercially viable. It was unlikely that the State, which had hitherto sustained the development of nuclear energy and research up until then, would be prepared to give the necessary financial protection that none but the very largest and most powerful concerns could secure for themselves without resort to commercial insurance. Initially, however, there was reluctance amongst insurers, particularly in the United States, to consider exposing their funds to such risks in the absence of any actual operating experience, without a very clear idea of the likely extent of damage arising from a nuclear accident. What they did know was that it could, and probably would, be very extensive and very costly in terms of claims settlements. However, early doubts were muted, if only out of practical necessity, since the insurance business could not be seen to be ducking out of what was going to become a field of industrial development of great importance. Thus, in the United States in 1955 the American Insurance Association set up an Atomic Energy Committee which duly reported on the need for and the possibilities of insurance provision. The American Insurers' Casualty Association also delivered a report to the United States Atomic Energy Commission in that year, and the Inland Marine Underwriter's Association set up a special Committee on the Industrial Uses of Atomic Energy which reported in September 1955. The main points were that:-

1. The risk of nuclear damage should be excluded from Inland Marine conventional covers.

2. Insurers should provide a market for the perils excluded.

3. The Joint Stock Insurance Companies should establish a syndicate to provide the required cover.

4. This syndicate should develop its own capacity and should be responsible for the distribution of premiums and losses.

5. It should be administered by the Insurance Association.

Not surprisingly, similar discussions and consultations were going on during that same year in the United Kingdom, the home of the world's largest international insurance market. Sometime during 1955 the British Insurance Association (the trade association of the majority of the insurance companies, as distinct from Lloyd's Underwriting Syndicates, operating in the United Kingdom) set up their "Atomic Energy Liaison Sub-Committee". Their terms of reference were "To study insurance problems associated with the development of Atomic Energy". Their work began in earnest in October 1955. Two months previously the Chairman of the B.I.A. had received an official approach from the United Kingdom Atomic Energy Authority in the form of a letter which referred to the rôle insurance was expected to play as regards the development of nuclear power. The Sub-Committee consisted, initially, of 6 experts drawn from various sectors of the insurance market under the Chairmanship of H.T. Silversides, the General Manager of the Yorkshire Insurance Company Limited. A.G.M. Batten of whom we have already heard, G.E. Bullock, the General Manager of the Vulcan Boiler and General Insurance Company Limited, R.L. Hervy (Barrister-at-Law) of the Commercial Union Assurance Company Limited, R.W. Musson of the Royal Insurance Company Limited and A.E. Sansom of the Iron Trades Employers Assurance Company Limited were the other members. These 6 gentlemen were to play a very important rôle in the development of nuclear insurance and international co-operation for many years to come after 1955.

The U.K. Atomic Energy Authority offered to provide consultancy arrangements in connection with the engineering and scientific aspects of the development of nuclear energy and also to arrange visits to nuclear establishments subject to the six members of the Sub-Committee obtaining the necessary security clearence.

The setting up of this group was reported in Novmber 1955 to all members of the BIA and also the members of what were known as the Sectional Committees, the various specialist bodies dealing specifically with fire insurance, accident insurance, marine insurance and so on. The Liaison Sub-Committee held their first meeting on 25th November 1955. Apart from visiting establishments such as the first commercial-sized power station at Calder Hall, much of the energies of the Sub-Committee were devoted to reading published matter and reports such as a long article entitled "Atomic Energy — Insurance Problems in the USA" published in the American "National Underwriter" of 10.11.55. This drew attention to the importance of limiting the liability of nuclear operators and, within that limitation, restricting the amount of compensation that would be payable per person in the event of an accident, although doubts were expressed as to the constitutionality of making provision for such limitations in Federal legislation. The conclusion reached at the time was that there was no dramatic, simple solution to the problems facing insurers in relation to the provision of cover for nuclear installations. The Sub-Committee also crystallised their objectives in terms of their activities, which were summarised as being:

1. to assess the risks likely to arise from the use of nuclear power for industrial purposes in Great Britain and overseas.

2. to consider the extent to which the British market could arrange cover for these risks.

They also resolved to obtain all the necessary advice from atomic scientists and to make recommendations based on such advice. They stressed the need for the limitation of liability with respect to Third Party risks and emphasised the importance of weighing the dangers of entering into the insurance of nuclear risks against the importance for British insurers of maintaining their leading position in the international insurance market.

Apart from the work of the BIA Sub-Committee, to which Lloyd's were invited to appoint representatives, and did so before the end of 1955, the European Insurance Committee, a federation of the Insurance Associations of most of the Continental European countries, began to consider the problems of atomic energy. They decided that the members of the National Associations should be advised not to cover atomic risks at present, while recognising that insurers might be asked to do so in the near future.

In December, 1955 it was decided to change the title of the Sub-Committee to "Atomic Energy Committee". The British Insurance Association, at the beginning of 1956, started to issue a newsletter to its members. The names of the Lloyd's representatives who had joined the Atomic Energy Committee were announced as being R. Hiscox (a leading and very distinguished Underwriter of the day) and M.J. Rogers (Barrister-at-Law), Legal Adviser to Lloyd's Underwriters Fire & Non-Marine Association, as it was then called.

January 1956 also saw the foundation of the Experts' Study Group of the European Insurance Committee to investigate atomic risks, according to the Newsletter. The "Financial Times" of 2.1.56 reported the planning of two new commercial nuclear power stations in the United Kingdom to be operated by what was then called the Central Electricity Authority. These were to be equipped with 4 power reactors of the PIPPA design and to be located at Bradwell on the East Coast and Berkeley at the estuary of the River Severn in the South-West. They were expected to come into operation between 1960 and 1961 and there were said to be plans for a further 10 reactors. Construction was to take place between 1955 and 1965.

Apart from the efforts of the insurance associations and the market leaders in Great Britain and Europe to grapple with the coming challenge to the insurance industry, academic interests were also devoting some of their energies to the subject. The London Insurance Institute, which is a local branch of the Chartered Insurance Institute, had as early as 1953 set up an Advanced Study Group. Their purpose was primarily to consider the possible impact of the development of nuclear energy on the conventional classes of insurance, notably Fire, Accident, Consequential Loss, Public Liability, Employers' Liability, Product Liability, Personal Accident, Motor and Contractors All Risks, up to the time when an installation under construction became "nuclear" upon the arrival of nuclear fuel on the site or the loading of a reactor. The rapid approach of the commissioning of Britain's first nuclear power plants added impetus to their work. The Group had a total membership of 18 experts drawn from both the underwriting and the broking sectors of the British Insurance market. By December 1956 they had produced what was to be the first edition of their report on the subject of "Atomic Energy — Insurance Problems Arising Therefrom". (Because of the developments taking place in the British market and in other countries in the actual provision of insurance for nuclear installations this report was later updated and a second edition came out in January 1961 which encompassed the latest developments, after the passing of the first British Nuclear Law, the Nuclear Installations (Licensing and Insurance) Act of 1959, which came into force on the 1st April, 1960).

By April of 1956 the B.I.A.'s Newsletter was reporting that, according to Sir John Cockcroft the eminent Nuclear Physicist, future nuclear power stations would be equipped with 500MW reactors using liquid fuel; that the first privately owned reactor was to be built by the Associated Electrical Industries at Aldermaston in Berkshire; and that there had been an accident in a United States reactor, involving the escape of radioactivity which was not sufficient to cause harm. (This report had appeared in the Financial Times of 7th April, 1956).

As evidence of the speed and determination with which the Atomic Energy Committee set to work, they were able by May 1956 to issue a circular to the insurance market on the subject of "Property & Liability Risks Arising from the Construction and Operation of Reactors". This promised the issue of a report in the near future pending which insurers were asked to agree not to give cover or quote for atomic energy risks or to grant any reinsurance or to extend any reinsurance treaties to such risks. Insurers were also told that it may well prove to be necessary to deal with all such risks on a net-line basis (i.e. meaning that insurers would have to retain their shares wholly for their own account without recourse to any form of reinsurance).

On 28th May, 1956 the B.I.A. issued a Press Release informing the world that British Insurance Companies and Lloyd's had set up a special committee. It was expected that in order to provide insurance cover for the first of the commercial nuclear power stations (to be operated by the Central Electricity Authority) it was going to be necessary to find material Damage capacity for up to £30M and Liability insurance capacity for up to £10M. It was stated that Insurers regarded the catastrophe risk as remote; recognised that the development of nuclear energy was of the greatest importance to

British Industry; and felt that they had a responsibility to afford cover in respect of the new risks.

On 31st May, 1956 a large meeting of the principal Insurance Companies (excluding Life Assurance Companies) was held under the Chairmanship of C.F. (later Sir Charles) Trustam, the then Chief General Manager of the Royal Insurance Group. It was explained on that occasion that although the CEA's new nuclear power stations were not expected to go into operation for some time, tenders for their construction were to be invited in a matter of weeks and therefore insurers had to decide how they were going to handle not only the insurance of the construction but also the ultimate operation of nuclear installations. The meeting was told that nuclear energy was expected to be the principal source of energy in the next 25 - 50 years, that the companies were to co-operate with Lloyd's in providing the necessary cover and the expected insurance amounts as already announced in the Press, were £30M for Material Damage and £10M for Liabilities. The ways of establishing this capacity were considered and emphasis was laid on the intention that the commitment of insurers would be on a net-line basis and that it was not desired to ask the State to take any part of the cover. In practice it was not expected that an accident would cause a loss exceeding £1M. The total loss of any one reactor of the type to be installed at the new stations was estimated to cost about £8M. The Chairman of the meeting stated "Our action for many years ahead may be determined by what we are doing now". This was plainly an historic meeting. The following month the professional Reinsurance market was approached with the request that they should make their resources available in support of the direct-writing insurance market.

More news came in of developments in the United States. It was reported that the Atomic Energy Commission (now called the Nuclear Regulatory Commission) did not contemplate putting any ceiling in financial terms on the liability of Nuclear Operators. It was also reported that the American Insurance market had now organised itself sufficiently well to be in a position to make insurance provision available. What they had done was to set up 3 syndicates. Two of these consisted of Joint Stock Insurance Companies and were to be concerned separately with Physical Damage Insurance and Liability Insurance. The third comprised the Mutual Insurance Companies and likewise was to deal with both these classes of Insurance. It was also reported that the German Insurance Market was considering setting up a special "pool", as it was called, to provide insurance for atomic risks.

By July of 1956 the Americans were looking for reinsurance support and the British Market was informed of a possible approach by Brokers, which it was thought might best be met by the formation of a British Atomic Risks Syndicate for the purpose of writing American Risks. However, this was not proceeded with because it was felt that it would delay the efforts of the Brokers concerned in obtaining reinsurance support from the London Market for the American Syndicates. It was becoming evident that the British market would also have to decide pretty quickly how it was going, collectively, to deal with the provision of insurance for nuclear risks because in this same month it was learnt that a research establishment in Belgium would be seeking insurance cover and the London market were expected to make a substantial contribution to their requirements.

Therefore, it was proposed that the insurance companies should consider participating in a syndicate or pool to be run by a Committee of Management on behalf of the Members. It was likened to two existing pooling arrangements which had been set up some years previously by the Company market. The first dealt with the fire insurance of Government stocks of commodities during and after the war; the second provided a comprehensive scheme of insurance for the Electricity Supply Industry when this was nationalised under the, then, Central Electricity Authority, in 1949.

It was emphasised that the participation of insurers would be on a net-line basis. That is to say, they would retain 100% of their shares of any insurances written, both Material Damage and Liability, strictly for their own account without recourse to any form of reinsurance. By this same token, of course, they could not be exposed to any unwanted aggregation, through incoming reinsurance, of their commitments on the nuclear risks written through their membership of the pool. It was also proposed that the pool should provide cover for foreign risks and that the participating Insurers should not be under any obligation to provide compulsory deposits in order to write business in any country.

On the 19th July, 1956 a meeting was held of interested insurers to appoint a Management Committee. By 2nd August it had been decided that this should be composed of the 21 largest insurance companies. Eventually this became 22.

These companies were drawn from the non-Life, non-Marine sectors of the British market and were representative of what were then three types of insurance companies, namely the Tariff Companies, the Non-Tariff or Independent Companies, and the Mutual Companies. Soon afterwards Lloyd's made two distinguished leading underwriters available to join the Management Committee. They were R. Hiscox and G.E. Thomson. In the case of the Companies, the Member of the Committee was, in fact, the

Company itself but each Company was required to nominate a Representative and an Alternate. The two Lloyd's Members and their Alternates are, and always have been, Members of the Committee in their own right and not as representatives of their firms. The original 8-Member Atomic Energy Committee (which started life as the BIA's Atomic Energy Liaison Sub-Committee) remained in being but it now became the "Advisory Committee", its purpose being to assist and guide the Management Committee in its handling of the new Syndicate. Membership of the Advisory Committee has always been on a personal basis, that is to say, each individual Member is on the Committee in his own right and not as a representative of his employing Company or, in the case of a Lloyd's Underwriter, his Syndicate or the Corporation of Lloyd's. The Chairman of the Advisory Committee is responsible for inviting its Members to join and they appoint an Alternate, normally from within their own Company or Organisation who would attend meetings in their absence. The Advisory Committee immediately set about preparing their famous Report which was to be published in the following year. This was to be the principal preoccupation of the first few months of the Advisory Committee's existence.

In the meantime, there was work to be done. Enquiries were coming in as to the possibilities of providing insurance cover for nuclear installations in Belgium and the United Kingdom, and obviously a great deal of preparation was required to fit the new Pool to be able to provide insurance for the first of the British nuclear power stations which, at the time, were thought likely to be coming into operation within five years. It was of great importance for the Committee to discover the extent to which the provision of nuclear insurance for Material Damage or Liabilities was likely to be supported by the British market and the amount of net-line capacity which respective Members of the intended new Pool would be likely to contribute. All this meant that the Management Committee were required to have an immense amount of authority to carry the necessary weight within the insurance industry in order to achieve their objectives. Thus it was that the membership of the Management Committee comprised no less that the Chief Executives or General Managers of the Companies, and the Lloyd's Members were very senior leading underwriters. The first chairman of the Management Committee was the General Manager of the Commercial Union Assurance Company, Sir John Makins. The other company Members of the Management Committee were the following: "Alliance", "Atlas", "Caledonian", "Eagle Star", "Employer's Liability", "General Accident", "Guardian", "London & Lancashire", "London", "North British & Mercantile", "Northern", "Norwich

Union", "Pearl", "Phoenix", "Prudential", "Royal Exchange", "Royal", "Sun", "Union of Canton", "Yorkshire" (and, later, the "Iron Trades Mutual"). When this Committee was set up on the 2nd August 1956 it was decided that there should be a much smaller Executive Committee which could take on more of the detailed work facing the new Organisation. This consisted of the 8 largest Companies, together with Mr. Hiscox of Lloyd's. The setting-up of these Committees formally marked the ending of the British Insurance Association's responsibility for atomic energy insurance matters.

The Management Committee decided that the necessary administrative arrangements for the proposed new Syndicate or Pool and for the Committee Members should be provided by the Secretariat of the already existing Associated Insurers (British Electricity) Management Committee, a small unit with offices in Cheapside in the City of London whose two-man Executive comprised a permanent Secretary, (at the time C.G. Pemberton) and Assistant Secretary (D.E. Kerridge) plus a small staff. The title of the new Organisation had not yet been settled by the time of the first meeting of the Management Committee on 13th August. They had in mind some such name as the "British Insurance Nuclear Risks Committee". By the 4th September it had been decided to call it "British Insurance (Atomic Energy) Committee". By January of 1957, the Executive Committee were grappling with the practical questions that were going to have to be solved if the Material Damage and Third Party Liability risks associated with the exploitation of nuclear energy were to be insured and insurers were to be attracted to support the provision of such cover. There were discussions with the ever-supportive U.K. Atomic Energy Authority on technical questions, one of the most pressing of which was the significance of the siting of nuclear installations near centres of population for the insurance risks associated with the provision of fire policies on, for example, private homes. The result of these discussions was that it became obvious to insurers that it would not be practicable to extend current insurance policies whether they were related to fire risks or third party liabilities to include the consequences of radioactive contamination.

Apart from this domestic issue, the committee were under pressure from the Belgian insurance market to give assistance with the prospective insurance needs of the first of the Belgian atomic energy research establishments. Representatives of the Executive Committee met the Belgians, together with the Swiss Resinsurance Company and the Zurich Insurance Company. The representative of the former was the formidable Dr. W.E. Belser, who was also acting as leader of the Study Group set up by the European Insurance Committee to consider the insurance problems associated with atomic risks. The result of this meeting was a decision to set up a Belgian Nuclear Insurance Pool similar to that which the British were to set up in that year. This enabled British representatives to say that they would provide reinsurance support for the Belgian case. The scope of the Third Party Liability insurance that might be provided was decided. It was agreed that unlimited cover was not possible and there must therefore be a limit both in amount and in time with no automatic reinstatement.

The British Government were also very much concerned at the time as to the insurance provision to be made, particularly in relation to liability to the public. Special legislation was then under consideration by the Board of Trade, who had decided that the operator's liability would have to be absolute, that is to say, that he would have virtually no defences to any claims arising from the release of ionising radiation from his site, except possibly where there was contributory negligence, and apart from that he would be solely liable, without proof of negligence. The Government were very anxious not to create public alarm by the measures they were to take or by the actions of insurers, and one area of concern was the insurers' intention to exclude from ordinary insurance policies the risks of damage or injury arising from radioactive contamination. (It was pointed out by insurers that such policies had never covered such a risk and certainly were never intended to). Even the amount of Liability cover that insurers were proposing to offer to nuclear operators, namely, £10M, seemed to cause some concern to the Government officials who feared that such great sums of money might give rise to public anxiety as to the potential cost, and therefore dangers, of a nuclear accident. Another area of anxious discussion at the time was what should be done about the payment of compensation if the insurance cover was not sufficient. Insurers were clear that they could not contemplate providing more that £10M, and eventually the Government decided that it would be appropriate for public funds to be made available to cover any excess compensation required above that limit.

One of the first actions of the Management Committee when it started to operate in August 1956 had been to establish what was called a Technical Panel. This was intended to give detailed consideration to, in particular, the drafting of the policy wordings that would be appropriate to the insurance of Material Damage or Liability risks for nuclear installations. The Technical Panel consisted of no less than 13 Company Members drawn from the Members of the Management Committee and 2 Lloyd's representatives: an Underwriter, P.R. Holford, and M.J. Rogers, the Legal Adviser to the Non-Marine Association, appointed previously to the Advisory Committee. An Engineering insurance specialist was also added to the Committee, representing the Inspecting Offices' Sub-Committee of Associated Engineering Insurers, which was a pool providing Engineering insurance for the conventional power stations of the Central Electricity Authority. They held their first meeting on 28th November 1956, the importance of which was underlined by the fact that the Chairman of the Management Committee in person, Sir John Makins, welcomed the Members and opened the Meeting. They immediately decided to set up two Sub-Committees, one for Material Damage and one for Liability matters, to deal with the domestic nuclear risks that were on the horizon. An Overseas Sub-Committee was established later. The very first technical meeting, that of the Material Damage Sub-Committee, was held on 5th December 1956. The Liability Sub-Committee met later that month. The 3 Sub-Committees of the Technical Panel were re-constructed in 1958 as Sub-Committees of the Management Committee. The Technical Panel was certainly in existence up to December 1957, but had no further meetings or business after that date.

In the meantime, the Executive Committee had not been idle. They had a further meeting with the Belgian insurance market representatives when they learned of the imminent formation of a Belgian nuclear insurance pool. Terms for the insurance of the research centre were discussed again, and it was agreed that once the reactor was commissioned, the Material Damage insurance must extend to the perils of radioactive contamination and the conventional damage perils of at least Fire and Explosion. There was to be no question of issuing separate policies for the different types of damage.

Another meeting took place with the Board of Trade in July 1957, when the Parliamentary-Secretary was present. Insurers were informed that the Government were contemplating bringing in legislation which would make the licensing of sites for nuclear installations compulsory, and would impose an absolute liability on the operators of nuclear installations. They had in mind fixing a limit of liability for compensation to the public of £1M with the Government taking responsibility for any compensation above that limit. They were prepared to support an insurance pool and accept the necessity for insurers to make a specific exclusion of radioactive contamination damage from their conventional insurance policies. It was also stated that Liability insurance was to be made compulsory for the licensees of nuclear installations. The Board of Trade offered to issue a Press Release to publicise these decisions but insurers felt this might be premature.

1957 — Annus Mirabilis?

This was to prove to be a year of the greatest importance in other directions also. It saw the holding of the first of the British Insurance (Atomic Energy) Committee's international conferences of insurers dealing with nuclear risks; the completion of the highly-important Report of the Advisory Committee, in April; and the setting up of the British Nuclear Risks Pool in the form of a voluntary association, with the signing in December of a formal Agreement between the Management Committee and the Companies and Lloyd's Underwriters wishing to participate in the insurance of nuclear risks.

The First International Conference

The approaches made in 1956 to the leading insurance companies to ascertain the degree of support for the provision of nuclear insurance had produced a loyal but very cautious response. It became clear that the co-operation of the insurance markets of other countries would be absolutely essential if the insurance industry, both in the U.K. and internationally, was to make adequate provision for the Material Damage and Liability insurances that would be required by nuclear operators. The Management Committee therefore decided to call a Conference in London of the Insurance Associations of the countries of continental Europe, and also a Conference of the leading professional reinsurance companies, to discuss ways and means of establishing a satisfactory form of insurance and to try to achieve some common ground as to what should or should not feature in the provision of such insurance.

The Conference of National Insurance Associations took place on 12th February 1957. It was held at the Great Eastern Hotel under the Chairmanship of H.T. Silversides, who at that time was Chairman of the BI(AE)C, with E.C.T. Carden of the Alliance Assurance Company Limited as Deputy Chairman. Eleven other countries attended: Belgium, Denmark, Finland, France, Germany, Italy, Netherlands, Norway, Spain, Sweden and Switzerland. Apart from the Chairman and Deputy Chairman, the British Delegation consisted of 10 Members, some drawn from the Advisory Committee, including 3 representatives of Lloyd's. The high-level nature of the U.K. representation was reflected in that of the European Associations and such distinguished names as G. Martin of Belgium; E.G. Lilius of Finland; G. Cheneaux de Leyritz of France; Professor B. de Mori of Italy; H.T. Asser of the Netherlands;

J.M. Sunyer of Spain; G. Kalderen of Sweden; and Dr. W.E. Belser of Switzerland, to name but a few, were present. The subjects discussed included the proposed constitution and operating methods of the British Pool, the need for co-operation with other national pools (although as yet few had been set up) and the bases on which atomic risks insurance might be managed. These covered such questions as rating methods, scope of cover, the need for net-line insurance, the respective merits of coinsurance and reinsurance as a means of assuring international support, settlement of claims, and so on. Legislative problems were also considered. The Conference, like all those that followed in the years ahead, was regarded as a private meeting between insurers: therefore its report was not circulated beyond the insurance industry although there was a full press release about the proceedings in general.

The second meeting, with the professional reinsurance companies, was held 2 days later on 14th February 1957 at the Chartered Insurance Institute. Seven of these from continental Europe, represented the reinsurance markets of Denmark, France, Germany, Italy, the Netherlands, Spain and Switzerland. Five leading British reinsurance companies also took part, as well as the representatives of the BI(AE)C.

Mr. Silversides took the Chair. The subjects discussed were much the same as those dealt with by the Insurance Associations with the added topic of the part to be played by professional reinsurers.

A considerable measure of agreement was reached at both meetings and this was to prove to be an extremely valuable basis for the development of nuclear insurance on both a national and an international basis in the years to come.

The Report of the Advisory Committee

The Advisory Committee completed their Report by April 1957 following several months of intensive effort.

After it was presented to the Management Committee in April 1957, the 18,000-word report was printed and published in June of that year. Some 5,000 copies were distributed, most of these within a few months of issue. About half were distributed to insurance companies, Lloyd's underwriters and other insurance interests at home and abroad. The remainder were made available for sale at a price of five shillings (25p) and could be obtained for many years after 1957 from the Secretariat of the British Insurance (Atomic Energy) Committee. The Report is now out of print.

The object of the Report was to examine with great care the nature of nuclear risks from the insurance viewpoint, and to decide whether it could be recommended that the insurance industry should indeed provide cover, and if so, on what lines. Its authors showed a remarkable prescience and insight considering the undeveloped nature of the art in those days. Even after thirty years much of what the Report has to say is extremely valid and of great practical use to Underwriters. Without any experience of actually having underwritten any nuclear risks the authors got the picture very largely right. It was a remarkable achievement. It attracted a great deal of attention not only in insurance circles, but beyond. It was the subject of a special Press Conference which was held on the 27th June and this brought the Report and its authors a considerable amount of publicity in the media.

The Report was divided into two parts: Atomic Energy; and Insurance. The introduction pointed out that controlled nuclear fission had made available a new source of energy involving hazards unlike those with which the world had long been familiar, in relation to which "the magnitude of the values at risk .... confined to a relatively small compass, together with the extent of the third party risk involved in the production of atomic energy necessitate new approaches by the Market if adequate insurance cover is to be made available." The Report was based on practice in the United Kingdom. It pointed out the worldwide nature of the problem. The general nature of nuclear energy and various types of reactors were described, including the first atomic reactor to operate in the United Kingdom, which was GLEEP at Harwell in 1947. Reference was made to this and various other reactors which were already in operation and had indeed been functioning for ten years or more, although as yet none had been presented to the insurance industry as requiring insurance. The Report pointed out that atomic reactors were by 1957 already operating in Belgium, Canada, France, Holland, India, Norway, and Sweden apart, of course, from the U.K. and the U.S.A.

Two special risks were identified. Firstly, the risk associated with a failure of the cooling system, which could lead to what they called an "overshoot" of temperature, resulting in a melting of the core. Also they saw a risk, if only a remote one, of a constructive total loss of a reactor due to what was described as a "runaway" or "melt" in the technical jargon of the day. A build up of radioactivity could accompany this, precluding the possibility of salvage and maybe even entailing the abandonment of the reactor. In lesser incidents the particular problem of access owing to the presence of radioactivity was expected to make repairs very costly. The escape of radioactivity causing contamination to the reactor site, as well as over wide areas surrounding it, was the second special risk associated with the insurance of nuclear installations. The Report laid emphasis on the importance of insurers insisting upon the best standards of training and discipline for the operators of the nuclear plant "Too much importance cannot be attached to the standard of operation, maintenance and inspection of reactors".

The first part of the Report continued with a review of some known reactor accidents, a description of various atomic reactor fuels, and consideration of the all-important question of radioactive waste products and their disposal and control. Radioisotopes were also examined in some detail. As has already been mentioned in this book, by 1957 these were not a new problem for insurers. Sources of radiation, and X-ray machines, for example, had been in use since well before the second World War. In fact the Report made no special recommendations and merely made the point that such hazards as exist in the use of radioisotopes had been absorbed by the insurance market freely over a period of some ten years.

There was an important examination of the hazards associated with radioactive contamination in the event of an escape. In assessing the possibility of such an escape, the main factors that the Report considered were:

a) the type and design of the atomic reactor

b) personnel factors

c) the safety margins allowed in the construction of the reactor vessel and the biological and thermal shielding

d) the geographical situation

Given that up till then there had been no known reactor accident involving the widespread dispersal of radioactive materials away from the site of a nuclear reactor, the authors of the Report demonstrated an astute understanding of the probable consequences of such an accident and the factors that would tend to maximise or minimise them. They were aware that the escaping fission products would be in the form of vapour or dust or a combination of both which if released to atmosphere would form a cloud. The strength of the prevailing wind would govern to some extent the area over which the fission products would be likely to fall out and it was pointed out that the stronger the wind the further away would damage be likely to occur. The Report recognised that rain falling at the time of release would cause a greater fallout in nearby areas with less likelihood of damage further afield. The quantity of radioactive fission products was related to the operating power and the length of time during which a reactor had been in operation prior to the incident. The conclusions of certain experts' studies as to the possible extent of the area likely to be contaminated were referred to, and the Report quoted opinions which suggested that possibly an area of 1 - 5 miles down wind might be adversely affected. This estimate seems to have been viewed with some caution by the Advisory Committee and they emphasised that it must be taken as entirely theoretical.

The likely damaging effects of radioactive fallout were also considered. It was expected that only the surface of buildings and property of a solid nature would be affected, although it was pointed out that property of any nature, including land, would be unusable so long as the contamination existed beyond tolerance levels owing to the emission of radiation dangerous to all forms of life, which would mean that both people and animals would have to be evacuated from the area quickly.

The Report also discussed the possibilities of decontamination. There had been some experience of these techniques in connection with the nuclear incidents that had occurred in the years preceding the issue of the Report, although nothing of a major nature. Cleaning surfaces by washing, manual or mechanical means or by scraping paint or grinding concrete, for example, were seen to be practical possibilities. The costs of such operations were expected to be economically worthwhile in relation to the capital value of the property. The Committee had been given an indication by experts that where property is of substantial monetary value the decontamination procedures would probably cost only in the region of 5% - 10% of the total value. With hindsight, one can say that the advice given to the Committee in those days was very wide of the mark in regard to decontamination expenses.

Turning to the second part of the Report, which dealt with the subject of insurance, it is clear that the Committee had really put all their efforts into determining how insurance could be provided and what form it should take, in spite of certain misgivings that obviously were felt amongst the insurance industry at the time as to whether these risks could wisely be undertaken by insurance underwriters. Considering the insurance of Material Damage, the Committee decided to recommend as wide a form of cover as possible, taking into account the new and unknown hazards. After stating that the alternative means of providing such cover would be:

1) An "All Risks" cover subject to detailed exclusions which would necessarily be of a complicated and extensive nature, or
2) By defining the exact nature of the risks to be included in the cover,

they reached the conclusion that it would be preferable to set out the perils which are to be covered so that insurers and insured could clearly understand the extent of the cover afforded. In other words, they came out against All Risks insurance for nuclear installations. This being so, they considered that the usual conventional risks should be included in such a policy, i.e. Fire, Lightning, Explosion, Storm, Tempest and Flood, Burst Pipes, Aircraft Damage, Earthquake, Riot and Civil Commotion and Malicious Damage. The new risks which were identified as requiring to be insured were as follows:

a) loss of coolant or moderator from the installation from any accidental cause;

b) damage to the reactor or its contents following "runaway" or "melt" — due to sudden, uncontrolled or excessive energy increase;

c) radioactive contamination of a reactor installation where the radiation emanates from the reactor itself and is occasioned by an accidental cause. (This applies to the risk of radioactive contamination external to the reactor vessel, but does not apply to radioactive contamination ordinarily incidental to the normal operation of a reactor).

Insurance practitioners will be aware that except in countries which do not specify the perils individually, the last two of the atomic risks identified above have been adopted very widely as part of the cover ordinarily given in Material Damage Policies covering nuclear installations. In some cases the first one — loss of coolant — is also to be found, although this is hardly appropriate where the coolant is ordinary light water. It should be remembered that when the Advisory Committee's Report was prepared the main consideration was the type of reactor adopted for the United Kingdom which used carbon dioxide as a coolant. There was knowledge also of the use of heavy water in certain other designs.

After recommending some of the underwriting considerations such as the risks that should be excluded like subsidence, wear and tear and gradual deterioration, and the need for excesses or deductibles the Report recommended the provision of a separate sum insured in respect of decontamination of roads, pathways, land, etc. within the perimeter of the installation, as these would not normally be described as part of the property insured. This was an important point and its significance will be considered again later in this book when the question of decontamination and the clean-up costs as an aspect of insurance cover will be covered in more detail.

Another important recommendation was that policies should not be issued for a period of more than 12 months and that at the end of this time a re-survey of the installation (which should of course

190

have been inspected by insurance surveyors before any cover was granted) was essential.

On the highly-important subject of Third Party Liability insurance, the Committee recommended that insurance cover should be provided to the reactor owner to ensure that he has available the maximum possible limit of indemnity to provide for such claims as may be made against him. Reference was made to pending legislation in the USA intended to ensure that if the prescribed Liability limits under Third Party policies were exhausted, the State would accept a responsibility for compensating the public beyond these limits up to a substantial amount. The Report referred to the opinion of the Comité Européen des Assurances (European Insurance Committee) that all nations should be placed under an identical system of indemnity and it was therefore desirable to harmonise national legislation in the field of nuclear liability as much as possible. The Comité also attached great importance to strict liability being the basis of legislation, which should stipulate the financial limits of liability and the period during which claims could be made. The Advisory Committee, in addition, recommended that insurers should try to ensure that the reactor owner assumed sole responsibility for radioactive contamination arising from his reactor. (It should be remembered that at the time of the issue of this Report, the British Nuclear Installations (Licensing and Insurance) Act of 1959 had not yet come into being nor, of course, had the Paris or the other International Conventions). Another suggestion of the Advisory Committee was that the operator's liability, on a no-fault basis, should apply to all third parties including employees. Furthermore, there should be no right of recovery against any other party, thus avoiding any question of complicated legal cross-actions to establish in individual cases who is legally liable for radioactive contamination.

With regard to the assessment and rating of risks, the Committee recommended with respect to Material Damage insurance that the following factors should be taken into conclusion:

a) The normal Fire and Special Perils risks

b) The atomic risks, dependent upon the
    i) type of reactor;
    ii) nature of fuel;
    iii) nature of moderator;
    iv) nature of heat transfer medium;
    v) control mechanism;
    vi) safety margins allowed in the containment design;

vii) geographical situation and prevailing meteorological conditions;

viii) operating safety code and training and discipline of the operator.

Regarding Third Party risks, the material factors were considered to be the following:

a) the normal Third Party hazards of the undertaking, i.e. excluding radioactive contamination risks, on the basis of ordinary underwriting considerations.

b) the possibility of the release of radioactive materials by taking into account factors b) i) to viii) above.

c) the nature and approximate value of property in the vicinity and the concentration of population in any area likely to be affected.

d) the direction and strength of prevailing winds, and the extent to which waters may be affected by the release of radioactive effluent.

The Committee made no special recommendations regarding Workmens' Compensation and Employers' Liability for reactor owners, stating that it was a matter of underwriting in individual cases.

Finally, in regard to the provision of insurance policies, the Committee said that normal rates of commission would not be appropriate for the large premiums to be anticipated in connection with reactor installations.

The nature of the factors taken into account in evaluating hazards and assessing risks for rating purposes as they are practised at the present day will be described more fully in a later Chapter.

Another important area of study undertaken by the Advisory Committee was the impact on ordinary conventional insurance policies of the advent of nuclear risks and the position that would arise if and when special insurance cover was made available to the operators of nuclear installations. Great anxiety had been expressed as to the possibility that ordinary insurance policies, particularly those covering Material Damage, might unintentionally pick up responsibility for radioactive contamination. The question revolved round the possibility that if an escape of radioactivity was the result of excessive temperature it might be argued that the latter was a form of "fire" and therefore a Fire insurance policy could be said to be liable to pay for radioactive contamination damage proximately caused by an insured peril. It was perfectly clear, as had indeed been explained to the Board of Trade during discussions during this year, that ordinary insurance policies did not cover, and were never intended to cover, radioactive contamination damage. The opinion of eminent Counsel was taken and it demonstrated that unless the standard wordings of conventional insurance policies were to be amended in some way the position would be obscure, and that the insurance industry owed it to itself, as well as its policyholders, to clarify the intention. As a practical consideration, particularly from the point of view of policyholders, the Committee pointed out that if ordinary policies were to give specific cover against radioactive contamination, this would inevitably lead to differential premiums, dependent upon proximity of the property to a nuclear installation and the type of reactor. Such differential premiums, they felt, would lead to public protest from property owners in the neighbourhood of existing or proposed reactors. It was therefore recommended that there should be a clear and specific exclusion of damage or liabilities arising from radioactive contamination; there would be no prejudice to policyholders because if their recommendations regarding the provision of substantial Third Party cover to nuclear operators were to be adopted, then the public would have sources of ample compensation to turn to.

In support of this attitude, the Report mentioned that the question of excluding radioactive contamination risks was under close consideration in the USA. On the Continent of Europe the Atomic Risks Study Centre set up by the European Insurance Committee had recommended a complete exclusion of all atomic risks, including those arising out of the use of radioisotopes, although they did not rule out the possibility of the re-inclusion of such risks against an additional premium. Their recommendation applied to all forms of property and liability insurance but not to accident and sickness insurance or to life assurance. It was pointed out by the Advisory Committee that for some years past in many European countries insurers had been using an atomic exclusion clause in various types of policies. The conventional property of a nuclear site licensee, whether on his site or elsewhere, could of course not be covered under a nuclear Liability insurance because he would not be "liable" to himself. Therefore it was recommended that such property should be insured against radioactive contamination by extension of the Material Damage policy covering the nuclear installation.

Apart from the factors that would have to be taken into account in relation to the assessment and rating of Material Damage and Third Party risks, the Advisory Committee also reviewed the considerations that would arise in the wider field of underwriting.

The drew attention, in particular, to the following considerations.

a) Some of the risks under consideration were new and would be difficult to assess.

b) For some time there would be few risks insured and, consequently, there would be difficulty in accumulating an adequate insurance fund.

c) Reactors would vary considerably in design, in purpose and in value.

d) Overriding all other considerations was the immensity of material values which often would be at risk, and the considerable concurrent third party liability which may arise from radioactive contamination.

In view of these considerations, the Committee decided that while reluctant to recommend departure from normal insurance practice, they were forced to conclude that in view of the need to marshall the maximum capacity of the insurance market, some special procedure would be necessary. They were particularly concerned that if normal procedures were followed, including the various types of reinsurance, this could result in reinsurers accepting Treaty business (which would not necessarily disclose the inclusion of atomic risks in the portfolio) through which they may become saddled with concurrent accumulations of liability under both Damage and Liability headings. The Committee's conclusion was that at the then stage of development, the only practical method of underwriting atomic risks would be on a net-line basis under which each insurer or reinsurer would accept an amount for his own retention and would not pass any part of that acceptance through any reinsurance or retrocession facilities. This, however, was not regarded as a complete answer to the problem of capacity since it was considered that the direct writing sectors of the Market could not provide sufficient.

Therefore, it was felt that there must be some means of enabling professional reinsurers to participate in the direct writing of nuclear risks. The ultimate solution was to set up some form of pooling arrangement. The object of this was not only to marshall the full capacity of the Market, having in mind the net-line basis, but also to enable such risks as were insured to be spread in such a way as to avoid the risk of serious loss on a narrow front. (In this connection it should be borne in mind that the numbers of nuclear installations expected to become available for insurance even within, say, a decade of that time, was so small that the normal process of spreading the risk through the insurance of very large numbers was not going to be available to the insurance industry).

As the Report acknowledged, by the time of its issue the British

Market had indeed already decided to set up a Pool, and the Report therefore contented itself with suggesting the importance of feeding to any such Pool as many insurances connected with nuclear reactors as possible, and also that it should not accept the risk of radioactive contamination divorced from the other insured perils. It was also recommended that the provision of Consequential Loss insurance should be within the scope of the Pools. Another strong recommendation was that there must be co-operation and reciprocity between Syndicates or Pools writing atomic risks in various insurance markets around the world, not only where these had been or were being formed — in the United States of America and elsewhere — but also that they should be formed in other insurance markets on the United Kingdom model.

The bulk of the Report dealt with the provision of Material Damage and Liability insurance for nuclear installation operators, and also with the importance of excluding atomic perils from conventional insurance policies; any damage would be compensatable by the operator of the nuclear installation under the legislation that was to be recommended and under the Third Party insurance which it was proposed should be provided by the Insurance Market Pools. However, some attention was also given to other classes of insurance, such as Life Assurance, Marine Insurance, Aviation Insurance, Personal Accident and Sickness Insurance, Workmen's Compensation and Employers' Liability Insurance and various other areas of business which might be affected by the impact of atomic energy. In general, it was considered that special arrangements were not necessary except in relation to Marine and Aviation Insurance, where the carriage of nuclear materials and possibly even forms of nuclear propulsion might present certain problems. Further reference to some of these considerations will be made later in this book.

At the end of the Report, there was a short but very important Chapter dealing with the problems of deposits, reserves, currency and taxation. It was considered necessary to draw attention to these aspects because it was going to be essential, if the magnitude of cover required for nuclear installations was to be provided successfully on an international scale, that insurers should not be under any obligation to set up special deposits or technical reserves, or to increase those already existing. It was unlikely that they would be prepared to do this merely to be able to participate in the insurance of nuclear reactors. Therefore it was considered that capacity would be necessarily restricted unless some means could be found to relieve insurers of these obligations. It was thought possible that if adequate insurance capacity on a worldwide scale could not be provided then industrialists might be unwilling to build atomic reactors if they could not be sure of this. Regarding the important subject of reserves, it was pointed out that these must of course always be provided in order to meet the unexpired risk — this is a normal insurance requirement — but that for nuclear risks, the amount of reserve would have to exceed that which was normal. It was recognised that the unlikelihood of a major atomic incident could mean that an insurance fund, even it it were specially designed to take care of atomic risks, might remain free from claims for many years but that even if an incident were to happen after a long period the amount to be absorbed in meeting claims could equal, or even exceed, the total premiums received over a period of years. The problem was accentuated by the fact that there would be relatively few insured reactors for some time to come. It was recommended, therefore, that the fiscal authorities in all countries should be asked to give special consideration to the taxation position so far as reserves for atomic risks were concerned and that the Governments should be approached in this respect without delay. There was also seen to be a need in some cases to modify the controls on the transfer of currencies. It was suggested that the universal creation of Pools, and a system of reinsurance between them rather than coinsurance, may well help in the solution of these difficulties.

This carefully-considered, well-presented and cogently-argued Report was to have a considerable influence, not only in the United Kingdom but internationally, on the development of nuclear insurance, and what was in the fullness of time to become a widespread international pooling system based upon the domestic Market Pools. These were eventually set up in about 25 countries, each of course on an entirely independent and national basis but co-operating closely, exchanging views and information through international meetings, and the International London Conferences in particular, and endeavouring to find common ground in regard to the nature and scope of the insurances, the broad aspects of assessment and rating, and in building up a dependable, solid, consistent and secure base for the insurance of all types of nuclear installations in many countries around the world.

Organisation of the British Pool

The third of the 1957 milestones in the development of nuclear insurance in the United Kingdom was the setting up of a Market Pool. This was a successful operation in that it was found possible to attract to the membership of the Pool a high proportion of the non-Life, non-Marine insurance companies operating in the British Market, as well as a large number of the Lloyd's Underwriting Syndicates, in both the non-Marine and the Marine field. With regard to the latter, they were not exclusively insurers of Marine risks and it was possible for them to apply capacity to the insurance of non-Marine risks. A number of professional reinsurance companies were able to join the Pool so long as they were not prohibited, by the terms of their authorisation to operate as insurers in the United Kingdom, from accepting direct risks. Those that were so restricted were able to take a share in the Pool through a "fronting" direct-writing insurance company. Even foreign insurance companies were able to join, providing they were admitted by the Government Authorities to operate in the relevant fields of insurance in the United Kingdom.

The status of this organisation was to be that of a voluntary association of insurers desirous of participating in the collective insurance of nuclear risks in the United Kingdom and in other countries on a co-insuring basis.

Membership of the Pool was to be renewable annually as at the 1st January each year. Participating insurers wishing to withdraw from the Pool may do so on giving not less than six months' notice. Each Member was to be individually responsible for his own allotted percentage share of the Pool, his commitment being on a several not joint basis. The rights and duties of each Member were to be determined by a formal Management Agreement which was to be the legal basis of the contract between each participant and the Management Committee. The Agreement defined the nature of the business to be contracted by the Pool, and the meaning of "nuclear installation" for these purposes. It set out the powers of the Management Committee with regard to the acceptance and under-writing of nuclear insurance business on behalf of the Members, the reinsurance of such business on their behalf, the fixing of rates and conditions, the obtaining of professional reports and advice, the determination of rates of commission payable to intermediaries, the receipt and payment of premiums on behalf of Members, settlement of claims, the handling of legal proceedings, the holding and distribution of monies belonging to the Members, the removal of Members, the apportionment of claims and expenses between Members, the variation of the proportionate shares of Members. The Agreement was to be a contract solely between each insurer and the Committee.

The original Management Agreement was open for signature on the 19th December 1957 and came into effect for the administration of business on 1st January 1958.

Subsequently a number of small amendments agreed with Members were consolidated into a Revised Agreement dated 1st June 1978. Apart from changes in the text of the Agreement, the main alterations over the thirty years since it was drawn up have related to the membership of the Management Committee. Due to mergers between insurance companies, and the establishment of larger Groups, less than half the original 22 companies remain. In recent years, there was one resignation and one new appointment. Changes in the Lloyd's Members had, of course, also taken place over the years. By 1987, the Members of the Management Committee were 10 Companies and 2 Lloyd's Underwriters.

The subscribing insurers originally comprised 91 companies and 137 Lloyd's Syndicates. By the end of 1986 50 companies and 240 Lloyd's Syndicates were participating in the Pool. The reduction in the companies over the first 30 years was due mainly to the number who joined to form larger groups which participated as a single member, or who lost their individual names as a result of mergers. Membership of the Pool is variable in any event because it is on an annual basis: some companies or syndicates may withdraw and new ones join every year.

In order to establish the Pool's capacity, each prospective Member was invited during 1957 to state the maximum amount that he was prepared to commit under the headings of Material Damage and Liability insurance for Home Risks, Foreign (General) Risks and, subsequently, Canadian Risks. Canada was listed separately because many British insurers had large interests in the Canadian Market and wished to reserve all or part of their capacity for the local Pool, the Nuclear Insurance Association of Canada, when it was formed in 1958: thus the British Pool's Canadian risks capacity was always to be less than for other overseas countries.

The United States was excluded altogether because British Insurers were already subscribing capacity to the American Pools which had pre-dated the British.

When all the indications of the amounts of capacity that Members of the Pool were prepared to commit on a net-line basis were received they were totalled and then each prospective participant was invited to confirm that they would accept their rateable proportion expressed as a percentage of the whole in each of the sections of the Pool they had expressed a desire to support. That percentage would of course determine their share of premiums earned, (which were to be distributed at six-monthly intervals), of claims paid, and of expenses incurred. Until the Pool began to receive an income, the expenses of running it were defrayed by means of occasional levies on the Members of the Management Committee.

The classes of business which the British Pool was to write, or reinsure, were defined as being Material Damage, i.e. the insurance of damage to the property of the insured, and Legal Liability.

Material Damage insurance was deemed to include the insurance of Consequential Loss occasioned by the damage insured.

Each Member of the Pool, whether it be an insurance Company or a Lloyd's Syndicate, has equal rights and responsibilities under the terms of the Management Agreement, subject to their various proportionate shares of the business accepted, the premiums earned and the losses and expenses paid. Premiums received are held on deposit on behalf of Members until the six-monthly payment date and thereafter distributed in full plus interest, less any losses paid and permitted expenses of administration, together with a copy of the independently audited accounts. In the event of a loss being incurred for which there were insufficient funds on temporary deposit with the Secretariat of the Committee, each Member would be obliged to pay a levy in proportion to his share of the risk concerned. Each Member is supplied with regular brief details of risks accepted on his behalf by the Management Committee and is responsible for setting up the necessary reserves and meeting all taxation applicable to his share of premium income.

The response of the various sectors of the Market to the request for contributions of capacity was good and indeed better than the earlier soundings had suggested might be the case. Of the several explanations for this, one was undoubtedly that by now prospective participating insurers could be better informed as to the nature of the potential business to be insured and the way in which the Management Committee intended to deal with it in the light of the Report of the Advisory Committee. It is possible that, whereas the original soundings in 1956 suggested that the Material Damage insurance would be written on this basis of "All Risks", the decision taken to adopt the named perils form of cover would be more attractive to most insurers accustomed to the British and European way of dealing with the insurance of property.

The Management Agreement, and the setting up of the British Pool, could be said to be a triumph for inter-Market co-operation in the face of a difficult challenge from which the British insurance market could not back away. At that time nobody in the U.K. had had any experience of underwriting the risks associated with the exploitation of nuclear energy nor, indeed, was aware of any large installations of a commercial nature in operation anywhere, except for the first of the Government-owned nuclear power plants equipped with Magnox reactors which had just gone into operation at Calder Hall: so the launching of the Pool was a bold decision. Although the prospects of a catastrophic accident were said to be slight, nevertheless the insurers were entering into unknown territory and could have been criticised for exposing their conventional insurance funds to possibly heavy claims arising from a field of activity which up till then had contributed nothing by way of premiums. Nevertheless, the insurance market was under pressure from the Government and from the nuclear industry to provide substantial, solid, dependable and continuous insurance cover to enable this important new source of energy to be commercially developed.

Committees

In the meantime, the Management Committee and the Executive Committee continued to hold important meetings, the former on no less than 12 occasions in the 2 years following their first meeting in November 1956. When it is remembered that the Company representatives attending these meetings were usually the Chief Executives themselves, and never less than very senior General Managers from the Company members as well as two very highly-placed Lloyd's Underwriters, the importance attached to the insurance of nuclear risks in the early years becomes very apparent.

By the middle of 1958, a number of what, by present-day standards, would be regarded as minor cases were coming forward for consideration, particularly from abroad. Rather more detailed matters than were appropriate for the high-level Management Committee were going to need attention. Although much of the specific underwriting questions were handled for particular cases by the Advisory Committee, it became necessary also to develop the existing specialised technical sub-committees, and these were re-organised in July of 1958 into what were called Standing Sub-Committees. There were three, each consisting of a small number of companies and a Lloyd's Underwriter: one each to deal with the more specific aspects of rating and policy wordings for the Material Damage and Liability classes of Home risks and one for Overseas business generally. A small committee of engineering insurance companies was also established at this time, not for the purposes of dealing with the provision of engineering or machinery breakdown insurance but to give highly-expert advice to the other technical committees on the evaluation and assessment of nuclear risks at home and abroad and to provide reports on individual nuclear installations.

Liaison with the various sectors of the conventional market continued. The committees were involved in assisting the other Market Associations in considering the appropriate wording to be applied to conventional insurance policies for the purpose of excluding damage by radioactivity arising from nuclear installations or nuclear materials in transit. With the peaceful use of nuclear energy being now a reality, the earlier inclination of the insurance markets to delay giving their attention to this matter was no longer appropriate.

It was known by now that the legislation the Government were planning to introduce would include provisions regarding the necessity for the licensees of nuclear sites to carry insurance or other financial security to cover their liabilities to third parties, and that this liability would be on a strict or absolute basis. It was intended that the amount of compensation would be very substantial, although the proportion to be carried by the operator under his insurance or other financial security would be limited to a reasonable amount, the remainder being provided by the Government. In these circumstances, and given the availability of adequate Liability insurance, there was consequently no need for ordinary insurance policies to attempt to duplicate the cover. Discussions continued over a long period of time, and Counsel's Opinion was taken. The BI(AE)C's Management and Executive Committees and Liability (Home) Sub-Committee continued from time to time during the 1958/59 period to give their attention to the technicalities of this matter, on which they were able to advise the so-called Sectional Committees, the FOC and the AOA, as well as Lloyd's.

Reinsurance considerations

With the creation of an active Pool able to underwrite nuclear risks, the Committees began to consider other matters, including the practical aspects of the insurances to be provided and the considerations to be observed in dealing with risks outside the United Kingdom, in particular the provision of substantial reinsurance facilities to the growing number of domestic Pools in other countries. The need for reinsurance support from other countries was also a matter of great importance. When the British Pool had been initiated, the capacity obtained from the participating Companies and Lloyd's Syndicates, although very respectable having regard to the net-line principle and the unknown nature of the risks to be handled, fell considerably short of the requirements for Material Damage cover, in particular for the coming nuclear power stations. It will be recalled that in 1956 the expected insurance amount was put at £30M. By April 1959, the Executive Committee were informed that the minimum sum insured was now likely to be £60M. Even though by now a number of Pools had been set up in other countries and the British Insurance (Atomic Energy) Committee was already in very close contact with insurers in many parts of the world, their considered opinion was that it would be unwise to expect at that time a total of more than about £45M of capacity worldwide for the

Material Damage insurance of any nuclear power station. This expectation included the possible contribution from the American Pools. However, events were to show that they were not ready then, nor for some years to come, to share in the insurance of nuclear installations outside North America.

Basic principles

This was one of the most pressing problems facing the Management and Executive Committees of the British Pool and it was becoming a problem for those in other countries. It was in the common interest both nationally and internationally, for insurers to do their utmost to establish and maintain adequate insurance provision and to try to ensure that all available resources were concentrated on meeting these needs. During the early years, a number of guiding principles was worked out. One of the most important of these had been that the interests of participating insurers should be protected by prohibiting reinsurance of their shares of any business accepted through a net-line Pool. Another was that their commitments should be very precisely determined so that there could be no possibility of each Member's maximum contribution per risk and per annum being exceeded: hence the rule that there should be no automatic reinstatement of cover following a claim payment. Fortunately for British insurers, the Government were prepared to accept that the financial obligation of a nuclear operator, and therefore of his insurers, should be fixed at one amount for the whole period of his responsibility, as we have seen in Chapter 5. Thus, there was a finite limit to the compensation that could be paid out in respect of each installation, as distinct from each incident. In most other countries, legislation did not support the "limit per installation" concept and therefore it was necessary for insurance policies to be based on such a limit regardless of what the "per incident" limit may be according to national legislation and the International Conventions. Another principle that was determined was the necessity for those insurers who opted to join the Pool to concentrate all their resources on that commitment and not to insure nuclear risks except through the medium of the Pool. It was not, however, considered to be either practical or desirable to attempt to impose a positive prohibition on Members in this respect. If asked to write the insurances of nuclear installations outside the Pool, they were expected to advise the Management Committee and to seek their concurrence but preferably to leave such business strictly alone.

Changes in Committee work

As the principles and practices that might be adopted in conducting the business of the Pool began to be clarified, and as the specialist Sub-Committees and, of course, the Advisory Committee expanded their activities, the frequency and the need for meetings of the Management and Executive Committees became less. In fact, by 1965, the need to involve highly-placed Insurance Executives and Lloyd's Underwriters in the work of the Pool through the medium of the Executive Committee was reduced to such an extent that it was discontinued. The Management Committee, as the ultimate authority in the management of the Pool's affairs, stayed although the frequency of meetings became less as the need for them reduced. By 1966, the technical sub-committees were elevated to full-scale Committees and the head of the Secretariat who, by now, was Mr. A.C. Miles, with the title of Manager and Secretary, was appointed Executive Chairman of the Material Damage (Home), Liability (Home) and Overseas Committees.

With the growth of business, and in particular overseas business, the work of these Committees increased substantially over the years. For a long period of time, the Overseas Committee was obliged to meet as often as every other week and, indeed, members had a regular committment to attend fortnightly meetings unless they were cancelled. The Home Committees had less business to deal with, since they were concerned only with domestic matters, and their meetings were held on an ad hoc basis. There were Standing Sub-Committees for the purposes of assessing and rating risks. In the case of the Overseas Committee, this usually met regularly between the full Committee Meetings. In the case of the others, they were called upon as necessary. The work of these Committees was very strongly supported by the full-time and increasingly experienced professional staff of the Secretariat, to such effect that by the Autumn of 1985 it was no longer necessary for the Companies and Lloyd's Under-writers to participate so fully in the work of BI(AE)C, and after some 20 years the three technical committees were disbanded. It had, in any event, become increasingly difficult for senior and experienced officials from among the participating insurers to find the time to take part in such work on a regular basis. However, the permanent staff of the Secretariat, not being otherwise involved in the day-to-day business of the insurance markets, could have been seriously handicapped on occasions if they were not fully up to date in regard to current practices. Therefore, leading Companies and Lloyd's Underwriters were appointed to act as contacts and consultants on all non-routine matters involving the underwriting, acceptance and reinsurance of nuclear risks at home and abroad.

The Advisory Committee continued to be a body of the utmost importance. The somewhat independent nature of its membership meant that it was able to address unusual problems and the broader questions affecting the BI(AE)C's operations and, with a degree of freedom, to consider innovative ideas, as well as performing its advisory functions for the benefit of the Secretariat and the Management Committee. Nothing stands still in the world of nuclear insurance and the rôle of such a forum should not be under-estimated.

Wider functions of BI(AE)C

It will be apparent from the early history of the BI(AE)C that its purpose was never solely to run a nuclear Pool even though this function absorbs a large part of the Secretariat's energies. The organisation also represents all insurers' interests in relation to nuclear energy in a variety of ways. They include, (as at the beginning) dealing with Government departments, now principally the Department of Energy, and with Treasury Solicitors on legislative matters. Liaison is also maintained with U.K. bodies such as the U.K.A.E.A., National Radiological Protection Board, NIREX (the waste handling organisation), the Nuclear Installations Inspectorate, and the British Nuclear Forum, on whose Management Committee BI(AE)C is represented. A member of the Engineering Committee is an independent member of the Health and Safety Executive's Advisory Committee on the Safety of Nuclear Installations (ACSNI).

There is also an important link with the Legal Division of the IAEA to whom the BI(AE)C has, since the 1960's, provided an informal service, without charge, of expert advice on insurance matters, including the provision of a speaker at the Agency's periodical Regional Training Workshops, Courses and Seminars (mainly for developing countries) and Symposia — notably that on Third Party Liability and Insurance held jointly with the OECD's NEA at Munich in 1984. BI(AE)C is also privileged to attend the occasional Vienna meetings of the IAEA's inter-Governmental Standing Committee on Civil Liability for Nuclear Damage, with Observer status only, although usually invited to comment on insurance questions. It has links also with the International Nuclear Law Association. Such occasions provide excellent opportunities for meeting people of influence from all over the world and for putting over the insurance viewpoint — even if only informally. Similarly, in conjunction with the General Committee for Atomic Risks Insurance of the European Insurance Committee, BI(AE)C is represented at the occasional meetings in Paris of the OECD/NEA Group of Governmental Experts on Third Party Liability. The representative at such meetings presents a report on the proceedings to the BI(AE)C and to other interested Market bodies such as the I.L.U. and B.I.I.C. (British Insurers' International Committee).

Apart from these representational duties, undertaken mainly by the General Manager or a senior executive of the Secretariat, information and advice on nuclear insurance is given to enquirers — insurers, brokers, and industry — from home and abroad. Considerable technical assistance is given to overseas Pools, particularly in the developing countries, including risk assessments, on-site inspections and professional advice on the setting up of their own pooling organisation — customarily without charge. This can involve long journeys but in view of the British Pool's substantial participation in foreign risks, usually as leading reinsurer, it is considered to be worth the effort on account of the advantages it brings to British insurance interests. Other leading Pools with the necessary resources provide similar help.

The BI(AE)C also contributes articles, on request, to insurance and other periodicals, and provides occasional speakers on specialised nuclear insurance topics for meetings of bodies like the London Insurance Institute, the American Atomic Industrial Forum and specially convened meetings of underwriting and broking interests and others including, on one occasion, the American Bar Association at its 1985 London Convention.

The Secretariat gathers and stores information on a wide range of nuclear topics to enable it to maintain its informal advisory service to all insurers and other bona fide enquirers.

Even if the need to manage an insurance Pool on behalf of the London market were to cease, the insurance industry and many other interests would still require the varied expert services of the BI(AE)C and the Secretariat in the nuclear field.

CHAPTER VII

INTERNATIONAL CO-OPERATION

The Pools would not have been able to achieve the progress they have made over thirty years without an immense amount of international co-operation and the benefit of the contribution of insurers in various countries in all sorts of ways. Within Europe, this was manifested in the work of the CERA — Centre d'Etudes du Risque Atomique (Atomic Risks Study Centre) — previously mentioned. This organisation functioned for several years in Zurich under the general control of what was then called the Atomic Risks Standing Committee of the European Insurance Committee. At that time, the British insurance market were not Members of the European Committee, having only Observer status. However, at a very early stage, the BI(AE)C were invited to participate in the work of the Study Centre. Various technical reports, "Green Reports" (from the colour of the paper they were typed on), were issued over the few years of the life of the Centre. This was strongly supported in the early days by the Swiss Reinsurance Company, who provided not only its Head, Dr. W.E. Belser, but a young English Cambridge Law graduate, J.W. Youngs, to assist. Eventually, the Paris-based European Insurance Commitee assumed a greater degree of financial responsibility for the Centre, which was moved firstly, to Brussels, where the Atomic Risks Standing Committee (now the General Committee for Atomic Risks Insurance) had their Secretariat and, finally, to Paris where it was wound up in 1967.

The Study Centre did some valuable work in the early days, producing numerous information Bulletins (still being issued by the Special Adviser to the Committee) and reports on many subjects, including methods of rating, the desirable scope of Material Damage Insurance cover, and such difficult questions as the protection that could be afforded against the costs of decontaminating property suffering nuclear damage, nuclear explosions and so on. British insurers regarded themselves as somewhat outside Continental Europe in those days (this was long before the U.K. joined the Common Market) but BI(AE)C nevertheless gave their support and contributed valuable expertise to the Zurich Study Centre.

In the nuclear field the need for international co-operation was already becoming worldwide, but in those days the European

Insurance markets did not have so widespread an international business as London which was, and remains, the leading worldwide insurance market. Thus it was that, being able to call upon the international knowhow of its leading Companies and Lloyd's, and not only because of the initiative taken in calling the first and subsequent London Conferences, BI(AE)C came to be regarded as the natural source of leadership and expertise on a worldwide scale.

It can reasonably be claimed that the mainspring and focus of international co-operation in the field of nuclear insurance have been the Conferences held in London from time to time, of which fourteen took place between the first meetings with Continental insurance associations and professional reinsurance companies in February 1957 and the 1986 Conference — which was not the last.

Other Pools and the international pooling system

By 1984, no less than 26 countries throughout the world had established Pools or Associations within their markets for the purpose of providing cover or reinsurance for nuclear installations.

This included a number of countries where there is very little or nothing in the way of nuclear risks, although their insurers were willing to provide support to the nuclear energy industry of the world by giving reinsurance capacity to those Pools that needed it for their domestic business. There are now nuclear insurance pools or associations in the following countries (with date of formation in brackets):

Australia	(1984)	Netherlands	(1958)
Austria	(1959)	Norway	(1957)
Belgium	(1957)	Philippines	(1983)
Brazil	(1977)	Portugal	(1964)
Canada	(1958)	South Africa	(1978)
Denmark	(1957)	Spain	(1968)
Egypt	(1983)	Sweden	(1956)
Finland	(1957)	Switzerland	(1957)
France	(1957)	Taiwan	(1974)
Germany	(1957)	Turkey	(1962)
Italy	(1957)	United Kingdom	(1957)
Japan	(1960)	United States	(1956 & 1957)
Korea	(1971)	Yugoslavia	(1979)

The two dates for the United States means that there are two separate Pools in that country, one comprising the Joint Stock Companies was the first to be set up, the second comprising the Mutual insurance companies came a year later. The Joint Stock Companies originally had two separate syndicates, known as Nuclear Energy Property Insurance Association (NEPIA) and Nuclear Energy Liability Insurance Association (NELIA). These two were merged in June 1974 into NEL-PIA — Nuclear Energy Liability - Property Insurance Association, and B.C. Proom was appointed General Manager. This body underwent a further change of name and a certain amount of reorganisation in March 1978 when it emerged as American Nuclear Insurers with B.C. Proom as President and, later, also Chief Executive. The Mutual Companies' Pool was known as the Mutual Atomic Energy Reinsurance Pool (MAERP) which included Mutual Atomic Energy Liability Underwriters (MAELU). This is nowadays known as the MAERP Reinsurance Association or MRA. For most of its life, until he retired in 1987, it was led by its Chairman of Committee, R.W. Newcomb of the Arkwright-Boston Insurance Company Limited.

The British Market's Syndicate — or Pool as it is commonly known — was not the first to be established, although as an organisation concerned with the insurance aspects of nuclear energy, the British Insurance (Atomic Energy) Committee and its B.I.A. predecessors were certainly very early indeed in this field.

Although the colloquial term "Pool" is widely used, and has been adopted into the languages of other countries, a number of the organisations do not use the word in their titles. Their correct designations and addresses can be obtained from any national Nuclear Pool or Insurance Association.

With such a wide range of size, the nature of the differing Pool organisations varies considerably. All are basically voluntary associations of the individual insurance companies plus, in the case of the United Kingdom, Syndicates of Lloyd's Underwriters. Each Pool is subject to a Constitution or a formal Agreement between a Management or Steering Committee, or whatever the controlling body may be called, and the participating insurers. Each operates on a strictly net-line basis and outwards reinsurance of risks accepted by the Pool on behalf of its members is undertaken only by that Pool, normally with other net-line Pools or similar net-line reinsurance facilities. In some countries, the participating insurers have a joint as well as a several liability, although only the latter applies in, for example, the case of the United Kingdom and the United States. Every Pool would be directed by some form of Management Committee or Board which, except possibly for the smallest, may be assisted by specialist Sub-Committees dealing with Material Damage and Liability risks and overseas business and, sometimes, a technical panel of specialists in nuclear engineering, nuclear physics, fire protection and other safety factors.

The nature of the day-to-day management of the Pools also varies considerably. The United States ANI, which probably has more business to handle domestically than all the rest of the Pools together, has a large permanent staff, which is understood to exceed 100 men and women, including engineers and personnel in the field. They have to service the needs of hundreds of clients as well as hundreds of members, and also to safeguard the interests of the Pool as a reinsurer of foreign risks by inspecting overseas installations in consultation and collaboration with the local Pool from time to time. Like the British Pool, ANI issues policies on behalf of its members in its own name, each member being a coinsurer with a fixed percentage share which is subject to variation each year in the light of their contributed capacity. Several other Pools issue their own policies, including the Brazilian, Canadian, Japanese, Korean, South African and Taiwanese, to take a few examples.

On the other hand, and particularly in the continent of Europe, more than half the Pools operate through one or more of their member companies. A company issues the policy of their behalf, then ceding the whole of the insurance 100% to the Pool, which redistributes the business in the normal way to each member in accordance with his percentage share. The reason for this is usually that a Syndicate or Association cannot legally conduct insurance business on its own behalf without establishing itself as a company and being duly authorised by the supervisory authorities to issue policies. In most of these countries, the "fronting" company would deal with the insured directly in the first instance, collecting the premiums as well as issuing the policy and handling claims, though on behalf of the Pool. This is not always an efficient procedure and can delay the eventual distribution of premiums to the participating members and the other Pools. Furthermore such companies, with business interests of their own to protect, may sometimes be vulnerable to pressures from clients or brokers which would be less likely to affect a collective body like a Pool.

The organisations which have to operate in this way are sometimes known as reinsurance Pools because the function they perform is, in effect, to reinsure the fronting company 100% and then to pass back to that company as well as to all the other members their appropriate shares. Where a Pool operates through a fronting company, the latter often supplies much of the management function and the administrative facilities needed.

The provision of administrative, accounting and management facilities and access to equipment by one of the companies is often a feature of the smaller Pool which would not be able to justify the maintenance of a full-time professional staff or the acquisition of expensive communication and electronic equipment of its own. The company which provides the necessary logistical support is as often as not a leading reinsurance company. However, it may be some other insurance association or even another specialist Pool. Very often the Manager is shared with another organisation or is else a Manager of one of the Companies and has to find time from his other onerous duties to look after the interests of the Nuclear Pool. He will usually be supported by other staff. The arrangement in the Philippines is interesting and does not seem to have been adopted in any other country. They have set up an incorporated company (Philippine Nuclear Insurance Pool Management Corporation) to provide the management function and this is duly established in accordance with Philippine Company Law. Nevertheless, the personnel concerned have to be drawn from the management of a leading insurance organisation which provides office facilities.

Each Pool is entirely independent of the others in terms of its management and operation. There is a considerable degree of inter-dependence from the point of view of exchanging reinsurance facilities and also a great deal of co-operation and assistance between Pools on technical and other subjects. The size of a Pool is no guarantee of a matching level of specialist resources. The financial restraints faced by those Pools which do not have the capacity to retain more than a very small part of their own business has been overcome for many years by a system of contribution to their expenses by the reinsuring Pools. However, it has always been axiomatic that the pooling organisations shall operate as economically as possible so that a very high proportion of the earned premiums shall be committed to the financial protection of the policy-holders.

Business acquisition costs are very low and it is not customary for a commission to be paid to Pool members who introduce business, although a fee may be payable for professional services rendered, such as site surveys and claims handling.

There has always been a great readiness amongst the Pools to pull their weight in the international effort that has to be sustained to ensure a reasonable amount of sound insurance cover for nuclear installations and the liabilities of their operators. The readiness of even smaller Pools to make a contribution to Working Parties and similar groupings is noteworthy, but resources in terms of facilities, as well as financial resources, vary greatly. For a number of countries it would simply not be practicable for the local Pool to organise a Working Party or some similar type of international meeting. Very often where the administration of the Pool is provided from resources of one of the leading Companies, its office facilities may have to be limited to little more than one room, or perhaps even the desks of the company officials who have been given responsibility for the organisation of the national Pool, the running of the business, the setting up of reinsurance and participation in international discussion. Others, of course, have much better facilities, and it is largely on this account that the venues for the international Working Parties and similar meetings other than the London Conferences have tended to rotate between the larger countries, such as the United States, Germany, France and Japan, although others have made frequent contributions to this common effort — Belgium, Sweden, Switzerland and Spain have hosted international meetings of one sort or another over the years and, in the past, Italy has been a valued contributor. There is a tendency for such meetings to be concentrated in Europe, which is not altogether surprising because the majority of the Pools are from European countries. Also it tends to be easier for delegates to make their way to a European capital from the far corners of the world, particularly as it is very often possible when they are drawn from participating insurance companies, to combine a trip to a Pool meeting with ordinary business in the same country or nearby on behalf of their own company. Inter-Pool discussions are always kept short, 1½ days being the usual maximum.

The facilities the Pools are able to provide in a number of countries owe much to the generosity of one or other of the large insurance or reinsurance companies which can put at their disposal meeting rooms, catering arrangements and the like. It would, however, probably be difficult for many countries to match the Conference facilities that the British Insurance (Atomic Energy) Committee was able to provide for more than two decades from the early 1960's. This was because in 1962 the Joint Secretariat which BI(AE)C shared with the Associated Insurers organisations mentioned earlier, were provided with a small suite of offices in then then new building erected to house the various Company Insurance Market organisations other than those serving the Marine and Aviation Markets, named after the neighbouring Wren Church, St. Mary Aldermary — Aldermary House. This contained a number of meeting rooms, including one large enough to provide for the increasing numbers wishing to attend the London Conferences until they rose to 70 or more, when conditions were a little cramped — and also to provide luncheon facilities for up to 100 Delegates and Guests. The convenience to the Secretariat of being able to hold their Conferences in the very building in which they worked compared favourably with the very early days when they had to use a hotel with Conference facilities.

Aldermary House is still flourishing although the organisation of the Market Associations has radically changed and all of them, including the British Insurance Association, have now been replaced by a large composite organisation, the Association of British Insurers, which absorbed several of the old market associations though not certain tenant organisations whose activities did not lie within the ABI's general purposes. Among these was the BI(AE)C who in December 1986 decided to move their Secretariat from Aldermary House to independent accommodation in Berliner House, a small building in Gracechurch Street.

The Pool Chairmen's London Conferences

The International Conferences on the subject of nuclear risks insurance held periodically in London are known as the Pool Chairmen's Conferences because the principal representatives from the various Pools, Associations, Syndicates or Consortia attending are almost invariably the Chairman or President of the national organisation concerned. They have always been well-supported by other very senior people, such as Chairmen of specialist committees, not to speak of the permanent Heads of the Administrations or Secretariats of the Pools.

The second Conference, which took place in February 1958, was again an all-European affair. Some of the countries represented had by then set up special nuclear pools although two of them, Greece and Ireland, in fact have never done so, since they have not developed nuclear energy or nuclear insurance capacity. The absence of countries beyond Europe was not due to any desire to exclude them. Although by now the United States Pools were well-established, they were not at that time showing interest in extending their activities to other countries. Yet others had not as yet begun to approach the question of insuring nuclear risks, largely because the question of providing reinsurance support to the Pools in other countries had not really been explored.

In the early years, there was much ground to be covered by the representatives of the insurers of nuclear risks in their search for an understanding of the problems, possible solutions and the establishment of common ground on the best methods of handling the provision of Material Damage and Liability insurances, although other classes of insurance were thoroughly discussed over the years, such as Machinery Breakdown, Consequential Loss, the liabilities of suppliers of goods and services, transport risks, and so on.

The reservations held by insurers all over the world with regard to the acceptability of nuclear installations and nuclear damage as proper subjects for insurance, coupled with a realisation that the insurance markets must, however, meet this challenge, meant that there was a strong desire on the part of those meeting from time to time in London to reach a consensus on essential issues so that there could be good exchange of reinsurance support and an interchange of expertise and technical resources. Uniformity was neither wanted nor would it have been desirable. In fact, every Pool being firmly based in its local insurance market obviously had to follow national practices, some of which were controlled by supervisory authorities. The objective all along has therefore been to find practical methods of working together, harmonisation rather than standardisation, and the development of broad principles and guidelines which would enable the different national pools to observe certain guiding principles which would ease the task of persuading other Pools to give them reinsurance support.

The Conferences have never dealt with individual cases, which are strictly a matter between the individual Pools and their clients. Nor have they ever attempted to lay down any tariffs of rates or premiums, since these are, again, essentially a matter for decision by national Pools and negotiation with their clients and with their prospective reinsurers in other countries. This has not ruled out exchanges of views and information from time to time on methods of evaluating hazards and assessing risks as a preliminary to determining rates and premiums, but there has never been any attempt at a centralised pricing mechanism which would, in any event, be illegal in many countries.

The range of topics covered by the London Conferences since they began in February 1957 is very wide indeed. Some 70 different subjects can be identified from the records of these meetings, as summarised in the confidential reports circulated to the participating Pools and the other insurance interests entitled to have such reports. These included insurance associations in countries which had not yet embarked upon the provision of facilities for insuring nuclear risks. The numbers doing so began to increase in the early 1960's, and they included not only countries where the exploitation of nuclear energy was going ahead but also those which did not have any major nuclear installations but desired to provide support to the Pools in other countries by way of reinsurance.

The representation of the Pools continued to be at a very high level. A number of Presidents or Chairmen of Pools attended continuously over many years — some right up to the 1986

Conference. They included G. Martin — Belgium (who was awarded the Plaque of Grand Officier of the Order of Leopold III in 1985); E. Lilius — Finland; the late H. Maury — France; Dr. C. Pfeiffer — Germany; the late Professor B. de Mori — Italy; D.G. Postma — Netherlands; H.P. Durant — U.K.; and R.W. Newcomb — U.S.A. to name just the veterans among many distinguished insurance leaders. They and others were supported by long-serving Pool Managers some of whom have now retired, like F. Lacroix — Belgium; S.H. Ayres — Canada; G. Hertel — Germany; M. Masaki — Japan; E. Englestedt — Sweden; A.C. Miles and H.W. Francis — U.K. Still in active service after many years in post are H. Wiser — Austria; K.M. Stroemmer — Finland; J. Deprimoz — France (since 1959); S.H. van Gijn — Netherlands; S. Øytvedt — Norway; J. Gomez del Campo — Spain; J.W. Youngs — Switzerland (since 1966); B.C. Proom, C.R. Bardes and J.M. Marrone — U.S.A.

Senior officials of the BI(AE)C always figure prominently at the Conferences being responsible for the organisation and keeping of records, gaining the experience and providing the continuity essential to the smooth running of these events.

The BI(AE)C's London Conferences, which are usually concluded within 1½ days only, have varied Agendas and have always attracted the enthusiastic support of Pool delegates, as well as insurance observers from countries contemplating entry into the nuclear insurance field. They have produced many highly practical recommendations and suggestions primarily aimed at expanding the insurance the Pools could provide both individually and collectively, subject to such expansion of their activities being compatible with the realistic insurance possibilities and the retention and the support of the participating insurers.

International Consensus — Some Conference Guidelines

a) **Keeping within limits**
In view of the difficulty of maintaining and increasing the capacity required for large nuclear installations, particularly with respect to Material Damage insurance, it was necessary for all Pools to give early reassurance to the actual or prospective participating insurers in regard to their protection against being committed unwillingly or unknowingly for more than the maximum net amount of. their subscriptions. Therefore, it was essential from the very beginning for it to be agreed that policies should not provide the right to automatic reinstatement of cover in the event of a claim. This did not rule out reinstatement achieved by special agreement. This explains a Resolution adopted in 1958 to the effect that sums insured

could not be reinstated in the event of these being reduced by claims, and that reinstatement if provided at all should only be considered on the merits of the case. This was re-affirmed as recently as 1981 with a slight clarification, since over the intervening years some uncertainty had arisen as to whether the non-reinstatement of "sums insured" was intended rather than non-reinstatement of the overall policy *limit*. The distinction had become very important once the capacity available, even on a worldwide basis, was not sufficient to provide full value coverage for a large nuclear installation, compelling insurers to impose an annual limit on the maximum losses that could be paid in any one year for any one risk as distinct from the total value of the properties at risk. Therefore, the old Resolution was amended to bring in a reference to "overall limits" as well as sums insured. In practice, the important element in this was the aggregate annual policy limit: the individual sums insured, being an expression of the value of the properties at risk, could in all probability be reinstated following a partial loss without putting in jeopardy the annual net line maximum commitment of individual participating insurers and the reinsuring Pools.

b) **Waiver of recourse against third parties**
Another important principle established by the early Conferences was the need to waive the right of recourse under Material Damage insurances against third parties. This, in a way was a close parallel to the concept of channelling of liability laid down firstly in the International Conventions and then in many national laws as well as in liability policies covering nuclear installation operators. The object was to protect the suppliers of goods and services against any liability they might have for physical damage caused to the nuclear installation and other property and plant on the site belonging to the operator or being used in connection with the operation or construction of the nuclear installation. Without such a waiver under Pool Material Damage Policies there would very likely have been an unmeetable demand from producers of nuclear components, suppliers of other materials used in nuclear installations or contractors for contingent Liability insurances, since the capacity of the Pools had necessarily to be concentrated on the needs of the nuclear installation operators themselves.

c) **Intentional Emissions of radioactivity**
Much attention was given also to the potential scope of Liability insurances, particularly those aspects of such Policies as related to the liabilities imposed on nuclear operators by national legislation and the International Conventions. By the early 1960's these had been signed although, as we have learned earlier, the Paris

Convention did not come into force until 1968, and the Vienna Convention until 1977. However, the Pool insurers in all countries affected by such legislation and the Conventions were naturally anxious to try to ensure some reasonable degree of harmonisation in their approach to the provision of the required nuclear liability cover. One feature on which they were fully agreed was that it would be inappropriate for insurers to accept liability to pay compensation for any damage or injury caused in consequence of the release of radioactivity within the permitted levels in the course of the normal operation of the plant. It was generally agreed that while one could have some faith in the judgement of the authorities in determining what might safely be released, it was not possible for insurers to be absolutely certain that no harm would ever result from such releases. Furthermore, there was always the possibility of intentional but unauthorised releases of radioactive matter in liquid or gaseous form taking place. Therefore, it was agreed that what was generally described as "intentional emissions" should, if possible, be excluded from the cover granted by the Pools under their Liability policies or, if this was not possible because the insurance cover provided had to match the operator's liabilities fully, a right of recovery from the operator should be negotiated.

d) Combination of nuclear and non-nuclear liabilities in one policy

Another important principle was that a Liability insurance policy should not be confined to what was sometimes called the "naked" nuclear risk. Insurers from an early date foresaw the possibility that a combination of nuclear and non-nuclear damage could arise from the same incident and that it would be almost impossible to separate out the claims due to the two or several causes. However, for the insurance policy to be a valid financial security the whole of the cover must be devoted to the compensation of the victims of *nuclear* damage or injury within the terms of the nuclear liability laws and Conventions, and no part of the insurance monies could be applied to the relief of non-nuclear claims. Furthermore it was unsatisfactory, for two different sets of insurers to cover the liabilities of the same operator with respect to the same installation separately. Therefore, it was decided that Pool policies should include the conventional liabilities as well as the nuclear liabilities, but for a separate amount. This practice is not followed in the United States and Canada, who determined their method of dealing with this problem well before they began to participate in the work of the London Conferences. However, they are satisfied that their cover is sufficiently widely-drawn to meet the situation where there is mixed damage arising from, or at the same time, as the occurrence of a nuclear incident.

217

e) Importance of underwriting data

From an early date, the Conferences also produced a wide measure of agreement that for the satisfactory development of nuclear insurance cover, and in particular, international reinsurance support, it was of the utmost importance that underwriters should obtain the maximum possible detailed information about the risks they were to undertake. It was agreed that such data should be obtained in the form of a Material Damage and Liability underwriting report which would be set out in accordance with numerous headings recommended by a Group of Experts called together by Dr. Belser of the Atomic Risks Study Centre which met in Zurich in February 1958. This "Questionnaire", as it is sometimes called, was presented to the 1958 London Conference and adopted by a good many Pools as a basis for their own presentation of underwriting information although modified by some.

f) Machinery breakdown

Another very important practical issue which received detailed consideration from time to time was the insurance of machinery breakdown risks in nuclear installations. The nuclear power stations contained boilers and conventional machinery, which could normally be covered against the breakdown risks under what in the United Kingdom were called Engineering insurance policies, but the nuclear reactors were a very different problem. It was generally considered from the outset that the risks of breakdown in a nuclear reactor were not insurable because of the presence of radiation. Where the levels of radiation were low because the equipment in question was outside the biological shield some degree of cover was considered to be realistic. It was generally agreed in 1966 that for the plant or equipment outside the biological shield, it should be possible to give cover preferably under a separate form of insurance and not part of the basic Material Damage cover unless that accorded with national market practice.

The Engineering Committee which provided technical assistance to the British Pool thereupon undertook a study of the problem and presented certain ideas and recommendations to the 1968 Conference. They identified three zones of radioactivity associated with a nuclear installation: the High Radioactivity Zone, the Low Radioactivity Zone, and the Zero Radioactivity Zone. It was considered that the first two were a better description than the old reference to the plant "within the biological shield": there were certain components within that shield which could be repaired because radioactive levels were not too high for access to be a possibility. The Zero Radioactivity Zone would normally be the area in which the conventional plant was contained and no radiation was normally there. It was decided that this whole subject required further study since the Pools were anxious, as far as possible, to meet the legitimate demands of nuclear reactor operators for Machinery Breakdown insurance. Therefore a Working Party was set up which met in Rome and London, duly producing a detailed report in 1971.

g) Decontamination expenses

Another important practical and technical problem which the International Conferences were able to examine in depth was the scope of cover to be provided against damage by radioactive contamination with particular reference to the additional costs associated with decontamination procedures, including the isolation or shielding of contaminated parts or debris and the removal of such debris from the site. This question had originally been looked at by the European Group of Experts at their Zurich and Paris Meetings in 1958 and 1959, and the topic was presented to the Pool Chairmen's 1959 Conference by Dr. Belser. The general view at that time was that the cost of removing radioactive contamination would probably not be great. Cover for damage by contamination by radioactivity meant that such costs would be met under a Material Damage policy but only up to and within the insured value of the damaged property. The inclusion of an additional costs item to meet any extra costs over and above that value was recommended as being possible and desirable at an additional premium, and in fact some Pool policies were already making provision for it.

The matter was looked at from time to time by the Pools, but as a general practice, not very much attention was paid to this in the development of Material Damage policy covers. In the United States, the Physical Damage All Risks policy did make specific reference to radioactive contamination and included a debris removal and decontamination clause as an integral element of their coverage. Elsewhere, there was at first little demand from policyholders for a separate item of cover for a fixed amount. Where a specified amount of cover was provided, the limits varied widely between, say, £10,000 and £1,000,000. These figures appeared to have no relationship to the probable true cost of carrying out the decontamination and other operations which was then not well understood.

In spite of earlier recommendations that, if provided, such cover should be for a fixed limit, the practice began of including decontamination expenses without specifying a limit, meaning that the policy would meet all costs subject only to the overall annual policy limit. This could mean, in practice, that insurers might be paying out a very substantial amount to meet the cost of decontamination, possibly much higher than the replacement value of the property, whereas the direct damage giving rise to the radioactive contamination in question could be in itself quite small. This caused concern to a number of the Pools for whom it was important to know exactly what they were covering and what their members' potential exposure might be so far as this could be assessed by the appropriate experts. It was also desirable that where a Pool in a particular country was giving this much wider form of cover for decontamination expenses, those in other countries should be forewarned and prepared to grant similar facilities to their own clients.

This was a fruitful field for international consultation and co-operation but there was no strong incentive to pursue it internationally, until with dramatic force the implications of the disastrous Three Mile Island accident became clear following its occurrence in March 1979 (see Appendix A). It was obvious that, but for the limit of $300M to which the policy issued by the American Pools was subject, the total pay-out, including decontamination and other clean-up costs would very probably have topped $1,000M under the terms of the insurance provided.

This realisation prompted a recognition that the way in which the insurance amounts provided under Material Damage policies were deployed as between indemnity for destruction of or partial physical damage to the property and for additional costs, particularly for decontamination and associated operations, must be reviewed with some care. At a Working Party appointed to study this question, which met in March 1982 in Spain, it was agreed that a detailed technical investigation was essential and a Sub-Group comprising technical as well as underwriting experts of the German, Spanish, Swiss, United Kingdom and the two United States' Pools was set up.

This was an excellent example of the willingness and the ability of Pools from various parts of the world to contribute technical resources and other expertise to finding answers to difficulties that might be helpful to all Pools. As a preparation for the work of this Sub-Group, the British Pool's Engineering Committee carried out a study of the whole question of the consequences of different types of nuclear accidents with particular reference to the decontamination and associated work that would have to be undertaken. Above all, it was desired to know what costs might in practice be involved. The results of this study were presented to a meeting of the Sub-Group held under the Chairmanship of the American Pools in San Francisco in July 1983 and for the first time insurers were able to focus their attention on some very objective considerations. The United States

Pools were able to contribute valuable practical experience of dealing with the payment of claims arising from clean-up operations, primarily on account of the Three Mile Accident, but also in connection with other, much smaller incidents that had occurred elsewhere in recent years. The payments for decontamination work were wholly disproportionate to the nature of the initiating event because direct damage associated with it would alone have amounted to a relatively small insurance loss. The studies undertaken by the British representatives identified the steps that would have to be taken to deal with incidents involving major radioactive contamination and costed the different levels of work that would be called for according to the nature of the initial accident scenarios which were related to a typical Pressurised Water Reactor. Costs were calculated on the basis of current U.K. labour costs and other prices as at 1982. The United States Pools contributed the cost estimates for the recovery of the TMI 2 reactor.

From such studies it emerged that the cost of dealing with decontamination and other recovery work, even following a moderately severe nuclear accident, were likely to be far higher than many insurers would have suspected, quite apart from what was already clear from the TMI accident. The expenses deduced for three levels of accident by the Working Party ranged from £200,000 to £500,000,000.

This is another illustration of the ability of the nuclear pools through their London Conferences and associated Working Parties to collaborate closely on highly practical and important projects aimed at, firstly, a better understanding of the nature of nuclear risks and, secondly, improving the scope of cover that they can offer both nationally and internationally to the nuclear industry, without exposing insurers to unrealistic financial commitments.

h) Material Damage Insurance Values

The detailed technical work undertaken by this Sub-Group on the subject of additional costs with particular reference to decontamination was only a part of a wider study undertaken by the Working Party established by the April 1981 Conference to review the whole subject of Material Damage insurance values. It had for some time become apparent that there was a lack of consensus on the appropriate bases for fixing material damage values for insurance purposes. It was essential to get this right because otherwise neither insurers nor their insureds could know what would be the correct basis for the settlement of loss payments. Differing national terminologies had added somewhat to the confusion; and, for very similar types of plant of similar age, considerable disparities had begun to appear as between the insurance values covered in one country compared with those in another, although the basis of valuation purported to be much the same. Accordingly this broad topic had first been raised at the London Conferences by the British Pool in October 1978 in the form of a paper entitled "The factors to be taken into account in establishing insurance amounts for nuclear power stations". This had pointed out: i) nuclear insurers are essentially concerned with the same considerations as in the case of traditional industrial risks; ii) the importance of agreement or understanding on the basis on which the insured expect losses to be settled; iii) the necessity for a regular review of insurance values to ensure that premium income increases in line with any increase in the insurers' exposure, particularly with respect to partial losses; and iv) the special considerations applying to the valuation of nuclear fuel during burn-up. This matter was referred then to a Working Party comprising representatives of Belgium, France, Germany, Japan, the Netherlands, Sweden, Switzerland, USA and the United Kingdom which was joined by Spain at a later stage. Meetings were held in Stockholm and in Berlin. More will be said on the question of Material Damage insurance values in a later Chapter. Suffice to say at this point that detailed studies by the Spanish Pool extended subsequently in collaboration with the Swiss Pool analysed the variations in insurance values attributed to similar plants in different countries and considered the various bases of valuation which could legitimately be regarded as a proper foundation for insurance cover. As a result of a report on this subject being presented to the 1981 Conference further studies were agreed to be necessary and it was this which led to the Working Party, who incorporated in their work the whole subject of the insurance of additional costs with special reference to decontamination mentioned above.

i) **Fire Protection**
Another excellent example of close and on-going collaboration between the Pools has been their work on the subject of the fire protection of nuclear installations. This subject had been examined in the first instance by what was known as the Fire Working Group of the European Insurance Committee at the beginning of the 1970's. It clearly called for specialised knowledge and experience in the nuclear field which that body did not feel it had the expertise to provide. At the suggestions of its then Chairman, the late G.C. Ackroyd, the Chief Technical Officer of the F.O.C., it was referred to the British Insurance (Atomic Energy) Committee to organise an inter-Pool study of the subject. This was led with great distinction by the Swiss Pool, who have contributed so much to the practical

aspects of nuclear risks insurance. The initial drafting of what was to become the "International Guidelines for the Fire Protection of Nuclear Power Plants" was undertaken by their Engineer, Dr. H.F. Enzmann. It was therefore arranged at the 1973 London Conference that the Swiss Pool's "model code", as it was then called, be reviewed. It was decided that it needed certain modifications to broaden its international appeal, since hitherto it had been the work simply of a European regional group. Consequently, a Working Party comprising Sweden, Switzerland, the United Kingdom and the United States was established to work on this project, in collaboration with the European Insurance Committee's Working Group which had initiated the first studies. Following a meeting in Zurich, the final Guidelines were agreed and distributed to all Pools for comment and support. Each Pool signified in writing that it was able to commend the Guidelines, and the first edition produced by the Swiss Pool was published in 1974, receiving very wide circulation. Well over 3,000 copies were issued.

Subsequently, it was agreed that there was a necessity also for a similar, though less detailed, companion study of fire protection for nuclear installations *other* than the power stations. These risks presented different considerations because they were smaller, did not have large generating plant, and some of them used materials and processes involving quite different hazards. The Working Party therefore prepared some draft material, most of which was contributed by the British and the American Pools, and proceeded at a meeting held in 1975 at Williamsburg in the United States to compile this into a short publication entitled "International Guidelines for Fire Protection at Nuclear Installations" which was sub-titled to show that it applied specifically to nuclear fuel plants and stores and research and teaching reactor establishments but not nuclear power stations. It was produced by BI(AE)C, presented to the 1976 London Conference and, when agreed by all the Pools, it was published on their behalf by the British in 1976.

Both publications were distributed primarily through the national Pools and insurance associations and also to enquirers applying directly to the two Pools which had undertaken the publication on behalf of all the Pools.

This successful international collaboration on the highly-important subject of fire protection encouraged the Pools to up-date and re-issue the main Power Station Guidelines, and the 1978 Conference entrusted this work to the experts of the French, Finnish, German, Swiss, United Kingdom and United States Pools. They decided that a complete re-writing of the Guidelines was necessary in view of considerable additional experience that had been gained in the intervening years, as well as the emergence of better knowledge and new methods of fire protection. Various revisions were put forward and these were discussed in depth at a full meeting held in Zurich in October 1980, which was attended by other experts from the countries concerned, as well as those provided by the Pools' own specialist staff or member companies. The amount and nature of the new material was such that it became necessary to entrust the job of editing the final draft of the new version to a much smaller Sub-Group which could literally review the new draft line by line and decide upon the best order in which the various Chapters, of which there were several additional ones, should be put together. A small final drafting group comprising the two United States' Pools, the United Kingdom (whose representative was the author of this book) and Switzerland met in New Orleans in January 1981, and after two full days of intensive work the new edition was completed to their satisfaction. More work was required before it was ready for publication, because it had been decided that the new edition should have a detailed index and a glossary of technical terms which were not in the 1974 version. The Swiss Pool undertook to prepare this material. In the meantime, the draft was circulated to all Pools for their comments and suggestions, which were co-ordinated by Dr. Enzmann. The revised edition was finally completed and ready for issue by the end of 1983. This is still in demand and many copies have so far been sold.

It is fair to claim that the degree of international co-operation on highly practical issues achieved by the International Conferences arranged by the British Insurance (Atomic Energy) Committee in London, and the Working Parties that have been held under the Chairmanship of the Pools of a dozen or more countries is probably unique in the long history of insurance. The meetings could never be characterised as mere talking shops. They are short and to the point. They all have a very useful and practical contribution to make. They have led to a close and valuable working relationship, both between the Pools as a community and small groups; and between individual Pools who may have special interests to discuss amongst themselves. By no means all meetings are necessarily under the aegis of the Pool Chairmen's Conferences. A recent development has been the establishment by the 1986 Conference of a forum for the working managers of the Pools to consider day-to-day matters of both immediate and medium-term concern which may either be too small or too detailed to justify reference to a full Conference or the creation of a formal Working Party.

CHAPTER VIII

TO POOL OR NOT TO POOL?

When insurers in many countries were faced in the mid-1950's with the certain prospect of having to meet the challenge of insuring nuclear risks, many experienced underwriters had grave doubts as to the wisdom of embarking on such a venture. As has been stated earlier, the hazards associated with nuclear energy were new and untried. They had no reason to believe that the nuclear industry would ever be other than highly responsible in the establishment of safety standards and would not be permitted to operate by the Governments if these were not entirely satisfied. Nevertheless, the studies insurers undertook in consultation with their experts and others were clear on one thing: radiation was a dangerous and somewhat unpredictable hazard, and the damage it could cause in the event of an uncontrolled nuclear accident could be immense. The immediate and long-term consequences of exposure to radioactivity, particularly for humanity, were unpredictable and there was no relevant experience from the insurance of other industries that could possibly help insurers to assess the probabilities except on a theoretical basis.

Another unattractive feature of the situation was that it was to be many years before there were sufficient nuclear installations in operation and insured even to approach the large numbers which any branch of insurance must deal with to be able to balance the risks and to generate sufficient premiums to be self-sustaining. There were some commentators who imagined that within 10 or perhaps 15 years the growth of nuclear energy and the use of nuclear reactors would be such that there would be large numbers of units insured. As we now know, this was not to be and 30 years after the formation of the first of the Pools there were still no more than about 200 nuclear power stations operating throughout the world, many of these not insured, and an unimpressive number of smaller installations, including fuel factories. These figures have to be contrasted with numbers like tens of thousands for conventional power stations, hundreds of thousands for manufacturing concerns, tens of millions for motor vehicles.

Therefore, from the outset, it was perfectly clear that there was no possible future for the insurance of nuclear risks unless the insurance markets were to co-operate fully and bring as many insurers as possible into the field so that to compensate for the lack of spread of risk in terms of numbers of insured units there would be a spread of risk through the participation of large numbers of insurance Companies and, in the case of Great Britain, also Lloyd's Syndicates. The case for pooling was unanswerable. The alternative would have been inadequate and probably non-existent insurance cover.

There were those who had their doubts about pooling, because insurance is a highly competitive business, some branches more than others, and insurers, particularly the leading Companies, do not like to subsume their individuality into some more or less anonymous body. There is liable to be strong opposition from the broking fraternity also since they obviously thrive on competition and the opportunities this provides to seek better terms for their clients and perhaps themselves, by matching one insurance offer against another. In good times, and in branches of insurance which are commercially successful, this is all to the good, but in bad times and with the less successful branches of insurance it can induce a high degree of volatility, a serious reduction in capacity and, sooner or later, an unsatisfactory market so far as the consumers are concerned: one which is extremely sensitive to bad results and the impact of a few very heavy losses, particularly when owing to the competitive situation it is commercially almost impossible for the insurers who carry the risks to correct the situation by improving their rates and premiums or reducing their commitments.

As we have seen, it was the leaders of the insurance industry who took the nuclear situation in hand from the very beginning, applying their great authority, expertise and experience to ensuring that a proper and stable system of insurance was set up in the 1950's to enable the nuclear industry and the Governments concerned to be reasonably sure that the necessary financial security would be forthcoming when required, that it would be reliable, that it would have the backing of the economic strength of the whole or greater part of every national insurance market which decided to enter into the insurance of this class of risk and to do it through a pooling system.

Of course the Pools mean that there is very little opportunity for competition, although there is no compulsion on any insurer to participate in any association set up to assure the provision of nuclear insurance whether in Great Britain or abroad; nor is it conceivable that anyone could be so compelled except by a desire to take part and to add their weight to the project.

The economic necessity for pooling, as distinct from individual competing insurers providing for nuclear risks, has been recognised

226

by the Governments concerned in every country where such Pools have been set up. In some there are strong safeguards against monopolies, against unfair trading, against restraints on competition, and against the abuse of dominant positions by particularly powerful operators in one or other sector of the economy and the commercial world. This is especially true of the United States with its powerful anti-trust laws, and in those countries which belong to the European Economic Community for whom the Treaty of Rome imposes strong controls on the restriction of competition through concerted practices. Nevertheless, this Treaty does recognise that there are instances where the control of competition may be justifiable in the wider interests of economic development. It makes provision for those enterprises whose activities may be thought to be in this category to notify details of what they are doing and to seek, if necessary, what is known as negative clearance. The nuclear insurance Pools in the Common Market countries, firstly those who were amongst the original six and then those like the United Kingdom and Denmark who joined later, voluntarily submitted themselves for scrutiny although they had no reason to think that they would be likely to be contravening Common Market rules. This was mainly because they had not taken any steps deliberately to monopolise the insurance of nuclear risks for a favoured few, nor to prohibit any reputable insurer from participating or setting up their own arrangements individually or in concert with others. When such a step is taken vis-à-vis the Common Market authorities, this leads to a thorough scrutiny by their officials. It is not possible to comment further on this matter because transactions involving the Commission are of a strictly confidential nature. Suffice to say that the nuclear Pools in the Common Market countries have encountered no complaint from the EEC about the way they conduct their domestic business and their co-operation with Pools in other countries in relation to the regulations of the EEC, the relevant Articles of the Treaty of Rome and the responsible authorities in their own countries who liaise with the appropriate EEC Directorate.

A country which might have been expected possibly to run into difficulties in this sphere is the United States of America. Here again, the situation is that there is no restraint on any insurer or group of insurers seeking to make provision for nuclear risks without their necessarily having recourse to membership of either the Joint Stock Companies' Pool or the Mutual Companies' Pool. There are, indeed, alternative organisations for the insurance of nuclear risks in the U.S.A. as we shall see when we come to examine the whole topic of insurance capacity in the next Chapter.

The international pooling system developed so effectively by the many different insurance markets of the countries concerned has served both the insurance industry and the nuclear industry extremely well. Since it began to gather strength after 1957 and found itself dealing with large nuclear installations by the late 1960's, it has been tested very severely by two not dissimilar events. The first involved a heavy insurance loss, the second might have done but it occurred in a country where there was no insurance. The events were, of course, the TMI accident and the Chernobyl accident which took place, respectively, in 1979 and in 1986. The insurance arrangements of any individual, large or small, being a confidential matter would never be disclosed without the authorisation of the policyholder. However, the position in respect of the TMI nuclear power stations has been widely and authoritatively publicised. It is therefore well known that the Material Damage insurance cover, provided jointly by the two American Pools with a large measure of reinsurance support from most of the other Pools throughout the world, was limited to a maximum loss payment in any one year of 300M U.S. Dollars. The basis of the cover was an All Risks policy form, which provided for protection against damage due to a variety of causes including radioactive contamination and it also extended to the costs of decontamination and debris removal. The nature of the accident at Three Mile Island in March 1979, and the subsequent damage and clean-up costs were fairly and squarely covered by the policy and therefore insurers were faced with a loss which totally exhausted the cover. The ultimate cost of this catastrophic event including decontamination, etc. is still not known because the operation is still in progress but seems certain to exceed $1,000,000,000 by a substantial margin.

However, the point is that the Pools withstood this loss without difficulty and indeed with a remarkable degree of sang-froid. A substantial proportion of the risk was reinsured with the foreign Pools by the two American Pools. Nevertheless, they were able to collect the payments as and when they required them, on time, and it is understood that only one reinsuring Pool was late in paying owing to certain exchange or remittance difficulties which were overcome. What is not always realised about this loss is that it was by far the largest payment that the insurance industry had ever had to meet in the whole of its history in consequence of an accident affecting just *one part* of the premises of one risk. Obviously major catastrophes such as earthquakes, floods and hurricanes affecting many properties, perhaps running into thousands, would cost a great deal more, but that is not the issue. To put this loss into proportion it is useful to compare it with the cost of the *total* fire damage for the *whole* of Great Britain in 1979 — £355 million.

The main reason undoubtedly for the ability of the nuclear Pools to take this massive loss in their stride was the net-line pooling system. This meant that every participating insurer throughout the world, large, medium or very small, knew with certainty that the maximum amount he could lose with respect to that particular installation in any given year of insurance was the net line that he had laid down, that is to say, his percentage share of the risk written by the Pool concerned which he knew to a precise number of Dollars and Cents. Unless anybody had broken the reinsurance rule that every participant in a nuclear Pool voluntarily accepts, there was no possibility of his subsequently being exposed to an additional share through his reinsurance treaties. Furthermore, although every participant in the business of the American Pools, whether a domestic Pool member or member of a reinsuring Pool, was able if he desired to withdraw his membership of the Pool or reduce his subscription at the end of the current year, those who exercised either of these options were reported to have been significantly few. Yet the insurers concerned had met a loss payment authoritatively estimated by those in a position to know as approximately equal to no less than three times the gross *worldwide* premium income derived from Material Damage insurances on all existing nuclear installations that were carrying insurance in 1979.

It would be foolish to deny that the Pools were dismayed at the size of this loss and the relatively insignificant initiating cause. It demonstrated vividly, what they had always suspected, that an accident of undramatic proportions in the first instance could nevertheless lead to a wholly disproportionate loss in terms of the costs of damage and decontamination. Apart from the fact that their financial resources had been able to respond very effectively, insurers were by now sufficiently confident in their technical know-how to realise that an exact similar accident was unlikely to recur and that the nuclear industry and the Governments concerned with controlling it would undoubtedly have learned the lessons of TMI and would insist upon the necessary remedial measures being taken in similar reactor systems elsewhere.

It is instructive to contrast the response of the insurers of the Three Mile Island power station to this loss with that of the insurers of space satellites to the loss of "Westar 6" and "Palapa" from the United States Space Shuttle at the beginning of 1984. The cost to insurers was variously estimated at the time as lying between US$180M and US$200M but it sent a shiver of anxiety through the circles of underwriters involved in satellite insurance and excited considerable comment in the financial press. Another interesting comparison is that the amount of the loss was thought to represent about twice the then current annual premium volume derived from world-wide satellite insurance. Much of the anxiety was engendered by the realisation of the insurers concerned that they could be exposed to larger amounts than their initial shares in these insurances because of commitments through their reinsurance treaties, as indeed seems to have been the case. (Eventually the leading Lloyd's Underwriters made the bold decision to have these satellites salvaged. They were duly recovered from orbit by NASA and sold by Lloyd's to reduce their loss). Satellites were covered in the normal way, unlike the international pooling system used for the insurance of nuclear risks with its accompanying benefits of net-line participation and the substantial spread of risk achieved by involving very large numbers of Pool insurers throughout the world.

The Chernobyl accident accident (see Appendix A) did not involve insurers in any claims, either for damage to the plant or compensation to third parties. Nevertheless it was a shattering event in every sense of the word. It could have severely shaken the confidence of the members of the nuclear insurance Pools, although by now they had recovered from the effects of the American loss. Once again, however, they were able to view the situation with some degree of calm because it was realised that, even if there had been insurance policies in force, the exposure of individual insurance companies and Lloyd's underwriters would have been on a strictly limited basis and no more than they had agreed to lose on that particular risk had it been accepted for insurance or reinsurance by any Pool in which they may be involved. They were sufficiently well advised on the technical aspects, also, to recognise that a replica of the Chernobyl accident could not be expected to occur in any Western design of power reactor. Therefore, although there might have been a tendency, particularly amongst the smaller insurers and their Boards of Directors, to want to pull out of the Pools because of this further reminder of the potentially catastrophic nature of a nuclear accident and the enormous cost of it, there has been very little evidence of any withdrawals or even significant reductions in subscriptions to the Pools around the world. This must owe something to the sense of security felt by those who choose to participate in nuclear installation insurances by this means. It probably also represents a growing level of sophistication in the face of the technicalities that have to be understood by those who have to evaluate and underwrite nuclear risks and by those who choose to follow their expert advice.

It does not, however, require a great level of sophistication to recognise that if the insurance industry had not set about the business of providing cover for nuclear installations through net-line Pools very little insurance might have been available at the beginning: it is more certain that if the business had been handled in the ordinary course of competitive underwriting, the impact of Three Mile Island would most certainly have resulted in a very severe reduction in capacity, coupled with a massive increase in rates worldwide. Neither, in fact, happened. And if that had not devastated a "free" nuclear insurance market, if such a thing had existed, then Chernobyl almost certainly would have done the trick.

A free-for-all was therefore never a likely option in the early approaches to the provision of insurance for nuclear risks. Far from wishing to compete against each other for the privilege of covering such risks, insurers needed a considerable amount of persuasion even to work collectively to enable the national markets to rise to the challenge. Had the growth of the nuclear industry, the number of installations available for insurance and the spread of risk been more extensive and more rapid in the first 10 to 15 years after, say, 1960 the development of alternative or "open" markets might have been a possibility. The loss experience up to 1979 was obviously good and by that criterion it could be said that the business was very profitable. However, prudent underwriters would not consider the surpluses that were building up year by year on that account as a "profit" in their or their shareholders pockets. They had to maintain by one means or other very substantial reserves in order to be in a position to meet the heavy loss that many believed to be inevitable sooner or later without the Insurance Companies and Lloyd's Underwriters endangering the performance of the general branches of their business.

Another choice might have been for one or more specialist insurance companies to be established by a group of insurers for the sole purpose of handling nuclear installation risks in much the same way as there are specialist consortium-run companies to deal with Export Credit Guarantees and Aviation risks for example. That might have been a possibility if there had been the prospect of thousands of reactor units to insure. However, if that had been done to the exclusion of other schemes, it may well be the case that such a Company would have attracted the displeasure of the supervisory authorities, particularly in the field of monopoly controls.

As we shall see when we consider the question of capacity, there has been a development since the early 1970's in the direction of captive insurance companies set up by the Utilities themselves. These provide a basis for mutual "self-insurance", and one such Company, Nuclear Mutual Limited, established in Bermuda by a large group of American electricity generating companies, operates in direct competition with the American Pools. Others, however, have been created primarily for the purpose of enabling the Utilities to participate in the covers provided through the pooling system on a co-insuring basis, an Excess of Loss reinsurance basis or the self-retention of a large first layer of the direct insurance by the means of a special in-house insurance fund for which a very substantial amount of reinsurance is placed directly or indirectly with the world's nuclear Pools. They, it may be said, are ready to collaborate in such arrangements when they are soundly based; when they offer at least as good a prospect of stability and continuity as the Pools themselves; when they do not add excessively to the administrative costs of providing such insurance; and when they are not likely to have a destabilising influence. The financial strength of the international pooling system is very considerable, and it should be remembered that worldwide the number of individual insurance companies participating in the national Pools almost certainly exceeds 1,000. Perhaps only in the United States with its very large domestic power industry would it ever be realistic for such an industry by way of a captive insurance company of its own to provide a totally viable alternative.

It is a tribute to the insurance markets of the world, and their Pools, that they have maintained such close understanding and collaboration in spite of many national differences and variations of practice and principle for thirty years. There seems to be no reason why they should not be able to continue the very high standards they have developed hitherto. No country, no insurance market, no Pool is too small to be admitted to membership of the "club" as some like to call it. The ideologies, the political systems, the countries from which they come, are no obstacle to working together. The personal relationships which have been developed and the resulting sense of mutual trust and good faith have been of immense value in ensuring that the nuclear industry will not lack adequate, sound and secure insurance provision for as long as they require it. The distinguished President of the Belgian Pool, SYBAN, M. Georges Martin, speaking in 1969, as quoted in the Belgian Pool's pamphlet "Twenty years of nuclear insurance in Belgium" characterised nuclear insurance as "a Common Market before its time and international by nature" — a statement no less apt than another sentence in this same publication: "never in the past when confronted with a new problem have worldwide insurers achieved such a common effort to resolve it".

Risks to be pooled

The Nuclear Pools were established to make various classes of insurance available to nuclear installation operators when the required cover could not be obtained in the conventional market.

Their primary objective was not to take over risks which could otherwise be adequately handled. National practice varies in the matter of the types of nuclear installations and classes of insurance to be undertaken by the Pools. Broadly speaking there is general agreement that they must be responsible for insuring the various categories of nuclear installations (and/or nuclear matter), as defined in the International Conventions and/or national nuclear laws, for at least material damage (including "nuclear" machinery breakdown) for both nuclear and conventional perils; and the operators' liabilities towards third parties both nuclear (in accordance with nuclear law) and non-nuclear. They must also relieve the conventional market, as necessary, of the obligation to provide insurance for consequential losses (or business interruption) following insured damage and breakdown, transport risks, product liability, professional indemnity, and other contingent risks to which suppliers of goods and services may be exposed; also personal accident and sickness insurances and accidents at work for employees (if included in Pool Liability policies), in some countries.

In order to facilitate the exchange of reinsurance it was decided at the London Conference held in May 1961 that there should be a better understanding of the nuclear risks that should be handled by the Pools and that national variations in practice should be examined. A Working Party of 8 Pools was set up and in a report prepared later that year they suggested a list of 7 such classes of risk, based upon the categories of nuclear installations referred to in the Paris and Vienna Conventions, but including, to cater for border-line cases, any establishment for which financial security is a statutory obligation. The recommended categories, which were reviewed and reaffirmed in 1978, are:

1. Land based reactors and ancillary buildings and generally all other property on the site.
2. Plants for any manufacture, fabrication or processing of nuclear fuel, other than natural uranium, including the reprocessing of irradiated nuclear fuel.
3. Plants for processing, or disposal of nuclear waste arising from the use of nuclear fuel.
4. Factories for the separation of isotopes of nuclear fuel.
5. Buildings concerned with the storage of enriched or irradiated nuclear fuel used or to be used in any reactor, or nuclear waste arising from nuclear fuel (not being incidental to or temporarily used in connection with transport of such nuclear fuel or waste).
6. Research establishments using nuclear substances which could cause serious claims for personal injuries or property damage.

7. Any other installation considered by National Law to be a nuclear installation and for which the operator is obliged to insure for third party risks up to the minimum sums set out in the Paris of Vienna Conventions.

It has always been accepted that, if additional categories such as sub-critical assemblies, radioisotopes or particle accelerators have to be pooled in a particular country and reinsurance is required, the other Pools will endeavour to assist, even though such risks would be insurable in the conventional market in their own countries.

The classes of insurance written by each national Pool are determined by its statutes, management agreement or other legal instrument setting it up. Pools cannot be so accommodating to other — excluded — classes in these cases. For example, although almost all insurance markets regard the transportation of nuclear matter to be the responsibility of their nuclear Pool, the London Marine and Aviation insurance markets, both Companies and Lloyd's Underwriters, have always been able to handle these risks themselves (under special net line arrangements). BI(AE)C therefore excludes all forms of transport insurance from its field of operations (except for the inland carriage of nuclear matter dealt with by the licensee as part of his site operations for which his statutory liability is inseparable from that applicable to the licensed site). Therefore the British Pool cannot reinsure other Pools' transport risks. In Germany, the Marine insurance market, as a matter of normal practice, handles nuclear risks but the German Pool is not precluded from covering or reinsuring transport risks, if desired. On the other hand, the German Pool (unlike any other) is precluded from writing or reinsuring nuclear Machinery risks even in the High Radioactivity Zone, except as part of an "All Risks" policy, because they are reserved to the specialist Machinery insurance market.

The construction of new nuclear installations, and the related Contractors' All Risks, Engineering All Risks or Builders Risk insurances, is handled only by the specialist conventional markets in all countries but not exclusively so in the U.S.A. There the Pools can also cover the construction risks from the beginning and usually do, the conventional market having no exclusive rights in the matter. In the United Kingdom, however, by agreement reached in 1961, the Pool would not begin to provide insurances for a newly constructed nuclear reactor until the commencement of fuel loading. Most insurance markets follow a similar pattern although some would initiate the nuclear Pool MD insurances for, at least, the usual specified perils and the nuclear part of the station, upon delivery of the fuel: others, notably Germany, not until after the fuel has been loaded *and* first criticality has been achieved in the reactor core. The Liability position may differ again, since in some countries the delivery of nuclear fuel would cause the whole site to be designated a nuclear installation by law, even though construction may not be completed for some years. (An interesting point arises here: the construction work is often delayed and progress is slowed through unforeseen problems whereas the manufacture and delivery of fuel elements is usually on schedule, resulting in the first fuel charge arriving long before the reactor is ready to receive it). When new buildings are constructed on an operational nuclear site, the "work in progress" would normally be regarded as part of the nuclear installation and therefore covered in the Pool MD policy. Straightforward conventional insurance on new plant under construction is, it seems, a class of business only the American Pools can accept. Because it is entirely non-nuclear they would have to seek reinsurance from non-Pool sources, as a rule. Similarly, in the case of a country like Finland, France or Switzerland, for example, where the Pool assumes responsibility for providing Personal Accident insurance, the scope for reinsurance from other Pools is very limited because so few are authorised to accept this class of business.

The United Kingdom is one of the few countries where the Pool insures Products Liabilities and similar contingent risks such as Professional Indemnities in relation to the nuclear industry. Most other Pools do not (nor do some of the conventional markets) but some are willing to provide limited reinsurance out of their Liability capacity. The general attitude is that such insurances should be unecessary because all *legal* liability arising from a nuclear accident is channelled to the operator. That applies to damage or injury to third parties — but financial responsibility can be partly or wholly transferred by contract to a supplier of goods or services. Furthermore, damage to on-site property cannot be compensated out of the insurance or financial security provided under nuclear legislation; so, if the operator or owner is not protected by a material damage policy, or his policy does not waive rights of recovery against another party, then that party is entitled to insurance protection for his liability to make good any damage or loss he may cause.

The reverse of the coin is seen when a type of risk universally regarded as a "nuclear installation" is retained wholly by the conventional market. This is the case with the material damage insurance of nuclear fuel factories in Germany which are potentially hazardous (there can be serious radioactive contamination risks and, in those concerned with reprocessing irradiated fuel, accidental criticality or over-heating may occur); but they are insured conventionally in much the same way as, say, a chemical factory, with no exclusion of nuclear damage. This caused certain problems in the international reinsurance markets when these cases were placed on Treaties, until steps were taken to protect Treaties by way of a special exclusion clause. Generally speaking, such risks would in other countries not be classified as "minor" and therefore would be a matter for their nuclear Pool unless the market decided otherwise.

Conventional material damage insurances (with a suitable nuclear exclusion clause) could however be written on establishments (not defined by law or the Conventions as nuclear installations) containing or handling radioisotopes, particle accelerators and the like.

One aspect requiring clarification was the position of a primarily conventional establishment such as a large research laboratory complex or a University which installs a reactor. Even if the licensing authorities were to designate the whole establishment as a nuclear installation, which is most unlikely, it would be regarded as good practice for insurers to delineate the truly "nuclear" area, so far as it is physically separable from the rest of the buildings, and concentrate the Pool insurances on that, with a suitable extension of the Material Damage policy to cover radioactive contamination of the adjoining non-nuclear property in the same ownership. The rest would then be insurable outside the Pool for conventional perils and liabilities, excluding nuclear damage.

Another situation in which conventional insurance (excluding nuclear damage) might be granted on the non-nuclear part of a nuclear installation would be a power station when, but only when, the owners do not insure the nuclear part, sometimes called the "nuclear island", at all, but request purely conventional cover on the separate generating plant and other non-nuclear facilities.

In all such cases, whether a new construction risk, a multiple occupation complex with a small nuclear sector, or a power station with the nuclear part completely uninsured, Insurers must be completely satisfied as to the integrity of the separation so there will be clear agreement on the precise demarcation between the two parts. However, in all their reviews of this type, the nuclear insurance experts have never wavered from their view that an exclusively non-nuclear policy should not be granted on nuclear installations; that the Pools should not insure only "naked" nuclear risks (i.e. nuclear and conventional perils must always be combined in the one insurance contract); and that the whole of the property, comprised within the legally determined boundaries of a nuclear installation, whether it be a power station or a fuel factory, must be included in the cover provided by the nuclear Pool.

Occasional dissenting voices are heard from interests who see some advantage in limiting Pool Material Damage insurances to nuclear perils only and/or the nuclear part only of a power station. Such proposals are always carefully considered but the strong practical and technical objections to such derogations from internationally agreed practices, formulated many years ago but regularly reiterated, have up to now held firm in all but a very small minority of the lesser types of nuclear risks. In these instances, when a group of insurers have chosen to go their own way there are no major obstacles except when other insurers, not of like mind, exercise their right to withhold their reinsurance support for such ventures.

Nuclear Exclusion Clauses in conventional insurance policies

Mention has been made from time to time of the specific exclusion of nuclear damage from conventional insurances and the reasons for this. The clause wording considered by the BI(AE)C in the late 1950's when advising the various market associations, was eventually finalised in 1959 by the Advisory Committee and was submitted to the interested parties with detailed recommendations and Counsel's Opinion. One of the main recommendations was that the exclusion should apply only to a limited range of classes of insurance, primarily those covering property damage and public liability. Other classes were specifically exempt.

Another recommendation was not to exclude damage due to radioactive contamination or ionising radiation arising from *minor* sources of radiation, such as radioisotopes used for medical, industrial or agricultural purposes or from particle accelerators or X-ray machines. This was achieved by focussing the wording on nuclear fuel and wastes arising from its being "burned-up" in a reactor. In this way, the wording picked up all the likely major sources of nuclear damage.

The wording adopted by market agreement by the Companies and Lloyd's Underwriters for compulsory application to certain classes of conventional insurance by those adhering to the agreement, known as the *Radioactive Contamination Exclusion Clause* (or R.C.E.C.) was as follows:

"This policy does not cover:

(a) loss or destruction of or damage to any property whatsoever or any loss or expense whatsoever resulting or arising therefrom or any consequential loss

(b) any legal liability of whatsoever nature
directly or indirectly caused by or contributed to by or arising from ionising radiations or contamination by radioactivity from any nuclear fuel or from any nuclear waste from the combustion of nuclear fuel".

237

Some 19 classes of insurance were exempted in the sense that it was left to Insurers to decide whether to apply the clause to them. Some of them involved narrow fields of insurance, such as Budget Risks, Missing Beneficiaries, Twins and Licence Guarantees, for example, which were unlikely to be exposed to atomic risks, anyhow. The more important exempt classes included Employers' and Workmen's Compensation; Life; Personal Accident and Sickness; Weather; Professional Indemnities (subsequently deleted, although some 25 years later Insurance Brokers' Indemnity policies were restored to the list of exempt classes at the pressing request of the British Insurance Brokers' Association); Marine and Aviation.

The option of keeping the Exclusion Clause out of Employers' Liability, Workmen's Compensation, Life, Personal Accident & Sickness policies is interesting. The thinking behind it seems to have been mainly that, although a very large number of such policies would be in force, the potential victims covered were widely dispersed. The personal risk to individuals was uncertain so a serious accumulation of immediate claims from one incident was not likely to result. This may not seem to be so valid for employees although it took into account the fact that the Liability policies issued to nuclear site licensees in accordance with the forthcoming Act of Parliament would give them equal rights to compensation as members of the public: Employers' Liability policies issued to nuclear operators may therefore have no need of a nuclear exclusion. In any event, in the considered judgement of the insurers concerned, such a clause was not essential in those classes of insurance.

Motor insurers decided to modify the clause slightly by adding the word "irradiated" before "nuclear fuel" when it first appeared in the standard wording. The reason was that the 1959 Nuclear Installations (Licensing & Insurance) Act applied to ionising radiation from something in the course of carriage only when it was *irradiated.*

The public was informed of these important decisions on 8th January 1960 by way of a joint announcement published in the press by the BIA and Lloyd's in the following terms:

"All new insurance policies which relate to the various forms of material damage to property on land or liability to third parties will, as from 1st April 1960, contain a clause making it clear that any injury to any person or any damage to any property arising out of ionising radiations or contamination by radioactivity emanating from nuclear fuel or nuclear waste is not insured. The Clause will be added to existing policies as they come up for renewal on or after the same date.

If an escape of radioactivity from an atomic installation covered by licence should occur, anyone who is injured or suffers damage to his property will be entitled by virtue of the Nuclear Installations (Licensing and Insurance) Act, 1959 to be compensated by the operator of the installation concerned. The operator will be enabled through special insurance facilities provided by the British Insurance (Atomic Energy) Committee to meet such claims for compensation. In these circumstances it will not, therefore, be necessary or indeed possible for the general public to insure against loss from this cause.

The clause does not extend to exclude other sources of ionising radiation such as radioisotopes, X-ray machines and particle accelerators. Those who use them in industry, agriculture, medicine, research and other fields will still be able to obtain the insurance they require.

The exclusion will not in general apply to life, pension, personal accident or sickness insurances. Policies covering the liabilities of employers to employees for personal injuries sustained in the course of their work will remain generally unaffected. Motor policies will be endorsed but the motorist's liability under the Road Traffic Acts will be fully provided for. The position under marine and aviation insurances is still under consideration.

The British Insurance (Atomic Energy) Committee was set up in August 1956 to mobilise the resources of the whole of the British Insurance market, comprising Tariff, Independent and Mutual Companies and Lloyd's Underwriters and can provide insurance cover to the operators of nuclear installations in respect of their liability to the public in accordance with the Nuclear Installations (Licensing and Insurance) Act, 1959.

The Committee does not, however, provide insurance against damage or injury caused by radioactive fall-out from the explosion of nuclear bombs or similar nuclear devices.''

The Irish Insurance Association decided to adopt the R.C.E.C. and published a similar advertisement (suitably amended) simultaneously. The British announcement was supported by the issue of a detailed Press statement explaining the background and, in particular, the new Act of Parliament as it affected the duties of nuclear site licensees and the public's right to compensation. This received wide coverage and the "Financial Times" followed it up the next week with a quite lengthy commentary by their insurance correspondent who did not think that the official information was sufficiently clear as to the insurability of radioisotopes used in industry and science.

By now, nuclear damage was being routinely excluded from conventional policies in at least 12 other countries round the world, usually under a simple but much wider form of words making no distinction between "major" or "minor" sources of radiation.

A point not always understood is that the nuclear installation insurances provided by the Pools are not directly related to any of the nuclear exclusion clauses. Their purpose has never been limited to filling the "gap" except for certain contingent liability insurances and their function would be quite inadequate if that were so. Equally it is true to say that the various exclusion clauses are not directly geared to the cover nuclear Pools can provide nor, in the case of Liability risks, the terms of nuclear laws. They exclude what the conventional insurance markets intend to exclude: some of these clauses, indeed, came into effect well before the advent of nuclear Pools in some countries. Numerous countries applying nuclear exclusion clauses to their policies still have neither a nuclear Pool nor nuclear liability legislation.

In the years following 1960 no changes have been made in the U.K. R.C.E.C. although it was carefully reviewed in the light of the 1965 Nuclear Installations Act. Some countries, however, notably France, have introduced new or modified wordings in recent years.

An important event in 1966 did, nevertheless, cause BI(AE)C to think again. This was the accidental dropping of unarmed thermonuclear weapons on and around the Spanish coast near Palomares. The British Advisory Committee reached the clear conclusion that damage or liability arising from such an event would not be excluded by the R.C.E.C. wording: the fissile material in a nuclear weapon (or an explosive device for peaceful purposes) could not be described as "nuclear fuel or nuclear waste from the combustion of nuclear fuel".

The exclusion of nuclear weapons material required a separate clause which should, desirably, extend to civil as well as military devices.

Valuable scientific and other advice was obtained from the UKAEA and a film about the American Plowshare project was seen. The potential damage from a nuclear explosion was analysed. It was realised from the Palomares incident that widespread contamination could be caused by even an unarmed nuclear weapon (i.e. one that did not contain the components needed to set it off) if it should be damaged or destroyed accidentally.

Apart from the inadequacy of the R.C.E.C. to protect conventional insurance policies from even the non-explosive hazards associated with nuclear explosive devices, it was realised that if one should fall into a nuclear site and release radiation, the licensee would be held liable under the Nuclear Installations Act because he has a duty to secure that no ionising radiation shall be released from *"anything"* on the site and must compensate anyone suffering injury or damage if it does. The Government confirmed that this was the legal position.

In June 1967, the BI(AE)C Management Committee agreed to advise the Companies and Lloyd's market associations to adopt a new exclusion, designated the "Explosive Nuclear Assemblies Exclusion Clause" (ENAEC). The wording had to receive clearance from the interested Government Departments, primarily the Board of Trade then, who consulted others. This took some months.

In the meantime, there was another incident involving unarmed nuclear weapons — four American H-bombs. "The Times" reported on 23.1.68 that a B52 bomber crashed when attempting an emergency landing at Thule, Greenland going through the ice on North Star Bay. The bombs, which were not "primed", sank to the bottom of the sea: there was no danger of an explosion but an escape of radiation into the sea was a strong risk if any of the bombs was sufficiently damaged to leak radioactive matter. This was said to be unlikely by the "Financial Times" Scientific Editor, writing two days later: he thought corrosion would eventually be a more likely cause of leakage.

Eventually a form of words was agreed and after consideration by market associations such as the Accident Offices Association, Fire Offices' Committee, British Insurance Association (all three are now merged in the Association of British Insurers) and Lloyd's Non-Marine Association, the following exclusion clause was adopted by market agreement:

"This policy does not cover:

(a) loss or destruction of or damage to any property whatsoever or any loss or expense whatsoever resulting or arising therefrom or any consequential loss

(b) any legal liability of whatsoever nature — directly or indirectly caused by or contributed to by or arising from the radioactive, toxic, explosive or other hazardous properties of any explosive nuclear assembly or nuclear component thereof".

It was also reported to the Pool Chairman's November 1968 Conference with a full explanation and received by the 16 other Pools present without comment. A press release was issued on 31st December 1968 in the following terms:

"INSURANCE AND DAMAGE FROM NUCLEAR EXPLOSIVES

As a gradual process starting after the 1st January, 1969 Insurers, both Companies and Lloyd's will be adding to their policies covering risks in the United Kingdom a clause that makes it clear that such policies do not cover loss or liability caused by or arising from nuclear explosives.

Examples of the kind of event contemplated are the accidental dropping of unarmed nuclear bombs in Spain in 1966 and the possible future use of nuclear explosives for civil engineering and other peaceful purposes. Policies were never framed to cover the effects of nuclear explosives and it is understood that Parliament has provided for compensation for the damage caused by accidents due to nuclear materials, including materials used in explosive devices.

Insurance policies of the kind which will bear the new clause already exclude radioactive contamination as well as damage arising from acts of war''.

The Explosive Nuclear Assemblies Exclusion Clause was widely adopted in 1969, usually by extension of the RCEC in the case of conventional policies since the opening words of both are identical. A number of other countries had similar wordings of their own by the time the British wording was under study though they were almost invariably related to nuclear weapons or other devices for military use and their Pools used these exclusions in their own policies. The British Pool does not apply the ENAEC to the Liability policies they issue to nuclear operators because, as explained earlier, their liability under the 1965 Nuclear Installations Act extends to ionising radiation from anything (even an explosive nuclear assembly) on the licensed site. The Pool cover has to match all the statutory liabilities in accordance with the Act. However, since the unarmed devices in question — if ever one did fall into a nuclear installation site — would come from military sources, operators or their insurers are indemnified by the Government for any claims they may have to meet, whether as a result of impact with explosion, or without.

The ENAEC is applied by the British Pool to the other classes of insurance they provide: the hazards associated with these devices — whether military or civilian — are still regarded as uninsurable even by the nuclear Pools.

NON-POOL INSURANCES

Marine & Aviation Risks

Any nuclear cover required under these branches of insurance would be provided in the conventional market in the United Kingdom.

Conventional policies on hulls and cargoes written by the London Marine Market do not carry the RCEC or any nuclear exclusion.

Aviation insurance policies may carry the standard RCEC which, in the case of policies issued by Lloyd's Underwriters, would bear the Lloyd's Non-Marine Association reference number 1670. Underwriters also utilise two other exclusion clauses relating to (1) damage arising from any source of ionising radiation carried in aircraft subject to the IAEA safety rules; and (2) radioactive contamination of aircraft engines (which is a normal and unavoidable phenomenon due to natural background radiation). These two exclusions do not apply to radioactivity levels below the limits set out in the IAEA's Health & Safety Series No. 6 covering the safe transportation of nuclear materials.

Construction risks

It has already been explained that except in the United States the nuclear Pools do not insure the construction of new nuclear installations particularly power stations, until at some point they come to be regarded as "nuclear" either by operation of the law or because of the arrival on site of nuclear fuel, or the commencement of loading of a nuclear reactor, or the achievement of first criticality of a loaded reactor. It follows, therefore, that the conventional markets specialising in these forms of insurance provide the necessary insurance services to contractors and suppliers, subject to appropriate demarcation between their policies and the forthcoming Pool policies in accordance with an agreed timetable related to the takeover of a completed premises and plant.

The construction work that may be undertaken on an existing operating nuclear power station or other installation once it is completely in operation and fully taken over by the operators would not normally then be regarded as a matter for the conventional market although in some cases this is a somewhat grey area in regard to the division of responsibilities. It is normal for a Pool Material Damage policy to extend to work in progress, on an operating nuclear site, but it would not necessarily cover All Risks. On the other hand, a conventional Contractors' All Risks or Builders' Risk insurance would carry the standard nuclear exclusion clause. It may be, in such circumstances, that Contractors' All Risks Insurers would issue a policy which excluded not only the risk of contamination by radioactivity but also all other specified nuclear and non-nuclear perils provided under the existing Pool Material Damage Policy, retaining the balance of risks. However, Insurers involved in both covers would then be exposed for more than their Pool net line.

So far as the liabilities of contractors are concerned, these would normally be assumed by the operator under the channelling of liability principles imposed by nuclear law, although the contractor may be obliged by agreement to accept an obligation to indemnify the operator with respect to his financial obligations to compensate third parties. Where a contractor is undertaking maintenance and repair work unconnected with the nuclear operations and outside the reactor block, control zone or whatever it may be called, and could not cause any damage giving rise to a nuclear occurrence, then there is no reason why any necessary non-nuclear Liability cover should not be provided in the conventional market. The presence of a Nuclear Exclusion Clause would not be a significant restriction of cover because of the remote, possibly non-existent, risk of the contractor causing any damage that could give rise to a release of radiation from anything on the site.

Conventional reinsurance

In the normal way, reinsurers would not wish to accept any nuclear risk, whether it be related to damage or types of property or liability. Provided they are fully informed as to the nature of the case there is little danger of reinsurers unwittingly assuming any nuclear risks under facultative arrangements. However, even though the assumption may be that all insurances relating to nuclear installations would only be covered under a net-line market Pool this is an assumption which, increasingly, cannot safely be made. We have seen already that different national insurance markets and Pools may classify nuclear installations and/or risks to be pooled in various ways.

The position became even less clear-cut with the development of captive or mutual insurance arrangements by the large Utilities and the availability of reinsurance, particularly Excess of Loss reinsurance, from outside the net-line pooling system which accompanied such developments. These features were not present in the mid 1960's, although inconsistent classification as to risks to be pooled was causing a number of participants in the Pools to become concerned about the possibility of picking up additional exposures with respect to risks in which they were participating through the Pool on their reinsurance treaties — "blind" treaties — which certain insurers might use for business written outside the Pools but which related to nuclear risks in one form or another. To relieve this problem the Pools attempted in 1967, through a Working Party, to develop an exclusion clause that would be appropriate for attachment to treaties. It went considerably further than the words that were commonly in use then, and for a considerable time afterwards, which tended to relate only to risks accrued *through a nuclear Pool*. However, this venture made very little progress. No generally agreed comprehensive form of wording was adopted by the reinsurance markets outside North America where since 1957 both Canada and the United States had had detailed exclusion wordings for attachment to treaties, which were widely used and which were designed to make it clear that they did not relate merely to nuclear damage or merely to insurances written through nuclear Pools.

By the early 1980's the Lloyd's reinsurance market, in particular, were becoming increasingly concerned over the likelihood that they were attracting additional nuclear exposures on their treaties without their knowledge. This was a particular problem for the LMX market which is the last refuge of all reinsurance transactions.

Therefore, a new and comprehensive Nuclear Risks Exclusion for treaties was devised in 1983 by Lloyd's Non-Marine Association, who in developing their wording had a certain amount of technical advice from the BI(AE)C. This clause, which bears the Lloyd's reference NMA 1975, is entitled "Nuclear Energy Risks Exclusion Clause (Reinsurance) (1984) (Worldwide excluding USA and Canada)". It is worded as follows:

"This agreement shall exclude Nuclear Energy Risks whether such risks are written directly and/or by way of reinsurance and/or via Pools and/or Associations.

For all purposes of this agreement Nuclear Energy Risks shall be defined as *all first party and/or third party insurances (other than Workers' Compensation and/or Employers' Liability) in respect of:*

(i) nuclear reactors and nuclear power stations or plant

(ii) any other premises or facilities whatsoever related to or concerned with:
(a) the production of nuclear energy, or
(b) the production or storage or handling of nuclear fuel or nuclear waste

(iii) any other premises or facilities eligible for insurance by any local Nuclear Pool and/or Association but only to the extent of the requirements of the local Pool and/or Association, it being the intention always that Reinsurers shall follow the fortunes of the Reinsured insofar as the Reinsured complies with the requirements of any such local Pool and/or Association.

However, this Exclusion shall not apply

(a) to any insurance or reinsurance in respect of the construction, erection or installation of buildings, plant and other property (including contractor's plant and equipment used in connection therewith):-

(i) for the storage of nuclear fuel — prior to the commencement of storage.

(ii) as regards reactor installations — prior to the commencement of loading of nuclear fuel into the reactor, or prior to the initial criticality, depending on the commencement of the insurance or reinsurance of the relevant local Nuclear Pool and/or Association.

(b) to any Machinery Breakdown or other Engineering insurance or reinsurance not coming within the scope of (a) above, nor affording coverage in the "high radioactivity" zone."

This clause was also considered by the Reinsurance Offices' Association who recommended their Company Members to utilise it on their own treaties.

The new clause very quickly began to take effect during 1984 and uncovered a number of cases of what were undoubtedly nuclear installations being written or reinsured outside nuclear pools which the Companies concerned were placing on their Fire treaties with Lloyd's and others. The wording used was sufficiently full and precise to exclude anything that could reasonably be regarded as a nuclear installation and extended it to include any other premises or facilities eligible for insurance by any local nuclear Pool and/or association.

Because of the generally-agreed situation, particularly in the United Kingdom, regarding the demarcation between Pool Material Damage insurances and conventional Contractors' All Risks insurances covering new construction work which may properly be written outside the net-line nuclear pooling system until the delivery or loading of nuclear fuel, the scope of the exclusion is appropriately restricted as set out in sub-paragraph (a). This exception advisedly does not embrace any construction work undertaken on the site of an operational reactor installation once nuclear fuel has been loaded into the reactor. This is quite right because once the premises are a "nuclear installation" they become a Pool risk and that applies to anything going on within the boundaries of the "nuclear installation".

The other exception to the Exclusion Clause relates to the insurance of Machinery Breakdown risks during the construction or erection of new plant prior to the arrival or loading of nuclear fuel *and* to any Machinery insurance written outside the nuclear Pool with respect to plant which is not within the High Radioactivity Zone.

Following the adoption of this Clause by the London Reinsurance

Market some other countries, including Belgium and Switzerland, adopted similar treaty exclusions of their own.

As for Liability risks, this exclusion is not intended to eliminate the reinsurance of conventional Liability policies covering the suppliers of goods and services, such as maintenance work, on a nuclear site which is *unconnected* with the operation of a reactor or the handling of nuclear matter and when the work could not possibly cause any nuclear occurrence. An example might be the activities of a plumber working in the staff canteen or an electrician replacing wiring in an office block.

So far as the wishes and the best judgement of most of the insurers themselves are concerned, there seems to be little doubt that their resolve to keep the main classes of insurance relating to nuclear installations or nuclear matter within the net line pooling system, subject to national variations, is no less than when they first approached this problem in the 1950's. In spite of the development of certain alternatives and of reinsurance facilities outside the pooling system, the position has hardly changed since the Pools were originally set up. There seems to be no realistic likelihood in the near future of individual insurers seeking to break away from the provision of nuclear insurance on a collective basis through net line Pools in order to compete against each other for such limited business as is available from the nuclear energy industry. If they did, the quality and the availability of insurance could probably not be sustained for very long and would doubtless disappear or become prohibitively expensive in the event of another Three Mile Island or Chernobyl accident. In that case everybody, not the least the nuclear energy industry, would be the losers. The international pooling system is far more likely in such an event to assure continuity of sound insurance protection at reasonable cost. Therefore, the answer to the question posed in the heading to this Chapter seems to be unavoidably that pooling must continue to be the main means of providing reliable and adequate insurance and reinsurance cover for some considerable time to come.

CHAPTER IX

INSURANCE CAPACITY FOR NUCLEAR RISKS

The assembling of enough capacity to provide adequate cover for the large nuclear power stations, particularly with respect to property damage and associated classes of insurance, has always presented considerable difficulties for the insurance world. For Liability risks, the problem has been far less because as a result of the intentions of the International Conventions, as we have seen, most national legislation imposes relatively modest limits on the financial responsibilities laid upon operators having to compensate third parties.

It was absolutely essential that the obligations of insurers, when first persuaded to participate in the insurance of nuclear risks, should be subject to very clear and positive limits. They had to be quite certain that their subscribed line in their national pool for any one risk in any given year of insurance would not exceed the figure they had laid down. This, as previously mentioned, was secured by adopting the net-line principle as a means of safeguarding insurers against unforeseen and unwanted accumulations of financial liability in relation to any particular nuclear installation, whether it be concerned with physical damage, consequential loss or liability at law. To achieve this objective it was essential to prohibit the placing of reinsurance by individual participants and, by the same token, to protect them against the possibility of their liabilities pyramiding through the acquisition of additional commitments under their normal reinsurance arrangements with other companies. In the normal way, when an insurer underwrites a risk, he fixes his desired share of that risk in accordance with his Company's or Syndicate's capacity for a particular class of business and reinsures the balance under one or other of the different types of reinsurance procedures. The size of his retention may vary very considerably and, even when the insurer is acting as a reinsurer, the final amount that he retains for his own account can be substantially reduced by further reinsurance or retrocession arrangements. Consequently, when the insurance companies and Lloyd's underwriters who decided to join the British Pool were required to fix their net retentions, these were in most cases relatively modest compared with the gross amounts or lines that they would put down for a normal conventional risk.

Paradoxically, however, many Pool participants fix net retentions for nuclear business at a higher level than those they would regard as acceptable for the conventional classes of insurance. There are several reasons for this, but the main one is that they know the amount they take on a nuclear risk cannot be exceeded by the influx of additional commitments through blind reinsurance treaties. Good risk control by the Pools and sensible rates are other reasons. There was never any possibility of more or less unlimited cover being offered for the insurance of nuclear risks by the Pools operating on a net-line basis.

In spite of very energetic efforts on behalf of the BI(AE)C to maximise the participation of the British Insurance market in the Pool in anticipation of the provision of cover for the first of the commercial power stations, and also to interest the foreign Pools that were in existence when such capacity was being put together in 1959/1960, the total subscriptions offered fell considerably short of the estimated sums insured on the Material Damage side. It will be recalled that these had been expected in 1956 to amount to something like £30M. By 1959 that estimate had had to be doubled to £60M. Even with foreign support, less than £30M became available for U.K. Material Damage risks when required a year or so later. Because of the sensible restriction upon the insurance requirement fixed by the national nuclear laws and the International Conventions, the same problem did not arise in regard to Public Liability insurance for nuclear operators. Nevertheless, it should be remembered that the amount of capacity subscribed on the Liability side had to be considered in the light of the Material Damage commitment because in the event of a serious nuclear accident there would undoubtedly be claims with respect both to property damage and to injury or damage suffered by third parties. Most Pools establish separate capacities for the two main classes of insurance. In a few countries the participating insurers subscribe a single amount which can then be split between the Material Damage and the Liability sides by the Pool management as required, sometimes subject to certain restrictions as to the apportionment of the total amount over the different classes of insurance.

Another very important principle, which was really bound up with the net-line approach, was the need to ensure that there could be no undue accumulation of liabilities with respect to a particular annual insurance policy: hence the objections to allowing any form of automatic reinstatement of cover following a loss described previously and universally accepted by the Pools as recommended by their Conferences. A similar requirement applied also to the Liability insurance. Although, under the United Kingdom legislation, there is an overall ceiling on the amount of claims that can be paid out with respect to any one nuclear installation throughout its lifetime, or at any rate during the full period of the responsibility of a particular operator known as the cover period, most other nuclear laws in line with the International Conventions determine the operator's financial commitment on the basis of a limit per nuclear incident. This is not universal, fortunately, and Switzerland, for example, has a "per installation" limit enshrined in its nuclear legislation. Insurers have always been firmly resolved to avoid the accumulation of liabilities under third party insurances beyond their maximum fixed capacity for any one installation regardless of the number of times the policy is renewed over a period of years. Consequently, quite apart from the statutory incident limit that has to be provided for under such insurance, it is the normal practice to fix an additional overall ceiling known as the "installation limit" which has to be reduced by the amount of each and every claim that is paid throughout the lifetime of the insurance cover. The fact that there may well be spare capacity to enable the policy limit to be reinstated after a claim has been met if the participating insurers agree to this does not invalidate the application of the net-line principle as an essential safeguard against the possibility of participating insurers being exposed to a commitment, however theoretical, that would take them beyond their maximum limit or share of the limit selected by their Pool for a particular case, without being consulted first.

Although the response of the British insurance market to the Management Committee's requests for subscriptions was not unreasonable, in view of the completely novel nature of the nuclear hazards and the installations to be covered, it clearly fell short of what was required even with foreign support. This led the Advisory Committee and the Management Committee to re-think the basis on which the Material Damage cover could be provided to see whether it would be possible in some way to stretch the cover beyond the limit of less than £30M, which appeared to be the most that could be expected. A possible solution was suggested by the very nature of the way in which the Magnox Nuclear Power Stations in the United Kingdom were constructed. There was a very clear and definite separation, with all the necessary engineered safeguards, between the nuclear part of the plant, known as the reactor block, and the non-nuclear buildings, mainly the Turbine Hall and associated facilities. This suggested to the Committees concerned and the engineers and fire surveyors consulted that the separation from the point of view of the possible spread of fire and explosion was such that the probabilility of such conventional damage orginating in the reactor block and spreading to the conventional property and vice versa was so small that they could reasonably be regarded as separate risks from the point of view of application of insurance capacity. Of course, the nuclear and the conventional parts together comprised one complete power station and had to be covered under one policy though not necessarily for the same range of perils. There was no possibility of any form of nuclear damage arising in the separate conventional buildings so the spread of radioactive contamination, for example, would only be associated with something occurring in the reactor block. This pointed to the solution because it was mainly the risk of nuclear damage rather than the more familiar conventional perils that made it difficult to acquire a large amount of capacity.

The answer was to divide the policy into two parts, each with its own insurance values and limits. Part I was to cover the whole of the reactor block and its contents and the nuclear fuel therein and, also, to cover any damage of a nuclear nature, primarily radioactive contamination, originating in the reactor block and spreading to other property belonging to the insured on the site, and indeed off the site for that matter. Part II would then provide exclusively non-nuclear cover for the normal range of perils subject to a separate sum insured or limit. It was considered extremely unlikely that major losses would arise separately under both sections of the policy in the same year, but to safeguard against that the whole of the policy could be subject to a further overriding annual limit.

To encourage support for this proposition, the subscribing members of the British Pool were invited to re-assess their contributions on the basis of two separate "slips". Slip 1 would coincide with the first part of the policy covering the whole of the reactor block, etc. for the full range of nuclear plus conventional perils. Slip 2 would apply only to the purely conventional cover on the purely conventional properties and plant. An important concession was that since the second slip applied exclusively to conventional risks the normal prohibition on reinsurance would be waived* — except in the case of Excess of Loss reinsurance, since that could have exposed professional reinsurers and Lloyd's market to the possibility of building up an unacceptable accumulation on the non-nuclear part of the station in addition to their commitments on the nuclear part. This innovative approach produced a very good

---

* This waiver was dropped by common consent in 1986: very few Pool participants had ever taken up the option to reinsure their Slip 2 shares.

response from the Companies and Lloyd's Syndicates participating in the British Pool, and as a consequence it was possible then to contemplate providing a much wider cover in terms of the amounts insured than would otherwise have been the case.

Of course even with the new system, there was no increase in the capacity available for the reactor blocks or, rather, block, because all the British nuclear power stations from that day to this have consisted of two reactor units which, except in the earliest stations, are in the same building. In the case of the early Magnox stations, the reactor blocks were some distance from each other. It was considered to be almost inconceivable that an accident in one block could cause a similar accident in the other but there could be a spread of radioactive contamination from one to the other. Consequently, it was considered that if the policy could provide a Part I limit sufficient to cover the full value of one reactor unit and its fuel, plus an amount to pay for damage due to radioactive contamination and the cost of decontamination of other property, together with a full value insurance (capacity permitting) on the conventional part of the station, the insured would have as good a protection as could possibly be provided given the limitations on the worldwide capacity for nuclear risks. While there could be no automatic reinstatement of any loss payments, there remained the possibility that subject to the nature and size of the loss some reinstatement might be possible subject to the approval of the participating insurers and the reinsuring Pools. However, that was not the main concern, and it seemed likely that if sufficient capacity could be provided to ensure that the Part I limit was not less than the value of one complete reactor unit and its fuel, plus an amount for spreading contamination damage, this proposition would have some attractions for the insured, particularly as it seemed unlikely that any limitation would have to be imposed on the Part II section of the policy. This, indeed, proved to be the case and thus, almost from the outset, the British Home Risks Pool has been based upon two separate subscription lists or slips for Material Damage, with a separate slip for Liability insurance.

Subsequently, the Slip 1/Slip 2 concept was adopted also for foreign risks, and the British Pool were then able to offer to other Pools an enhanced level of capacity providing the layout, construction and technical features of the station complied with the Part I/Part II requirements.

Although the layout of the mainly PWR and BWR stations built in other countries was different and there was no separation in space between the reactor block and the turbo-generating plant and buildings containing it, the separation from the point of view of the potential spread of fire and explosion was entirely adequate largely because Light Water Reactor stations have a massive concrete shell or sphere built round the reactor block which would be a very effective bar to the spread of such conventional damage.

Another advantage of this system was that in the event of a loss being limited to the conventional part of the station subject, perhaps, to a very small spread of damage to the nuclear part, it could be settled in full without reducing the much more "sensitive" nuclear cover.

With the gradual growth of worldwide capacity, and the fact that the nuclear power stations built in other countries were in the early years almost invariably equipped with only one reactor, the problem of finding adequate Material Damage cover was not acute, especially when the British Pool were able to offer an additional subscription for the conventional properties on the station. However, as time went by, the values of the nuclear power stations, because of increasing size and also, in some countries, substantial inflation, began to rise very steeply and to outstrip the available international Pool capacity. It thus became essential to fix with respect to each annual policy an overall limit, called in the United Kingdom the annual aggregate loss limit, which could not be exceeded under the policy covering a particular year of insurance regardless of the size of any one loss or series of losses. Twin-reactor stations and stations with even 3 or 4 or more reactors also began to appear, pushing the insurance values into very high levels. However, so far as the potential loss was concerned, it was still the case that in a twin or multi-unit station, the likelihood of more than one reactor unit and its nuclear fuel or, conversely, one turbo-generating set being substantially damaged or destroyed in any one year was remote. This was considered to mean that, if the total capacity available could at least cover the worst conceivable loss, which would be the total loss of the most costly reactor unit and the fuel in it and the spreading contamination damage, the insured would have adequate financial protection against all foreseeable contingencies.

However, at this time, relatively little account was taken of the likely expense of clean-up operations following a major contamination accident, including decontamination, isolation of contaminated debris and waste and the removal of such contaminated matter from the site. When specific fixed amounts of cover were given for such expenses on a first loss basis, they were usually for rather modest sums which, as the TMI case demonstrated, would have been entirely inadequate to meet such costs in excess of the insured value of the contaminated property. On the other hand, even in those cases where full decontamination expenses *were* included in the cover, subject only to the overall annual policy limit, such limits may not have provided adequate protection.

By the early 1970's, although some of the Pools were adopting the British Part I/Part II policy concept as a means of stretching capacity, serious concern was being expressed at the lack of Material Damage capacity worldwide. This led to the BI(AE)C to present a paper to the April 1973 London Conference drawing attention to the inability of nuclear insurers to provide even a satisfactory amount of cover for Material Damage risks, not to speak of any additional demand that had arisen for Machinery Breakdown insurance, and even Consequential Loss cover. In addition a similar problem would arise, of course, if there were to be any spread of the North American practice of providing All Risks insurance on nuclear power stations. The paper drew attention to the growth of partial self-insurance by the large nuclear operators in the form either of captive insurance companies or the adoption of substantially larger deductibles or excesses than were usual until then, and called for increased efforts to secure larger subscriptions from participating insurers. The means included giving them fuller information regarding the nature of nuclear installations and the potential hazards, while at the same time assuring them of an intention to keep rates and premiums at reasonable levels. The British Pool's dual Slip approach to the provision of Material Damage capacity was explained and commended to other Pools in cases where the nuclear and non-nuclear parts of a power station could be regarded as separate risks for underwriting purposes in respect of the potential spread of conventional damage such as fire and explosion.

During the course of the discussion, various Pools mentioned the bases on which they sought subscriptions from their members who were recommended to fix their contributions in accordance with the size of their premium income for general business. Figures such as 3% for large companies and 5% for small companies were mentioned. While agreed upon the absolute necessity of expanding worldwide capacity for Material Damage risks and associated classes of business, the Conference recognised that there were limits to the extent to which net capacity could be stretched, whatever expedients may be adopted. The Pools were not unfavourable towards the notion of persuading the policy-holders to take a share in the Material Damage covers, the preferred method being that they would become partners with the insurers by perhaps retaining a 10% coinsurance participation for their own account. This would mean that they would have a share in the premiums, the losses, the expenses and, indeed, any notional profit on exactly the same basis as the insurers themselves. It would also give them an interrest in maintaining good loss prevention standards.

It was decided to remit the whole question to a working party comprising the Pools of 10 countries, who were to meet as early as possible and to issue an interim report thereafter.

The Working Party met in Florence at the invitation of the Italian Pool. They studied in some depth the possibilities of making better use of existing capacity through the sub-division of suitable types of nuclear power stations on the British pattern although they considered that this required more study by the technical experts. They also studied the possibilities of partial "self-insurance" which would mean the large electrical utilities with the necessary financial resources carrying a fixed percentage share of each risk themselves, possibly quite a large share, as an alternative to an insurance based on full value subject to a lower annual aggregate loss limit.

It was generally agreed that the preferred method of participation by the insured would be from the basis of a percentage coinsurance share, meaning that the insured would contribute a fixed proportion to every loss payment and retain the same proportion of the annual premium less a small percentage to account for a reasonable contribution to the administrative expenses born by the principal insurers. A share of 10% was considered to be realistic, this having in fact been already adopted by one or two of the large Japanese utilities with respect to the Material Damage insurances written by the Japanese Pool on their nuclear power stations.

Another method by which the insured could share in the cover would be by means of his carrying a large excess or deductible whereby he would pay the first part of any loss up to a stated limit or percentage. The Pool policy would then be written as an excess insurance for maximum capacity above the amount retained by the insured; or, alternatively, for the maximum limit that insurers could provide subject to an agreed percentage being deducted from each loss payment. The objective of the voluntary participation of the insured, either by way of a coinsurance share in the policy or a large excess or deductible, was to reduce the amount of cover that would actually have to be provided by the insurers, thus relieving the pressure on their limited capacity. This approach had some attractions compared with the enforced application of a loss limit which would be substantially below the aggregate full insurance values. However, it was considered that such participation should be at a modest level, and at that time (1973) the Working Party were reluctant to contemplate agreeing to an excess or deductible larger than the equivalent of, say, US$1M (later doubled). To go beyond that, it was felt, would encourage the removal of a substantial portion of the business from the Pools and could even result in their share of the insurances ultimately falling to a level well below that which they could provide as a result of increasing their capacity. It was considered that the net-line principle could be at risk if the retention of relatively large shares of Material Damage policies on nuclear power stations by the insured were to result in their seeking to reinsure such retentions outside the pooling system, possibly by way of a captive or mutual insurance company set up by the electrical utilities themselves.

That this was a practical possibility had been demonstrated during that year in the United States by the establishment of a captive mutual insurance company by a number of the large private enterprise electrical utilities. This was Nuclear Mutual Limited, an off-shore company installed in Bermuda by, initially, some 14 power companies. Its purpose was not to collaborate with the Pools in America to add additional capacity but to enter into direct competition primarily by offering a discount off the rates charged by the American Pools for their Physical Damage All Risks covers. The Mutual did not engage in any form of Liability insurance. The American electrical utilities were, of course, far more numerous and more powerful than those of any other single country. They had the financial resources to fund what was initially no doubt a somewhat risky financial operation, even though they were able to obtain a certain amount of protection from the traditional reinsurance markets.

The Working Party followed up their Florence Meeting with another in Brussels in January 1975 under the Chairmanship of the President of the Belgian Pool. In the interim, all Pools had been urged to make great efforts to persuade their participants to increase their subscriptions so as to narrow the gap between the full values of large nuclear power stations and the maximum net-line Material Damage capacity that the international pooling system could supply. Further attention was called for, primarily because, by the time of this meeting, the International Union of the Producers and Distributors of Electricity (known as UNIPEDE after the French title of this Brussels-based organisation) had, with the assistance of a leading firm of London Brokers, begun to study the possibilities of setting up a captive Mutual Insurance Company in Europe for the benefit of the Union's member organisations who operated nuclear power stations in various countries. The objective of this project was, initially at least, relatively benign, and they declared that they were not concerned to compete against the established insurance markets and nuclear Pools: rather, by contributing a certain amount from their own resources, together with reinsurance which they believed they could obtain from markets not tapped by the Pools, they would be able to produce new capacity. This they would utilise by issuing a policy of insurance, in coinsurance with the Pool insuring the particular nuclear power station in which they were interested. However, at this stage of the proceedings, UNIPEDE were also referring to an intention to put pressure on the Pools to reduce their rates although this would seem to be a somewhat irrelevant side issue since the main declared objective was to enable Material Damage policies to be written for larger limits than were otherwise achievable by the use of the primary capacity of the nuclear Pools. Lower rates were, furthermore, hardly likely to appeal to their prospective reinsurers.

If the proposed European Mutual were to be set up with the objective simply of co-operating with the established Pools by issuing a coinsurance policy as a means of increasing cover this was felt to be something with which Insurers could and should co-operate. Even so, the general view was that the participation of the Utilities by this means should preferably not exceed 10% and that there should be a reasonable reduction in their share of the premium to allow for a realistic contribution by the insured to the costs of setting up and administering the original insurance cover incurred by the Pool concerned.

Regarding the provision of First Loss insurance for amounts within the available capacity, related, say, to the value of the largest unit of property exposed to risk on a nuclear power station, probably the Reactor Block and its contents, there were some reservations about this. It could result in insurances being written for amounts significantly below the available cover which could militate against the drive for the increased capacity still needed for those insured who were not satisfied with a First Loss cover for large installations. It was agreed to recommend that insurance subject to a loss limit should be avoided unless necessitated by an insufficiency of world capacity, in which case the limit should be related to the amount of capacity available. However, if the insured particularly desired his cover to be limited to a lesser amount, each case should be dealt with on its merits.

This was among a number of recommendations presented to the next Pool Chairmen's Conference in February 1976, which confirmed that coinsurance on a quota-share basis with the insured carrying up to 10% of the risks was an acceptable proposition provided the insured would undertake not to seek to cover his own participation by way of additional insurance elsewhere. The limitation of deductibles to, preferably, not more than US$ 1,000,000 was confirmed, as was the recommendation concerning insurances subject to a loss limit below that which could be provided by the full use of worldwide capacity, although in these cases insurers would be expected to have due regard to the total insured values and the maximum probable loss in each case.

Apart from considering such expedients as a means of reducing the pressure on capacity, while at the same time giving those insured who desired it the opportunity for partnership, the Conference continued to lay great stress on the primary objective of increasing worldwide capacity. Their target had been to get together from all the Pools £100,000,000 for Material Damage risks by the date of this Conference and, from reports received, it seemed that this had largely been achieved.

The other means of improving the amount of cover that could be granted in the face of capacity limitations were also considered, the most promising being the sub-division of large installations into separate sections, where on technical and underwriting grounds these could properly be treated as separate risks. The arguments for this approach were advanced almost entirely by the British Pool, based upon their own practice. Some Pools were doubtful about the concept, particularly when considering the possibilities of an aggregation of losses as a result of a single *external* cause such as an earthquake or a crashing aircraft, or possibly even terrorist acts causing simultaneous damage to more than one of the sectors which for the purposes of applying capacity had been designated a separate risk. However, this was a problem that could be and is overcome easily enough by applying appropriate interlocking limitations over the separate insurances applying to the complex in question. Consequently, there is now a wide measure of agrement that a Pool's capacity may be applied fully or almost 100% when a risk can be sub-divided in the following ways:-

   (i) in the case of a single power station by treating the Reactor Block or nuclear island and the remaining properties on the site as separate risks providing the necessary physical separation criteria are met;

  (ii) by treating two or more self-contained nuclear power stations on separate plots on the same site as separate risks for the application of capacity, providing of course that the distance they are apart is reasonable and there is no communication such as by way of bridges or tunnels carrying services which could be a means of spreading damage from one to the other;

 (iii) in the case of a large fuel factory, where there is good separation between the different parts of the plant, sub-dividing it into as many sectors as the technical experts would regard as prudent and practical from the point of view of the risk of spreading damage whether this be nuclear or conventional.

These methods of making better use of available capacity developed fairly gradually over the decade or so following the 1976 Conference. Particularly in the case of the smaller power stations and the fuel factory-type of risk, they have led to a very considerable improvement in the insurance protection that can be offered. However, especially with the multi-unit power stations, there is still a considerable gap between the total insurance values, especially when assessed on the basis of value as new, and the annual aggregate loss limits that have to be applied to the section of the policy covering the nuclear properties.

World-wide capacity

By 1987, the combined efforts of the Pools had succeeded in increasing the net-line primary capacity for Material Damage insurances to an amount ranging between about £350,000,000 and £450,000,000 according to the size of the domestic capacity an individual Pool could contribute towards the Material Damage insurance of its own risks and the extent to which reinsuring Pools would accept risks in certain countries. It will be appreciated that the resources of each Pool vary very considerably falling between roughly £1,000,000 and £100,000,000. The maximum capacity available to nuclear installations in different countries is not uniform also, because most Pools are unable to provide as much capacity for the reinsurance of foreign risks as they are able to provide for their own cases. The figures mentioned relate to the position outside North America and also only to capacity applicable to Material Damage insurances and the related Machinery Breakdown and Consequential Loss classes to the extent that an individual Pool is prepared to provide cover or reinsurance for these two classes. In a few cases, the capacity available from a Pool is on a combined Material Damage and Liability basis. In order to estimate a worldwide figure for Material Damage capacity, a proportion of that combined amount has been taken.

Machinery Breakdown and Consequential Loss capacity

So far as concerns Machinery Breakdown and Consequential Loss insurances written alongside a Material Damage policy under separate contracts of insurance, the required cover has to be supplied from the general Material Damage capacity. In the case of large risks, this inevitably means either that no capacity can be made available for these additional covers or, more likely, it has to be spread over the different policies in one of two ways. One is to ensure that each policy is subject to a separate annual aggregate loss limit of such amount as combined with the other one or two policy limits will not exceed the total capacity for Material Damage risks. The other is to apply the full limit, or as much as is required, to each of the policies but to make them subject to a common overriding limit by means of a suitable cross limitation clause that subjects the two or three covers to a stated maximum in any one year of insurance.

As mentioned earlier, normally the scope of a Machinery Breakdown insurance would be limited to the plant in the High Radioactivity Zone with perhaps part of that in the Low Radio-activity Zone, the remainder of the cover being written outside the Pool in the conventional Machinery insurance market by specialist insurers who are able to provide separate capacity although they do not have capacity for Machinery Breakdown in the High Radio-activity Zone. Only in Germany where all Machinery Breakdown cover on nuclear installations is a non-Pool business is there a limited amount of separate capacity available for the High Radioactivity Zone from the specialist market.

If Machinery Breakdown is written as part of an All Risks Policy, then of course the overriding limit for that policy would apply equally to the breakdown damage subject to any sub-limit that may be imposed for that within the Policy.

There has been very little demand for separate Machinery Breakdown or Consequential Loss insurances for nuclear power stations, and in some countries these classes of insurance are not available from the nuclear Pools. The reasons for this lack of demand may be due partly to the wish of the nuclear operators to concentrate their insurance cover on the direct physical damage and clean-up costs, partly because the capacity is not really there anyway, and partly perhaps because of the relatively high cost of applying these classes of insurance to nuclear power stations, although this would be less of a problem in the case of non-reactor establishments such as fuel fabricating or reprocessing factories. These, in any event, can be treated much more favourably from the point of view of applying capacity, because of their capability of being in most cases sub-divided into several risks. In a number of cases these may have a value well within the available capacity, thus releasing a margin for the provision of Consequential Loss insurance. Machinery Breakdown insurance is not very likely to be required for that class of nuclear installation.

Example

Considering the practical questions which arise when cover has to be provided for a large, high-value nuclear power station, the following hypothetical example may help to illustrate the sort of numbers involved:

The risk is a modern twin-PWR power station of recent construction for which insurance is required up to the highest limit possible related to the insurance values applicable to replacement as new in the event of destruction or damage. The station is constructed to the highest standards, with an effective containment shell round the reactor units, each of which is housed separately. The necessary separation criteria as between the nuclear plant and the non-nuclear facilities are met in full. Therefore, subject to survey and consideration of the technical data, this is a case which would qualify for the application of dual capacity either on the British Slip 1/Slip 2 pattern, or by means of Pools applying their normal capacity twice, subject to being satisfied with respect to the possibilities of aggregation between the two parts as a result of simultaneous external causes or spreading damage from one to the other.

A proper valuation has been undertaken, and from this it is shown that the full replacement cost of each Reactor Block, including its auxiliary buildings and the fuel therein, is £400,000,000. The value attributed to the Turbine Hall and all the other non-nuclear property is £250,000,000. The Insured want as much Additional Costs cover as possible to meet the expenses of decontamination, isolation and removal of contaminated debris and waste in the event of a nuclear accident involving significant radioactive contamination.

In this illustration the input of the local Pool is substantial and there is no limitation on the amount of reinsurance they can take up. Therefore the assumed maximum worldwide Material Damage capacity can be deployed. Consequently, the insurance is written on a Part I/Part II basis with a Part I limit of £450,000,000 as against a total of £800,000,000 plus the Additional Decontamination Costs cover which it was agreed should be limited to £100,000,000. Thus, as against a potential exposure of £900,000,000 under Part I, the capacity available is exactly half. The likelihood of the destruction of more than one of the two units, since they are separately housed within their own substantial containment buildings, is very low; on the other hand, the amount that will have to be paid out, if any, for decontamination operations is almost unpredictable, but under the terms of this insurance would not exceed £100,000,000. Therefore, the protection afforded against the *most likely* loss would be close to 100% in all probability: even in the worst accident it is unlikely that no part of the nuclear plant could be recovered, so the worst loss would probably be within £450,000,000.

As far as the non-nuclear part of the station is concerned, given that the majority of Pools, including the imaginary domestic Pool concerned, are able to provide additional and separate capacity for this, there would be no problem over providing full value insurance for the £250,000,000 declared value.

However, if this Insured wants also to cover Machinery Breakdown on the High Radioactivity Zone, and in addition a suitable form of Consequential Loss insurance to indemnify him for the additional cost of supplying electricity from an alternative source in the event of his station being shut down for a long period due to an accident, the Pools would not be able to supply this cover unless one of the aggregate loss limitation methods mentioned above were to be adopted. The amount of insurance that would be given for Machinery Breakdown of specified components in the High Radioactivity Zone would depend on very many factors, as would the amount for the additional costs of access and repair due to the radioactive environment. There would be not only an imposed loss limit in any event, regardless of the capacity available, but there would also be a fairly substantial deductible. Nevertheless, it may well be that the additional cover needed would be of the order of £100,000,000. That required for the Consquential Loss insurance could equally be of the order of, for the sake of argument, £50,000,000.

To enable such covers to be written within the available capacity, it would be necessary therefore to issue the separate policies and impose an overriding limitation clause on each to ensure that the payments made in the aggregate arising from one originating cause could not exceed £450,000,000 with respect to damage in the nuclear part of the station, and £250,000,000 in respect of damage in the conventional part, although the latter consideration would arise with respect only to Consequential Loss cover. Otherwise, the £450,000,000 of capacity available for Part I would have to be reduced in order to release, say, £100,000,000 for a separate Machinery insurance and further reduced to provide the £50,000,000 required for Consequential Loss insurance, the result being a Part I limit of £300,000,000 instead of £450,000,000. However, since there is ample spare capacity with respect to the non-nuclear part of the station, which would be insured for conventional damage only of course, there would be no need to reduce that on account of the Consequential Loss insurance so far as that relates to financial losses arising from damage in the conventional part of the station.

If the situation were one in which there were two separate but adjoining nuclear power stations on the same site and the necessary criteria in that respect were met, there would be no reason not to apply the full capacity under both parts separately. In this way, for one complex consisting of what are generally known as A and B stations, the potential capacity limit would be £900,000,000 subject to any necessary overriding limitation regarding damage spreading from one to the other which could arise in relation to contamination by radioactivity. In such a case, the normal practice would be for the damage caused by one station to the other to be covered under the policy applying to the station where the damage originates. In that case there would be no claim under the policy covering the other station. Conversely, if the insurance was provided in such a way that damage originating in Station A and affecting Station B were paid under the policy covering Station B, then there would be no claim for that damage under the policy covering Station A. Thus the limitation of aggregation where a single originating cause affects both would be preserved.

If one takes the case of a large nuclear fuel fabricating or reprocessing factory covering many acres and consisting of several different processes housed in separate well-protected buildings which represent separate risks from the point of view of the spread of damage other than damage by radioactive contamination, the same concept can be applied in order to maximise the use of the available capacity. Assuming that as a result of a thorough inspection and investigation of all the technical data, the plans and the construction features and the engineered safeguards, it is decided that this plant can be safely sub-divided into five separate sections, then there is no reason, in principle, why the available international capacity cannot be applied five times over. In practice, this may not always be achieved because some Pools take a much more cautious view of the possibilities of this multiplication of the capacity than others. Nevertheless, assuming the worldwide capacity would again be £450,000,000 it should be possible to contemplate providing as much as £2,250,000,000 of cover under *separate* policies for this installation. In fact, the maximum aggregate values would probably be less because the different sectors may not be of equal value. It is possible that one or more sectors might be valued at more than £450,000,000, in which case a limit would have to be applied: others may be much less. The question of spreading radioactive contamination damage would be dealt with in the same way as would usually apply to a nuclear power station. Any damage suffered by an adjoining sector would be paid for under the Policy applying to the section in which the damage originates. If necessary, there could be an overriding limitation with a suitably worded clause on each policy to safeguard insurers against the possibility of simultaneous damage arising from an external cause such as earthquake.

While the practice of individual Pools varies in regard to the stretching of net-line capacity by one or other of the means described, there is a considerable degree of flexibility and a willingness to take all reasonable steps to mitigate the limitations on capacity resulting from the very necessary net-line principle which was no less important in 1987 that it was in 1957, although experience has shown ways of easing the constraints it imposes on insurers.

Excess capacity

The potential worldwide Material Damage capacity for nuclear installations is primary capacity, that is to say, it is subscribed for the purpose of providing insurance cover from the ground upwards in terms of values. It was never intended to be used as Excess reinsurance in any form of layered cover. For this purpose an *additional* source of capacity has been developed in the United States mainly in response to the Three Mile Island accident which demonstrated the need for Excess of Loss capacity in view of the inadequacy of their $300,000,000 policy limit (which was of course first layer or primary capacity) compared with the total cost of this accident.

For various reasons, the United States Pools did not attract as much international reinsurance support as most other countries' Pools, although this situation was remedied to some extent in the years following 1979. Responding to the great concern felt by the American nuclear industry, the Government, and the Nuclear Regulatory Commission in particular, the American Pools pledged themselves by one means or another to increase the potential insurance coverage to at least $1,000,000,000. Over the next few years, through a vigorous campaign amongst their own participating insurers, the reinsuring Pools and certain Reinsurance markets outside the nuclear pooling system, they succeeded in increasing their own primary capacity to about $500,000,000. The Utilities were also involved, and those which were not tied to the Nuclear Mutual Limited captive insurance company established their own as a means of contributing about another $500,000,000 to the general pool of capacity for American nuclear power stations. This was further topped-up by the establishment of a second layer of capacity by the American Pools to be brought in on an Excess of Loss basis above the aggregate amounts supplied by the Pools' primary layer plus the nuclear industry's secondary layer. Eventually the maximum potential limit under Physical Damage insurance in the USA was raised to more than $1,000,000,000. This capacity is not available for Business Interruption insurance.

Secondary Pool Capacity

The capacity subscribed to the net-line Pools all over the world was intended to be used as primary cover. It became apparent by the mid-1970's, but particularly after the TMI accident, that there were sources of secondary capacity or Excess of Loss reinsurance. This could be judged by the success of the American Pools in setting up a secondary layer within their own net-line system, and of the captive companies (of which more will be said later) in attracting such additional capacity from other markets including specialist reinsurance markets not involved in the national nuclear Pools. Their function as Excess reinsurers precluded them from participating in primary layers of insurance. A potent source of such reinsurance capacity was a specialised sector of the Lloyd's market, known as the LMX (= "London Market Excess").

There was some hestitation on the part of the BI(AE)C and others over seeking to follow the American example of establishing a second source of capacity, an Excess of Loss Pool, within their own membership because of fears that this might lead to a flight of capacity from the primary to the secondary layer. The assumption was that in spite of the evidence of the Three Mile Island loss, insurers would consider it unlikely that claims would reach such levels in the wake of a nuclear accident as to involve the secondary layer to any great extent. This, at any rate, swayed the British Advisory Committee against attempting to establish some Excess of Loss capacity for Material Damage risks on top of the basic Material Damage Pools when a proposal to that effect was considered at one stage. Subsequently, this decision was changed and the existing Pool participants were approached with a view to their subscribing to a second layer of capacity on the understanding that in so doing they would not deplete or terminate their subscriptions to the all-important primary layer. This produced a very limited response from

Companies, and none at all from Lloyd's where the specialist reinsurance sector had already decided to commit themselves to the support of the various captive insurance companies.

This question was subsequently considered by a Working Party of the Pools set up following the 1983 London Conference to examine the whole area of "self-insurance", captive companies and mutual associations and the development of nuclear capacity outside the net-line system. Here, it was considered that it should be possible for the Pools to supplement their primary capacity by tapping the Excess of Loss reinsurance facilities that were undoubtedly available elsewhere, although the first objective should be to increase the primary capacity. The conclusion was that it would be unwise to expect this move to generate any substantial amount of additional capacity but that the Pools should consider developing excess layers on the usual net-line basis providing this could be achieved without depleting the primary capacity which they saw as their first duty to provide for their clients.

It was this Working Party which extended earlier thinking on the possibilities of increasing the participation of the larger policy-holders, on a coinsuring basis, and developing partnerships on even a 50/50 basis. Large deductibles continued to be regarded with considerable caution although there was a readiness to contemplate the possibility of going as high as £25,000,000 in the case of large, very high-value installations where the insured would have the financial resources to meet at least that amount in the event of a serious accident. Nevertheless, voices were raised against such a concept, the view of some being that insurers may be placing themselves in an almost impossible position when seeking to meet repeated and often unreasonable demands for rate reductions on the grounds of good claims experience because large deductibles meant that the payment of small or moderate losses by insurers would be virtually eliminated.

Self-insurance by way of Mutual insurance schemes or Captive Companies

References have been made from time to time to the establishment of captives by groups of large electricity utilities. The first of these, Nuclear Mutual Limited of Bermuda, set up in 1973, has already been mentioned. This had the clear purpose of providing an alternative to normal insurance from the American Pools and of competing with them on rates. This Company insured only the nuclear power stations operated by the participating utilities, the number of which initially was about 14. They were able to set up a substantial fund over the years although their method of operating would be to pay claims on the basis of a post-accident assessment, which in the early years would mean making a levy on the participating utilities. Through good luck as much as good management, the NML has been able to develop very substantial resources sufficient to meet quite a large loss without straining their finances. They were also able to attract quite substantial reinsurance support without great difficulty since they only covered risks not insured with the ANI and MAERP, and their supporters were not therefore exposed to an accumulation of commitments as a result of their also being supporters of the Pools. For this very reason, there might have appeared to be possibilities of the Mutual providing reinsurance support to the Pools and of the Pools' reciprocating by providing reinsurance support where needed for the power stations within the NML sector. Certainly, in the early years, the Pools and NML regarded each other as strong competitors who could not be expected to collaborate. This is a situation which appears to have changed in recent times.

Two other Mutual insurance companies for the purpose of dealing with nuclear installations have been set up since 1979 in the USA by virtually all the American electricity utilities. These are known as NEIL I and NEIL II (NEIL stands for Nuclear Electrical Insurance Limited and like NML they are established in the British Crown Colony of Bermuda). NEIL I was set up rather urgently after the TMI loss in order to provide some protection to the General Purpose Utility Company who owned that station in regard to their heavy financial loss through the interruption of their business. Therefore, NEIL I provides insurance protection for Business Interruption risks for which there is no additional capacity available from the U.S. Pools.

NEIL II was developed somewhat later and works in collaboration with the U.S. Pools to provide a secondary layer of Material Damage capacity. It is through this organisation that the American nuclear industry has been able to provide the middle layer of the three-layer capacity set up by the American Pools in collaboration with NEIL II.

Apart from the USA, there are now two other captive companies providing additional capacity for nuclear installations although they confine their resources to Material Damage risks only. The first of these was established in 1978 by the Brussels-based International Union of Producers and Distributors of Electricity mentioned earlier — UNIPEDE. This was set up with the assistance of a large British firm of international insurance brokers who provide the management for the organisation and place their reinsurance needs. It is entitled the "European Mutual Association for Nuclear Insurance"

(EMANI) and is a mutual insurance association established under Belgian Law with its Head Office in Brussels. It was approved by Royal Decree on 20th October 1978 for the purpose of practising the insurance of fire and natural elements and other damage. Its declared object was to cover all or some of the risks of Material Damage in operating nuclear installations. Its rôle was not to compete with the Pools but rather to act in the capacity of coinsurer. It was considered that the Mutual would be a means of enlarging the capacity of the insurance market. Its founders saw this to be necessary because in some cases the capacity available from the international pooling system was substantially exceeded by the amount of cover required. This problem was expected to be exacerbated further with the growth in European countries and elsewhere in the levels of Liability insurance which the operators of nuclear installations were required to provide.

EMANI usually operates by providing a coinsurance policy alongside the policy written by the national pool concerned on the same terms and the same rates of premium. The insureds would then pay a rateable part of their premiums to EMANI who would, in their turn, pay them a rateable share of any claims. In the case of some of the Pools EMANI agreed to a small percentage of their share of the premiums being contributed to the administration costs borne by the original Pool although it apparently was left to the actual policyholder to decide whether or not this sum should be paid over to the national Pool concerned. Some refused to do so.

Initially, the shares of large nuclear installations insurances allocated to EMANI were very small as a percentage of the total because they had very limited capacity even including the reinsurance their Brokers were able to obtain for them. Their capacity, consisting of a combination of a small retained share contributed by the participating utility companies and a fairly substantial reinsurance obtained from Lloyd's and other reinsurance markets gradually increased. It took a spectacular leap upwards in 1985 as a result of a decision by the leading underwriters in the Lloyd's LMX market to give substantial support on an Excess of Loss reinsurance basis to EMANI: so much so, that by 1986 they were able to put together something like £50,000,000 of capacity consisting of their own Members' small contribution, a certain amount of reinsurance and a third layer of Excess of Loss reinsurance. In a number of the Material Damage insurances in which they were involved the capacity available from the Pools, particularly when the insured chose to have a limit in his policy below the maximum capacity available, was such that there was certainly no need for such a large contribution by way of coinsurance from EMANI. By developing their total resources they were going considerably beyond the original objective of only supplementing the capacity which the Pools could provide when this was not sufficient to meet the requirements of the policyholders. Nevertheless, the latter, as members of UNIPEDE and participants in the EMANI company insisted on increasing the percentage shares placed with EMANI, who are now therefore, in effect, in competition with the Pools for the proportion of those risks for which the Pools do not need as much support as EMANI insists upon providing.

This situation might make more sense if, when the amount of cover which could be provided by the combined resources of the Pools and EMANI and their reinsurers would enable cover to be written for a higher limit, some of the operators of the nuclear installations concerned would not insist on lower limits. In view of the constantly-voiced criticisms of the insurance market for not being able to provide for full cover or a larger percentage of the total values at risk, this is difficult to comprehend unless it is because they feel they are saving premium by so doing. Nevertheless, it makes the efforts of the Pools to respond to the demand for more and more capacity seem rather pointless if the capacity is not going to taken up.

EMANI is involved in only a proportion of the insured nuclear power stations in Europe: some of the Utilities do not belong to EMANI at all and therefore do not place any business with them; others do participate in EMANI but do not place business, either because they do not insure their nuclear power stations against Material Damage or they do not wish to involve EMANI.

The most recent captive insurance company set up for the purpose of providing Material Damage cover for nuclear power stations was established in 1986 in the Isle of Man as a result of a combined effort by the two British nationalised electricity producing and distributing corporations, the Central Electricity Generating Board and the South of Scotland Electricity Board. This is known as EPIC (Electricity Producers Insurance Company) and it deals with all types of power stations, not only nuclear ones. It confines its activities to the properties of the two Electricity Boards in Great Britain.

Quite unlike the other Mutuals that have been mentioned, although perhaps resembling NML to some extent, the objective of EPIC is to provide insurance covers at the primary layer for a substantial amount, reinsuring the Excess up to a fixed limit where the insurance values are beyond their own retention. Although the reinsurance is placed with a group of Companies, the major part of any reinsurance capacity required for the nuclear power stations can only come from the international pooling system. It is an unusual arrangement and EPIC are perhaps fortunate that the Pools are prepared to co-operate with their reinsurers instead of dealing directly with them.

Captive or mutual insurance companies set up by the electrical utilities or others are useful if they generate real additional net line capacity. If they obtain reinsurance protection from sources which do not retain their shares of nuclear risks wholly for their own account the confidence of insurers that the net line system is "leak-proof" will be undermined. Such a situation may be counter-productive for the Pools' efforts to increase their capacity.

Liability Capacity

Little has been said so far about the provision of capacity for Liability insurance on nuclear power stations. This is because until fairly recent times, the limits set by the Governments in their legislation in the field of nuclear liability were, in accordance with the spirit of the International Conventions, at a modest level. Generally speaking, these tended to average around £30,000,000 to £40,000,000 equivalent, although less in some cases, as in the U.K., where the statutory limit was no more than £5,000,000 until 1983. In the U.S.A., substantially higher limits were insured by the Pools, but they had always had a large capacity for Liability risks and were, in any event, not expected to provide cover beyond that which could be sustained by the available worldwide Liability insurance capacity. Consequently, while they were always anxious to improve their performance in this respect and for that reason sought as much additional capacity as they could obtain from the other Pools they were not faced with a critical problem nor, indeed, were any of the other Pools until in 1983 the Swiss Government decided to make a very substantial increase in the compensation limits payable by their nuclear operators under the Swiss Nuclear Law. Although most Pools have separate subscriptions for Material Damage and Liability risks, and in most cases for Transport risks, both Damage and Liability, the limits placed by individual Pool members on their subscriptions for the two main classes of insurance are obviously linked, because more probably than not, a serious Material Damage accident will involve a Liability claim as well. The reverse would certainly be true. The main difficulty is, and always has been, to provide adequate Material Damage capacity for large nuclear power stations and fuel factories which are extremely costly to build and to replace and which are growing in size and insurance value almost annually. This, together with inflation means that it is impossible for anyone to control the amount of insurance cover that is going to be needed to give adequate, if not full, protection against material damage risks. It seems to be unfortunate, therefore, that in the areas where the insurance requirement can be controlled, and that is in the field of nuclear liability, very large increases are being demanded by the legislators in a few countries which must have the inevitable effect of pulling down the capacity that could be made available to cover Material Damage losses and, of course, the associated Machinery Breakdown and Consequential Loss exposures.

In the Liability field, apart from the provision of Third Party cover to meet the requirements of the nuclear legislation and common law, the Pools do not face much demand for other classes of insurance except in North America and the United Kingdom. These other classes would include Product Liability for the manufacturers and suppliers of components and materials to nuclear installations, Errors & Omissions insurances for the designers of nuclear reactors and components and those who provide special inspection or maintenance services and the liabilities of contractors and others working on nuclear sites, Professional Indemnity insurances for Consultants and Advisers of various kinds. All of these may incur liabilities for which they have a legitimate insurance need which cannot be supplied by conventional insurers because of the nuclear risk element and the application to conventional policies of most of the types involved in providing such covers, of a nuclear exclusion clause. Cover for such contingent Liability risks can only be supplied by the nuclear Pools therefore out of their Liability capacity. In most countries the demands of the nuclear operators (which must obviously have priority) are not such as to exhaust the capacity available and therefore it is possible for the Pools who write or reinsure such risks to reserve a part of their capacity for the needs of such clients. Nevertheless, the amounts that can be provided would in some cases fall considerably short of the expectations of the individuals concerned in view of the very heavy damages that are awarded these days in the Courts to the victims of professional negligence.

Therefore, in considering the Liability capacity field, the whole picture, and not merely that related to the needs of the operators of nuclear installations, has to be borne in mind. As has been explained previously, the concept of channelling of all liability to the licensed operator of a nuclear installation does not remove the need for provision for contingent Liability insurances for other parties. Providing for these needs is an additional burden upon the capacity of the Pools, because in the event of a nuclear incident involving the liability of both the operator and the supplier of goods or services there could be an accumulation of claims under the different insurances which could not normally be subjected to a single overriding limit applicable to the various policies involved, although this situation may vary somewhat from one country to another.

Ways and means of increasing Pool capacity

From what has been said of the repeated efforts of the Pool Chairmen's Conferences and Working Parties to face up to the problem and to encourage all Pools to respond to the growing needs of their clients and if possible to improve upon past achievements, it will be apparent that the efforts directed towards this objective have been unremitting. This is certainly true on a national scale, and all Pools make an annual effort to increase the subscriptions of their members and indeed the numbers of their members by recruiting from reputable new companies or established companies which have hitherto hestitated to participate in the insurance of nuclear risks. On the other hand, equal attention is paid to ensuring that the membership of the Pool shall be of very good quality. Participating insurers must be fully authorised under the commercial and insurance laws of their countries. They must demonstrate their financial probity and solvency. They must in brief be able to pay their share of any losses at all times.

One of the factors facing the Pools is the natural caution of experienced and prudent underwriters, including those who have been participating in nuclear risks for many years, when they consider the possibilities of heavy losses; those who make the decisions must be assumed to be well-informed and objective and should certainly be given full information by their Pool managements. They are also human. They cannot shut their eyes to events like the Three Mile Island accident and the Chernobyl disaster and they must weigh up the possible impact on their own financial position should they be called upon to pay a share of such a claim. It has to be remembered also that the premiums contributed to their general income by their participation in the insurance of nuclear risks represents only a tiny proportion of their business, whereas potential losses are disproportionately large. Therefore, the cost of a claim could have an impact on their general business and this for many companies in recent years has not been running very profitably in either the Property Damage or the Liability branches on account of excess capacity and severe rate cutting — a situation that cannot last.

The unremitting search for ways and means of developing capacity on a net-line basis involving reputable insurers and reinsurers has produced a number of useful ideas, some of which were recommended to the Pool Chairmen's Conference in 1983 as a result of the efforts of a Working Party appointed at the previous Conference and which held meetings in Zurich under the Chairmanship of the Swiss Pool, and in Brussels under the Chairmanship of the President of the Belgian Pool.

The recommendations were forward looking and not merely pre-occupied with the merits of the Pools as the only way of adding to the insurance capacity, and commended such new ideas as the need to explore additional markets which would be willing to accept the net-line principle and able to guarantee financial security, including the surplus and excess line markets and individual companies in countries without nuclear Pools (although it would usually be regarded as preferable if those companies and their Markets could set themselves up as a net-line Pool or Association similar to those in other countries). The Life Assurance Companies were felt to be a possible source of additional capacity, having in mind that in the United States some of them had committed their capacity to the Pools through the Casualty Companies. Another possible source of supprt was seen to be the State-owned monopoly insurance companies in the Centrally-Planned Economies (to use the IAEA term) or Socialist countries such as the Peoples Republic of China, the USSR, and other such countries without competitive insurance markets. Attention was also directed to the developing insurance markets in Asia, the Pacific Basin and the Middle East.

It seemed likely that a number of the members of individual Pools could be persuaded to be a little more venturesome in their approach to the insurance of nuclear risks, since it was apparent that the response of individual participants in terms of their potential varied considerably. It was found that only a minority of Pools offered guidelines for the determination of subscriptions to the Pool.

The contributions of individual Members to their national Pools when related to understandable bench marks such as their gross non-Life premium income, their reserves or assets, or the maximum net loss they would accept for some conventional form of catastrophe such as a windstorm disaster, were found to vary considerably. The judgement to be made by the individual underwriters, managers or Boards of Directors in determining how much they should contribute to their national Pool for nuclear risks insurance on a net-line basis is a personal matter, and there could be no question of issuing any directions as to how they should make their decisions. However, it was felt that if some of these findings could be brought to the attention of the responsible senior management, including the apparent fact that the bigger Pools were producing rather less impressive performances in proportion to their size and the resources of their Members than the smaller Pools, it may be that there could be some relaxation of the restraints being imposed on the maximum net lines available to the Pools.

It was noted that there were usually, though not in every case, wide variations between the size of the capacity contributed by Pool Members for domestic risks compared with those available for the reinsurance of foreign risks. This was understandable to some extent, particularly in the case of insurance markets which are not accustomed to taking substantial shares of foreign business through their reinsurance or coinsurance operations in the conventional fields of business. Nevertheless, it was felt that a greater degree of parity and more flexibility was a reasonable aim.

Reinsurance and Coinsurance

The worldwide capacity for Material Damage risks has been estimated at £350,000,000 to £450,000,000 in 1987. The Liability capacity by the same token would be in the region of £100,000,000 to £200,000,000. These figures pre-suppose that the maximum possible capacity will be harnessed and they must take account of the extremely wide variations in the input that individual Pools can apply to their own risks owing to the wide disparities in the resources of the national insurance markets which have set up nuclear Pools.

Inter-pool reinsurance is a vital part of the picture. Except in the case of the business offered by the American Pools, of which more will be said later, every Pool is able to consider each case individually, on its merits, on the basis of information which can be, and should be, as full as they desire. There is a strong presumption amongst the Pools that they will support each other with their maximum available capacity in any case which meets the generally-accepted criteria in terms of quality, and for which the policy conditions and rates of premium lie within broadly accepted tolerances. No Pool is obliged to accept a risk which they do not like; no Pool is expected to make available to every individual country the same amount of reinsurance. Judgements will be made in this respect, having regard to the experience of the members of a particular Pool in underwriting risks in some of the more distant parts of the world, or lack of experience. Political and economic stability in a particular country may well be a factor. Many Pool Members would also have regard to the amount of ordinary business in which they are able to participate in a particular country when determining or influencing their managements as to the possible need for certain limitations in particular countries compared with others. In some cases the reinsurance capacity offered will be affected by the scope of the insurance. It might be reduced if the perils insured include such items as Earthquake, Windstorm and Volcanic Eruption, for example. Some Pools reduce their participation below their normal percentage because they are not satisfied with the premiums offered. Others, including the British Pool, would regard this as somewhat illogical: if the terms offered to the reinsurer are regarded as unsatisfactory it does not seem good sense to accept a reduced share nevertheless, and along with it a reduced share of an inadequate premium.

Since inter-pool reinsurance transactions (except for American business) are on a facultative basis, every Pool is entitled to consider each request for reinsurance support strictly on its merits. While it is in the interests of all parties concerned for insurers to maximise the capacity they can offer collectively, Pools cannot be undiscriminating in the way in which they utilise the subscriptions of their participating insurers. They are obliged to accept their percentage share of every insurance or reinsurance written on their behalf by their Management Committee and the Pool administrators to whom they have given the necessary powers of acceptance and rating. Since the individual Pool Members cannot pick and choose between the risks accepted on their behalf, they are entitled to look for a growing premium and ever-widening spread of risks if they are to respond positively to annual demands for higher and higher capacity. By maintaining, and if possible increasing, their reinsurance cessions to other Pools each national Pool can make a valuable contribution to the achievement of these objectives, but this may in itself pose a dilemma for the larger Pools with substantial capacity and high retention limits. Their Members are not likely to be satisfied if they do not make full use of their domestic capacity first, taking up reinsurance from other Pools only when theirs has been fully deployed. It is understandable that the Members of each national Pool wish to retain for their own benefit as much as possible of the premium generated by their domestic business, while at the same time increasing their income from other countries. It may sometimes be acceptable to cede larger shares of a Pool's own risks than is strictly necessary from the point of view of their own retention limits. Flexibility in this respect may be politic for a Pool with a limited amount of business to offer to other Pools, both because they are writing relatively few nuclear installation insurances and because of their own large domestic capacity.

Reciprocity, in the sense of achieving a balance in the amounts of business ceded and received through inter-Pool reinsurance is a reasonable objective, but in most cases impossible to achieve. This is because some of the Pools which pay out the largest proportions of their premiums to reinsuring Pools do so for the simple reason that their own capacity is relatively small. Consequently, their ability to accept large shares of another country's risks is very limited. Reciprocity is, therefore, only a practical prospect where a small Pool is exchanging business with a large Pool which has a very substantial number of risks on its books, small shares of which will produce in the aggregate a substantial reinsurance premium for the small reinsuring Pool.

Another consideration which must weigh heavily with Pools reinsuring substantial portions of their business, is the del credere risk which their Members must carry. While it is almost inconceivable that a Pool set up and supported by the national insurance market of any country is likely to fail to meet its obligations as a reinsurer, it cannot be ruled out, particularly in the case of countries which may be subject to serious political or economic instability. Even so, since they started discussing these matters together in 1958, the Pools have been concerned to ensure that by one means or another the default of individual Pool Members would not be permitted to reduce the ability of a national Pool to meet its obligations towards other Pools. The basis on which the participating insurers are committed differs from country to country. In some their responsibility is both joint and several; in others it is only several. There is a general commitment amongst the Pools to ensure that their obligations are fully met, but the means by which they achieve this is considered to be a domestic matter. This is a particularly important question for the smaller Pools, who are obliged to cede a very high percentage of their risks because of their own limited capacity. This obviously exposes their participating insurers to a potential commitment, even if somewhat theoretical, of many times their net line should the reinsurance from other Pools fail to materialise or, for some reason, their contributions to loss payments cannot be collected. It is hardly conceivable that even in the worst imaginable circumstances a small Pool which may have to cede 90% or more of its risk to others would not be able to collect in the event of a big loss. Nevertheless the possibility cannot be ruled out, and even a relatively small deficiency on the part of the reinsuring Pools, or some of their Members, if not safeguarded against could pose serious problems. Various measures can be taken to mitigate the risk. These may include the conclusion of formal bilateral reinsurance agreements between individual Pools under which it may be possible to ensure that in the event of a significant accident occurring they will send a deposit based upon their share of the estimated loss; or that they will provide Letters of Credit on an acceptable bank. Such agreements may well be very much in line with conventional reinsurance practice.

Another protection adopted by some of the Pools, including the

British, is to limit the extent to which reinsurance may be taken up from other Pools. The Pool's Management Agreement or Constitution may contain a prohibition against the placing of, say, more than two, three or four times the net retention of the Pool. The drawback to this method of protecting the Members of the Pool against an excessive del credere risk is that it limits the ability of that Pool to make full use of worldwide reinsurance capacity when this exceeds the stated multiple of the original Pool's own capacity.

Reinsurance of American Risks

The American Pools were first in the field with the writing of substantial nuclear insurance business and the need to take up reinsurance from other markets because, when they started, there were no Pools actively in operation in other countries. They obtained their reinsurance, as mentioned earlier, by offering quota sharing treaties to the traditional reinsurance markets elsewhere. Their traditional supporters were the London Market, with a large contribution coming from Lloyd's Underwriters. Support was also available to them through the American organisations of leading foreign companies, particularly British, who were able to participate directly in the American Joint Stock Companies Pool (ANI). By operating on a Treaty basis, the American Pools were spared the need to place each individual risk facultatively and the role of the placing insurance brokers was limited to making an annual approach to the underwriters and companies by offering a Slip based upon the terms of the Treaty. Even when the majority of the Markets from which they were obtaining reinsurance support had established net-line Pools, the use of reinsurance brokers as intermediaries continued — at some cost to ANI, since they had to pay reinsurance commission. This continued until a few years ago when the anomaly of operating through brokers — whereas all other Pools were able to carry out their international reinsurance business on a direct Pool to Pool basis — became unacceptable, and the broking operation was amicably brought to an end.

This, however, did not apply to the London Market. The placing of reinsurance on behalf of the American Pools in the London Market preceded the setting up of the British Pool. When this was achieved, in December 1957, the wish of those concerned was not to disturb the direct reinsurance relationship established by the Lloyd's Underwriters and the Companies participating in the American Slip which was working well. This arrangement continued for many years, although it meant that the British Pool were the odd men out in that they had no reinsurance relationship with the

American Pools. This suited the participants who had become used to the arrangement, particularly Lloyd's Underwriters, and the BI(AE)C because some of the methods followed by the American Pools were incompatible with the practices and policies laid down over the years by the Management Committee of the British Pool. The most important difference was that they were pledged to operate reinsurance on a strictly facultative basis enabling them to decide whether or not they would accept any particular foreign risk offered to them. This also involved the right to demand full technical and underwriting information from the ceding Pool in any case on which they required it. Under the American Treaty arrangements there would be no possibility of exercising choice nor, indeed, of scrutinising the premium rates and other conditions in every individual case although in practice the Americans used standard policy conditions and their rates were broadly in line with an established Guide. A further difficulty was that all Physical Damage insurances written by the American Pools were on an All Risks basis, which the British Pool's Management Committee had never regarded with favour.

There were other practical difficulties in the way of extending the Foreign Risks sections of the British Pool to embrace American risks, one of these being that the amount of capacity available for other countries could not be applied to the USA, partly because some of the largest Company participants were already fully commited through their American organisations to a direct participation in ANI. Another reason was that quite a number of the Companies participating in the General Foreign Risks section of the British Pool did not wish to write American risks. Those who did were not prepared to commit as much capacity for various reasons, among these being that they had in many instances suffered poor experience in relation to their conventional American business and were apprehensive of extending their nuclear commitments to that country. Another possibility might have been to extend BI(AE)C's Canadian Risks Pool, which was for a substantially smaller amount of capacity than for foreign risks in general, mainly because of the direct commitment through their participation in the Canadian market of a number of Companies and Lloyd's Underwriters to the Nuclear Insurance Association of Canada.

A consideration was that if the British Pool's Management Committee did decide to set up an American section, the Lloyd's Underwriters concerned in the existing reinsurance arrangements did not wish to alter these. Consequently, they would not be able to participate and thus the existing combined Company/Lloyd's Market Pool could not insure American risks. However, a number of the leading Companies, including some who were not participating in American risks to the full extent of their capabilities, were for various reasons not satisfied with the arrangements available under the London Slip. They were strongly of the opinion that support for the American Pools should be arranged on a normal net-line pooling basis. The American Pools themselves were not averse to such a development.

Thus a new Pool was established in 1985 with a completely separate membership from the main Pool, restricted to Companies, with its own Management Agreement and its own Management Committee. With respect to the problems which would have inhibited the extension of the main Pool to the USA, they were able to take a fresh look at the situation and to seek the specific approval of the prospective members of the new Pool to departing from certain essential principles in relation to such questions as the acceptance of a quota-sharing Treaty arrangement in place of facultative reinsurance and certain other systems peculiar to American practice and which if the Pool was ever to do business with ANI and MAERP would obviously have to be accepted.

Thus it was that for the purpose of reinsuring American risks (although in principle they could be written direct if this ever became necessary) the Company market established the British Insurance (Atomic Energy) Committee for American Risks (to accept reinsurance as from 1st January 1986) which now provides reinsurance cover to the U.S. Pools on a normal direct Pool-to-Pool basis.

Currency Problems

In the early years of the Pools, exchange rates were relatively steady for most countries, although some currencies were very much stronger than others. However, the relationship between the hard currencies like the American Dollar, the German Mark and the Swiss Franc and others were fairly stable until countries such as the United Kingdom became obliged in the late 1960's and beyond to de-value their currencies very considerably. In the ensuing years, considerable volatility has grown up in relation to the relative strengths of many of the important currencies, including the U.S. Dollar, and this has played havoc with the reinsurance capability of some of the Pools in relation to others. However vigorously the national Pools may pursue their objective of increased capacity, which is almost invariably subscribed in their own currency, it is impossible for the annual increases to keep in step with the rapid appreciation of some of the major currencies in which the large nuclear power stations and other installations are insured. Japan is a very good case in point.

This is a country with a large and growing number of very important nuclear power stations for which the operators seek the maximum possible cover. The Japanese Pool are naturally most anxious to meet these requirements as fully as they can. Although a strong Pool, they depend on a substantial amount of reinsurance support from the other Pools around the world. The value of the Yen has appreciated enormously in recent years. In 1972, the year in which the BI(AE)C sent its first delegation to visit the Japanese Pool, the exchange rate was approximately 1,000 Yen to the Pound Sterling. 15 years later, the rate was less than 250 Yen. Even though the capacity of the British Pool has grown very significantly over these 15 years, it could not be increased by as much as 300%. Therefore the value to the Japanese Pool of the British Pool's reinsurance support, large though it is in Sterling terms, has dropped considerably. The same situation arises in other countries, although the Japanese are perhaps in the most unfortunate position because not only has their currency increased greatly in value, but one of their principal sources of reinsurance support, the American Pools, have seen the U.S. Dollar dropping substantially.

The situation is universal — it is not a peculiarity of the insurance of nuclear risks, although it is exacerbated by the fact that the Pools provide their capacity on a net-line basis and cannot therefore cover themselves against currency fluctuations by utilising any form of reinsurance. Rapid movements in exchange rates create other problems. The share of a risk in a strong currency country such as Japan, Germany or Switzerland, which a particular reinsuring Pool is able to accept at the outset of the insurance period concerned, would certainly be within their capacity calculated in their own currency; but if the foreign currency in which the insurance is written appreciates during the year, that limit will clearly be exceeded. It is the accepted practice that reinsurers honour their commitments, notwithstanding the effect of fluctuating exchange rates, until such time as they can re-arrange their participation. Nevertheless, when the increase in the commitment in the national currency is substantial, this puts the reinsuring Pool in a difficulty vis-à-vis the obligation to ensure that a Member's *financial* limitation on his participation in the Pool shall not be exceeded. To safeguard against this eventuality, a number of the Pools nowadays have had to adopt the expedient of maintaining a margin between the capacity they have for foreign risks and the amount they actually offer to a foreign Pool in case the exchange rate moves against them. This is not satisfactory because it means that if the expected currency movements do not take place, that margin of capacity is in a sense being wasted.

There is no simple answer to this problem other than the

achievement of much greater stability in exchange rates which only Governments and the international organisations concerned with monetary affairs can tackle. Nevertheless, for some countries it is obstructing the maximisation of inter-Pool capacity which is so badly needed. If any means can be found of relieving the situation there is not doubt that, with the degree of co-operation and collaboration which the Pools have achieved over the years, they will surely do their best to find an answer.

CHAPTER X

ANALYSING AND ASSESSING THE RISKS

The risks associated with nuclear energy, the potential cost of damage to plant and to the environment and the burdens imposed by the exceptional legal obligations which have to be covered by Insurers mean that they must be able to assess most thoroughly and expertly every aspect affecting the commitments they are called upon to assume. This demands the provision of very detailed information by the concern to be insured and by the Insurers' own engineers and risk surveyors. This data must be analysed by professional specialists capable of presenting objective reports and evaluations which can be interpreted and priced by those who must prepare the insurance contracts and calculate rates and premiums.

With so much at stake if there is an accident, there can be no justification for being satisfied with superficial data or adopting blanket methods which neither heed significant facts nor differentiate between the characteristics of the various reactors and installations, locations, operating experience and commercial considerations.

The basis of the assessment must always be a full and accurate statement of information, backed by on-site inspection and discussion whenever possible, and access to technical data such as the Official Safety Report or Hazards Analysis that has to be compiled by the designers, constructors and operators of every nuclear installation before it gains Government approval in whatever country it is located.

Information required

In the first place insurers and their experts will focus their attention on the reactor when that is the central feature as it will be of almost all the establishments to be insured. The minimum information required in the case of power producing reactors by a Pool's technical experts will be as follows:

Technical Data

I   **Details of Reactor**

(a)   Type and purpose (including details of experiments if these are planned)

(b)   If reactor is a prototype or, if of approved design, whether new features have been incorporated. If similar to existing types these should be cited.

(c)   A general description of the reactor, including details of the core pressure vessel, core configuration.

(d)   Particulars of the primary, secondary and other coolant circuits, including general details of any circulators or pumps, pressure vessels, heat exchangers, turbines and any other plant in the circuit.

(e)   Description of the control rod operation system under normal operating conditions and details of their operation during "scram". Details of any other reactivity control arrangements should also be given.

(f)   Details of signals causing reactor "scram".

(g)   Details of containment systems, including design pressures, temperatures and leak rates.

(h)   Full particulars of the major accidents considered in the official hazards report, together with the relevant details on powers, temperatures, pressures and the consequences involved including estimates of the possible fission products released.

(i)   Details of the fuel charge and discharge arrangements — on-load or off-load refuelling.

(j)   Details of any auxiliary circuits affecting safety, such as:-
          (i) Core flooding system
          (ii) Core spray system
          (iii) Poison injection system
          (iv) Clean-up circuits etc.

(k)   Particulars of the electrical supply to the reactor and its auxiliary equipment and details of emergency electrical supply arrangements.

II   Reactor Parameters

The following details are required as a minimum:-

(a)   Thermal power output

(b)   Electrical power output

(c)   Particulars of coolant with temperature and pressures

(d)   Details of fuel with enrichment and details of canning

(e)   Temperature reached during service by fuel and canning

(f)   Control rods — number, material, individual reactivity investment

(g)   Moderator data

(h)   Reflector data

(i)   Full details of reactivity balance including control rod negative reactivity investment

(j)   Expected values of nuclear coefficients.

For other types of nuclear reactors (e.g. research) the list would be suitably amended. It is irrelevant to fuel factories.

Material Damage and Liability Insurances

The basic underwriting information would, typically, be arranged in accordance with the following pattern based upon the "Questionnaires" devised internationally in the early days, mentioned previously. (A single form is used because some of the details relate to both forms of cover). It should be suitably modified for "non-reactor" establishments.

"UNDERWRITING QUESTIONNAIRE"

(A)   General Details

1.   Name of

    (a) Operator

    (b) Owner (if different)

    (c) Principal Contractor

2.   Full address of the installation

3.   Details of the purpose of the installation (including processes and uses for which it is intended).

4.   Estimated dates of

    (a) arrival on site of nuclear fuel or materials

    (b) start of loading fuel in reactor

    (c) reaching criticality

    (d) handing over by Contractors to Operators (if this is after criticality a note of the legal position between parties to be included).

(B) Site

5. General geographical and hydrographical description of the terrain, including meteorological conditions, with history of windstorms, floods and earthquakes

    NOTE: A copy of the detailed report leading to the selection of this site should be attached, if available.

6. General description of the surroundings, i.e.

    (a) Adjacent towns and villages including distances

    (b) Population

    (c) Water courses, canals, rivers, lakes, reservoirs or sea

    (d) Nature and approximate values of neighbouring properties and land

    (e) Regular aircraft routes and nearest airfield/airport.

    NOTE: An extract from a map of the district should be attached (with scale used).

(C) The buildings

7. Description of each range of buildings, type of construction, use, processes, plant and other property on the site.

    NOTE:
    (i) Full details should be given of reactor buildings, "Hot" and "Cold" laboratories (including nature of work done), process buildings, and nuclear fuel stores.
    (ii) Brief details of "non-nuclear" buildings will suffice,
    (iii) A site plan showing lay-out and North Point, with scale used, should be attached.

(D) The Reactor(s)

8. (a) Name of reactor type.

    (b) Name of manufacturer and supplier.

    (c) Detailed description including thermal capacity, type of fuel, moderator, coolant, operating temperature and pressure, safety devices, biological shielding, containment vessel.

9. Name of Licensing Authority

10. Details of Code of Practice or Rules of Operation including
    (a) by whom prepared
    (b) features covered thereby
    (c) whether it is mandatory
    NOTE: A copy should be attached if available.

(E) Other Nuclear Equipment

11. Details and location of critical and sub-critical assemblies, particle accelerators, separation plant and other nuclear equipment, including purpose of their presence.

(F) Nuclear Fuel

12. (a) Type, with degree of enrichment, and material used for cladding
    (b) Name of supplier
    (c) Quantity in reactor
    (d) Quantity in storage with storage arrangements and location
    (e) Arrangements for removal from reactor, cooling and storage of irradiated fuel
    (f) Re-processing arrangements

(G) Other Hazardous Nuclear or Non-Nuclear Substances

13. (a) Description, quantity, location and storage arrangements
    (b) Uses of such substances.

(H) Radioactive Waste

14. Details of disposal or storage arrangements for waste materials on the site and also when discharged from the site
    (a) solid
    (b) liquid
    (c) gaseous

(I) Safety Features

15. Details not included under other headings, e.g.

(a) Air monitoring and sampling

(b) Health inspections of personnel and visitors

(c) Security of radioactive zones on the site, and of nuclear fuel stores, from unauthorised persons including thieves and terrorists

(d) Authority for safety and frequency of official inspections by such authority.

NOTE: Confirmation should be obtained that suitable records are made and retained of the results of such operations and official inspections (including, for personnel, health records of previous employment involving radiation hazards).

(e) Details of emergency plans made for dealing with a nuclear incident should be given.

(f) Results of any probabilistic or source term assessment.

(J) Staff

17. Details of experience in handling nuclear reactors and materials of
(i) Physicists, chemists, engineers
(ii) others who control personnel

18. Details of safety committees and other arrangements to ensure control of reactor operation and other hazardous nuclear operations by properly trained personnel including, for example, duty rosters.

(K) Material Damage Insurance Details

19. Name(s) of parties to be insured

20. Commencing date and renewal or expiry date

21. Estimated full value of property to be insured and basis of valuation for each separate building or range of buildings (identified by plan references or description), subdivided under the following headings

Plan ref (or description)	Buildings	Nuclear Fuel	Plant, equipment & other contents	Total Value

22. Details of supplementary cover (with amounts) required in respect of
    (i) cost of decontamination of surrounding property belonging to the Insured (giving description and full value thereof) and decontamination of land roads and paths on the site of the installation
    (ii) cost of isolation and/or removal of radioactive debris
    (iii) other costs (to be specified)

(L) Liability Insurance Details

23. Details of any nuclear legislation on liability for damage to property or injury to persons

    NOTE: A copy of the relevant law should be attached.

24. Nature of cover (if any) required in respect of injury to employees, including right of recourse (if any) by government or private insurers of workmen's compensation and/or employer's liability.

25. (a) Limit of liability required to be insured under nuclear legislation (if any)

    (b) Limit of Liability to be covered in respect of non-nuclear accidents (and also for nuclear accidents if there is no nuclear legislation applicable.)

    NOTE: Details of any sub-limits, e.g. for any one person, which apply in the country concerned, should be given.

    (c) Limit, if any, on legal and other costs if not normally included under (a) and (b) above.

26. Details of official Emergency Plan.

Machinery Breakdown Insurance

Where specialised Pool Machinery Breakdown cover is required (confined to the High Radioactivity Zone in most countries) the basic underwriting data would need to be supplemented on the following lines:

1) Detailed list of each item to be insured including Replacement Value as new.

2) Full loss experience including cause, extent and whether plant repaired or replaced since completion of the station including

pre-acceptance test and any operating period. If plant insured at time then full details of insurers' name and claims reference to be submitted.

3) Full details of any known defect at the time of the enquiry.

4) Overall plan and elevation drawings of the buildings and containment vessel.

5) Regular inspection programme carried out by the licensing authorities and/or insurers for the items to be covered.

In the light of the information supplied, further details may be called for.

Where items in the Low Radioactivity Zone are to be included the above list would provide the necessary information. However when an "All Risks" type of policy is issued as in Canada or the USA, this could embrace also boilers and other pressure vessels, turbines, alternators and so on which would require the same special inspection and report as for such conventional property anywhere (Comments on "zoning" will be given later).

Except where machinery breakdown cover for nuclear power stations is an integral part of the "All Risks" form of physical damage insurance (as habitually provided in North America but elsewhere only, and very recently, in the United Kingdom) there has been little demand for this specialised form of insurance.

Other classes

Two other classes of insurance related to damage and liability risks may be written by most of the Pools, notably Consequential Loss, Business Interruption, and Suppliers Liability, including professional indemnities. The type of information that should be assembled before these aspects can be assessed will be described later but before going further it would be useful to comment on some key aspects of the details required for the main classes of Material Damage and Liability insurance.

Some comments on key items in the information required (Numbers correspond to those in the "Questionnaire").

Question (A)   Dates

The various *dates* are particularly important in the case of a new reactor installation because it is necessary to have a clear demarcation between the ending of the policy covering the construction risk (unless this is provided by the Pool itself) and the beginning of the Pool

Material Damage and Liability policies. With a large complex, particularly a power station, the phasing out of the CAR insurance and the phasing in of the Pool insurances may be done in steps if there is a staggered handover of the completed property and plant by the contractors to the operators.

Question (B)   Site

The *siting* of a nuclear installation is of the greatest importance. Owing to the strict controls imposed by the Safety Authorities in all countries, the site will undoubtedly have been selected with very great care, especially in a country which may be prone to severe weather, earthquakes and volcanic eruptions. Proximity to the sea or rivers which may overflow and cause flooding is also important, on both the Material Damage and the Liability side. Floods could be a means of spreading radioactive matter which has escaped from its proper containment. Location is clearly a crucial question from the point of view of Third Party Liability because the nearness of centres of population or industry or important agricultural or silvicultural areas can greatly influence the judgement of underwriters as to the possibility of numerous claims arising in the event of an escape of radioactivity from the site. Water courses, rivers and the like can be a means of spreading fission products much more widely if nearby. The sea may always be a means of spreading radioactive matter along a coastline and this may cause problems to a fishing industry or populations dependent on fish for food which could add to the potential burden of claims for damages.

Seismological and geological reports must also be examined to enable the risks of earthquake, subsidence, landslip etc. to be evaluated in relation to the site of the nuclear installation whether or not these perils are to be specifically insured.

Information about *aircraft routes* and the proximity of airfields is important not simply because of the possibility of such property suffering damage but also because of the risk of damage to the plant through crashing aircraft or objects falling from them. It should be said, however, that in most countries the overflying of major nuclear installations is prohibited and this should be looked into when obtaining underwriting information.

Question (C)   Buildings

Apart from details of the *buildings,* plant, processes and materials that may be on the site supplied by the insured or his representative, insurers will almost invariably require to make their own site inspection and their surveyor's plan and report would cover all this information in the manner required.

Question (D)   Reactor(s)

Technical details of the *reactors* are absolutely vital and must be very full indeed. As mentioned earlier, such information should be readily available from the Safety Reports and other official documents which have to be prepared to satisfy the Licensing Authority. It is useful to know something about the *Licensing Authority* because that may assist Insurers to make a judgement as to how strict the controls are likely to be, since national practices vary in this connection. Rules of operation or codes of practice are likewise highly important, and these would almost certainly be obtained by the inspecting engineer who, when visiting the site, should have discussions with the operators and perhaps the constructors of the plant.

The other details covered under Sections (E), (F), (G) and (H) in the Questionnaire are self explanatory.

Question (I)   Safety

The detailed *Safety* features sought under Item 15 are plainly of the greatest importance, particularly from the point of view of public safety and the safety and protection of persons working on the site. The keeping of records of individual personnel showing their exposure to radiation, much of which may be perfectly safe and within the normal requirements of their work, is essential, as are records of any monitoring or air-sampling of the environment that may be maintained as a routine practice regardless of whether there are any untoward incidents. Such records are important from the point of view of prospective delayed claims from persons who may receive a dose of radiation, whether as a result of an accidental or intentional release of radioactivity. Such records almost certainly will be rigorously maintained in all countries and carefully stored until the periods allowed for the bringing of claims following an incident have been exhausted. (In practice, in almost every country the State is responsible for providing compensation to victims whose right to compensation from the operator or his insurers has expired under the usual 10-year prescription rule so it is very likely that local regulations will require such records to be maintained for very many years, possibly permanently).

Question (J)   Staff

Details of staff and their qualifications and experience are very important indeed, a point strongly emphasised by the TMI and Chernobyl accident histories. Operating methods are also an important factor to consider from the point of view of the safety of the plant, not the least being the numbers of personnel, both graduate engineers and other technicians on duty at any one time, especially overnight.

Question (K)   Material Damage details

A detailed specification of every building and its contents, stores, equipment and above all their individual values, is of great importance for Material Damage insurance. A separate valuation of the nuclear fuel is also necessary and the considerations relating to this will be referred to later. The provision of a detailed list of the buildings and contents should be regarded as a normal obligation. Some of the nuclear Pools appear to find difficulty in obtaining proper information, particularly when it comes to specifying the individual insurance values. Providing such information should not be difficult and all the Pools have the means of giving advice and guidance based upon some detailed studies undertaken by one of their Working Parties which will be referred to later. Consequently, Insurers are entitled to insist upon this information and should not be dissuaded on the grounds that it is too complicated or expensive to provide. A blanket value covering the whole of a nuclear installation or even one large section of it such as the nuclear island is not satisfactory: at the very least, there should be a split between the main zones of a large installation, the fuel values and any additional cost items.

If there are any good reasons for not insisting upon a full value insurance with detailed breakdown of values, a First Loss or, as it is known in some countries, a First Risk cover may be acceptable to insurers providing a realistic value can be established. This should normally be related to the maximum foreseeable loss as assessed by the experts, although if capacity imposes limitations it may have to be fixed at the maximum obtainable, and rated on a normal First Loss insurance basis.

Details of the *Additional Expenses* for which supplementary cover may be required, as called for under Item 22 in Question (K) are nowadays regarded as much more important than they used to be.

Because the costs of cleaning up after a nuclear incident may be very heavy and quite out of proportion to the initial damage in many cases, it is vitally important to know exactly what costs associated with these operations are to be specified and included in the cover. As actual experience and the technical studies mentioned earlier have demonstrated, decontamination and the associated operations can be extremely expensive and may greatly exceed the value of the property damaged or destroyed. The insurers and their clients must be absolutely clear as to the basis on which such expenses are to be settled and, therefore to be insured, and in particular the amount for which they are to be insured. This may be a fixed First Loss amount; it may be for a special sub-limit within the overall policy limit; or it may be for an indeterminate amount subject only to the annual aggregate loss limit of the policy. (In view of the high importance of this subject, further comments will be included later in this Chapter under a separate section).

The question of any other Additional Costs to be covered is also important, although the sums involved are likely to be far less than in the case of decontamination. It may be that the policy will be so worded that expenses such as architects' and surveyors' fees, removal of debris which is not contamined by radioactivity, replacement of records and similar extra costs are to be included within the overall cover, without specific limit. On the other hand, they may need to be separately specified for an agreed amount or percentage. This may be necessary in the case of extra expense which might need to be incurred in order to complete any necessary repairs or replacements within a definite time scale: i.e. the insurers may agree to pay certain additional labour costs if overtime is to be worked or cover may be granted for "expediting expenses". These would represent the extra cost of delivering urgently required spare parts by means, for example, of air-freighting.

The intended scope of cover in relation to eventual expenses of this nature will doubtless be apparent from the wording of the policy (which will be discussed in the final Chapter). If they are to be the subject of an extension under the policy, then they must be properly itemised and valued.

Question (L)   Liability details

Most of the details called for in relation to *Liability* insurance will be self-explanatory. However, one point which needs further attention is the question of the payment of claims arising from intentional releases of radioactivity from the nuclear site. These may occur quite properly within the course of normal operations, providing they are in accordance with the terms of the operating licence and within the permitted safe levels. On the other hand, intentional releases may occur as a result of unauthorised practices not amounting to an accidental occurrence. Ideally, insurers will wish to exclude totally any liability for such releases but may not be able to do so if, in order to be acceptable as a financial security, the policy has to match fully the obligations of the nuclear operator under his national legislation. If, as is to be hoped, a right of recovery for claims paid under this heading can be negotiated with the policyholder, then in determining the insurance limits and other similar factors it would be necessary to be clear as to whether this may be for 100% of claims paid or whether the insured will be willing to meet a percentage of such claims or up to a certain limit, or conversely, whether the insurers would meet the excess of such claims beyond a figure to be set by agreement.

Decommissioning

There is a relatively new aspect of Material Damage and Liability insurance cover particularly in the case of ageing or obsolescent reactor installations which the Pools have explored. This relates to *decommissioning,* that is to say, the procedures involved in the final shutdown and eventual mothballing (or cocooning), dismantling or entombment of a nuclear installation, particularly a reactor. When this procedure is to be carried out, normally as a planned end-of-life operation, it is more than likely that the Pool Material Damage and Liability policies will have to continue for some time although the risk would have to be newly assessed and rated. The normal underwriting information enquiry form would not cover this because it is designed to deal with new installations.

However, there is an aspect which has to be considered: that is the insurance of costs involved in the decommissioning process which may be very heavy and possibly as high as the original construction costs. When the procedure is pre-planned following the final shutdown of an old plant, insurance of such costs would not be a question for an ordinary Material Damage Policy but it may be reasonable for insurers to consider providing for such costs when they occur unexpectedly as a consequence of an accident. In such circumstances, the operations involved in *premature* decommissioning may be very expensive indeed. If, therefore, there is any question of making provision for such additional costs, this point must be borne in mind when underwriting information is obtained. More details of the whole question of decommissioning operations and their cost will be given later.

Premature decommissioning does not appear to call in question the continuation of the Liability insurance because the installation operator, or whoever be licensed to undertake the decommissioning procedures, will continue to require insurance or other financial security in accordance with national nuclear law. Here again, the ordinary underwriting information questionnaire would not cover the situation and special enquiries would have to be made as to the nature of the work and the potential hazards which may be considerable, particularly for employees and other workers. If some form of dismantling is to be undertaken, insurers will also need to know what limits will be required to be insured on a per incident/per installation basis, as for normal operational insurance cover.

295

Material Damage Insurance Amounts

This is a topic of considerable importance. It is essential for insurers and their clients to be agreed as to the basis of valuation and loss settlements of which there may be several choices. It is also necessary to explore more fully the general topic of additional costs with particular reference to the cost of decontamination and other clean-up operations and those associated with premature decommissioning following an accident as has just been mentioned. Fortunately, the Pools are able to obtain some valuable guidance on all these topics as a result of the excellent work put into studying them by their Working Parties. It is very largely on the basis of their work that the following advice is proffered:

a) Property Values

When a nuclear installation is built, it is of course thoroughly costed. The price of everything is, or should be, known and therefore its insurance value. Occasionally, this may be exaggerated if those undertaking the valuation include also the costs incurred in civil engineering and in meeting the fees of architects, consulting engineers and also the contingency costs of the contractors. Costs of this nature should not enter into the calculation of the values to be declared for the purpose of Material Damage insurance.

The Working Party set up by the 1979 and 1981 Pool Chairmen's Conferences uncovered some very practical issues underlining the need for Pools to insist upon incorporating correct insurance values in their policies. The recognition that there are several different bases on which values may properly be constructed sprang from proposals put before the 1979 Conference by the British Pool which identified the main variants as being as follows:

1) the cost of replacement as new ("new for old");

2) the cost of reinstatement of damaged plant which is not very new to the condition it was in immediately prior to the accident, i.e. taking into account the depreciation for wear and tear, obsolescence, etc.;

3) indemnity value meaning that in the case of plant that would not be worth repairing or replacing in the event of severe damage, perhaps because of its age or its general condition, insurers would pay no more than the agreed value of the property as a depreciated asset.

4) a first loss amount agreed between insurer and insured not directly related to a specific valuation but reflecting the probable cost of a significant accident.

When the final reports of these Working Parties were presented to the 1983 Conference, they included a useful Swiss Guideline providing a practical method of arriving at a realistic value for a nuclear power station, together with a programme for use with computers which Pools could use to assist themselves or their clients to establish proper insurance amounts.

Another very sensible practice is to make use of indexation based on one or other of the official Price or Cost of Living Indices published by most Governments or other authoritative sources of statistical data. France and Belgium, for example, regularly up-date the insurance values of their Material Damage policies although it does mean that for policies renewable at the beginning of the year the Pool and their clients have to wait some months before the official figures emerge. Each year's index is based upon the data for the previous year. However, the indicators are usually sufficiently clear to enable the Pools concerned to fix provisional sums insured on renewal and to adjust the premium. In line with these percentage increases, the figures can then be readjusted as necessary when the official index is available. In the USA, the Pools utilise what is known as the Handy-Whitman Index to up-date the insurance values for most of the property and equipment on a nuclear power station.

In other countries, although the terms of the insurance may not necessarily involve automatically aligning the insurance values annually in accordance with a specified official index, such indices would nevertheless be used as an aid in agreeing the new sums insured. The importance, particularly to insurers, of having accurate values on a recognised basis, is such that if all else fails it may be worth considering a practice followed, for example, in France, whereby, in return for agreeing to a professional valuation of his property, the insured is granted a small automatic discount off his rates.

Valuing nuclear fuel

The valuation of the properties, equipment and most of the materials on the site of a nuclear installation can be undertaken, although it may require time, effort and money to achieve, but it is generally recognised by the nuclear Pools that the valuation of nuclear fuel presents particular problems. Such is the price of uranium, and in particular, enriched uranium, that the fuel represents a very high value. It is easy enough to determine what that value should be in the case of new, unused fuel since the market price can be ascertained. The case of nuclear fuel within a reactor undergoing what is known as "burn-up", i.e. while it is actively producing energy and in the process being depleted, is much more difficult. There are certain formulae by which nuclear physicists and the operators of nuclear reactors can assess the state of their fuel at various stages during burn-up from the initial loading to the final removal and they may be able to give insurers a valuation based on such assessment. When this is possible, the insurance of fuel can be on an adjustable basis. On the other hand, it may be equally sensible not to attempt the difficult process of periodic valuation and simply to insure it for its value as new, since if it is damaged then replacement with new fuel will be necessary. However, in some countries the nuclear insurers require periodical statements of values, at least quarterly. Following the practice of conventional insurance, a predicted average value would be agreed at the beginning of the year of insurance and an appropriate adjustment of premium, either an addition or a rebate, would be arranged at the end of the year when the actual stock quantities are known.

Another factor in the valuation of nuclear fuel is the quantity of irradiated fuel that may be on the site at any one time. In many countries, there are no national facilities for the reprocessing of spent fuel; or it may be the policy of the Government not to reprocess it but eventually to dispose of it as waste. Even when reprocessing is to be undertaken, the available worldwide facilities are so limited that the operators may have to retain considerable quantities of used fuel elements in their storage ponds for a period of years. Because these used fuel rods contain valuable, extractable materials such as plutonium and certain other radiochemicals they should be capable of being priced.

However, when this question was most recently reviewed at the time of the detailed studies on the whole subject of Material Damage values, it was concluded that the only practical advice to give was that the insurers and their clients should make every effort to establish a realistic valuation but in view of the complexities the best that could be hoped for was that they would fix an agreed value so as to avoid difficulties at the time of a loss settlement.

This would be good advice on the whole topic of establishment of correct property values for the purposes of Material Damage insurance whatever basis of cover and settlement of losses is agreed upon. It is important to avoid the kind of situation that arose not long ago in one European country where the client wished to declare the values on the basis of reinstatement of property at its current value but to have losses paid at the cost of replacement as new.

Consequently, although he was only prepared to pay the lower premium related to the value of his property less depreciation, he expected his compensation to be for the cost of new building, contents or materials.

Average

Finally, on the subject of values and limits, there is sometimes a misunderstanding as to the effect of the condition of Average or, as it is called in some countries, the proportional rule. This is the basic insurance principle whereby if the insurance values to which the rates are applied, are found, when a loss has to be settled, to have been under-stated, then the insured will only obtain compensation in the same proportion as the declared value bears to the true value as ascertained at the time of the loss. In the case of a Material Damage policy covering a large nuclear power plant or other major installation for which full value insurance cannot be provided, partial loss settlements are not scaled down because the annual aggregate loss limit is only a proportion of the total values. Partial losses below that limit are fully covered and would always be settled in full. If the Average condition is applicable to that particular policy, it would be brought into effect only if the values of the individual items damaged or destroyed were found to have been under-stated, according to the previously agreed basis of valuation.

b) Decontamination and other Clean-up Costs

The value of the technical work undertaken by the Sub-Group of the Working Party set up in 1981 cannot be over-stated. On the basis of the detailed investigations undertaken initially by the Engineering Committee of BI(AE)C and other contributions, notably a study of the costs of the TMI accident and others from the United States Pools, it became possible for insurers to achieve a realistic appraisal of the likely work that would have to be done following various typical nuclear accidents and, more importantly, the potential cost of such operations.

The majority of nuclear power stations were and are equipped with Pressurised Water Reactors and therefore to keep the study within reasonable bounds the British Engineers and the Working Party concentrated their attentions on accident scenarios related to that particular reactor type.

For three selected degrees of severity of accident, the potential expenses that could be incurred in carrying out the necessary work to recover the reactor, estimated at 1982 prices were thought likely to be as follows.

A) Water & High Temperature Damage to Equipment, Cables, Structure, Instrumentation, etc. Clean-up of mildly-active coolant   £200,000-£750,000

B) More extensive plant and structural damage than Accident A. No problems with removal of defective fuel.   £60,000,000

C) As B) but no possibility of normal removal of fuel.   £500,000,000

The study pointed out that the estimated costs, manpower requirements and outages of the reactors must vary widely due to specific circumstances of the accident or design of the plant. The figures presented were orders of magnitude estimates for P.W.R.'s. Not all the costs would necessarily be insurable or insured under a Pool Material Damage policy.

Plainly there would be national variations, perhaps to a considerable degree, due to local labour costs and for the reconstruction or replacement of damaged property and new parts whether manufactured locally or imported.

As a matter of interest, a study has also been undertaken by the British Pool on the costs that might be incurred in dealing with serious accidents for the AGR and Magnox reactor. The figures suggested were of a lower order than those used in pricing a PWR accident. The length of recovery time and therefore the man-hours or man-years required could have a considerable influence upon the costs. Putting the times at between 6 months and 3 years, according to the severity of the accidents, access problems, whether or not Machinery Breakdown is caused and the amount of decontamination work actually required, orders of magnitude ranging from £50,000 for the least serious to £210,000,000 for the worst case were assessed with intermediate figures for various degrees of damage and time-tables.

It will be clear from this that under any policy, whether it incorporates a special item to meet the specified costs of decontamination, isolation, the removal of contaminated waste or debris and any other justifiable expenses associated with recovering a damaged reactor, or merely includes the indemnification of such costs within the policy cover for nuclear damage, a very substantial amount may have to be insured if it is to give adequate cover and the premiums are to be assessed upon a realistic aggregate sum insured, but judging the right amount is never easy.

Therefore, in ascertaining the necessary information for underwriting Material Damage risks it is vitally important to go into the question of decontamination and associated clean-up costs and the extent to which they are intended to be insured. When the scope of cover for these costs has been agreed it is clearly necessary to ensure that insurers, reinsurers and the client are ad idem by describing it unequivocally in terms that can be incorporated in the contract of insurance — especially the monetary sub-limits, if any, within the overall sums insured and/or the policy's annual aggregate loss limit. Because the costs can be so high, the possible loss payments following a nuclear accident will be much larger than under a policy giving no extra cover beyond the actual property value: hence the paramount importance of avoiding any misunderstanding as to the expectations of the insured, the insurer and the reinsurers.

(c) Decommissioning Expenses

Although the term "decommissioning" is commonly used to describe the operational activities involved in taking a nuclear installation out of service when it is finally shut down, this is strictly speaking an administrative procedure. The operations themselves may take one or more forms following a period (sometimes called Stage 1 Decommissioning) during which the installation is put into a safe state under routine maintenance and surveillance. The options may be summarised as follows:

1. *Mothballing:* encapsulation or sealing of parts of the installation for a period of years to reduce radiation hazard prior to dismantling or removal (fuel would be removed from a reactor). This may also be described as cocooning or lock-up with surveillance (known as SAFSTOR).

2. *Dismantling:* complete or "prompt" safe removal of the whole installation after dismantling — including the reactor pressure vessel and shielding around it to allow, eventually, unrestricted access to a completely vacant site ("unrestricted site release") (May be combined with a preliminary mothballing stage).

3. *Entombment:* permanent burial of the hazardous parts of the installation, most likely the concrete reactor shield and possibly the reactor pressure vessel. Minimal surveillance of the burial site would be necessary including radiological checks.

The least expensive operation would be mothballing: the most expensive (and probably the most desirable) prompt dismantling.

This is the most likely option when it is preplanned for an installation reaching the normal end of its life. The cost might be as much as 12 times that of mothballing: entombment perhaps 3 times as much as mothballing.

It is of interest that, on evidence given to the Public Enquiry into the Sizewell B power station project, the CEGB estimated that a twin-reactor Magnox station would cost between £150 millions and £270 millions to completely decommission — i.e. up to dismantling and removal. The OECD's Nuclear Energy Agency, in 1985, assessed the cost of prompt dismantling for, say, a 1300 MW(th) — (400 MW(e)) Light or Heavy Water-moderated reactor, at between US$103 millions and US$144 millions, but more detailed estimates of between $95 millions and $185 millions, for a wider range of options, including multi-unit sites, were published in the OECD's NEA Newsletter in 1986. (These figures related to *normal,* pre-planned operations, not the cost of unforeseen post-accident work).

The expense of pre-planned or programmed decommissioning does not come within the likely scope of a Material Damage cover since it is not a fortuitous event. Being essentially administrative it would be financed by the owner/operator of the installation — in some countries under an obligatory funding scheme.

When associated with a post-accident situation, decommisioning would almost certainly be premature and the operator may have insufficient funds to deal with it, even when he has started putting money aside for planned decommissioning. There may have been too little time to accumulate the large sum required to pay for premature, post-accident decommissioning which would be far more costly. Therefore, he would be faced with a fortuitous and unforeseen loss which he ought to be able to insure as an Additional Cost under a Pool Material Damage policy.

Detailed studies, based partly on some work of the U.K.'s Engineering Committee, undertaken by a Pool Chairman's Working Party which met in Paris in April 1984 under the Chairmanship of the French Pool's Manager, Monsieur Deprimoz, indicated that *post-accident* decommissioning was likely to cost up to 6 - 8 times as much as pre-planned decommissioning. For a 1000 mw(th) Light Water Reactor this could mean expenses in the region of US$800M — US$1,000M.

The conditions on which at least partial cover might be given by extension of a nuclear Pool Material Damage policy requires further discussion. In the present context, if cover is to be considered, there must be a detailed analysis of the operations that might be paid for and, when cover is defined, it must be carefully and expertly costed. Since the amount involved may be as high as the replacement value of a large power station (less any funding set up by the operator) it may be that meeting the Additional Costs of premature, post-accident decommissioning would be an alternative to indemnifying the physical loss of the installation — to be covered in the same policy, subject to a specified amount and an annual overall policy limit.

So far as is known, no such arrangement has yet been entered into. The problems associated with devising a suitable insurance contract should not be underestimated but the situation may have to be faced when insurers and their clients are considering the values, including additional costs, to be insured under a Material Damage policy.

"Zoning" in property damage insurance

It is always necessary to break down the properties on a large nuclear installation into zones. This may be to facilitate differential premium rating when there are material differences in the hazards presented by different sections of the plant; or it may be used to sub-divide a large complex into technically separable areas to enable insurance capacity to be more fully and efficiently deployed.

(a) Material Damage

In the United Kingdom, as we have seen, capacity for large nuclear power stations was subscribed on a dual basis, the first list of subscribers and their proportionate shares, (Slip 1), being related to the insurance of the nuclear parts against nuclear and non-nuclear damage; Slip 2 providing capacity to cover the quite separate conventional properties and plant against non-nuclear damage only. The two sections of the power station and of the corresponding Material Damage policy are known as Part I and Part II respectively and separate insurance values are fixed.

This also enables necessarily differential rates to be charged on the two types of property and in that connection, the concept of zoning was further developed in other countries in the early 1960's when the somewhat dissimilar power stations using Light Water Reactors began to come into operation. Zoning was not used in the USA where the Pools arranged their All Risks Physical Damage insurance differently.

The system used almost everywhere outside North America and the U.K. involves allocating the properties on a nuclear power station to 3 zones: Hot, Warm and Cold. This was almost certainly first adopted by the Italian Pool who wished to differentiate, for rating purposes, between (1) the reactor unit proper (the heavy concrete shell constituting the containment building and its contents) and (2) the adjoining auxiliary buildings and facilities concerned with the nuclear operations, but not involving the production of nuclear energy and the high levels of radioactivity associated with the reactor.

This group was described as the Warm Zone, being less hazardous from a nuclear viewpoint than the parts within the containment which were therefore designated as the Hot Zone.

The conventional part of the station, providing it was completely separated by space or constructional features and engineered safeguards, and would never contain any radioactive matter (unless by accident) was then designated as the Cold Zone.

Typically, in a station equipped with a Pressurised Water Reactor system, the main components of those zones would be:

Hot Zone Reactor containment building and contents, including nuclear fuel, fuel handling facilities, storage of new and irradiated fuel, radioactive waste system.

Warm Zone Service or auxiliary buildings, including control room, change room, health physics department, decontamination facilities, low activity waste disposal, laboratory, etc.

Cold Zone Turbine building and contents, emergency diesel generators, pumphouse and water intake and treatment facilities, switchyard, administration buildings, canteens, etc.

Pressurised Heavy Water Reactor (CANDU) stations would be similar but for stations equipped with direct cycle Boiling Water Reactors, there is one important difference: the Turbine Hall is included in the Warm Zone because the turbines are driven by steam which comes directly from the nuclear reactor and may contain radioactively contaminated water droplets. Thus there is no absolute separation between the reactor containment and turbine building.

For Gas-Cooled Reactor stations, the containment is different and so the Reactor Building and other associated facilities would normally be treated as one group for rating assessment and the typically "cold zone" property as another providing the fire/explosion separation criteria are met.

(b) **Machinery breakdown**

Plant insured against breakdown risks may also be zoned for hazards evaluation, rating and insurance coverage purposes. Those adopted for this class of insurance do not coincide with those applied in material damage insurance and their purpose is a little different. This is mainly because they identify and classify the various items of plant according to the importance of the surrounding radioactivity levels in regard to access and repairability.

The zones are designated, respectively, High Radioactivity Zone (HRZ); Low Radioactivity Zone (LRZ); and Zero Radioactivity Zone (ZRZ). They are broadly defined as follows:

High Radioactivity Zone

The vessel or structure which immediately contains the core (including its supports and shrouding) and all the contents thereof, the fuel elements and the control rods. (For each reactor system the exact extent of this zone should be precisely defined).

Low Radioactivity Zone

Those parts of the reactor system outside the High Radioactivity Zone in contact with the primary coolant or other radioactivity, where special precautions are necessary due to the radiation level when inspections or repairs are carried out.

Zero Radioactivitiy Zone

Any other part of the site.

It will be apparent that, compared with the other zoning system, the Hot Zone covers much more than the plant assigned to the High Radioactivity Zone, but includes only part of the Low Radioactivity Zone equipment, the rest of which would be in the Warm Zone of a power station. The Cold and the Zero Radioactivity Zones more or less coincide although the latter only applies to certain specified plant and equipment.

Since the machinery breakdown insurance zoning is not identical for every type of power station, the following generally accepted classification, devised by some of the technical experts of the nuclear Pools in 1971, should be helpful:

MACHINERY BREAKDOWN INSURANCE ZONING OF PARTS OF VARIOUS REACTOR SYSTEMS

1. Pressurised water reactor

High Radioactivity Zone

Reactor Pressure Vessel   Reactor Internals
Fuel   Control Rods

Low Radioactivity Zone

Heat Exchangers	Pressurisers
Circulation Pumps	Auxiliary Circuits
Control Mechanism for control rods	Ventilation
Travelling Crane	Loading Machine and Transfer Machine

Zero Radioactivity Zone

Turbo Alternators	Condensers
Control Panel	Transformers
Pump and Re-heaters	

2. Boiling water reactor

High Radioactivity Zone

Reactor Pressure Vessel	Reactor Internals
Fuel	Control Rods
Control Mechanism for control rods	

Low Radioactivity Zone

Primary Circuit:

Steam Drum

Turbine
Condensers — Although these Items are in the primary circuit, experience indicates that any contamination present only contains isotopes with a short half-life and that the limiting time for repairs is that necessary to open up the casing. Any additional costs and decontamination costs which may arise in normal operations will be very small as compared with the costs of opening up.

Feed Pumps	Re-heaters

Other parts:

Auxiliary Circuits	Travelling Crane
Loading Machine and Transfer Machine	Ventilation

Zero Radioactivity Zone

Alternators	Control Panels
Transformer	Cooling Water Pumps and Equipment

3. **Gas cooled reactor (Magnox)**

(i) **Steel Pressure Vessel**	(ii) **Concrete Pressure Vessel**
High Radioactivity Zone	
Reactor Pressure Vessel	Parts of Reactor Pressure Vessel unshielded (e.g. top inside boiler shield wall)
Graphite Core	Graphite Core
Fuel	Boiler shield wall
Control Rods	Fuel
	Control Rods
Low Radioactivity Zone	
Boilers	Boilers
Gas Ducting	Parts of Pressure Vessel shielded from the direct radiation
Gas Circulators	
CO_2 Clean Up Circuit	
Charge/Discharge Machines	CO_2 Clean up Circuit
	Charge/Discharge Machines
Zero Radioactivity Zone	
Turbo Alternators	Turbo Alternators
Condensers	Condensers
Feed Pump	Feed Pump
Re-Heaters	Re-Heaters
Transformers	Transformers
Control Panels	Control Panels

4. **Heavy water cooled & moderated (CANDU type) reactor**

High Radioactivity Zone	
Calandria Vessel	Pressure Tubes
Control Rods	Fuel
Low Radioactivity Zone	
Heavy Water Moderator & Coolant	Heat Exchangers
Control Rod operating mechanism	Auxiliary Circuits
	Fuelling Machines
Reactor building ventilation system	Dump Tank

Zero Radioactivity Zone

Turbo Alternators
Control Equipment
Re-heaters
Vacuum Building,
  Vacuum Pumps and
  associated equipment

Condensers
Transformers
Cooling water equip-
ment

The radiation levels around LRZ equipment, and therefore accessibility and repair costs, are usually considered to be low enough to permit of its being insured under a conventional Machinery Breakdown policy, along with the ZRZ, where there is a specialised Engineering or Machinery Insurance market with the capacity to provide a suitable form of cover. In practice, some of the LRZ equipment like the control rod operating mechanism and part of the fuelling machines may be so closely associated with the reactor unit as to be more appropriately included in the nuclear Pool Machinery Breakdown policy covering the HRZ. The rest could be separately insurable with the ZRZ plant because the insurers are concerned only with selected items, covered for damage not included in a specified perils Material Damage policy under different policy conditions, in a specialist market able to provide additional insurance capacity from its own resources, although the arrangements may vary from country to country. If a Pool is to provide Machinery Breakdown insurance on the High Radioactivity Zone (with or without part or all of the Low Radioactivity Zone as well) a breakdown of the equipment into these two classes, together with values fixed on an appropriate basis, will be an essential part of the required underwriting data referred to earlier.

Fire Hazards Data

Another extremely important aspect of risk assessment in relation to nuclear installations is the risk of fire. The recommended criteria will be explained later in this Chapter, but to ensure that the underwriting information required for Material Damage insurance is produced, in addition to or possibly in the absence of an on site inspection, particulars on the following lines should be supplied, together with a detailed plan showing the layout of the buildings and the location of fire protection equipment.

BUILDINGS

Full details for each major building on the site, from the fire hazard aspect, of:

1. a) Walls
   b) Roof
   c) Floors
   d) Linings and insulation
   e) Internal partitions
   f) Separation from adjoining buildings

2. Windows, fanlights or skylights, etc. constructed from combustible materials and their total surface area as a proportion of the wall or roof area concerned

3 Lightning conductors

4. Encasement of structural steel

5. Fire resistance of load-bearing elements of the structure

6. Smoke, heat or explosion vents

7. Space heating plant

8. Water drains and scuppers

OIL STORAGE

Details of:

1. Types and quantities of oils on site

2. Bulk storage arrangements
   a) in separate detached buildings
   b) in fire resisting compartments within buildings
   c) in the open
   d) capacity of catchpits in relation to the capacity of the storage tanks.

HOUSEKEEPING AND SECURITY

Details of:

1. Steps taken for the disposal of non-radioactive waste

2. Frequency with which floors, passages and stairways are swept.

3. Whether smoking is totally or partially prohibited and notices are posted.

4. Penalties imposed on any employee found smoking in a prohibited area.

5. Security measures against entry of unauthorised persons.

FIRE BRIGADE

Details of:

1. Nearest Public Fire Brigades and arrangements for attendance.
2. Approximate time taken to reach the site, including possible causes of delay.
3. Fully trained private fire brigade on permanent call on site.
4. Adequacy of access to the buildings for fire-fighting vehicles.
5. Training in special techniques for fire-fighting in radioactive areas received by fire brigades.
6. Water supplies for fire-fighting.

FIRE PROTECTION

1. Specification of parts of the Buildings and equipment protected by:
    i) Automatic or manual sprinklers and/or drenchers
    ii) Local emulsifying water spray
    iii) Automatic or manual local water spray
    iv) Automatic or manual dry powder or vapourising liquid systems
    v) Automatic or manual Co_2 systems
    vi) Internal hose-reel and hydrant systems
    vii) Heat and smoke detectors

Detailing
    a) the nature and type of the protection
    b) whether automatic devices are connected to annunciator panels in main control room and to public fire brigade
    c) whether warnings are audible as well as visual.

2. Full details of portable Fire Extinguishing Apparatus, stating:
    a) Type
    b) Quantity of each type
    c) Location

FURTHER DETAILS TO BE SUPPLIED IN RESPECT OF TURBO-GENERATOR HALLS, WHERE APPLICABLE

1. Sub-division of the building, including construction of partitions and protection of openings
2. Arrangement of turbo-generators, i.e. in line or in parallel and distance apart, or details of dividing wall.

3. Type of oil pressure lines, i.e. whether welded joints or otherwise, with particulars of protection against vibration.

4. a) Separation between oil and steam lines and whether steam lines are isolated and/or insulated.
   b) Precautions to prevent oil dripping or spraying onto steam lines.

5. Whether (a) all openings around ducts and pipes, including those for cables, are sealed and (b) fire stops are fitted where appropriate.

6. Nature and capacity of catchpits or bunds provided under or around equipment.

7. Location of oil service tanks.

8. Steps taken to prevent oil entering cable ducts.

9. Nature and frequency of physical and chemical checks of lubricating oil.

10. Warning devices fitted and whether linked to main control room.

11. Frequency of inspection of equipment, including cables, i.e. daily or weekly.

12. Cable insulation and protection.

13. The following section is required only where there is Hydrogen cooling:
    a) Where Hydrogen cylinders are stored
    b) Whether generator casings are explosion-proof or explosion vented.
    c) What checks are undertaken to ensure over-pressure is maintained and that no leaks exist.
    d) Whether venting from apparatus is external.
    e) Frequency of gas purity checks.
    f) Nature of automatic checks relayed direct to main control room.
    g) Precautions taken in filling or draining Hydrogen-filled components and related pipes and ducts.

Whereas the evaluation of the nuclear hazards should be undertaken by engineering specialists in this field, the other Material Damage hazards would be considered in the normal way in the light of the opinions of Fire Surveyors and other experts. Where extraneous perils are involved, such as windstorms, flooding, earthquake and, in some overseas countries, volcanic eruption, bush fire, tsunami and so

311

forth, it would be necessary in some cases for specialised reports to be obtained and examined by specialists in some of these fields of hazard. Without expert help, one may misinterpret the earthquake data, for example. From time to time insurance companies and others issue publicity material illustrating the incidence and severity of such potential natural catastrophes in various parts of the world, earthquake risks and the pattern of hurricanes being a favourite. It is too easy to deduce from the rather broadly drawn and colourful maps of, say, the earthquake regions of the world that a particular location may be rather more (or less) exposed than it really is.

Siting of nuclear installations all over the world is considered with the utmost care by the licensing authorities, the manufacturers and constructors and the operators. No electrical utility, still less its Government, wants to place a nuclear installation in an area where it is likely to be damaged by an earthquake. If the possibility of earth tremors were to be a disqualifying factor for the building of nuclear installations, none would ever be built in some countries. In practice, the experts in a country like Japan have a very full knowledge of what the risks really are. The construction of the nuclear power stations can incorporate good, although expensive earthquake-proofing devices. The risk of damage therefore is minimised both from the point of view of the siting as well as the construction features. Underwriters must rely upon the reports of local experts on seismology and tectonics to satisfy themselves as to the measure of the earthquake risk, if any. Such reports can always be supplemented by further investigation and advice from independent consultants from academic and research institutions. This is just one example of the consideration that has to be given to some aspects of the conventional damage to be insured although quite frequently in countries which are exceptionally exposed to natural disasters the Pool policy would not include such perils in their normal cover.

The Fire Risk — Prevention and Protection

The most important aspect of the assessment of conventional perils, however, is the Fire risk and the extent and quality of the fire protection arrangements. This is a subject on which the nuclear Pools have a high level of expertise as demonstrated by the work done on the Guidelines described earlier by international Working Parties of specialists in this field of risk control. There are few countries which do not have detailed fire protection rules and regulations laid down by Government Departments, Safety Authorities and the insurance industries themselves. There are not many with specific application to nuclear installations. In these cases it is possible that the

Government concerned will have adopted the regulations recommended by the International Atomic Energy Agency in their publication, "Fire Protection in Nuclear Power Plants" (Safety Series No. 50/SG/D2).

However, for practitioners in the field of nuclear risks insurance the principal work of reference is undoubtedly the "International Guidelines for the Fire Protection of Nuclear Power Plants" (revised edition 1983) published by the Swiss Pool for the Insurance of Nuclear Risks, Zurich on behalf of the Nuclear Risks Insurance Pools and Associations. This is obtainable from all the national Pools direct, or through insurance companies and associations. It aims to facilitate the application of the best and most up to date standards of fire prevention and protection in the design stage of nuclear power plants, but also to be of assistance for those responsible for subsequent risk assessment and safety surveys. It also helps to facilitate consideration of fire protection modifications in existing operating plant.

For nuclear installations other than power stations, there is the companion Guideline, also mentioned previously, "International Guidelines for Fire Protection at Nuclear Installations" edited and published by the British Insurance (Atomic Energy) Committee on behalf of the national nuclear insurance Pools and Associations. This covers nuclear fuel plants, nuclear fuel stores, teaching reactors and research establishments as well as any other facilities using significant quantities of radioactive materials. Like the Guidelines for Power Plants (parts of which may also be valuable in connection with the larger other types of nuclear installations) this publication recognises that there may be local statutory requirements, building and fire protection regulations and insurers' rules which have to be given precedence in some countries. Nevertheless, the intention of both Guidelines is that their recommendations should be followed except where local rules may be more stringent. However, because of the radiation hazards of nuclear installations and the inherent risk of accidental criticality in nuclear materials subject to spontaneous fission, certain standard fire protection measures may be incompatible with nuclear safety. In these cases, the measures to be applied to nuclear installations may then have to be considered in consultation with the controlling authorities and other experts.

Both publications contain very detailed recommendations of great practical importance both to the designers and the operators and insurers of all types of nuclear installations. In considering the assessment they are to present to the underwriters and reinsurers of the risks to be covered, the engineers and fire protection specialists should pay very careful attention to the Guidelines. Well-qualified experts will be familiar with much of the ground they cover, when concerned with the more conventional aspects of fire prevention and protection, since much of the property and plant at a nuclear installation, especially a power station, and some of the processes, have similar characteristics to those at non-nuclear premises. But not all experts are specialists in the factors which are affected by the nuclear hazards, with respect to which some aspects of fire protection have a special importance.

The uncontrolled release of large quantities of radioactive substances generated in a nuclear reactor whilst it is in operation is an ever-present possibility when fuel elements are seriously damaged, perhaps as a result of insufficiency or lack of cooling. This should be preventable by the multiple independent safety systems provided but if these are to be reliable they must be properly protected against a major fire. The diverse nuclear safety related systems must be continuously available. There must be redundant safety systems, i.e. they must be duplicated, or triplicated, and to ensure that the benefit of such redundancy is not lost, special attention must always be paid to risk separation. Known incidents prove the importance of this. It involves the use of solid concrete walls, separating the different fire areas, as other measures dependent on power, water or similar supplies requiring actuation may not be reliable enough. As the International Guidelines for the Fire Protection of Nuclear Power Plants points out in the Preface to the Second Edition, certain lessons have been learned from nuclear incidents which concern fire protection, as follows:

a) those that apply to some plant facilities which after such an incident may have to operate for longer and under heavier demand requirements than normal;

b) those that deal with the equipment at installations that are brought to the site and temporarily erected in connection with decontamination and repair work;

c) those that are demonstrated by the influx of temporary personnel and their space requirements. (Furthermore, besides office space, rooms for changing protective clothing, for the calibration and maintenance of radiation survey instruments and for the installation of health physics, control posts will have to be provided);

d) those that concern fire protection installations that may have been affected by the incident which need servicing and replacement.

Among the special problems affecting fire protection at nuclear power plants which must be considered is the need to ensure that the outbreak of fire will not endanger the safe shutdown and cooling of the reactor. The presence of various radioactive substances, whether solid, liquid or gaseous, is an obvious problem also. They are responsible for the sub-division of the premises of most nuclear installations into what are sometimes called the "controlled" and "uncontrolled" areas, the purpose of which is to limit the exposure to radiation of employees working in different parts of the plant. This also affects the arrangement of the fire protection and the design of ventilation systems. The presence of gaseous or airborn radioactive matter requires pressure differentials to maintain the flow of air from the less towards the more contaminated rooms and regions and smoke extraction methods must accommodate this principle, also.

The Guidelines point out that the manual fire-fighting in a nuclear power plant may be difficult and time-consuming because the fire-fighters have to be given sufficient protection against radiation exposure and this may involve limiting their exposure time or the wearing of special protective equipment. Another factor to be borne in mind is that because most nuclear power plants are constructed in isolated locations the response of public fire brigades which would have to be called in for a serious fire may take a long time. So far as on-site fire-fighting is concerned, this may sometimes be of fairly limited value because the large modern nuclear power stations can be operated with relatively small numbers of personnel. Nevertheless the provision of properly-managed and organised on-site fire-fighting measures is of the utmost importance.

There is no substitute for a thorough study of specially prepared fire protection manuals such as the two Pools' Guidelines mentioned. However, if one were asked to pick out the most important considerations in relation to fire protection, both passive and active, for a nuclear power station (all of which are covered in great detail in the Guidelines) they would be as follows:

1. **Passive Fire Protection**
    (i) Use of non-combustible and fire-resisting materials in construction.
    (ii) Risk separation and compartmentation of key and high-risk buildings, e.g. reactor block, turbine hall and ancillary buildings.
    (iii) Fire cell division within these main buildings.
    (iv) Fire sealing, between cells, of:
        - cable penetrations
        - pipes and ducts
        - ventilation ducts

    (v) Oil systems:
        - use of phosphate ester low flammability
          oil whenever possible,
        - double pipe system for high-pressure systems.
   (vi) Fire-resisting construction with fire breaks for cable
        tunnels and basements

2. Active Protection

    (i) Sprinkler protection for cable flaps and the area
      below the operating floor of turbine sets;
   (ii) Halon 1301 systems for control rooms, computer
      and instrumentation rooms;
  (iii) Automatic fire alarm protection in switchrooms,
      control rooms, cable tunnels and ducts and nuclear
      fuel storage areas;
   (iv) Good water supplies;
    (v) Adequate fire pumps;
   (vi) Suitable fire-fighting teams and brigade.

Fuel stores

With regard to the storage of nuclear fuel, whether this be new (or irradiated), some additional special considerations arise. Large quantities of new fuel are likely to be stored both at reactor establishments and at fuel factories. In the former, the store is likely to be part of the reactor block, and if so it should be in a separate non-communicating compartment of fire-resisting construction, with non-combustible linings and used only for the storage of nuclear fuel. At fuel factories, the finished fuel should be stored in separate, properly-designed buildings of similar fire resisting construction used only for this purpose. Proper containers and racking made of metal should be provided, the storage building should be compartmented and the arrangements should be such as to preclude accidental criticality under all conditions including fire extinguishment. Fire detection devices should include audible and visual automatic fire alarm systems linked to a central control point, including smoke detectors in ventilation or ducting systems actuating automatic shutdown of air-conditioning. First aid fire-fighting provisions should include hose reels to enable fires to be tackled promptly.

Irradiated, or spent, fuel removed from the reactors is normally stored in cooling ponds under a good depth of water so the only danger from fire would arise in the event of loss of water coupled with a sudden and excessive increase in the temperature of the fuel elements. Therefore there should be provision for monitoring the temperature levels in the pond. However, the advent of dry irradiated fuel stores presents different problems. Very few are likely to be encountered in practice but the engineer or fire surveyor inspecting the premises should pay special attention to these.

Security

Another safety area on which underwriters will expect to have satisfactory reports and assessments from their experts is *security*. Special attention is paid to this aspect in the International Guidelines in the interests of good fire protection although, as reactors are possible targets for terrorists or extreme anti-nuclear organisations, a very much higher level of security than would normally be sought will usually be present anyway because of the requirements of the licensing and safety authorities. Nevertheless, this consideration may be less important in some countries than in others, so it is necessary for insurers to be satisfied that there is a minimum level of security capable of deterring prospective intruders and detecting their approach. The most important points to look for include the following:

Security Fence. This should be strong enough to prevent easy access and high enough to prevent entry over the top. It should also extend sufficiently below ground level to prevent any intrusion by digging. A high steel palisade fence would normally be suitable.

Main Entrance. This should be manned at all times, and preferably protected by a manually or electrically-operated barrier. Other entrances should be protected by doors or gates of similar construction to the fence, secured by high security locks when not in use.

Lighting. At the perimeter this should be installed inside the security fence directed outwards. Floodlights should be installed at the main entrance with appropriate illumination of other areas.

Intruders. The perimeter fence, or area close to it, should be protected by installations capable of detecting any person approaching the fence. Closed-circuit television cameras should also be installed at sensitive points within the premises to detect not only intruders but unauthorised personnel or unauthorised activities by those otherwise entitled to be present.

––––––––––

The foregoing section illustrates some of the many features relating to the Material Damage hazards and, conversely, the measures taken to minimise them, that must be examined in detail and objectively assessed by properly qualified experts before the Managements or specialist Committees serving the Pool can begin to consider the acceptability of the risks for insurance purposes and to secure a proper evaluation which can form a satisfactory rating basis, whether this be related to Material Damage, with or without Machinery Breakdown; Public Liability (both nuclear and conventional) or any other form of insurance written by the Pools. If this includes Transport risks, the special factors to be examined would be primarily related to the nature of the nuclear matter being carried, the packaging and how it is stowed on the means of transport, together with methods of detecting abnormal radiation or heat.

Consequential Loss Insurance

This generic term includes not only what in the U.K. is usually called Consequential Loss or Loss of Profits insurance but also what are known elsewhere as Interruption Risk, Business Interruption or Additional Working Costs (or expenses) insurance: in other words, those forms of cover intended to indemnify an insured against various form of pecuniary loss following physical damage.

These occurrences can be very expensive, particularly when they are the consequence of nuclear damage which may necessitate a much longer shutdown than in the case of conventional accidents. Pools considering granting any form of interruption insurance will therefore need to have very full information which should cover the following items as necessary although some of the details will have also been supplied for the underlying Material Damage and, in some cases, Machinery Breakdown insurances:

1. **Basic details**
    1.1. Name of Insured
    1.2. Business address
    1.3. Location of installation
    1.4. Type of installation (plus detailed plan and specification)
    1.5 Electrical and thermal power (power stations only)
    1.6. Age of installation (and in the event of damage, whether likely to be regarded as obsolescent)
    1.7 Date of start-up
    1.8 Date of transfer to present operator
    1.9 Governmental involvement (e.g. ownership, regulatory control, etc)
    1.10 Contractual agreements (suppliers, customers, etc) and penalties for non-fulfilment

1.11   Financial year

1.12   Unscheduled shutdowns since date of transfer (total and partial)

1.13   Incidents due to any of the perils to be insured against since date of transfer.

2. **Underwriting information (power stations)**

    2.1   **Inception hazard** — the parts of the power station which are essential to the generation of electricity and, of these, which are expected to suffer more damage than the remainder by:-

    2.1.1. nuclear perils

    2.1.2. fire and explosion

    2.1.3. catastrophe perils, e.g. flood, windstorm, earthquake, riot and civil commotion, terrorism

    2.1.4. other perils

    2.2.   **Interruption hazard** — the organisation of the power station, with particular reference to:-

    2.2.1. number of reactors, steam generators, turbo-alternators

    2.2.2. different types of interconnection (e.g. reactor, turbo-alternator, etc)

    2.2.3. number, situation and use of computers (including storage arrangements for duplicate tapes, etc. and location relative to media in current use)

    2.2.4. capacity (maximum and normal operation) /demand ratio.

    2.3.   **Recovery potential** — the possibilities of:-

    2.3.1. implementing pre-determined contingency planning so as to maintain supplies (within constraints of property loss prevention standards, whether imposed by Insurers or by prescribed codes — e.g. American, national — with details of these standards for each separate risk within the power station)

    2.3.2. replacing machines and component parts, taking into account the policy of the power station regarding the maintenance of spares, and the value of these spare parts relative to the value of the power station itself

    2.3.3. replacing raw materials, with special regard to the replacement time and the number of sources of supply (plus the countries of origin in the case of imports).

2.4 **Dependencies** — particulars of the more important suppliers

3. Underwriting information (manufacturing installations)

3.1. **Inception hazard** — the parts of the establishment which are essential to the operation of the business and, of these, which are expected to suffer more damage than the remainder by:-

3.1.1. nuclear perils

3.1.2. fire and explosion

3.1.3. catastrophe perils e.g. flood, windstorm, earthquake, riot and civil commotion, terrorism.

3.1.4. other perils.

3.2. **Interruption hazard** — the organisation of the business, with particular reference to:-

3.2.1. the number of separate interruption risks there are (including percentage each contributes to the total earnings of the business)

3.2.2. the interdependency, or otherwise, of the various manufacturing processes.

3.2.3. the existence of continuous processes (automatic or semi-automatic)

3.2.3. the use and purpose of computers (e.g. for production control, stock control, storage/disposal of waste products control, monitoring of radioactivity levels, general administrative work, etc) and storage arrangements for duplicate tapes, etc. and location relative to media in current use.

3.3. **Recovery potential** — the possibilities of:-

3.3.1. implementing pre-determined contingency planning, within constraints of property loss prevention standards whether imposed by insurers or by prescribed statutory codes

3.3.2. extemporisation within the insured's own premises

3.3.3. replacing buildings rapidly (it is assumed special buildings are essential)

3.3.4. replacing machinery (including components) and plant (nuclear and non-nuclear)

3.3.5. replacing raw materials, with special regard to the replacement time and the number of sources of supply (plus the countries of origin in the case of imports)

3.3.6. obtaining alternative sources of power, etc.

3.4.   **Dependencies** — the extent to which the insured is dependent on suppliers or customers, with special regard to:-

3.4.1   the dependency of the business on a particular supplier (including details of any contract between the insured and the supplier under which the supplier is subject to penalties or fines, commensurate with the importance of the contract, if he fails to provide the goods or service)

3.4.2. alternative suppliers

3.4.3. the amount of raw materials and components stock-piled by the insured

3.4.4. the dependency of the business on a particular customer (including details of any contract between the insured and the customer under which the insured, as supplier, is subject to penalties or fines, commensurate with the importance of the contract, if he fails to provide the goods or services the customer requires)

4. **Details of cover**
    4.1.   Type of cover
    4.2.   Perils covered
    4.3.   Amount to be covered (annual basis)
    4.4.   Maximum Indemnity period
    4.5.   Limitation of Loss
    4.6.   Deductible — monetary, percentage of sum insured, or time.
    4.7.   Period of insurance

Contingent Liability Insurances

As already explained, suppliers of goods and services to the nuclear industry may require cover for liability they can incur in the event of their being held responsible in law for nuclear damage caused to a nuclear installation or property used or being constructed in connection with its operation. This is because such damage cannot be compensated out of funds compulsorily provided by licensees under nuclear Third Party Liability insurance or other authorised financial security. Although such damage can be, and usually is, covered under a nuclear Pool Material Damage policy, without recourse against the responsible party, it may not be insured at all.

It is also possible for a supplier to be obliged, under the terms of his contract, to indemnify the licensee of a nuclear site for claims he may have to pay to Third Parties in spite of the channelling provisions of nuclear legislation which can in this way be overridden so far as the financial obligations are concerned. In the latter case, if the licensee of the nuclear installation is insured by the Pool they should have sufficient information to make an assessment of the supplier's financial commitment arising from his contractual obligations. It is quite likely that a monetary limit will have been agreed — desirably a much lower figure than the operator's statutory liability under nuclear legislation. However, a copy of the contract will be examined, together with a legal opinion if necessary. Since the Liability policy issued to the supplier will be on the basis of his liability at law this must not be in doubt.

Consequently additional questions may have to be put to clarify this issue.

Apart from a general Third Party Liability insurance, tailored to his needs, a supplier of goods and services will need either a Product Liability insurance or an Errors & Omissions/Professional Indemnity policy. The latter would be relevant to firms or individuals supplying design, planning or consultancy services, inspections and, a comparatively recent service, decontamination, demolition and removal operations for decommissioned nuclear installations.

For Product Liability cover, technical and underwriting information on the following lines is required:

Product Liability Insurance

1. **The Proposer**

    a) Name and Address

    b) Nature of business

    c) Is proposer registered in the United Kingdom?
    If not, country of registration?

    d) Is proposer a subsidiary company?
    If so, name of parent company

    e) Has the proposer any representation outside the United Kingdom?
    If so, nature of representation and countries concerned

2. **The Product(s)** for which insurance is required

    a) Schedule required giving details of each product supplied for or used in land-based nuclear installations and supplement with brochures

b) In the case of products supplied by the proposer,
    i) which are standard products
    ii) which are individual designs
    iii) to whose specification these are produced
    iv) whether similar products are manufactured for use otherwise than in nuclear installations.
    v) previous experience of manufacturing these and other products

c) Conditions of sale

d) Conditions of purchase by the proposer of manufactured products, if any

Supply either copies of conditions or extracts showing provisions relating to indemnities or hold harmless agreements.

3.   If liability arising from the installation or servicing of products is to be included, estimated annual wages for such work

4.   Have any incidents occurred involving products for which insurance is required (whether a claim was made or not) ? If so, following details required

Date of occurrence	Brief details	Cost (if any) of claims paid	Estimated outstanding

5.   In respect of products not supplied for or used in nuclear installations,
    i) Estimated total annual turnover
    ii) Claims arising out of occurrences during the last 5 years

	Number	Amount
Claims Paid		
Estimated outstanding		

6.   Limit of Indemnity required

The *schedule of products* to be attached should set out the following details:

Full description of each product
Situation and function in nuclear installation
Nuclear installation for which supplied/used
Manufacturer (if not proposer)

Estimated annual turnover (Home and Overseas)
Countries to which exported.

Errors & Omissions or *Professional Indemnity Insurances* would require somewhat similar data, though a schedule of products would not normally be relevant. The enquiry form would have to be tailored to fit each case, but essential points would include, apart from details of the above and (if giving professional service) of qualifications and experience, the location of the nuclear installation, the nature of the work to be carried out there, an extract from the Contract conditions relative to the applicants' legal liabilities and the value of the contract or amount of professional fees. A history of any claims paid on account of professional negligence, whether insured or not, would also have to be disclosed.

It is unlikely that insurance would be provided without evidence of an actual contract either awarded or tendered for. A supplier of general products (such as valves or lubricants) or services such as design work, which are not specifically for the nuclear industry but *may* be used in connection with nuclear installations or materials, may nevertheless want some protection against the possibility of being involved in an action for damages arising from a nuclear incident, which would be excluded from his conventional insurance cover. Nuclear Pools able to write these classes of contingent liability insurance should be prepared to consider sympathetically any request for "gap" cover in these circumstances, and assess it as such in the light of the assessment of the underlying conventional cover.

Chapter XI

EVALUATION AND RATING

From the beginning insurers recognised that their main problem in assessing risks from the point of view of their acceptability and for rating purposes would be to understand and put a correct value on the atomic perils as distinct from the familiar perils such as fire, explosion, storm, etc. Secondly, they had to be able to measure nuclear installations against the more familiar hazardous industries and against each other to arrive at an equitable basis of premium assessment which fairly reflected the risks to be undertaken by underwriters.

Shortly after the second Pool Chairmen's London Conference in 1958, the Atomic Risks Study Centre met to exchange ideas on how this might be tackled. The material before them included proposals worked out by the BI(AE)C and also the French Pool. Other representatives contributed their own suggestions. There seemed to be a general consensus that the different types of reactors, particularly those that would be used for power production, known at the time could and should be classified according to various elements in their design and behaviour, the type of fuel, moderator and coolant, containment and thermal power indicating that the degree of probability of an accident and the severity should it occur meant there were distinct differences between the reactor types. Therefore the nuclear hazards related to the different reactor types could be set out in an ascending order of severity and could be quantified by some simple notation. This could be sufficiently flexible to allow for variations from the norm to be accounted for enabling the technical experts to allot to each case a specific number of points which could then be converted into an insurance premium or rate by the underwriters. A similar system was also adopted at the time by the United States Pools. Practices and methods vary from country to country. Some Pools have a more sophisticated approach than others or may rely upon others to assist them in the assessment and rating of their risks; but it is fair to suggest that the basis used nowadays for all nuclear risks is very much in line with the original methods put forward in the late 1950's.

This has certainly always been the British Pool's approach although it has, naturally, been improved and refined with experience over the years. As soon as all the necessary technical and other under-writing information has been obtained on the lines described in the preceding pages, the data concerning the reactor or other nuclear materials involved (for example, nuclear fuel undergoing manu-facture, processing, re-processing or storage), it would be referred to the Engineering Committee. Where one of the engineers has personally inspected the risk and obtained data locally, they may have practically all they require but in any event they would be sent copies of all the other information which may influence their thinking and advice.

Evaluation

Their first step would be to place the reactor, if that is the installation involved, into the appropriate group according to type and according to the severity of the potential hazards associated with operating that type of reactor. The least hazardous would be those falling within the categories of educational, research and testing reactors, the thermal power of which would be within the range of zero to five megawatts. The groups in ascending order of importance are as follows in accordance with U.K. practice:

Group 1
1. Critical assemblies,
2. "Eversafe" type (zero to 100 kW(th)),
3. Swimming Pool, tank and other types (100 kW(th) to 1 MW(th)),
4. Swimming pool, tank and other types (1 MW(th) to 5 MW(th)).

The second and more important group relates to reactors for power and other purposes with a thermal power range of 1 to 1000MW. These are classified in the following groups in ascending order of potential hazard:

Group 2
1. Low pressure Light Water Cooled and Moderated reactors,
2. Gas-cooled Carbon-moderated and Heavy Water-moderated reactors,
3. Carbon-moderated Organic Liquid Cooled and Organic-moderated and Organic Liquid Cooled reactors,
4. Pressurised Water and Boiling Water reactors,
5. Homogeneous Light Water and Heavy Water reactors,
6. Fast Reactors and Breeders and Liquid Metal-cooled reactors.

With respect to Group 2, the next consideration would be the use to which the reactors are put: this could include power production, educational and demonstration purposes, industrial processes and research testing.

Having placed the reactor in the appropriate group, the engineers undertaking the analysis would then allot certain points values. While it is not practical to list these in detail, it can be said that so far as Group 1 is concerned, these being the smaller and less hazardous reactors which would not ever be involved in the production of power, the range would probably be between 2 and 25 Points minimum. For Group 2, the range could be between 20 Points and, say, 75 or even more. These are minimum values which would be increased if the thermal power is above the lowest for that particular type (or, conversely, discounted if it is substantially lower than normal). So far as Group 2 is concerned, there would be variations according to use.

Finally, after they have examined all the many features of a particular reactor installation, including those listed in the Statement of Required Information given earlier, and the extra details produced by an analysis of or extracts from the official Safety Report, the Engineering Committee or their representative would then make what is called an Engineering Assessment of the design factors, which would result in a percentage variation of the Points Value already calculated. The factors to be taken into account would include the following:

Fuel and fuel containers,

Control and safety gear,

Reactor supports and foundations,

Fuel coolant, containment and primary heat exchanger (if any)

Moderator

Moderator coolant

Power Production Heat Exchangers and connecting ducting to Reactor,

Mechanical Equipment

Internal fire and explosion

Other Conditions.

Having carefully weighed and assessed these factors in accordance with expert judgement as qualified engineers with a special knowledge of nuclear matters, they would then arrive at a final figure. For a power reactor system this might be anywhere between the low 20's and 100 Points or even more at the top end of the scale.

Several other countries use rather similar methods of basic evaluation of the nuclear hazards, although they may differ in their grouping and classification of reactor types and their judgement of the comparative importance of the risks presented by the different designs and uses of reactors. However, there is unlikely to be any fundamental disagreement between properly qualified engineers, particularly those with an understanding of the assessment of risks for the assistance of insurance underwriters. The majority of those concerned would very likely have gained this understanding and experience by working in a specialised Engineering or Machinery Insurance company in the conventional field.

So far as concerns *non-reactor establishments*, methods of assessment may be rather less developed than those applied to reactors, and some insurers are inclined to regard, say, fuel factories as comparable to chemical works with or without metal working facilities, with which they are familiar in the conventional industrial field. However, such risks can present unusual hazards and it is unwise to relegate them to a low-risk category. The number of such risks insured compared with reactor plants is, of course, relatively few, and for many Pools they are not an important class of business. However, for those who have to deal with large fuel fabricating or reprocessing factories, it is considered essential that they should have equally careful analyses carried out by their technical specialists. The problem is complex and the considerations involved in assessing such risks objectively are substantially different. It is, perhaps, largely a matter of viewing them in the first place as a non-nuclear factory or laboratory where the dominant risks are of a conventional character as, for example, in a chemical works. It is then necessary to acquire some idea of the aggravation of these risks due to the presence of fissile or other nuclear materials whether irradiated or unirradiated. A comparative value which will be much smaller than applied to the assessment of a reactor can then be suggested by the experts.

The classes of risk which would qualify for this type of assessment would be as follows:

(a) Laboratories concerned with the examination and testing of non-irradiated or irradiated nuclear fissile materials;
(b) Factories concerned with the manufacture of nuclear fuels and nuclear fuel elements;
(c) Factories concerned with the reprocessing of irradiated nuclear fuel elements or the enrichment of nuclear fissile materials.

A consideration that must be taken into account in evaluating the hazards associated with these materials is the form in which they are present. In ascending order of importance of hazards, they are (1) solids, (2) powdered and ceramic, (3) liquid, and (4) gaseous, and are considereably aggravated if the material is irradiated.

From the point of view of the nuclear hazards the main ones are the risks of accidental formation of a critical assembly and the spread of radioactive contamination. Additional recovery costs would obviously be involved as well in the case of fissile and other material.

In assessing points, the same standards would be adopted as when dealing with a reactor, but the values would be very much less, in many cases only a fraction of a point, although the more dangerous forms of such materials could range between something like 2 points when in store to a minimum of perhaps 20 points when they are being processed in a laboratory or factory workshops. As in the case of assessing a reactor, the materials used in the various establishments covered by this part of the evaluation process would be subject to variations according to any additional assessments that the engineers may consider advisable.

The Points Assessments produced by the technical experts provide underwriters with a methodical and objective evaluation of the nuclear hazards to be taken into account when assessing their rates. They are the means of obtaining a consistent and systematic measure of the hazards and can be applied logically and impartially to each case. This makes it possible to adopt an even handed approach when considering risks of a like nature and to apply carefully judged variations of values when it is necessary to take account of significant material differences between unlike installations.

It is for the underwriters to convert their Points Values into a price or rate appropriate to the atomic perils to be covered in a Material Damage policy, or the risks of damage or injury to third parties arising from ionising radiation or contamination by radioactivity in the case of Liability insurance.

Various systems of rating nuclear risks for insurance purposes have been developed by the different Pools, although where the local insurers have limited technical resources and nuclear expertise at their disposal they would commonly look to one of the experienced Pools for assistance in the inspection and evaluation of their nuclear risks and for advice on rating and premium assessment. It is more than likely that their preferred source of such advice would be their leading reinsurer, since that Pool would be carrying a greater proportion of the risk than themselves or, indeed, any other. Consequently, the BI(AE)C has played a considerable part in giving technical assistance in this field, although it should be emphasised that whatever rating proposals may be suggested the ultimate decision on rates in negotiation of acceptable terms with their clients and the procuring of support for these terms from their reinsurers is wholly the responsibility of the national Pool.

ASSESSMENT OF RATES AND PREMIUMS

Material Damage Rating

Since insurers had no experience of dealing with nuclear hazards in 1957 they could not obtain any guidance from past experience of the rating of such risks. The expertise they could bring to bear on the assessment of non-nuclear perils, while useful in dealing with that aspect of Material Damage cover for nuclear installations, had little to offer them. Various possibilities were explored by the Atomic Risks Study Centre of the European Insurance Committee and attempts were made to produce rather elaborate tariffs using coefficients and other more or less mathematical formulae related to an analytical approach to the evaluation of the new hazards. By different paths insurers who studied the question between 1957 and 1959 reached rather similar conclusions. These had in common an acceptance of the fact that the approach to the rating of such risks must be based largely upon a theoretical appreciation of the objective evaluations presented by the engineers and other experts. We have seen already that these could easily be quantified using a flexible scale of values or points able to give a fair indication of the differences between the various reactor systems or other types of nuclear installations and to demonstrate the differences within a particular class of installation due to thermal capacity or size, use, a whole range of safety features; or the absence of desirable characteristics. Converting this information into a rate per cent on value or a premium then simply called for the application of a suitable formula. American thinking which was carried out with little or no input from European insurers produced a similar result. Experience and practice over the past 30 years has evolved flexibility and increasing sophistication in the application of this method. But most still use the same approach, i.e., to get a figure, a factor or a value from an expert analysis which can then be applied to a basic price or some other coefficient to produce a rate per cent or per mille to be applied to the property values to be covered.

This is the system that has always been used in the United Kingdom and therefore forms the basis not only of their own rates for Material Damage risks but also of advice to others seeking their assistance. At first, since there was no experience on which to base the pricing factor, the BI(AE)C sensibly took the view that since nuclear energy was potentially very hazardous, although the degree of hazard varied from one type of reactor to another, the price factor to be applied to the Points Evaluation should be such as to produce for the most hazardous types of reactor a rate comparable with that which would be charged in the conventional field for the most hazardous types of industry, such as oil refineries, dangerous chemical factories and plastics factories. The figure chosen in 1958 was 1.5% for a reactor which carried the value of a 100 Points. This was right at the top of the possible scale for the most hazardous category of power reactor in the list devised by the Committee's engineers. In practice, the Magnox type of gas-cooled graphite-moderated power reactors that were to be installed in the first of the British nuclear power stations came nearly two-thirds down the scale.

It is not possible for reasons of commercial confidentiality to quote any actual rates, since these are a private matter between the insurers and their clients. The notional price of 1.5% for 100 Points can, however, be mentioned because that figure is long out of date for risks like power stations or large research establishments. Present day practice is very much more flexible and, in any event, for such major risks the basic rating levels have been systematically and resolutely reduced by insurers themselves in the light of growth of business and satisfactory experience over at least the past 15 years.

However, to illustrate the method, it would not be betraying any confidences to use that rate since it is no longer relevant in current practice. It would now be susceptible to considerable discounts according to the quality and experience of the nuclear operator, the type and design of his reactor establishment, and other very cogent and reasonable considerations. The final rating incorporates appropriate amounts for the conventional insurance aspects according to the range of perils insured. In some countries, these would be limited in number and probably confined to Fire, Explosion, Lightning, Aircraft Damage and possibly Riot and Civil Commotion. In other countries, the perils may be more numerous. The conventional element of the composite rate would be determined largely on the facts and would have regard to local market rates or, in some countries, fixed tariff rates applicable to comparable non-nuclear industries or establishments.

Rating illustrations

(a) Power station

Taking an entirely hypothetical case of a modern PWR station equipped with a typical reactor design, let us assume that the Committee's technical experts have fixed an Engineering Points Assessment of 60 (this is not necessarily a figure that would apply to anything in real life) and that the old original "price" of .015% per point applied. (This relates to the reactor installation and not to other parts of the station.) For the reactor, the atomic perils rate would then be calculated by multiplying 60 Points by 1.5% (per 100 Points) to produce a reactor rate of 0.9% (or 9 per mille in view of the very high values to which rates have to be applied). The rate decided upon for the conventional forms of damage insured would then be added to that figure. Say this were to be 1.5 per mille, the resulting basic composite rate would then be 10.5 per mille. In practice it would probably be rounded down because there is possibly some overlap between causes of fire under the nuclear and non-nuclear perils. However, this being a station equipped with a Light Water type of power reactor "differential" rates are required, based on the 3-Zone system, so consideration also has to be given to the extent to which the atomic perils element of the composite rate could be cut down for the Warm and Cold Zones. (Conversely, with respect to the generating plant, it may be necessary to consider having a higher rate for the conventional perils in view of the comparatively greater risks of fire and explosion in, say, a Turbine Hall, compared with a Reactor building.)

In considering the differential to be applied to the atomic perils rate with respect to the other Zones, underwriters would be influenced by the efficacy of the containment building within which the reactor hall and other parts of the reactor installation are housed. This is because one aspect of the potential nuclear damage affecting the rest of the site would be the possibilities of an escape of a substantial amount of contaminating fission products in the event of a nuclear accident in the reactor. However, in considering the properties in the Warm Zone, it would have to be remembered that this part of the station also contains a certain amount of nuclear matter. This may itself be capable of causing radioactive contamination not only within the Warm Zone but to the outside of the buildings in the Hot Zone and to the rest of the site, but to a far less degree than the reactor. In considering the nuclear risks to which the Cold Zone would be exposed, account would have to be taken not only of the possibility of radioactive contamination originating in the Reactor Block but also to a small degree that which might originate in the ancillary facilities in the Warm Zone. It would also be relevant to consider the separation between the non-nuclear parts of the plant and the Reactor Block as a mitigating factor in assessing the risk of spreading radioactive contamination.

The advice of the engineering experts would almost certainly be required in order to make an objective judgement of the potential for nuclear damage to the Warm and Cold Zones.

Supposing the advice from these experts indicates that the vulnerability of the Warm Zone to nuclear damage is 40% of that for the reactor unit, and for the Cold Zone, 15%. These factors would then be applied to the basic 9 per mille rate for the Hot Zone to produce atomic perils rates of 3.6 per mille and 1.35 per mille, respectively, for the other 2 Zones.

Regarding the conventional perils aspect, it is decided, after considering all the details regarding the Cold Zone and in particular the fire protection for the turbo-generating plant which is not of the best standard, that the conventional perils rate here should be 2.5 mille instead of 1.5 per mille.

The following rating pattern can then be set out:

		‰
Hot Zone	Atomic perils (60 × .15 per mille)	9
	Conventional perils	1.5
	Total	10.5
	(Round down to 10‰)	
Warm Zone	Atomic perils (60 × .15 per mille) (less 60%)	3.6
	Conventional perils	1.5
	Total	5.1
	(Round down to 5‰)	
Cold Zone	Atomic perils (60 × .15 per mille) (less 85%)	1.35
	Conventional perils	2.5
	Total	3.85

To arrive at the premium it would then of course be necessary to have an accurate sub-division of the full value of the plant into the insurance amounts for the 3 Zones to which the separate rates could then be applied. The total insurance values for the sake of illustration may be put at £750,000,000. This value would then be split up over the 3 Zones and differently rated to produce the following premiums:

		£
Hot Zone	£375,000,000 at 10 per mille	3,750,000
Warm Zone	£ 75,000,000 at 5.0 per mille	375,000
Cold Zone	£300,000,000 at 3.85 per mille	1,155,000
		£5,280,000

It should be stressed that this is a totally *fictitious* example, valid only for demonstrating the method. In reality, the basic rates for a normal commercial PWR station, and therefore the premium, would be much lower. The figures are for full value cover without limits, or any deductible or excess other than a small amount that might be compulsorily imposed as part of the policy conditions. Furthermore, there is no provision in the cover for additional costs of decontamination, isolation or removal of contaminated debris, so such expenses would be met only within and up to the declared value of the contaminated property.

If this exercise were related to a policy written on the Part I/Part II basis, i.e. with the conventional or Cold Zone property insured exclusively for non-nuclear perils, and with cover for radioactive contamination spreading from the reactor block being included within the Part I cover for some additional premium, the rating pattern would differ to the extent that the Part II rate would not contain any element for the atomic perils. The total premium would be unlikely to be very much less, though this would depend upon how much cover was to be included by extension of Part I of the Policy to meet the cost of radioactive contamination damage spreading to the rest of the site.

Although the above illustration shows a breakdown of the atomic and conventional rates and between the different Zones, it is the invariable practice to quote a composite rate for each Zone which is *not* necessarily just the sum of the parts. In some countries, the Pool would quote only a premium without any indication of the breakdown of the separate rates. Alternatively, they might convert the total premium into a single average rate. This method is not very often used because in the event of a substantial later variation in the relationship between the values applicable to the three rating Zones, a new average rate would have to be fixed every time such changes took place.

(b) Other types of reactor installations

The rating of other types of reactor establishments, such as research centres or the nuclear laboratories of a University, is simpler in that there would almost never be a zoning aspect to be taken into consideration. A small swimming pool or tank-type reactor would not require special containment and there is unlikely to be any significant separation between it and the adjoining laboratories or other workshops. The Engineering Points Assessment would be on a much lower scale, as we have seen. To take a typical example, the installation might be rated at something like 15 Points, on which a fictitious rate of 0.15 per mille per Point would produce an atomic perils rate of 2.25 per mille. The addition for conventional perils would, as in the case of power stations, depend upon the range of these perils and the assessment of the relevant hazards. Sometimes where laboratories are involved, the Fire and Explosion risks, in spite of precautions, may be above average. Given a limited range of extra perils, the conventional element might therefore be set at something like 1.75 per mille, giving a total of 4 per mille on full value assuming there are no limitations on the cover other than a small compulsory excess.

(c) Fuel Factory

For an installation involved in the fuel cycle, the Engineering assessment would again be carried out in exactly the same way as for any other type of nuclear installation but the values, as we have seen, are much lower than for a power reactor, varying widely between a fraction of a Point, and perhaps 20 Points where irradiated fuel elements are being processed and there is a significant risk from gaseous radioactive substances. The few radioisotope-producing or processing factories which require special insurance arrangements, because they are classified by law as nuclear installations on account of the level of radioactivity and/or quantity of isotopes involved, may be coupled with this type of installation for which the dominant rating factor is always the conventional perils element. There is no particular formula for rating these, other than the rating scales or tariffs which may be available in some countries for conventional comparable industrial processes such as chemical and metal-working factories. In the U.K., the BI(AE)C would take advice as necessary from those experienced in the underwriting of such risks. For a full range of "dry" and "wet" conventional perils, the rate might be 2‰ and typical Points assessment 6, giving a basic Atomic Perils rate (at .15 per mille) of 0.9 — total 2.9 per mille which might then be rounded off at, say, 2.75 per mille for full value insurance.

Flexibility

Once insurers in the United Kingdom had acquired some 10 or more years experience in the assessment and rating of nuclear risks, they felt able to develop their techniques in a direction giving more favourable technical rating treatment in the case of power reactors of proven design at commercial generating stations of exceptionally high standard in all respects, particularly when these were operated by experienced national or international concerns who could demonstrate an outstanding record of safe and successful operation of several installations over a period of years. For these, the *basic* price per Point was in future to be subject to a range of discounts to be judged according to the quality of the risk in relation to these factors. The logic behind this was that before the Pools had acquired any experience of how safe nuclear power reactors were going to be they had to assume that all the factors which led to the assessment of the nuclear perils most commonly insured, that is to say, excessive temperature within the reactor and contamination by radioactivity, were equally weighty pointers to the likelihood of nuclear damage occurring and the consequent loss payment experience to be foreseen. The price per point is not capable of being precisely analysed into different elements but clearly it covers a range of possibilities. These run from the worst credible accident such as a loss of coolant with overheating and melt-down of fuel, a massive release of fission products and heavy radioactive contamination, right through the range of other possibilities, including minor damage to perhaps just one or two fuel elements and a small degree of external radioactive contamination.

The possibility of a very serious accident due to the "heavy" end of the spectrum of nuclear risks causing a total insurance loss cannot be excluded, particularly since TMI and Chernobyl. So the part of the price per point (say 50%) notionally reserved to the generation of premium to meet the possible catastrophe must remain intact whatever the quality of the installation and the operator. However, damage associated with the "light" end could be discounted for the good quality cases because experience indicated that losses due to the lesser radioactivity incidents or minor fuel damage for example, were few. In other words, frequent small claims which may justify charging as much for that aspect of the nuclear hazards as the rare catastrophe, were simply not arising in the proven commercial power reactors.

This element could not, however, be wholly eliminated from the rating assessment so part of the price per point must always be preserved for the "light" nuclear damage aspects.

Consequently if the irreducible "catastrophe" element were put at .075 per mille where the price per point was .15, this could not be reduced; but for a "top quality" client the other 50% may be reduced but never wholly eliminated. Therefore, a minimum net price per point may be, on these figures, something like .009 or even .008, but never as low as .075 per mille.

This easing of the technical rating factors was, however, confined specifically to the large experienced operators whose status met the standards of excellence mentioned above.

In subsequent years, the BI(AE)C developed this philosophy to the extent of permanently reducing the basic rating factor for commercial-scale installations whilst still preserving the option of special further rate reductions on technical grounds for clients meeting their "quality" standards. Large research institutes managed by national or international concerns with a very good record may also qualify for a special technical discount on grounds of excellence.

Once the basic rates have been determined by these means, other technical factors also come into consideration according to the individual case. These may involve additions or loadings to the basic rate or further discounts. Some of the main considerations are as follows:

(1) Rate-loading factors

(a) Testing of new plant
It is frequently the case that a new reactor, particularly a power reactor, has to undergo a series of rigorous tests and trial runs once it is loaded but before it can be finally handed over to the power station operator as being ready for commercial operation. This period of operation, which may be relatively short, not normally more than a matter of months, can involve additional hazards which fully justify a temporary increase in the basic rates, particularly those applicable to the reactor unit. The size of this would be a matter for consideration by the underwriters and their experts, but would commonly be in the region of 20%.

(b) Building construction
When new facilities are erected on the site of an operating nuclear installation or existing plant undergoing major modifications, these activities may introduce additional hazards which would not have been taken into consideration in the initial assessment of the risks. In such cases, some addition to the rate during the period of construction may be necessary.

(c) The "ageing" factor
In the case of a reactor which has been in continuous operation for perhaps 15 years or more, its age may be a safety factor. If the technical hazards are correctly evaluated by the appropriate experts they will obviously take this into account because age-related processes can affect safety unless preventive measures have been taken. These will involve the assessment of the capacity of older plant components to perform their safety function in normal practice.

(d) Additional costs
The insurance sum to be provided will be a matter for discussion with the insured. The required cover could be for a relatively modest fixed sum on a First Loss basis, in which case the rating will be

relatively straightforward for experienced underwriters depending on what the policy is intended to pay for under this heading. There may, on the other hand, be a requirement to provide a very high level of protection against such expenses. The limit could be up to the aggregate amount of the sums insured on, for example, the whole of the reactor block, or even the total sum insured for the whole station, or the annual aggregate loss limit under a particular policy when this is less than the full values.

Compared with a policy which does not cover these additional costs or limits them only to a modest amount, the cost of an accident when there is extensive cover for clean-up operations will be very much greater. The originating cause of an escape of radioactivity causing heavy contamination does not have to be of dramatic proportions. These costs may therefore be several times the cost of making good the direct physical damage.

There is no perfect method for the technical rating of additional decontamination and associated costs. A logical way to look at it is to consider by how much the insurers are exposed to greater loss when they cover them. In the view of some experts, the best measure of this additional exposure is to consider the extra margin of loss that may be incurred compared with a policy which covers only the actual damage, including contamination and decontamination costs only up to the specific value of the property or zone affected. The margin would be the difference between that value and the total sums insured or annual limit under the policy. The required additional premium would then be determined by applying a rate to that margin.

Another, and in the view of some, more realistic, way of dealing with it, is to regard the extra exposure as being an aggravation of the risks associated with the peril or radioactive contamination. The reasoning is that decontamination and all the directly-associated operations can only be a direct consequence of such contamination in the first place. Furthermore, any of the property on the site which is insured against the peril of radioactive contamination is therefore liable to be involved in clean-up operations which would enhance the cost of making good damage. Therefore, the atomic perils element of the reactor rate should be increased to reflect the aggravation of the radioactive contamination aspect of that part of the cover, thereby yielding the appropriate additional premium since it will be charged on the values of the properties at risk.

(e) "All Risks"

The Material Damage rating system which has been described is related to the "named perils" forms of Material Damage insurance and takes into account the fact that the range of damage covered is specifically stated (and may in some policies be accompanied by definitions) and that which is not to be covered is explicitly excluded.

However, if an All Risks form of policy is to be used, this may not be sufficient. In spite of the sometimes quite long list of exclusions these policies incorporate, there will always be a somewhat indeterminate area of damage to which the policy will have to respond in the event of an accident. Nuclear damage could in this way go beyond the consequences of accidental excessive temperature or radioactive contamination external to the areas where radioactivity is normal. The policy will also be likely to cover undefined forms of accidental damage and to extend to machinery breakdown, particularly in the High Radioactivity Zone. So far as Machinery and Boiler risks are concerned, with which an Inspection contract may be associated, that ought to be separately rated by suitably-qualified experts in that field of insurance, but for the rest — the extra risks to be covered after one has extracted the perils that would be named in any other form of policy — some additional rate must be charged. Since this could cover either nuclear or conventional perils it has to be assessed separately in consultation with the Pool's technical and other experts. It is then added to whatever composite rate emerges from the type of exercise described earlier, although care must be taken to give credit for the longer list of exclusions which is likely to be found in an All Risks policy compared with a named perils form of cover.

(2) Rate-discounting factors

There are three main areas which justify reductions in the basic technical rates and which involve underwriting as distinct from commercial judgements. They are:

(a) Discounts for Deductibles or Excesses

Where an insured elects to carry the bottom slice of the Material Damage for his own account, he is entitled to a discount off his basic technical rates. It is difficult to devise scales for nuclear damage, although in the conventional insurance field these are very often applied routinely. In dealing with nuclear risks one has to give realistic consideration to what the effect of the deductible or excess may be from the point of view of (i) the expense that will be incurred by the insured by reason of the reduction of his loss payments and (ii), conversely, the saving that will be achieved by insurers which has to be set against the loss of premium.

The relative size of the deductible or excess compared with the total values at risk and the values of individual items of property is an important consideration. What might seem to be a large amount in connection with small or non-nuclear risks may not be a very significant means of reducing the loss payment when applied to a large nuclear installation. For this reason, some underwriters prefer to express the deductible or excess as a percentage rather than an amount. Be that as it may, it is reasonable to grant a flat discount of all the relevant rates when the amount is low. In the case of the very large excesses which are now beginning to appear (a point discussed earlier) the rating becomes a far more difficult exercise. This is one of the main reasons why many nuclear insurers are loath to agree to provide insurances on the basis of a very high deductible or excess, i.e. one amounting to millions of Pounds or Dollars, possibly going even as far as £50,000,000.

For the insured, this is a very heavy commitment but, for the insurers, when compared to the potential cost of a serious nuclear accident it represents quite a small proportion of their potential loss. The discounting of the rates therefore requires a more sophisticated approach than the application of a simple flat reduction. The reason is that if one takes, for example, a deductible of £10,000,000 the impact of this on potential loss payments is going to vary enormously according to whether the damage is purely conventional, or nuclear, or a combination of both. It would also involve different consider-ations according to whether one is assessing the potential damage that could be suffered due to, say, fire or explosion in the turbo-generating plant compared with similar damage in the reactor block. It therefore is advisable for insurers to dissect their composite rates and to apply different levels of discount to the different parts. The resulting reduced rates can then be re-assembled into a single net composite rate for each Zone or item of property. However, this is not an exercise that can be done in consultation with the Insured — the chances of amicable agreement are remote in the extreme!

While it is impossible to suggest any particular discounts in an exercise of this kind, even by way of illustration, as a general guide it may be said a figure like £10,000,000 would justify only a very modest discount when applied to the element of the atomic perils rating which reflects the catastrophe potential, i.e. the major nuclear accident, such as has happened at Three Mile Island and Chernobyl. This could undoubtedly involve a total loss, particularly if the cost of decontamination is included. Taking the replacement cost of a modern powerful Light Water reactor as possibly £450,000,000, clearly a reduction of £10,000,000 in the loss to be paid by the insurers is of little significance. On the other hand, an excess of £10,000,000 would substantially reduce, if not eliminate, any payment for the fire or explosion damage that might be suffered by a massive reactor containment building except, of course, if it is blown apart as happened in the case of Chernobyl. In this situation it would be justifiable for the conventional perils element of the basic rate for the reactor block to be much more heavily discounted than the atomic perils element.

Taking the Cold Zone properties, and in particular the turbo-generating plant, a conventional accident could cause heavy and costly damage perhaps running into tens of millions of Pounds. On the other hand, following a nuclear accident, the extent to which the turbo-generating plant would be likely to be contaminated is probably small and the damage might even be confined to the exterior of the Turbine Hall. So in that case, a deductible of £10,000,000 would very possibly eliminate a claim for contamination damage, particularly if there is no extra cover for clean-up costs.

It should be emphasised that the question of discounts off the basic technical rates to account for a deductible or an excess, however small or large that may be, can only be tackled after the basic rates have been settled. It would be illogical, for example, in a case where the policy is on an All Risks basis, not to increase the basic rates on that account on the ground that a large deductible or excess will probably eliminate any payments that might be due to the indeterminate additional risks. What would have to be paid for under an All Risks policy is difficult to predict until something happens. Further, the discount for an excess applies over the whole range of rates, and it would in effect be double-counting first to cut out the notional portion of the Atomic Perils rates because the damage to which it relates might be eliminated by a large excess and then to give further credit for the large deductible or excess whether this be £5,000,000 or £50,000,000.

It is a tricky area of rating but it is most important for insurers to recognise that as the heavy loss potential lies with the possibility of a serious nuclear accident, much the greater proportion of their rate or premium is related to that eventuality. This cannot be disregarded in determining discounts to be allowed for a large deductible or excess which, as a *proportion* of the potential claims costs, is in fact modest or even small.

(b) Loss Limitation

This is another area where the determination of an appropriate premium reduction in recognition of the imposition by insurers of a loss limit appreciably below the total values at risk is very difficult. In spite of the shortages of capacity, there must be very few even large nuclear power stations, for which insurers are unable to provide sufficient protection to cover at least the replacement value of one complete reactor unit, including the containment building, all that is within that, and the nuclear fuel, plus something in addition. This is especially so when the plant and the form of insurance are such that the Pool's capacity can, by one means or another, be applied additionally to the separate, non-nuclear parts of the station.

A number of nuclear power stations nowadays are equipped with 2, 3, 4 or even more reactor units and their associated generating plant. Even if one takes the nuclear plant alone, the maximum limit available from insurers compared with the aggregate of all the values at risk will represent a relatively small proportion, possibly as low as 25% or 30%. This is equally true of the small number of gigantic nuclear fuel manufacturing or reprocessing plants although they may be susceptible to sub-division into separate sectors, to each of which full capacity can be applied, as explained earlier.

However, even if the capacity in a multi-unit nuclear power station represents only 30% of the replacement values of 4 reactor units and their ancillary buildings, this must be set against the very low probability of more than one such unit being lost in the course of one year of insurance. There is unlikely to be a second severe accident if only for the reason that the whole of the plant would be likely to be shut down for some period in the event of a disastrous nuclear incident. Therefore, the whole basis of rating and the levels of premium that are charged take this situation into account. While even the highly improbable cannot be ruled out as every insurer knows, and some of the risk assessments which have been applied in recent years by the experts in predicting the incidence and severity of nuclear accidents may be somewhat suspect, there are areas of probability which can be fairly well trusted. This is one of them, i.e. that on a multi-unit nuclear power station the maximum foreseeable physical damage loss is the total loss of one reactor unit and its fuel plus some degree of spreading contamination. It is only if the policy gives a very wide measure indeed of cover for clean-up costs that this expectation may be discredited.

The point, then, is that the margin between the insurance capacity and the limit this allows for on the annual aggregate loss basis, and the total values of all the properties at risk, may be wide but the loss of protection, in all probable circumstances, to the insured is in fact somewhat illusory. In other words, even if the gap is 40%, 50%, 60%, or 70% there can be no question of reducing rates or premiums in anything like that proportion.

The way this is commonly approached, and it is the practice of British underwriters, is firstly to consider the margin between the policy limit or limits and the total values at risk. Where the limit represents less than, say 75% or 80% of the total of all the sums insured a small discount would be granted as a token recognition of the fact that the cover expressed in the annual aggregate loss limit compared with the total values of the properties on the site is well below the full value. This might go to as much as 5% if the limit is as low as 50% and a little more if it goes below that. Only if the limit is below the sum insured applicable to the most highly-valued block of property, i.e. the "maximum loss" (excluding additional decontamination costs), would any further discount related to the rating of that particular block of property or properties be appropriate.

The result of this approach is that, except possibly where a very wide measure of cover is required for the additional costs of decontamination, the level of discount that can be contemplated for a loss limit must be modest.

It has been argued that if this practice is followed, then insurers may find themselves in some difficulty in charging higher rates if they are able to obtain substantially increased capacity and thus raise the limit substantially. However, it certainly does not follow that because the reduction for a lower limit may be modest, the increased rate that may be justified for raising that limit should be of the same proportions. It has been argued that if the discounts for limits were increased, then in those cases where additional capacity becomes available allowing for an increase in the limit, the level of the discount could be converted to a loading for the same percentage, thus acquiring a larger premium increase for insurers. This proposition assumes that the policyholder will readily take up the increased limit and pay a higher premium than he might otherwise have done. The probability is that in these circumstances the insured will decline to take an increase if he feels adequately protected by a lower limit unless for some reason he is under an obligation, due to other commitments, to do so.

(c) Rate Reductions for Fuel Loading Phase

It is customary for insurers to apply a discount of up to 50% of the rate or premium applicable to a newly-constructed reactor when it is undergoing the loading of its first fuel charge. This is because from the beginning of the operation up to a certain point during the process there may be insufficient fuel in the reactor core for there to be any possibility of accidental criticality occurring even if the control rods were to be withdrawn. After that point, even though there may be no intention to start up the reactor, there is a critical mass of uranium, particularly enriched uranium, but it is generally regarded as fair that the rate or premium applicable to the reactor undergoing loading should therefore be cut by 50% compared with that for a fully loaded and operating reactor. In the case of a power reactor of well-established design, experienced operators can usually complete the loading of the core in a matter of weeks so the impact on the first year's premium of such a reduction is not significant as a rule.

In addition, the following factors may also have to be considered:

(d) Rate Rebates for Reactor Shutdowns

It is normal during the operation of any nuclear reactor, particularly power reactors, for them to be closed down from time to time to allow for routine maintenance, inspections and refuelling to be undertaken. Such outages would very possibly not last more than 30 days and are recognised by insurers as being a normal feature of the operating life of a nuclear installation. Such interruptions are taken into account in the Hazards Assessment and Rating process. While the risks associated with the reactor are reduced while it is completely shut down and out of action and has perhaps had the fuel taken out of it, there are some additional hazards associated with re-starting a reactor which has been shut down. No adjustment should be made to the rates to account for these occasional outages.

On the other hand, however, a reactor may have to be shut down for repairs following a breakdown or damage of one sort or another. If such repairs are of a relatively minor nature they can probably be held over until the routine maintenance shutdown but they may have the effect of prolonging that beyond the normal period. On the other hand, repairs may become urgently necessary following a major breakdown or the occurrence of damage which is not insured under the policy, either in the reactor or in the generating plant which, of course, would mean that the station cannot produce electricity and the reactor must be shut down for the period of that interruption. In these circumstances, providing the outage exceeds a certain minimum period (fixed by some nuclear insurers at 30 days, although in other cases a shorter period may be allowed) a reduction of the rates or premium, particularly that part applicable to the reactor unit, would be sympathetically considered. It would be necessary of course for any work to be undertaken on the reactor to be of a type that did not present exceptional hazards, and insurers would have to be satisfied that it was incapable of being operated even accidentally, such safeguards as the locking in of the control rods and, in some cases, removal of the nuclear fuel being mandatory. Providing these criteria are satisfied, a premium reduction would then be granted for the term of the shutdown, usually in the form of a rebate. It would be necessary for insurers and their technical experts to have full details of the work to be undertaken during the outage and of any necessary safety arrangements over and above the normal ones, but providing everything was satisfactory it is likely that a discount of 40% to 50% would be justified from the date on which the qualifying period starts.

A different set of circumstances which may result in a discount off the normal rates would arise when a nuclear installation has to be shut down for such a long period that the whole nature of the risk is altered. This may occur in the event of a serious breakdown of either the reactor or other plant meaning that it has to be shut down for a year or more. Providing the shutdown is not due to insured damage for which a claim will be paid by insurers, it may be possible for the whole installation to be re-assessed as if it were not an operating reactor and down-rated accordingly.

In general, the nuclear Pools are very willing to act reasonably in situations like this, since they attach importance to matching the rating levels to the nature of the hazards as evaluated for each individual nuclear installation according to whatever state it may be in.

(e) The "reactor/years" factor

A measure of experience favoured by, among others, the probabilistic theorists, and also used by technical experts and others as a measure of the level of "know-how" and operating experience, is the factor known as reactor/years. This is arrived at by multiplying the number of reactors in operation and the number of years for which they have operated.

When this factor produces a substantial number, it is sometimes advanced as justifying a *technical* discount off the normal basic rate for a particular reactor installation. It is a means of making comparisons between one nuclear installation operator and another. Its value as an objective rating element, however, is somewhat questionable, although the number of years a particular operator has been functioning, or the number of nuclear power stations he operates, is a relevant consideration. It is of limited value in assessing the hazards from the point of view of Material Damage rating. This becomes apparent when one considers that the reactor/years are the product of two factors. One has to ask whether an operator with 10 reactors operating 6 years is any better or worse than an operator with 3 reactors that have operated for 20 years. Both of course produce a factor of 60 reactor/years.

Most nuclear insurance underwriters would probably regard this as of no more help in determining the parameters that go into the objective assessment of Material Damage rating than is the use of the reactor/years factor as an aid to predicting the probable frequency of major nuclear accidents. The notion that, for example, the frequency of a major catastrophe may be one in, say, one thousand reactor/years, is possibly satisfying to the statisticians but they cannot say in which of the years making up the one side of this equation the major loss is going to occur; yet insurers must have the necessary financial resources ready at any time to deal with it, whether it occurs at the beginning or at the end of the cycle.

(f) Credits for Multi-Unit Sites

Another technical consideration that is sometimes advanced as a justification for applying a discount to a basic rate is the presence of two or more units on one nuclear power station. The thinking behind this seems to be that, because the rate is applied to the sum insured to produce the premium, the higher premium generated by the inclusion of the values of more than one reactor should be abated because of the likelihood that only a small part of the total inventory of a multi-unit site is likely to produce a loss compared with a single unit nuclear power station.

Whether this is a genuine rating factor is somewhat debatable. It goes without saying that the more units there are in operation, the more chances there are of something going wrong, and therefore the higher is the risk to which the policy limit is exposed. As against this, it might be averred that a nuclear power station equipped with several reactor units is a better prospect because if one of them breaks down and has to be taken out of service, the utility operating the station can still produce a substantial amount of electricity from the others. Consequently, they would be under less pressure to try to keep an ailing reactor going, with the possible risk of an accident, than would be the case of an operator with only one reactor on the site. There may be something in this theory, but it seems highly likely that the supervising and inspecting authorities, if they are doing their job properly, would insist upon the shutting down of a reactor with defects or operational difficulties which might lead to an accident occurring, quite apart from the safety standards that any self-respecting power station operator would insist upon. Nevertheless, there may be something in this idea when one is considering nuclear power stations in countries where the standards may not be of the best.

(g) Single Overriding Limit for Separate Stations

In spite of the desire of the great majority of nuclear power station operators and the financial concerns who provide very large loans for the building of such stations and insist upon their being fully insured, there are large utilities whose owners seem more concerned to obtain cheaper insurance than to be adequately protected against loss. One of the ideas for achieving this is that a group of quite separate nuclear power stations in the same ownership should be covered under a single insurance policy with a single limit regardless of the aggregate values of the separate plants. Alternatively, although a separate policy would be issued for each there would be a single overriding limit per loss per annum and in the aggregate over all the stations which, it is argued, justifies a massive discount off the rates.

This proposition does not bear very much close examination. It has to be understood that in pitching the basic level of their rates, even in the earliest years, insurers did not expect to have to pay a total loss on any one station with respect to the whole of the properties insured and as distinct from the reactor unit alone, although the latter could certainly be a total loss. Nor did they expect, in the case of a client with more than one nuclear power station, to be paying more than one major loss in any one year. Even if there were to be a severe accident in one of the stations which may suggest the possibility of a similar occurrence in another, the cancellation conditions written into the Material Damage policies were such that in most countries the Pool would be able to extricate itself and its members from a continuing exposure for more than, say, one month with respect to what then may have become an unacceptable group of risks.

It has been explained already that when the policy limit, whether it be imposed by insufficiency of capacity or for some other reason, is enough to meet the cost of, say, one reactor unit plus some additional spreading contamination damage, the insured can be regarded as being very well protected against all but the remotest of eventualities although of course the insurers are fully exposed. This is why the margin between that sort of annual aggregate loss limit and full values at risk in relation to the nuclear part of the station does not justify more than modest rate reductions, or conversely, more than a modest rate increase if the margin can be narrowed. (This may not be relevant in the event of a very substantial amount of cover for additional costs of decontamination operations being included in the policy.)

It is no more likely that prudent underwriters could justify a large rate reduction when a single overall limit is applied to the values represented by a group of quite separate nuclear power stations in different parts of the country individually insured under separate policies. A large utility which has been operating for a good many years may have numerous reactors covering a wide range of values and possibly different reactor systems. The bases of valuation may vary between a very low indemnity value for those which would not be replaced or repaired in the event of severe damage because they

347

are old and obsolete; and a high value for those of recent construction which would be covered for full replacement cost subject only to the limits imposed by the availability of insurance capacity. If the total value of this group of nuclear power stations were to be, say, £3,000,000,000 in the aggregate, and the limit proposed by the insured or his brokers were to be put at a maximum of £400,000,000 per annum per station and in the aggregate over all the stations, it might seem that the insurers were, in effect, in a highly favourable position because their limit would represent less than $13\frac{1}{2}\%$ of the total values at risk — a very plausible case for a massive rate reduction. Seductive though this may seem to the inexperienced or unwary nuclear underwriter, a massive rate reduction cannot for one moment be justified. Just as insurers do not expect to have to pay for the total loss of a complete nuclear power station save in remote and almost unimaginable circumstances, nor have they ever expected realistically to have to pay for more than one total loss in any one year for a single client. If they did, rates would have to be much higher!

Furthermore, when a single limit is applicable, then the more times it is exposed to possible loss payments through the multiplication of the units or power stations coming within that limit, the more likely it is that that figure will have to be paid out in full in response to a series of lesser incidents even if not for one catastrophic event. Therefore, the rating considerations in a situation like this are very little different from those which arise when a single nuclear power station, even if it has more than one reactor unit, is insured under a policy subject to an annual aggregate loss limit which does not greatly exceed the value of one reactor unit.

Consequently, in a case where the aggregate insurance values of a group of separate nuclear power stations in the same ownership are subject to a single annual loss limit over the whole group regardless of the number of loss payments in the aggregate, this consideration can justify only a token discount off the net basic technical rates applicable to any one station as a gesture, acknowledging that under this scheme in the extreme eventuality of more than one total loss arising for one nuclear operator in any one year the insurers would be exempt from further payments unless a reinstatement of cover could be arranged.

MACHINERY BREAKDOWN RATING

Assessing the risks of mechanical and electrical breakdown, particularly in nuclear reactors, calls for specialised underwriting skills. Whilst it is the responsibility of those in the Pool organisations to whom rating authority may be delegated to finally determine the rates to be quoted, they would certainly be well advised to seek the assistance and advice of Engineering insurance specialists. In the case of a Pool which has either the necessary in-house technical resources or can call upon member companies to undertake the necessary rating assessments, appropriate techniques will no doubt have been worked out. In other cases, it is very desirable that the advice of Machinery or Engineering insurance companies should be sought because the methods used to assess straightforward Material Damage rates would not be appropriate.

In the case of the British Insurance (Atomic Energy) Committee, the Engineering Committee mentioned previously undertakes the assessment of the nuclear hazards and evaluates these according to a system which enables the Material Damage underwriters to calculate appropriate rates for reactors or other types of nuclear installation. However, the work of this Committee is limited to its technical responsibility and therefore if Machinery Breakdown insurance has to be rated this is undertaken by a panel of experts drawn from the Engineering Insurance Companies based in Manchester. They have the techniques derived from generations of experience for assessing suitable insurance rates for boilers, pressure vessels and other major items of plant, which can be adapted to nuclear reactors. Except for the cover included in the All Risks policies written by the American, British and Canadian Pools and the non-Pool insurance written by the specialist Machinery insurance market, the portfolio of nuclear stations insured for Machinery Breakdown is very small. Consequently, actual experience of dealing with insured losses is very limited, although a certain amount can be learned from examining known cases of such damage as reported in the technical literature even when they are not subject to Pool insurance policies. Some of the damage suffered would not in fact be insurable in any event. Although few such events have been the subject of known insurance claim payments, something can be learned of the repair costs and the time involved in undertaking such repairs, which is a crucial factor.

It goes without saying that the costs of repairing or replacing damaged components in a nuclear reactor, particularly in the High Radioactivity Zone, are high. Leaving aside the major catastrophe, one is thinking in terms of costs of probably tens of millions of pounds, and repair times of a year or more. Apart from this, a highly important factor is the additional expense incurred as a result of having to deal with damage in a radioactive environment. This can account for substantial additional costs which would not be recoverable under the ordinary Material Damage insurance because the radioactivity in these areas is a normal feature and not the result of an accidental occurrence. Nevertheless, it has to be dealt with either by the use of decontamination procedures or shielding, the use of remote control equipment or severely limiting the time that operatives are permitted to be in the area, even if wearing protective clothing. Therefore, the Rating Panel will be proposing terms which take into account not only the cost of replacement as new of each item destroyed or damaged but also an Additional Cost item to account for extra costs of working owing to access difficulties. The latter would certainly have to be subject to a loss limit but to ensure a realistic level of cover this should not be less than some millions of pounds.

So far as the cover for the actual damage and replacement is concerned, this should be subject to an overall limit which is sometimes assessed at, say, one and a half times the value of the largest single item of plant which would almost certainly be the reactor pressure vessel. In order to assess an appropriate premium the engineering insurance specialists will require a breakdown of values, not only for the reactor pressure vessel but also to account for the value of the lid on the reactor, control rod drives, the control rods themselves and other reactor internals. A further requirement will be a substantial deductible for which an appropriate allowance would be made. If needed recommended discounts may be obtainable from the International Machinery Insurance Association.

It is not possible to go further in describing the rating process other than to say that the range of rates charged per mille on the value of the various major components would be very wide. The reactor pressure vessel, which is most unlikely itself to suffer severe damage, save in the event of a disaster of Chernobyl proportions, would carry a relatively low rate, whereas equipment such as the control rod drives might, according to the type of reactor system, be very much more highly rated. Other equipment, particularly that in the Low Radioactivity Zone, which is much more likely to suffer breakdown such as main pumps in Light Water reactors and circulators in Gas-Cooled reactors and also the fuel loading and transfer machinery in all types of reactors, would have to carry a much higher rate. Turbines and other plant in the Zero Radioactivity Zone would be rated in accordance with appropriate Market rates for such plant at conventional power stations.

So far as the deductibles or excesses are concerned, the Rating Panel may very well advise different levels according to which radioactivity zone is under consideration. It may be that the insured would wish voluntarily to carry a larger excess than that which would be imposed by insurers as part of the rating package. Similarly, they may opt for a lower annual policy limit than that which would be regarded as a necessary feature of the premium recommendations. In these cases special consideration would have to be given to these factors as a possible justification for discounted terms.

"EXCESS OF LOSS" RATING

It is necessary to give some consideration to this question because of the possibility (a reality in the United States) of Pools providing an additional layer of cover in excess of the limits provided by the primary insurance; or in excess of a secondary layer provided by either a Captive or Mutual insurance arrangement or by professional reinsurers. Since such layered insurance contemplates different levels of loss potential, the exposure at the upper levels in the conventional insurance and reinsurance fields is usually considered to be much less than at the primary level. It is, in effect, a catastrophe protection. As such, and depending on the maximum limits to which the primary insurance goes, the secondary layer may be exposed to claims only on very infrequent occasions. Underwriters specialising in this field are able to examine the experience of many decades in determining how much cover they will provide and the terms on which they will provide it. However, the experience of rating non-nuclear Excess of Loss covers may not be of very much assistance when considering nuclear risks. Several factors, of course, will have to be considered, first among these being the extent to which the primary cover is likely to be exposed. If the underlying policy or policies are written on the All Risks basis, including Machinery Breakdown, with perhaps a substantial amount for Additional Costs of Decontamination and other clean-up operations, and is subject to a limit significantly below the cost of a serious accident, it is quite likely that even a moderately severe nuclear accident will cause the ceiling on the primary cover to be breached sooner or more often than would be the case in the conventional field.

It is not practicable to give any objective guidance on the pricing of such Excess of Loss covers. This may, in any event, be different according to whether the reinsurance is written within the international pooling system or is placed outside in the professional reinsurance markets through the usual broking facilities for which a substantial commission is likely to be charged. Also, outside the Pools, there is no certainty of the reinsurers retaining net lines.

From what little experience there is of Excess of Loss covers or similar reinsurance arrangements, particularly when placed outside the pooling system, it is apparent that underwriters are looking for a substantial rate, probably close to the average rate applicable to

351

the underlying primary insurance. When a Pool is persuaded to write their policies on the basis of a very high excess (meaning a self retention for up to £50M) they should bear in mind that this is not going to give them much protection against the consequences of even a moderately severe nuclear accident, the cost of which would be aggravated if the policy is on an All Risks basis or otherwise includes Machinery Breakdown cover which might be involved in the same incident, with a substantial amount of cover for the additional costs of decontamination operations. So, even if such an arrangement is looked upon as an Excess of Loss reinsurance, it cannot be discounted to anything like the extent to which an insurance written in excess of £50M may be in the conventional insurance field. In the event of a nuclear incident of even moderate severity, cutting out even the first £50M of a loss payment may reduce the cost to insurers by only a very modest percentage. Furthermore, in assessing their rates and premiums for reactor installations in particular, the greater part is attributable to the more severe forms of damage covered by the policy for even a very large deductible or excess. This therefore is not reasonably reducible by more than a modest discount, so the net effect on the overall rates or premiums on which the Excess of Loss premium is to be based cannot be large.

CONSEQUENTIAL LOSS RATING

As in the conventional field, insurance for consequential losses, business interruption, loss of profit or additional costs of working written by the Pools protects the policyholder against financial loss in one form or another, resulting directly from physical damage which causes the shutdown of the plant and interruption or cessation of production. It is desirable, as in the conventional field, that any form of Consequential Loss insurance should be related to exactly the same insured perils as are covered under an underlying Material Damage policy. Whether or not this would be insisted upon, or even whether any form of underlying Material Damage policy would be a necessary pre-requisite, must be a matter for policy decisions by the insurers concerned.

In assessing rates for Consequential Loss insurances in the nuclear field, it would be usual to follow the same practices as would apply to conventional insurance, that is to say, an average rate for the whole of the property insurance would be worked out and would then be subject to a percentage loading according to the indemnity period, i.e. the number of months over which the insurers will meet the financial loss according to the basis on which it is computed up to a certain maximum limit.

The assessment of the limit of cover under the policy requires careful consideration in close consultation with the insured. As in conventional insurance, it would depend very much upon the basis of cover selected. For nuclear power stations, this is quite likely to be related to the cost of replacing lost electrical output. Most Utilities have a statutory or contractual obligation to maintain a minimum annual supply measured in kilowatt hours when the particular power station concerned is damaged to the extent that production cannot be maintained, and the shortfall must be made good either by increasing production from another power station owned by the same Utility or by "buying-in" electricity from another supplier. If the former solution is adopted, it may well be that the power station from which the alternative supply has to be provided is more expensive to run, e.g. it might be oil-fired, so that the cost of producing electricity would be higher. In such a case the difference between that price and the price of the electricity from the nuclear station would be a measure of the operator's financial loss. Cover may of course be required on another basis, or in addition to the additional working costs basis. There may be a need for an item to cover standing charges such as the continuing payment of wages to employees.

The scope of the insurance will to a large extent determine the rating. It has to be remembered that the time required to repair a damaged nuclear reactor may be very much longer than for comparable conventional plant. Quite apart from normal under-writing considerations, there may be an insufficiency of capacity to provide enough financial cover to allow for a very long period of outage. Therefore, such cover as may be granted is likely to be much more highly exposed than in the case of a conventional power station. However long the indemnity period, it is highly probable that even if it were to be as long as 2 years (which may be a desirable maximum) it will be fully exhausted before the plant is able to return to full-scale production. A further adverse consideration which will affect the level of rates is that because of the risks to the public associated with nuclear damage, the licensing authorities are likely to be much slower to authorise the resumption of production even when repairs are completed, not only on account of safety considerations but also for political reasons. However, undue prolongation of an inter-ruption for administrative reasons should probably be regarded as uninsurable when they are unreasonable and the policy conditions will no doubt limit the cover in regard to this aspect.

The conclusion must be that whatever Consequential Loss rate results from the application of the usual percentage addition for the selected Indemnity Period and taking account of any deductible whether this be in the form of a monetary amount or a period of time (waiting period) over and above any compulsory restriction of this nature, an additional loading will have to be applied to recognise the special problems associated with nuclear hazards. There are very few cases in which Consequential Loss insurance has been written on nuclear power stations by the Pools and no general body of practice has been built up. Nor has there been sufficient experience for nuclear insurers to look for common ground in regard to such matters. However, in the opinion of some experts, anything up to a 100% addition would be justified to bring the premium for a "nuclear" Consequential Loss insurance up to a reasonable level compared to that which may be charged for a conventional power station.

In the case of nuclear fuel factories and such very large radio-isotope-producing factories as would qualify as nuclear installations, the treatment of Consequential Loss Insurance rating would be much closer to that appropriate to a conventional chemical or metal-working factory, since the dominant element in the underlying Material Damage rates (except possibly for a factory reprocessing irradiated fuel and extracting plutonium) would be related to the conventional perils insured.

THIRD PARTY LIABILITY RATING

As in the case of the Material Damage insurance, the provision of very full underwriting and technical information is of the utmost importance. It is equally important that this is evaluated by Liability underwriters with the necessary experience and expertise to deal with the nuclear aspects, and this includes a thorough knowledge of the national legislation and International Conventions concerning liability in the field of nuclear energy.

However, the starting point in the Third Party evaluation in accordance with the methods practised by the BI(AE)C whether assessing British or foreign risks, is the Engineering Points Assessment. The reason for this is that before any damage or injury can be caused to third parties (which may include employees on the site) there must be an incident on the licensed site resulting in irradiation or contamination by radioactivity of the property or persons of third parties. Consequently, the first measure of the risk must be the possibility and severity of an incident.

However, it is not possible to evaluate the Third Party hazards on this basis alone. In the case of a reactor incident the damage could be totally confined to the reactor containment building presenting little or no risk to the outside environment although employees working on the site or having to go into the containment building may be at risk. On the other hand, taking the possibilities at their worst, there may be an accident of such severity, including an explosion, that a disaster of Chernobyl proportions could occur with widespread effects on the environment. Therefore the environmental factors are of extreme importance, although others will also affect the assessment.

All these factors can be quantified if sufficient information is available resulting in a figure for Supplementary Points which can be added to the Engineering Points to produce a basis for assessing Third Party premiums which will reflect the special features of each risk.

To evaluate the environmental factors, specific features should be considered and given a value in Points which should be fixed by the underwriters. Whatever scale is adopted, the standard price to be applied to the total Points assessed will be adjusted to produce the desired premium levels. As in the rating of Material Damage risks, the objective of this evaluation is not to produce an absolute and rigid rate or premium for each risk but to provide underwriters with a systematic approach to the rating which will enable them to evaluate the differences between risks in a sensible and consistent manner and to reach the appropriate technical "plateau" from which to make their final premium assessment.

The following are the principal factors that must be considered. The number of Points to be attributed to each will depend upon whatever scale is selected. To give proper recognition to the differing degrees of importance, it is suggested that 3 levels be adopted, although the scale of I-III used below should be translated into a suitable range of supplementary Third Party points with maxima of, for example, 20, 10, and 5.

	Level of importance
(a) Environmental Features of the Nuclear Installation	
(1) Population distribution within $\frac{1}{2}$ mile, 2 miles, 10 miles and beyond.	I
(2) Employees and others on the Site — i.e. including students, trainees and visitors, potentially subject to direct exposure, who would be entitled to compensation under nuclear legislation in the same way as third parties.	I
(3) Property and land, including animals, within 2 miles, 10 miles and beyond.	I

355

(4) Proximity to rivers, canals, sea coasts, etc. — this would include reservoirs, water collecting areas and fisheries, which could become contaminated. II

(5) Meteorological data — prevailing winds, rainfall, frequency of inversion, unusual meteorological conditions such as exceptionally strong winds, flood, tornado, typhoon, tidal wave. II

(6) Geological data, including earthquake — i.e. giving particulars of substructure, reclaimed land, mining operations, incidence of landslide, landslip and subsidence. II

(b) On-site factors

(1) Quantity of fuel in store — could have a bearing upon the immediate concentration of radioactivity. III

(2) Qualifications of Personnel — extent of training and experience as well as academic qualifications. III

(3) Hazards from radioactive waste — method of (a) Storage and (b) Disposal, including safety measures. III

(c) Miscellaneous

(1) Political stability — possibility of riots, etc. I

(2) Transit — nature, frequency and quantities of movements of radioactive materials. I

(3) Any exceptional features — including, e.g. close proximity to industrial complexes, special uses including medical, isotope production, products liabilities involving indirect liabilities to the public which may be channelled to the operator by statute or otherwise. variable (no upper limit)

Note: I is "high"

(d) Additional conventional cover (Third Party and Employers' Liability)

To be assessed in each individual case.

356

NB 1. There may be exceptional cases where any of the above allocations may have to be specifically increased.

2. For critical assemblies and small reactors of under 1 MW thermal power the area of contamination in the event of an incident may be so limited as to require a negligible points allocation for Third Party risks.

Factors (a), (b) and (c) all relate to the nuclear risk, which must also be related to the nature of the legal liability under individual national laws. The value attributed to each individual section may have to be adjusted on that account. For example, in some countries grave natural disasters are excluded from the causes of nuclear incidents for which the nuclear operator would be held liable. In others that is not the case. Again, in some countries the operator's liability to pay compensation would include economic loss suffered by members of the public even when they or their property are not directly affected affected by nuclear damage: for example, he may have to meet the cost of precautionary evacuation of homes and industrial premises and consequent financial loss of the people concerned when a nuclear accident threatens but does not in fact occur. There is another category of expense which the operator may have to meet and that is the cost of minimising the effects of a nuclear accident other than measures he himself would take to reduce the potential material damage on site.

Some countries' legislation, however, does not permit such payments to be made out of the compensation reserved for the victims of nuclear incidents, although the site operator would be liable under common law to pay compensation to third parties or perhaps in some instances to the local authorities for their expenditure to reduce the effects of an incident. While such claims would undoubtedly be due to a nuclear incident, cover for them would have to be provided separately and not in that part of the policy reserved to provide the operator with an indemnity with regard to his strictly statutory nuclear liabilities. Assessment of this type of extension would be difficult to handle on a Points Evaluation basis and the required additional premium would have to be considered by underwriters on the basis of (i) the best information they can obtain as to the likelihood of claims arising and (ii) the amount of the separate limit of cover granted.

Additional conventional cover

Nuclear liability legislation normally circumscribes the payment of compensation out of the insurance or the financial security that has to be provided under the Law. Consequently, claims may be met

357

only when they arise from incidents due to the radioactive properties of nuclear matter or a combination of its radioactive, explosive, toxic or other hazardous properties. The protection afforded by such legislation to third parties may, as we have seen, extend to certain indirect or "economic" loss. However, any other damage or injury would be a matter for common law or, possibly in some countries, other Statutes. To be fully protected, therefore, the operator's Liability policy must include a separate indemnity limit to enable him to meet claims for compensation which are not brought within the terms of the Nuclear Liability legislation. This part of the cover is commonly regarded as "conventional" liabilities although in some circumstances the source of the damage could very possibly be a radioactive substance which escapes the provisions of nuclear legislation. It may, as in the United Kingdom, for example, be declared to be "excepted matter" by the licensing and controlling authorities because it is a "small quantity" or of low radioactivity. When the excepted matter is on the site of a licensed nuclear installation it is subject to the nuclear law, however. Excepted matter which is still the responsibility of the licensee of the insured nuclear installation and is *elsewhere* than on any licensed site or in transit does not come within the provisions of the nuclear law. Therefore compensation for any damage it may cause may not be paid out of the financial security which has to be provided by the licensee under the Act.

However, when insurers consider the conventional liabilities included in a Pool policy covering the operator of a nuclear installation, they are primarily concerned with the ordinary Third Party liabilities that would be imposed by Common Law on any individual. A nuclear installation, be it a power station or a fuel factory or a research establishment, obviously contains the potential for any number of non-nuclear mishaps which could cause injury or damage to employees and the public. Additional cover will have to be provided for these ordinary liabilities. Because they do not differ greatly from those associated with conventional Public Liability insurance, the assessment of the appropriate premium to be charged for that section of the Pool Liability Policy would normally be handled by the Pool's Liability underwriters who would have regard to current Market practice.

Cover for liability towards employees may or may not be included in the statutory nuclear cover. This would be dependent upon the provisions of the national legislation. It is usually not included in the conventional section of the policy because the necessary insurance is available under Employers' Liability or Workmen's Compensation insurance arrangements from the ordinary market. However, if the local Market decides that the conventional Employers' Liability risk should also be the responsibility of their nuclear Pool, then of course an appropriate extension of cover would be included in the conventional section of the Pool policy at an appropriate premium which would be determined in consultation with the underwriters specialised in this field.

Legal Expenses and Other Costs

It is almost the invariable practice under nuclear Liability laws to exclude legal costs and sometimes other expenses and interest charges from the monies that may be paid out of the statutory compensation limits. So far as such costs relate to nuclear claims they would, if cover is required, have to be included in the Pool Liability policy by way of a separate section for a fixed amount. This adds to the total indemnity payable with respect to nuclear incidents and the premium would then be adjusted to take account of the increased indemnity payable overall.

Legal costs incurred in connection with the purely non-nuclear claims would not necessarily be the subject of additional cover, since premiums charged in the conventional Third Party insurance field normally take such additional costs into account.

PREMIUM ASSESSMENT

The starting point in assessing an appropriate premium would be the figure arrived at by adding together the Engineering Points and the Supplementary Third Party Points calculated in accordance with the above guidelines. However, it is not, as in the case of Material Damage rating, then simply a matter of applying a flat price per point. There are many other variables which would affect the pricing. The two most important are the thermal power of the reactor if that is the type of installation insured, and the Indemnity Limits to be covered.

In determining the scale of prices, it will be assumed that the statutory indemnity limit will be a standard figure according to national law. Because the levels of compensation for which insurance cover must be provided vary enormously from one country to another, the standard price per point according to thermal capacity will have to be keyed in the case of each country to the normal indemnity limit. This would usually be the highest limit applicable to a large nuclear installation. Thus the standard scale is centred on what might be described as the 100% price which would be subject to increases or decreases according to the extent by which the indemnity limit rises above or falls below the norm to accommodate any additional limits for an overall "installation" limit or, say, economic loss and the non-nuclear cover. As in the case of conventional Liability insurance, the percentage increase in premium would be less than the percentage increase in cover. A scale of limits, in steps, and the relevant loadings should be prepared; also, a graph to enable intermediate figures to be accurately identified.

1. Statutory Nuclear Cover

The price per point will have to be selected from an agreed scale expressed in the currency in which the insurance cover is to be provided. The pricing levels included in these scales should be subject to regular review to take into account inflation and other economic factors although problems with fluctuating exchange rates would be avoided if the local currency is always used. Claims experience will obviously be another consideration. Mercifully, claims from nuclear incidents are few and far between and may be very long delayed even when a known incident has occurred, so it may be very difficult to take this consideration into account objectively. Some attention may be paid to the claims experience in the general Liability insurance field. This could be relevant in considering the part of the premium attributable to the non-nuclear cover. However, it is unlikely to be relevant in assessing the majoi part of the premium which is that attributable to the statutory nuclear cover because this class of insurance has not shared in the general experience of Liability under-writers, which, it must be admitted, has in many countries been very poor in recent years.

It has always to be remembered that when the pricing levels for nuclear liability insurance were originally established, they were deliberately pitched at a relatively high level for the same reasons as those which determined the rating of Material Damage risks. In most countries they have been gradually reduced or at any rate not increased to reflect inflation. They were not subject to the savage rate reductions which in the years of over-capacity and excessive competition resulted in many liability insurance premiums being reduced to totally unrealistic levels. Being to a large extent insulated from Market movements, the Pools have avoided the volatility and instability experienced elsewhere and should hesitate before reflecting substantial rate increases applied to conventional business for reasons which are not related to the experience in the nuclear field, although entirely justified in those areas of Liability insurance business where insurers have had the courage to apply corrective rate increases.

The prices and scales applied must be very much a matter of the expert judgement of the Committees and others who determine these matters in the individual national Pools. While a common experience will suggest that there is likely to be some degree of harmonisation in Liability premium levels as between the different countries, there can be no question of uniformity because of the many and various local factors to be taken into account.

The first task of the Pool underwriter and their technical experts is to classify reactors according to thermal capacity and use. The following categories are recommended:

(a) large commercial power reactors
   up to 1250 MW(th)
   up to 1600 MW(th)
   up to 1900 MW(th)
   up to 2500 MW(th)
   up to 3000 MW(th)
   over 3000 MW(th)

(b) other than commercial power reactors
   less than 100 kW
   100 kW but less than 250 kW
   250 kW but less than 1 MW
   1 MW but less than 5 MW
   5 MW but less than 30 MW
   30 MW but less than 150 MW
   Above 150 MW

These stages have been selected because they correspond closely with the sort of power levels which are encountered in practice in teaching, materials testing and research reactors.

The premium to be charged per Point would then be fixed in steps, one level for each category according to thermal power.

Nuclear Fuel Factories

In the case of nuclear fuel factories which do not have a thermal power to refer to, "size" would be determined by the throughput or output of nuclear material measured in tonnes. Underwriters would have to work out a suitable scale in consultation with their technical experts according to (a) the annual capacity of the plant insured, and (b) the materials handled. A suggested rising scale for tonnage would be up to 10t; up to 50t; up to 200t; and over 200t. The classification of materials handled, in rising order of potential hazard would be:

Natural uranium
Up to 6% enriched uranium
More than 6% enriched uranium
Plutonium or irradiated fuel

361

It is not considered practicable to apply to non-reactor establishments the system of assessment developed for nuclear power stations and other installations equipped with energy-producing reactors even though the more hazardous types of fuel in fact might carry an Engineering Points Assessment for Material Damage above that for a small critical assembly used for educational purposes.

Premium scales according to indemnity limits

Even in the case of a country where the insurance is for only one fixed indemnity limit which would never be varied, it is valuable to have a scale based on percentage increases or decreases, particularly if the Pool concerned wants to make a check of the premium offered by another Pool for reinsurance against the pricing that they themselves would expect to apply to the risk in question.

Once the appropriate price per point has been selected, it would be applied to the sum total of the Engineering Points Assessment and the Supplementary Third Party Points to produce the nuclear portion of the premium for the risk. If the indemnity limit is different from that which has been used to select the appropriate price, at this point the necessary percentage reduction or percentage loading would be applied. It may be, for example, that although the indemnity limit required under the Act is a standard figure, it applies on a per incident basis which would be the case under most nuclear laws (although not in the U.K. or Switzerland, for example). However, the policy cover to be provided will be subject to an overall limit for the lifetime of an installation which would normally be for a figure above the "incident" limit — possibly twice as much, and may include additional cover for costs and "economic loss". Therefore, even if the correct price per point has been charged in accordance with the statutory limit, it will have to be increased to account for the overall "installation" limit. The amount of the increase will be a matter of judgement and it would be less than as for a higher "incident" limit. It represents some increase in exposure because it is possible that during the currency of the insurance period there could be more than one incident and that this could occur before the policy is terminated under the cancellation conditions. Such an eventuality is of limited significance and therefore the addition to the basic premium to account for the overriding installation limit need not be substantial: perhaps something between 10% and 20% according to the figures involved.

Technical factors justifying basic premium variations

1. Premium-loading factors

(a) *Intentional Emissions of Ionising Radiation*

The reasons why the deliberate release of radioactive matter from a nuclear site cannot be regarded as normally insurable have been explained earlier. Such releases may occur in two ways:

(1) A deliberately controlled emission of small quantities of liquid or gaseous wastes to the environment or a disposal of low-level waste on to other sites when the level of radioactivity is within the permitted safe levels according to the operating licence and the regulations of the ICRP and the IAEA.

(2) Similar releases in excess of permitted levels when the emission is by design and not a sudden fortuitous and unforeseen event.

Although the safety levels are such that human beings or animals should not suffer any harm as a result of exposure to radioactive matter in these circumstances, there is no certainty, even among scientific experts, that for every individual there is such a thing as a totally safe level. Even if the individual emissions are safe, it may be possible for the matter concerned, whether it be solid or liquid, though less likely if it is gaseous, to accumulate somewhere and gradually build up to a quantity which emits an unsafe level of radiation. It is well known that persons who are exposed to radioactivity or ingest radioactive matter may suffer serious illness, although radiogenic diseases may not emerge for many years after the time of the exposure. Diseases that may be suffered would include somatic injuries like leukaemia and other malignant diseases, cataracts, damage to skin, impaired fertility and possibly ageing which leads to premature death although it cannot be attributable to a specific cause. Thus, if insurers are obliged by some means to meet claims arising from intentional releases from nuclear installations they must treat this as a serious addition to the Third Party risk covered under the nuclear part of the Liability policy.

Whatever the insurance position may be, such is the nature of the liability imposed upon a nuclear operator in accordance with the International Conventions and national legislation based on these, that whether or not his actions are negligent, when a dose is absorbed by members of the public or their livestock in consequence of even a controlled and permitted release a claim may have to be met. There are very few defences in law against the payment of such compensation. Accordingly, under a Liability policy which is unable to carry an exclusion of the consequences of intentional emissions or cannot recover claims paid against the policyholder, a substantial additional premium should be charged according to the nature of the additional financial commitment involved, whether it be for the full indemnity limit, or for a part of it, or for the excess of a portion of the financial commitment retained by the policyholder for his own account.

Since this additional commitment amounts to an aggravation of the risks associated with the release of radioactive matter on the site, it is very likely that underwriters would deal with it by a percentage additional to the normal basic premium calculated in accordance with the guidelines given.

(b) *Exceptional Transport Liabilities*

The carriage of nuclear matter independently of the operation of a nuclear installation whether by the operator himself or an independent carrier would normally be the subject of separate insurance underwritten either by the Transport section of a nuclear Pool or in the Marine insurance market. The inclusion of a certain amount of transportation with the activities associated with the operation of a nuclear plant, however, is quite normal and would be included within the liabilities and financial obligations attaching to the operation of the installation itself. The sort of Transport risks that would be regarded as normal would be the despatch from the site of spent fuel, of nuclear waste and possibly of irradiated specimens or quantities of radioisotopes produced in the reactor as an addition to the normal commercial operations, in quantities which do not allow them to be exempted from the operation of nuclear legislation. Provided the transportation of such materials is carried out within the territorial limits of the country where the nuclear legislation is located, this may be treated as a normal part of the risks covered by the Site Liability Policy. The rating system recommended would allow for this feature to be taken into account by the addition of an appropriate number of points to the Third Party assessment. Transport risks are featured separately because there may be cases in some countries where no movements of nuclear matter to or from the site would need be covered under the Liability policy since they would be subject to separate insurance arrangements (subject to a separate overall indemnity limit "per voyage").

Nevertheless, underwriters should be alert to the importance of an exceptional frequency of movements of nuclear material from, and possibly to, the licensed site for which the operator is legally liable under the relevant nuclear law, especially when such transits are out of the ordinary. It may be that nuclear waste is transported both by land and sea to an offshore disposal site. This situation may require special consideration and the premiums to be charged for such movements may have to be assessed with advice from Marine insurance experts.

(c) *Economic Loss and Cost of Preventive Measures*

Under the provisions of national nuclear law, a nuclear operator may be obliged to meet such expenses as part of the compensation he must pay to Third Parties in consequence of a nuclear incident. The Points assessment should take acount of this when considering the scope of legislation, adding extra points for exceptional features where necessary.

However, under some nuclear laws, and this would include the British Nuclear Installations Acts, the funds to be provided for the compensation of Third Parties may not be used to meet economic loss claims except where these are a direct consequence of exposure to radioactivity of the third party or his property, nor any expenditure incurred in order to prevent or minimise a nuclear accident.

The operator would however be liable at law to meet any claims arising from these factors. The underwriting information, if it is properly prepared and sufficiently comprehensive, ought to give a reasonable indication of what additional expenses may have to be met. The insured, too, should have a good idea and will no doubt fix the amount of additional insurance that he wants to meet these aspects. This would be provided for in a separate section of the policy for a specific limit in addition to those provided for statutory nuclear liabilities and ordinary common law third party liabilities.

Since the additional exposure would be the consequence of an actual nuclear occurrence in most cases, the additional premium should be in proportion to the basic normal premium although it may be necessary to give some consideration to the possibility that such expenditure may be incurred as a result of precautionary measures taken when in the event there is no nuclear accident.

Since the legal position is liable to differ sharply between one country and another it should be carefully scrutinised before the additional premium is finally assessed.

(d) *Cross-Liabilities*

Insurers will occasionally encounter a situation in which there are two nuclear installations in completely separate ownership on adjoining or nearby sites. Owing to the very high value invested in such plants, this greatly increases the potential third party exposure in relation to spreading nuclear damage. Consequently, there is a significant cross-liability as between the two site operators which may have to be reflected in a considerable addition to the Third Party Supplementary Points when each case is assessed by the underwriters in relation to the Environmental Factors.

It is sometimes possible to overcome this problem by arranging for the two establishments to agree not to exercise their right to claim against each other with respect to any damage due to radio-active contamination or irradiation arising from an incident at the other's site. Whether or not the consequences of such damage can be included in each operator's Material Damage insurance is another question: some Pools' policies explicitly exclude nuclear damage arising from sources outside the insured site.

2. Premium-discounting factors

(a) *Discount for "quality" of operator*
As in the case of Material Damage rating, a special reduction off the scale premium per point may be justified in the case of commercial power stations equipped with reactors of proven design of exceptionally high standard, particularly when these are operated by experienced Utilities of first-class standing who form part of a major national nuclear energy industry and who can demonstrate an outstanding record of safe operation with several installations over a period of years. Any credit allowed in the rating for these considerations can properly be regarded as technically based because it does seek to measure objectively favourable technical considerations.

A special allowance of this nature might also be justifiable for other types of reactor establishments such as those engaged in nuclear research and development which are operated by experienced organisations of first-class national or international standing who have an outstanding record of safe operation over a period of years.

(b) *Allowance for Containment*
Reactor systems which involve the construction of a massive outer containment shell pose a considerably reduced hazard to the environment than reactors which have little or no such additional containment. It would be necessary to take advice from the Pools' technical experts as to the efficacy of the particular containment in individual cases as a barrier to the escape of fission products in the event of a nuclear accident. Assuming it is sufficiently strong to be proof against being breached by a conventional explosion within the reactor hall or by external missiles such as crashing air-craft, the presence of such containment is likely to be a favour-able feature in the assessment of the risks to the environment. Consequently, where the containment meets the necessary criteria,

the premium for the nuclear part of the cover would justify a reduction for these technical reasons of up to, say, 25%.

(c) *Discount for "common" site limit*
When a nuclear installation comprises two or more separate reactor units and, according to the national nuclear legislation, the whole installation is treated as one in determining the amount of financial security to be provided by insurance, it is reasonable to apply a reduction to the aggregate premiums that would be chargeable for each reactor. The reason for this is that regardless of the number of units which may contribute to the risk of an accident causing damage or injury to the public, only one overall limit applies under the policy. 2, 3, 4 or even more reactors may come under the one indemnity limit and in these situations a discount of anything from 10% to, say, a maximum of 20%, could be considered. It should not be more because to be set against the reduced financial exposure is the consideration that the greater the number of the reactors operating on one site the greater must be the possibility of an accident.

(d) *Premium reduction during fuel-loading phase*
As in the case of Material Damage rating, the Liability premium may be discounted by up to 50% during the period of the first loading of a reactor with fuel. The reduction may be less, however, because premiums may not be broken down in the same way as the Material Damage rating structure to enable the reduction to apply only to that part of the cover which relates to the reactor unit.

(e) *Rebates for reactor shutdowns*
The same criteria as those explained in the case of Material Damage rating, would be applied. The liability premium rebate should be for a lower percentage, however, because there are residual risks of injury or damage to Third Parties (especially if employees are included) arising from the presence of irradiated fuel and wastes. These would be a less important element in the assessment of material damage to the reactor during an outage.

Rating of Conventional Liability

As explained above, this would be largely a matter of judgement according to the nature of the non-nuclear liabilities involved, the limit of indemnity and whether or not employees have to be included. When this premium has been agreed, consideration will then be given to the combined overall premium to be quoted.

OVERALL OPERATOR'S LIABILITY PREMIUM

This final premium to be quoted is not necessarily the result of adding the product of the "technical" nuclear Liability premium, the premium for the conventional part of the policy, and any other additional premiums required for legal costs, economic loss, loss minimisation expenses and the like. Because there may be a certain overlap between some of the liabilities which have to be covered in accordance with national nuclear legislation and the common law liabilities covered under other parts of the policy, it may be appropriate for underwriters to review the resulting aggregate in the light of their judgement of the totality of the Third Party risk before deciding on the right overall "technical" premium.

CONTINGENT LIABILITY INSURANCES

(a) Product Liability Insurances

Although in some countries, notably the United Kingdom and North America, there is a growing experience in the provision of Liability insurance relating to products supplied to land-based nuclear installations, the variety of risks and possibilities is so considerable that it would be impracticable to try to develop a standard basis for a rating scale. It is normally well within the competence of experienced Product Liability underwriters to apply their talents to the assessment of products which are used or may be used in nuclear installations, or even complete nuclear installations. In determining basic premium rates, it will be implicit that such rates would need to be compatible with current Market levels, probably higher. All the necessary underwriting and technical information will have been elicited if the type of questionnaire described earlier is used.

What the underwriters assessing the premium will be looking out for, as well as the nature of the product, will be the type of injury or damage it could cause, and the locations where it is used. They will also be concerned with the country or countries in which the product is to be used because it is quite possible that the policy to be issued will apply to several countries to which the products may be supplied apart from the domicile of the manufacturer concerned. Therefore, they will take account of the legislative position, and the possibility of a supplier of products being obliged to accept some degree of legal liability for damage to the public notwithstanding channelling under normal nuclear lesislation; his contractual obligations regarding any damage he may cause to the property of his client; and so on. Their assessment for premium purposes will also have regard to the legal climate surrounding the settlement of claims arising from damage or injury caused by defective products.

In this connection, the reputation and the conventional claims experience of the policyholder will be highly relevant. Finally, the financial aspect, both in terms of the turnover of the product or products concerned, and the limit of indemnity to be provided under the Product Liability Policy issued by the Pool, will be essential factors in enabling a premium to be assessed.

(b) Errors and Omissions, and Professional Indemnity Insurances
For the other types of contingent Liability insurance which might be provided by a nuclear Pool, such as Errors & Omissions policies and policies covering Professional Indemnity, similar considerations would arise except of course that normally a product as such would not be involved. It requires a considerable amount of expertise assisted by the skill of technical specialists to evaluate the risk of damage arising as a result of, say, inspection activities, decontamination work or design work, and the professional competence of consultants in the nuclear engineering field.

CONSIDERATIONS JUSTIFYING SPECIAL TERMS (ALL CLASSES OF POOL INSURANCES)

(1) Credits for good experience
A form of special rating which some would regard as having a commercial rather than a technical base is the granting of regular discounts related to the claims experience over a period of years subject to an overall maximum for a particular client, or even collectively for the whole of the nuclear industry or such part of it as buys commercial insurance from the Pools. Such credit schemes may apply to Physical Damage or Liability insurance, or both, and usually involve granting an automatic annual discount or bonus every year to a pre-arranged scale based on the percentage loss ratio, i.e. the amount paid out in claims as a proportion of the premiums paid in to the Pool. When claims exceed a fixed percentage all rates are increased, however. When applied on an industry-wide basis to the totality of policyholders it may work to the advantage of some and to the disadvantage of others. Except in the USA, where there is a better spread of domestic risks than elsewhere, the erratic pattern of losses experienced in connection with the small number of insured nuclear installations makes it very hard to assess the significance, as an objective rating factor, of such claims as may be paid from time to time. Regular experience discounting in accordance with a set formula is practised systematically by no more than 2 or 3 other Pools outside the United States.

Whatever is done, it is extremely important that, while rating levels ought to reflect good loss ratios, increasing overall premium incomes and a greater spread of risk worldwide, the lowering of basic rates must be done in a systematic, methodical and well-thought-out manner in order to preserve a proper stability within the nuclear pool system; to recognise the impact of inflation; and to sustain and increase the support of the subscribing Pool Members.

The BI(AE)C have preferred to avoid such schemes, feeling that periodical reviews of rating levels which can be reduced to respond to a continuing satisfactory claims experience, maybe coupled with special commercial discounts in suitable cases, is a preferable method.

Insurances subject to large deductibles are unlikely to be suitable for experience credit-rating schemes because of the elimination of significant loss payments by insurers and the consequent masking or distortion of the claims experience: a problem unlikely to arise in a country where large deductibles are not favoured — as in the U.S.A. where experience discounting is a well established system of special rating.

(2) Commercial Discounts

When dealing with a large portfolio of good-quality risks, particularly when this relates to a group of nuclear installations owned and operated by one Utility or industrial concern, there may be good grounds for making special concessions in the net rates and premiums offered. It is more than likely that a very large and powerful concern, particularly if it be a monopoly, will be looking for special terms and will be able to bring various pressures to bear in the course of negotiations. In cases where the insured are paying in all a very large bulk of premiums each year, and qualify for all the possible credits on technical grounds, they may well merit a discount off the normal technically-based net rates or premiums. Such concessions cannot, of course, be catered for in any form of rating guide or scale since they must be dealt with by the negotiators according to their best commercial judgement. Whatever concessions a Pool may decide to grant to a particular client, it is desirable to seek to maintain a reasonable relationship between these and such special terms as might be allowable to another of comparable standing. The extent to which a Pool may be prepared to concede special reductions will be influenced to some extent by the importance they attach to maintaining the goodwill of their client and retaining his business. On the other hand, it has to be recognised that since there is very unlikely to be an adequate alternative to the insurance available from the Pools, this situation might be exploited by a difficult client.

However, in the interests of maintaining and if possible increasing the number of insured risks and the spread of business, providing the quality of the business is good, most Pools will be prepared to consider special concessionary terms for a particularly important client or group of clients prepared to remain loyal to commercial insurance. In an exceptionally attractive and important case as much as 25% off normal net rates or premiums might be justified.

In others it is possible to consider granting a commercial discount in return for an undertaking on the part of the client not to seek further rating concessions for a period of, say, 2 or 3 years. Since it is commercially attractive to insurers not to have to undergo an annual bargaining session, a rating standstill with a discount of perhaps 2% or 3% may be granted subject to review in the event of a severe loss.

It is not unknown, when a large and powerful establishment is aware that they have concessionary terms, for them or their Brokers to demand ever-lower premiums even in return for ever-increasing cover; but there must come a point when in the interests of the stability of the business and the ability of the Pools to continue to attract adequate capacity from their Members they must be ready to draw the line. Even the largest client may not be worth retaining "at any price" if this will damage the wider interests of nuclear Pools generally and threaten the continuing support of their Members.

It is true to say as a result of this steady and controlled process of reductions over the years, the average level of Material Damage rates for large nuclear power stations and other major commercial nuclear risks has fallen by some 40% or more, compared with typical rates when the Pools were writing their first risks in the early 1960's. Liability premium rates have also eased although comparisons with the past are more difficult in this field owing to the impact of inflation and, more importantly, the considerable increases in many countries in the indemnity limits which have to be insured to enable nuclear operators to meet their statutory obligations. Material Damage premiums, as distinct from rates per cent, have risen only when very much higher values have required nuclear operators to purchase so much more insurance protection that the rate reductions are overtaken by the resulting premiums even though these are substantially less than they would have been in the past for the same amount of cover.

Even so, the insurance costs have greatly eased through the readiness of the Pools to scale down their rates considerably even when competitive pressures are absent, and often ahead of consumer-driven demand. In spite of sometimes unfair criticism from some quarters, Insurers deserve praise for their responsible attitudes to pricing in a situation where they might have taken advantage of the absence of adequate alternatives to pooled insurance cover. This is especially true in view of the importance of maintaining a satisfactory premium flow from this very small and risky sector of their business.

Insurers must be the pacemakers on rates, anticipating reasonable demands for easement, but not being pressured into granting exaggerated concessions by interests invulnerable to an unfavourable loss experience and with little or nothing to lose from uneconomic insurance terms.

After all, though catastrophic accidents are likely to occur only rarely, the potential cost of claims is enormous; yet, even after nearly 30 years, the premium income from nuclear insurance is but a fraction of one percent of the insurance industry's total income from the related branches of conventional insurance.

CHAPTER XII

NUCLEAR INSURANCE POLICIES

Contracts of insurance covering nuclear installations and the liabilities associated with their operation are, for convenience, described as nuclear insurance. This should not be taken to imply that "nuclear insurance" is an independent branch of the insurance business as, for example, marine insurance, motor insurance, life insurance, and so on. What the Pools provide are ordinary forms of insurance adapted to cover extraordinary types of risk. Thus, a Material Damage is basically a Fire insurance or Property insurance policy with certain extensions, exclusions and variations. A Pool Machinery Breakdown policy, a Pool Consequential Loss policy, a Pool Third Party Liability policy, a Pool Product Liability policy, a Pool Transport Insurance policy, and so on are all likewise based on conventional forms of cover.

One of the main reasons for this is that for a large part of the wording of any such policy there is no need to depart from standard practice. Many of the general conditions will be exactly the same as for a policy covering a conventional risk. Another reason would be that the insurers participating in these policies are ordinary insurance companies, or, in the case of the United Kingdom, also Lloyd's Underwriters, who will not wish to depart from normal practice and may indeed by under some obligation to comply with certain wordings which are the subject of market agreements or customary practice. A third reason is that in many countries the wordings of all types of policies have to filed with and formally approved by Government insurance supervisory authorities, State insurance departments in the U.S.A. or other controlling bodies.

Therefore, the purpose of this Chapter will be to consider the special perils or liabilities which have to be insured and any special conditions, restrictions or exclusions which insurers find it necessary to incorporate in nuclear insurance policies. There is a wide measure of agreement internationally as to the nature of these variations from standard insurance practice although their form and content may vary. Because of the influences of national insurance practices, customs, principles and, in many cases, legal requirements, standard wordings for the use of all nuclear pools would be quite impracticable, even if the insurers concerned desired it. Even so, in the mid-1960's EURATOM — the European Atomic Energy Community — persuaded the European Nuclear Insurance Pools to collaborate with them in the preparation of model Liability insurance conditions, although the insurance interests pointed out that these could only be used by them as a guide because they could never be imposed upon Pools who had to observe the necessary legal requirements in their own countries as well as the established customs and practices of the local insurance markets. EURATOM also commissioned a study by German consultants into Material Damage insurance of fixed installations published in 1965 as an official document, bearing the reference number EUR3174. This examined specimen wordings provided by the French, German, Italian, Netherlands, Swiss, United Kingdom and United States Pools. The object of this undertaking was to lay down guidelines on which the EURATOM Commission intended to rely in its negotiations with insurers, the industry, and electrical producers in the Community.

They were greatly concerned to be satisfied that adequate insurance provisions could be made for the nuclear energy industry which at that time was in the early stages of development. This concern had been manifested in previous years as a result of which a number of meetings had been held with representatives of the insurance Pools and the nuclear industry, the most recent of these, at the time, having been what was described as the Fourth Colloquium. Although this study did not attempt to produce a standard or model insurance policy, it made a number of sensible comments, one of these being that it was advisable to combine nuclear and conventional risks — Fire, Lightning and Explosion — because in the event of these perils occurring simultaneously it would be far from easy to make a clear distinction between the types of damage resulting therefrom. They approved of the sub-division of the nuclear risk into, to use their words, "excessive temperature on the occasion of the phenomenon of nuclear transmutation" and "radioactive contamination" although they did not think it necessary to specify, in addition, "ionising radiation" as a nuclear peril. They had quite a lot to say about the general topic of excessive temperature although did not consider it appropriate for the policy to limit the cover to a sudden manifestation of excessive temperature, considering it sufficient that it be described as resulting from an unintentional and uncontrolled occurrence. However, they did think it necessary to provide for cover in the event of excessive temperature resulting from a breakdown of the reactor cooling system though not if it resulted from a breakdown of the moderator, since that risk should be regarded as excluded. They also considered that excessive temperature occurring in radioactive substances situated outside the reactor, or even outside the insured site, should be covered. As for costs of decontamination incurred in order to make contaminated property serviceable again, they did not regard it as necessary to specify this if the policy provided cover for expenses incurred for the reconditioning of the damaged article. They also considered that salvage costs and the expenses incurred in preventing damage should be covered.

They made many other comments, one of the most important being their approval of the concept of the waiving of rights of recovery against third parties. They regarded this as being of particular importance for sub-contractors and stressed the necessity for all policies to take it into account.

It may be said that while the Pools, particularly those of the countries belonging to the European Community, considered the report of EURATOM very seriously and with due respect, they had, by 1967 reached a wide measure of agreement as to the basic provisions of the Material Damage policies that they would be prepared to write even though the individual Pools' wordings varied in matters of detail.

Another international organisation, UNIPEDE, (the International Union of the Producers and Distributors of Electricity previously referred to) made a request in 1971, through the Belgian Pool, that Pools should all use a standard list of definitions in their policies covering nuclear power stations. When this was considered by the Pool Chairmen's London Conference in April 1971, considerable doubts were expressed as to the feasibility of such a proposition either because the policy wordings then in use were considered adequate and they had been acceptable for some years to the insured nuclear operators in particular cases, or because such standard definitions may conflict with statutory definitions observed in some countries, or for other legal reasons.

However, it will be clear from interventions of this nature that not only the insurers were aware of the need for a reasonable degree of harmonisation, if not standardisation, between the terms and conditions of the policies they were to issue. The principal points on which common ground has been achieved or recommended for the various classes of nuclear Pool insurance policy are described below.

MATERIAL DAMAGE INSURANCE

Nuclear perils

The range and description of these perils varies from country to country. However, all Pools except those issuing an All Risks form of policy specify excessive temperature as one of them. All include contamination by radioactivity.

a) Excessive temperature

The term Excessive Temperature seems first to have been introduced by the BI(AE)C and the British wording is therefore of interest. It reads "Excessive Temperature within any nuclear reactor insured hereunder consequent upon a sudden, uncontrolled, unintentional and excessive increase or release of energy, or upon the total or partial failure of the cooling system." There are other examples: "Excessive Temperature within the reactor"; "Abnormal temperatures which are not provided for in normal operation and which arise from accidental generation or release of atomic energy by the installation or the radioactive substances insured"; "Excessive Temperature inside a reactor insured hereunder if the build-up of this temperature shows abnormal characteristics, i.e. sudden, fortuitous and involuntary"; "Excessive rise in temperature during the nuclear fission, if not foreseen in normal operations, caused by increase or release of energy in an uncontrolled and accidental manner or by the failure of the cooling system". These come from several parts of the world. Other countries use a wording which is close to the British Pool's version, which is unsurprising since for many of these countries a British specimen policy would have been used as a basic model for their own.

b) Contamination by radioactivity

There is a number of variants according to national preference in regard to this peril. BI(AE)C policies utilise more than one version. The most straightforward of these reads "Contamination by radioactivity due to accidental escape of ionising radiations from the nuclear reactor or from any nuclear fuel which is on the site causing damage to

    (i) the outside surface of the external shield of the nuclear reactor or of the primary circuit

or

    (ii) any of the property described in the Schedule which is outside the external shield of the nuclear reactor or outside the primary circuit."

(If the plant insured is not a reactor, then the appropriate description of the installation would be used).

It is common practice nowdays to couple with the term "Contamination by Radioactivity" the term "Irradiation". Contamination implies the deposition of fission products in some form upon the contaminated object. However, damage can be caused by exposure to radioactivity or ionising radiation which can affect the properties or the chemical structure of various materials in a

376

harmful way. Other Pools tend to use somewhat similar wordings, for example, "Accidental radioactive contamination of insured property" defined as meaning the "accidental presence of a radioactive substance in a place or in contact with material where it is undesirable. However, radioactive contamination suffered by anything contained within any reactor vessel and primary circuits, including their internal surface, is not covered unless the decontamination measures are rendered necessary to allow the repair or replacement of property damaged as a result of one of the incidents mentioned ...." (the incidents referred to are the other insured perils). This particular example goes on to include "damage resulting from the effects of radiation of the insured property, i.e. an appreciable change in their physical characteristics under the effect of ionising radiations, etc."

Another Pool, in insuring "accidental radioactive contamination" describes this as meaning the presence of radioactive substances which are either in contact with a surface or within given surroundings. They also cover accidental irradiation, meaning the effect of ionising radiation on a material substance. Neither of these perils is covered if the damage is suffered by the reactor vessel and its contents and the primary cooling circuits and their contents, the only exception being damage to the outer surfaces of the said vessel and primary circuits. Elsewhere, radioactive contamination is covered and described in the policy as occurring "when the insured property has become wholly or partially unsuitable or unusable and has to be abandoned or does not lose its radioactivity within a reasonable period without decontamination measures. Insurance cover is subject to the incident having arisen accidentally from the installation or radioactive substances insured". The policy excludes contamination damage within the biological shield and to installation parts which by definition are exposed to radioactivity unless such contamination has been caused by one of the insured perils.

In another example, radioactive contamination or irradiation caused by an accident are covered in the following terms — "radioactive contamination means the presence of the radioactive substances which are either in contact with the surface of or situated within a given environment. Radioactive contamination is deemed to have occurred through any accidental escape of radioactivity from the said nuclear reactor or from anything which is on the site but is not within a nuclear reactor. Irradiation caused by accident means the effect of ionising radiation on material substances. Such perils are covered only if they cause damage to the outside surface of the external nuclear reactor shield or primary cooling circuit; any of the property described in the policy which is outside the said nuclear reactor shield or primary cooling circuit''.

It will be seen from these examples that there is a wide measure of similarity between the descriptions of the peril of contamination by radioactivity with which damage due to accidental irradiation is frequently included. Most policies use similar terminology. Instead of ''irradiation'' ''activation'' is sometimes used.

In addition to Excessive Temperature and Irradiation and Contamination by Radioactivity, at least one Pool recognises as a specific nuclear peril ''Accidental modification of reactivity''; ''Accidental criticality'' may also be covered, particularly in relation to nuclear fuel risks.

Conventional perils

The range of non-nuclear perils included in Pool Material Damage policies covering nuclear installations varies considerably from country to country. It is determined very largely by the custom and practice of the conventional Fire insurance or Property insurance market in the country concerned. However, not infrequently, some of the forms of damage, particularly those due to natural phenomena which might be insurable for a conventional industrial risk, would not be covered in the case of a nuclear installation. The commonest conventional forms of damage insured in Pool policies in all countries are Fire, Lightning, Explosion and Aircraft, by which is meant damage due to aircraft or objects falling from aircraft. (This may also include objects falling from spacecraft or satellites). One would expect to find these forms of damage included in all specified perils forms of policy. They would not be likely to be excluded from an All Risks form. Many other perils may by included either as standard or as additions which can be incorporated by arrangement for an additional premium. Policies covering British nuclear installations issued by BI(AE)C would cover the following additional perils as a matter of course:

Earthquake or subterranean fire;
Riot, civil commotion, strikers, locked-out
workers or persons taking part in labour disturbances
or malicious persons, but excluding loss, destruction or
damage resulting from (a) cessation of work (b) theft
by malicious persons;
Storm, tempest or flood excluding destruction or
damage (a) caused by subsidence or landslip (b)
of or to loose stocks of materials, loose plant and
the like in the open;
Impact of a vehicle but excluding destruction of or
damage to vehicles or to property in or on such vehicles.

The list may be varied, added to or reduced according to the requirements of the client and the circumstances of a particular risk. In other countries similar forms of damage would quite commonly be included. In addition, perils which are indigenous to the country are also encountered: one might find included in the policy: avalanche; entry of rain or snow; falling rocks; landslide; rolling stones; weight of snow; burst pipes; freezing pipes; leakage of heating apparatus. The reasons for most of these will be understood when one considers the climatic conditions of some countries. However, it is more than likely that the siting of nuclear power stations would be such that there would be little or no risk of damage due to avalanche, falling rocks, rolling stones, and so forth.

There may, however, be exceptions to this. In a country prone to earthquakes and tremors, this form of damage might be quite specifically excluded from a Pool Material Damage policy as would volcanic eruption and tidal wave following earthquake or seaquake; flood, overflow of the sea, tidal wave; landslide, subsidence or collapse. It is easy to see that these are forms of damage to which a nuclear reactor may be particularly susceptible to the extent that if they were to be included it is very unlikely that a Pool in such a country could obtain support from reinsurers in other countries.

Acts of violence, sabotage and terrorism

This was one of the topics which received particular attention from a Working Party set up by the Pool Chairmen's London Conference in February 1976 to consider the scope of cover available from Pools. It was composed of representatives from the Pools of 11 countries, and was initially divided into four sub-groups who reported their findings and recommendations to a full meeting of the Working Party held in Tokyo of April 1977.

One of their findings was that very few of the Pools specifically excluded violent acts. Others, like the British Pool, normally included Riot and Civil Commotion, etc. and Malicious Damage in their policies, in accordance with Market practice. It is standard practice to exclude war risks, including civil war and other armed conflict although practices vary in detail from country to country. It would be generally agreed that such exclusions would not extend to isolated acts of violence or terrorism. There are known legal definitions in various countries to deal with these different manifestations but the terminology used and the scope of the definitions may vary enormously and there seems to be no practical possibility of adopting any which would have international application. Nevertheless, the Working Party expressed the desire that some attempt should be made by the Pools to work out agreed definitions in consultation with their national insurance markets. Nuclear installations, whether under construction or in operation, are considered to be likely to form targets specially attractive to individuals and groups of individuals who may be incited to commit acts of sabotage or terrorism on them for political, social, ecological or other motives. It was considered that cover could not be refused when desired and that Pool Material Damage policies should grant cover for damage resulting from acts of sabotage or terrorism whether committed within a concerted framework or not but only when adequate rates, deductibles and security could be assured. Pools should be willing to reinsure such risks but only if policies extended to include them conformed with the practices followed in the national markets with respect to the insurance of conventional industrial risks.

The inclusion of Terrorism as such is not widely practised, although it would generally be regarded as being encompassed within cover against various forms of malicious damage, sabotage, etc.

Cover for additional costs

In the case of Material Damage policies covering nuclear installations or materials, it is common practice for the additional costs of decontamination, isolation, removal of contaminated debris and similar operations to be included either for a limited amount on the basis of a first loss cover or for a substantial amount which may go as far as the overall annual policy limit — a topic already discussed in an earlier chapter.

Additionally, on the conventional side, a Pool Material Damage policy would be likely to include additional expenses of the type normally found in conventional insurances in the country concerned. These may include the cost of clearance, of demolition and of debris removal; architects' and surveyors' fees; fire brigade charges; loss minimisation expenses; the cost of fire extinguishment undertaken by the policyholder; the replacement of models, plans, moulds and records; the cost of compliance with Government or Local Authority requirements when these are imposed in the interests of safety; extra labour costs incurred through employees working overtime in order to complete essential safety work quickly; expediting expenses, i.e. the additional costs incurred in arranging for spare parts or replacements to be supplied by the quickest rather than by the most economic method of delivery.

Whether or not conventional additional costs of these types would be incorporated in the cover with or without limit and/or additional premium would be a matter for compliance with local custom and practice. It is not to be expected that the nuclear insurance Pools would give their clients any more favourable treatment in these respects than would be granted to the policyholder in the case of conventional industrial risk.

Explicit exclusions

So far as the cover against nuclear perils is concerned, the principal explicit exclusion which all Pools would apply and which has always been regarded as essential, is any damage incurred as a consequence of irradiation or contamination by radioactivity occurring in the normal course of operations. For the inside of a nuclear reactor, the inner surfaces of the primary cooling circuit and any other parts where radioactivity is a normal part of the environment, the policy could not be expected pay for loss or damage occasioned by the presence or the occurrence of radioactivity. This would not apply when such contamination or irradiation were of abnormal proportions and the consequence of an insured peril.

Other exclusions which have a particular nuclear connotation and which are encountered in some Pool policies include the harmful effects of decontaminating agents, radioactive contamination coming from sources outside the nuclear installation insured, damage due to nuclear weapons and, frequently, explosive nuclear assemblies used for peaceful purposes, losses occurring when the safety controls of a reactor have been put out of action (usually during inspections or tests).

On the conventional side, the exclusions would, in most cases, be in line with those applicable to insurances of property of a non-nuclear nature according to the custom and practices of the national insurance market concerned. However, in some cases where certain types of damage may be particularly unacceptable when related to a nuclear installation, they may be added to the traditional exclusions. Such damage may include earthquake, earth tremors, hurricane, volcanic eruption, overflow of the sea and similar natural cataclysms when these are particularly prevalent in the country concerned. In a number of cases, as well as war risks, political risks and terrorist activities would be specifically excluded. (It must be remembered, however, that even though the direct damage that could result from such events may be excluded, the radioactive contamination or other nuclear damage which may be proximately caused by them might not be though national practice varies).

Among the other common policy exclusions which may have a

particular significance in relation to nuclear installations are the following:

(a) Theft — this is usually excluded from Material Damage policies because it is dealt with by most insurance markets as a separate class of insurance. (However, if the theft were to involve radioactive substances this may pose problems and a nuclear Pool may therefore be prepared to waive that exclusion and give specific cover for this). Damage caused in the course of Theft or attempted Theft would probably not be excluded.

(b) The cost of making good wear and tear, gradual distortion or deterioration — if not excluded, such costs could be very heavy in the case of a nuclear reactor. (In any event they are not accidental).

(c) Consequential Loss — this would be invariably excluded because it is a separate class of insurance. If not specifically excluded it could involve heavy financial loss aggravated by the complications due to the nuclear hazards.

(d) Order of public authorities — loss or damage due directly or indirectly to any act done by order of any Government, Public or Local Authority is a common policy exclusion in some countries, although it would not usually apply to such acts as fire-fighting. (On the other hand, costs incurred in complying with the requirements of Local Authorities e.g. in connection with building regulations, may actually be included in a Pool Material Damage policy).

(e) Sonic boom — damage or destruction directly occasioned by pressure waves caused by aircraft and other aerial devices travelling at sonic or supersonic speeds.

(f) Excess (or deductible) — the compulsory exclusion of a small proportion of the loss payment for certain forms of damage to discourage lack of care on the part of the insured is common-place but may acquire a particular significance when related to damage due to contamination by radioactivity. (This is a separate issue from the use of voluntary excesses as a part of the rating process).

Policy conditions

A great majority of the conditions found in a Pool Material Damage policy will be in accordance with standard insurance practices in the country concerned. Many of these conditions cannot be varied because they are in a form approved by the insurance supervisory authorities in the country concerned. There may, however, be special conditions or other requirements which also have a special relevance to nuclear risks.

Examples are:

Annual aggregate loss limitation In view of the capacity limitations and the obligations of Pools towards their Members to ensure that their net-line subscriptions cannot be exceeded this is a very important requirement. Suitable provisions, which should be in a prominent position in the policy document, would be as follows:

(1) The liability of the insurers shall in no case exceed in respect of each item the sum expressed in the said Schedule to be insured thereon or in the whole the total sum insured hereby or such sum or sums as may be substituted therefor by Memorandum hereon or attached hereto signed by or on behalf of the insurers.

(2) The liability of each of the insurers individually in respect of such destruction or damage shall be limited to the proportion set against its name or such other proportion as may be substituted therefor by endorsement hereon or attached hereto signed by or on behalf of the insurers.

(**Note**. The second paragraph is particularly important in the case of Pools whose members have a several or a joint and several liability; it may not be applicable where liability is joint only.)

Cancellation clause

The normal provisions enabling a policyholder to cancel his insurance at short notice would be found in most Pool Material Damage policies. It is of particular importance, however, that insurers' rights of cancellation should be clear and unequivocal because, in the event of a nuclear incident occurring, it is very possible for a further incident to follow that either as a result of the original damage done or in the course of operations that may have to be undertaken to recover the damaged reactor, or to make it safe, or to undertake decontamination operations. The period of cancellation may very quite considerably according to national practices or in some cases the legal requirements of the country concerned. It should preferably be not more than 30 days but a longer period, say two months, may have to be conceded. In many countries there is an automatic right of cancellation by the insurers immediately following a loss. The usual proportionate return of premium would normally be allowed.

Notification of loss

It is important to incorporate an appropriate condition to ensure that in the event of a nuclear incident, however small, and whether or not it may lead to the presentation of a claim, insurers will be immediately notified or as soon as possible thereafter and will have access to the site of the damage.

Tacit renewal

In some countries, notably in continental Europe, an insurance policy is deemed to continue in force year after year unless formally cancelled. Cancellation by the insurers may require as much as 6 months' notice. If such a condition is incorporated in the policy, awareness of it is very important particularly to reinsuring Pools whose membership is subject to annual renewal and who cannot, therefore, guarantee what their capacity, if any, will be at the beginning of each calendar year.

Warranties

This term, which is not used in all countries, is intended to apply to a policy condition which must be complied with, on penalty of the cover being automatically rendered void. Where it is legally permissible to impose such a condition, it is of particular importance in the insurance of nuclear installations as a means of ensuring that there has been no change in the use or safety rules applying to a particular installation and that obligatory inspections and record-keeping are complied with.

A suitable wording would be as follows:

1. It is warranted that there shall not be
    (a) any change in the design, specification or use of the within-mentioned nuclear reactor;
    (b) any alteration in the Code of Practice for the safe operation of the nuclear reactor or ancillary plant unless it be admitted by Memorandum signed by or on behalf of the insurers.
2. It is warranted that all buildings and plant in respect of which there is imposed upon the insured a liability by any authority or by the insurers for inspection are so inspected and records are kept and that any requirements arising therefrom be promptly complied with.

Rights against third parties

Mention has been made previously of the importance the Pools attach to eliminating, as far as possible, the necessity for concerns such as suppliers of goods and services to the nuclear industry having to take out their own insurance policies to cover themselves against any liability they may incur for damage to the property of a nuclear operator. This, in principle, is an extension of the channelling philosophy of the nuclear liability Conventions and laws. Consequently, there is a wide measure of agreement amongst the nuclear Pools that when they provide a Material Damage insurance there should be included in their policy a waiver of rights of recourse against such parties, to the extent that the policy provides cover for at least damage due to the 2 of 3 nuclear perils usually insured together with Fire or Explosion. Such an undertaking cannot apply to any uninsured damage, including that which would come within the terms or an excess or deductible. A suitable form of words, which should be incorporated in a prominent position in the Material Damage policy, is a follows:

In respect of —

(a) destruction of or damage to any property hereby insured caused by:—

   (i) contamination by radioactivity however arising, or
   (ii) fire explosion or excessive temperature each originating within the Nuclear Reactor, and

(b) destruction of or damage to the Nuclear Reactor, heat exchangers or blower houses or to buildings containing the Nuclear Reactor caused by fire explosion or excessive temperature however arising wherever originating

The Insured by the acceptance of this Policy warrant that to the extent that they are entitled to be indemnified under the Policy they will not claim indemnity from any person whatsoever whether or not such person has been guilty of fault negligence or breach of Condition or Warranty express or implied;

and

The Insurers agree that they will not enforce any rights and remedies or seek to obtain any relief or indemnity from other parties to which they would otherwise become entitled or be subrogated.

A detailed survey of the nature and contents of the Material Damage policies used by all the Pools which insure nuclear installations would be a very lengthy undertaking, although all the main wordings have in fact been closely compared by BI(AE)C and the results, which have been tabulated, are in the possession of each Pool to whom enquiries can be directed.

MACHINERY BREAKDOWN INSURANCE

Relatively few policies covering nuclear reactors against the risks of mechanical and electrical breakdown have been issued. Electrical breakdown is very occasionally provided by extension of a Material Damage policy. As with any policy covering nuclear risks, it is extremely important that its intentions and limitations are clearly and precisely stated. Advice on the drafting of policy wordings should always be sought from the specialist Engineering or Machinery insurers. In some respects, the policy will have some of the features of an All Risks insurance because the actual insurance of damage to plant would be expressed in rather broad terms as a rule and then clarified and given shape by the incorporation of a list of detailed exclusions. The basic damage cover may be expressed in the following terms:

"Sudden and unforeseen physical damage to any item of plant described in the Schedule which occurs at the location during the period of insurance and necessitates immediate repair or replacement before normal working can be continued"

Some policy wordings may seek to enumerate the causes of damage to be covered.

An equally important part of the cover which preferably should be provided under a separate section with a separate limit and if applicable a separate excess are the Additional Costs that may be incurred and for which insurers may properly be liable. Such Additional Costs (including costs of expediting repairs) may include the following:

(i)   investigating on the site the cause of the damage;
(ii) obtaining access to effect repairs (including costs of remote working and personal protection due to radiation levels);
(iii) decontaminating property within the external nuclear reactor shield or primary cooling circuit to effect repairs;
(iv) complying with obligatory inspections called for by the licensing authority after making good the damage.

Among the many exclusions that may have to be imposed are the obvious ones such as the forms of damage which may and should properly be covered under another form of insurance, e.g. Material Damage. The consequences of depreciation, wear and tear and deterioration, corrosion or rust and, very importantly, in connection with the reactor vessel, loss or damage caused by slowly-developing cracks and fractures, deformation, distortion, blisters, flaws, grooving or defective joints or seams are all necessary exclusions. The exclusion of Explosion, which would be damage covered under a Pool Material Damage policy to a limited extent, would not be regarded as encompassing such events as the bursting or disruption of turbines, compressors, engine cylinders, fly wheels or other parts subject to centrifugal force, transformers, switches or oil-immersed switchgear.

It would be usual also to exclude damage to concrete structures, masonry and civil engineering works or foundations, and the cost of temporary or provisional repairs, or of modifications, alterations or improvements.

The policy, as has been indicated earlier, would undoubtedly have to be subject to a relatively low limit on the damage cover and a fairly substantial excess or deductible. The additional costs, which could be very substantial, must also be subject to a clearly expressed limit.

General conditions, such as those relating to disclosure of information, reporting of losses, cancellation and, possibly, rights against third parties, would be similar to those which would be applied to Pool Material Damage policies.

ALL RISKS INSURANCE

This form of insurance, as has been mentioned previously, is normally used to cover physical damage to nuclear installations in the USA and Canada. Elsewhere many insurers have some reservations as to its suitability for such risks. In the case of these two countries where it is a common type of insurance for industrial risks the Pools and their members were accustomed to this system from the outset. No other national Pool has been tempted to provide All Risks cover for nuclear power stations except for the BI(AE)C and others as reinsurers of certain non-Pool insurers. Such covers are very occasionally encountered outside North America in relation to the installations other than power stations, or possibly to cover the tail-end of a construction risk after the installation has become ''nuclear'' and a subject for Pool insurance.

The feature of such policies is that they give a very wide basic cover which must then be modified and clarified by the application of a detailed list of exclusions. In the best-drafted of such policy wordings there would be some quite specific definitions as to the forms or causes of loss intended to be covered. The basic cover would probably best be expressed as being an insurance against "All Risks of direct physical damage to the property insured by any cause of loss specified as covered provided such physical damage takes place during the policy period". It would normally also specify additional costs of decontamination and debris removal providing such costs result from direct physical damage or for which the insurers are liable to indemnify the insured. The costs of expediting or temporary repairs and possibly extra expense which may be incurred in an emergency shutdown of a reactor might also be specified.

Otherwise, apart from the specific exclusion of certain forms of damage or causes of damage, the exclusions and general policy conditions and other provisions such as rights against third parties, cancellation, compliance with codes of practice, disclosure of aggravating circumstances, reporting of incidents and so forth would be in accordance with those referred to in the discussion of Material Damage policy wordings.

CONSEQUENTIAL LOSS INSURANCE

Policies covering the Interruption risk, the characteristics of which have been described earlier, particularly as they relate to the operation of nuclear power stations or fuel factories, would be broadly in line with the wordings that would be applicable to this branch of insurance in the conventional markets of each country. However, there are certain common criteria which inter-Pool studies have suggested should, if possible, be observed in the wording of policies applicable to nuclear installations, particularly if the national Pool concerned expects to obtain support from others. The general requirements and restrictions that such policies should contain may be as follows:

1. **Material Damage Warranty**

    A Pool Consequential Loss policy should contain a warranty to the effect that, before liability is admitted under the policy, there is in force a Pool Material Damage policy covering the premises against the same perils and also that the insurers on the damage insurance have admitted liability. If a material damage loss is not paid because of the existence of a large deductible, the consequential loss insurers would not normally regard this as non-fulfilment of the material damage warranty.

    For the above purposes, material damage would include machinery breakdown.

2. **Standing Charges**

If cover is given on net profit and standing charges, it is desirable to specify the charges by name rather than use an expression such as "all standing charges of the business". Any savings in standing charges after a loss should accrue to the benefit of the insurer.

3. **Average**

If the sum insured proves to be inadequate when a loss occurs provision should be made for the insured to be his own insurer for a proportionate amount. If cover is on specific standing charges then any amount payable as increase in cost of working must be proportionately reduced if the insured omits to include a standing charge. If the insurance is limited to additional expenses, there should be a limit per diem or for other suitable time and period.

4. **Increase in cost of working**

When this is payable as an alternative to loss of gross profits, steps should be taken to ensure that the amount does not exceed that payable as gross profit if the expenditure has not been incurred.

When the cover is on an increased cost of working basis (i.e. for electricity generating stations) this should be arranged on a per diem or other unit basis with a maximum time limitation. The coverage would only respond to the actual expenditure incurred beyond the cost of normal operation for the time period necessary to repair or replace the damaged portion of the plant with due diligence. Significant waiting period deductibles are desirable in considering this coverage for nuclear power stations.

5. **Adjustments Clause**

The policy should make provision for adjustments to be made in loss settlement to take account of any special circumstances occuring during the indemnity period or during any other period with which comparisons are being made.

6. **Statutory Authorities**

Liability for loss relates to the time necessary with due diligence to repair or replace the portion of the installation or plant damaged by an insured material damage peril. Liability through a loss resulting from delay in re-starting damaged installations or plant due to restrictions imposed by statutory nuclear safety Authorities should be limited to such period as is reasonable to enable the insured to comply with their requirements regarding that portion of the installation or plant that was damaged by an insured peril.

7. **Other Production**

If production is partially or wholly maintained by alternative means this must be brought into account in any loss settlement, except under a policy covering Increased Cost of Working only.

8. **"Valued" Policies**

These normally provide for the payment of a stated amount per unit of lost production. The following provisions should be applied where appropriate:

i) any production from other sources should be brought into account

ii) a "material damage warranty" should be applied;

iii) any special circumstances affecting the business should be considered in calculating the fall in production.

Pool Consequential Loss insurance policies would usually incorporate the usual General Conditions appropriate to the type of insurance and the market in which the national Pool is operating.

CAPACITY LIMITATION

It has been mentioned earlier in discussing the problem of capacity that a Pool's Material Damage capacity can only be used once for any individual nuclear installation or risk. This means that, unless there is a special subscription from the Pool's members to cover Machinery Breakdown or Consequential Loss insurances their capacity must be spread over these classes of insurance if they are required as well as the underlying Material Damage policy. If the decision is not to sub-divide the capacity into separate portions, the only solution to the risks of aggregation in the event of a nuclear incident giving rise to claims under both the underlying Material Damage policy and any associated Machinery Breakdown and/or Consequential Loss insurances is to apply to each policy what could be described as a "site capacity limitation" clause.

A generic wording for such a clause might be in the following terms:

The total amounts payable to the Insured during the Period of Insurance shall be limited in the aggregate to £   in compensation of all claims for any damage costs or consequential loss arising from one and the same occurrence or series of occurrences having the same originating cause whether insured by this Policy or any other Policy of Insurance in respect of any property belonging to or the responsibility of the Insured on the site of the Property insured subject always to the maximum losses payable by this Policy being limited to the amounts stated hereon. It is further agreed that the Site Capacity Limit and, insofar as it shall not be less, the maximum Limit under this Policy shall stand reduced by the amount of all such payments until reinstated by the Insurers.

In the above wording, in place of the words "or any other policy of insurance" it would be appropriate and perhaps better where the relevant other policy or policies have been issued by the Pool, or possibly another Pool, to identify by number and date.

THIRD PARTY LIABILITY INSURANCE

Whether or not they have ratified one or other of the International Conventions, most countries now have special legislation relating to the liabilities of the operators of nuclear installations and those responsible for the carriage of nuclear matter. The provision of a specified amount of financial security normally in the form of insurance is obligatory. This places a special responsibility upon the insurance Pools to provide forms of cover which will satisfy the controlling authorities as well as the operators themselves that their legal and financial obligations are fully protected and that the necessary funds to assure compensation of the victims of any nuclear incidents will be available at all times. In view of the special features of the liabilities imposed upon nuclear operators, the wording of the relevant policies must go further than simply stating that they cover the legal liability of the Insured in relation to nuclear occurrences. It will generally be necessary to specify the nuclear legislation applicable and perhaps even particular sections of the relevant law. The required financial security relative to nuclear incidents must be reserved for the payment of claims properly brought in accordance with nuclear legislation providing a special regime of liability, the principal features of which are that it shall be strict or absolute, that it shall be channelled solely to the operator of a nuclear installation responsible, that it shall be limited in amount and time and that it shall be subject to a single jurisdiction. These features must, therefore, be recognised in the section of the policy which provides the necessary nuclear cover as well as other requirements of national nuclear law and the international Conventions.

In addition to these basic requirements, the insurers have to establish an overriding limit on their financial commitment for any one nuclear installation, even though in most countries the compensation payable by a nuclear operator is for a fixed maximum for each and every incident that may occur. The amount of the overriding or "installation" limit as distinct from the "incident" limit will depend upon the amount of insurance capacity available and the requirements of the insured. A common choice for the installation limit is twice the incident limit but, in some cases, this may be less and may even be equal to the incident limit. Providing the insurance policy meets the basic statutory requirement any insurance limit which equals or exceeds the operator's financial obligation will normally satisfy the controlling authorities as meeting the requirements of an operating licence. The importance for insurers of the ability to impose such a limit, without automatic obligation to reinstate any claim payment (unless a margin for this is provided for in the policy limits), has always been widely recognised by the international organisations such as the IAEA, the OECD and EURATOM.

In the mid-1960's as in the case of Material Damage insurance, EURATOM considered a model third party liability insurance policy for operators of fixed nuclear installations. This followed the Colloquium on nuclear risk insurance held in May 1964 between them and the nuclear insurers; and a further similar meeting, in July 1965, attended by the EURATOM Commission, the insurers, various industrial sectors grouped in the Union of Industries of the European Community, and the International Union of Producers and Distributors of Electrical Energy. The British and other Pools made a considerable contribution to this work and the model policy was published in 1966 under reference EUR 3127 in English, French, Dutch, German and Italian. This was useful although by then most of the Pools had established their own.

The concept of a limited and reducing cover earned official approval in EURATOM's commentary on their wording which declared the amount of cover as being "degressive in proportion to the number of incidents occurring whatever the third party liability admitted by the operator, for a fixed period which is normally the period of operation of the installation in question".

Essential features of nuclear liability insurance cover

The limitation in the length of time allowed to a victim to notify a claim to ten years from the date of the incident or, if there has been a series of incidents arising from the same cause, the date of the last incident in the series, is almost universally provided for in nuclear legislation but where it is longer the Pool Liability policy will normally fix a 10 year limit nevertheless.

The limitation in financial amount, and provision for the

reduction, of the indemnity limit and the amounts paid out in claims is a feature common to all the Pools' policies and it should be set out in a prominent position in the "nuclear" section. The following is a simple but appropriate wording:

"The aggregate liability of the insurers in respect of all claims for which indemnity is provided by [Part I of] this policy or by any previous policies or by any policy issued in substitution therefor shall not exceed [insert here the overall installation limit] which shall be reduced by the amount of every payment made by the Insurers irrespective of the number of periods of insurance for which the said policies may be or have been in force".

The limitation in time may be expressed as a straightforward exclusion of "any claim which is made against the insured more than 10 years after the relevant date".

It is also essential for the nuclear part of the policy (which may be referred to as "Part I") to limit the cover to the consequences of a nuclear incident occurring during the currency of the insurance which is normally for a 12 months' period. Cover cannot be given on a claims-occurring basis. It is therefore perfectly possible, although the insurance may have ceased for one reason or another, for a claim to be met long after termination of the cover providing it is notified within the 10-year period of prescription and pursued within such further period as may be allowed for the bringing of actions (two to three years at most, according to the relevant nuclear law).

Exclusions from nuclear cover

The insurance cover must match the requirements of the nuclear law. Therefore, it is likely that very few exclusions will be permissible. However, this may sometimes present severe difficulties when any part of the liabilities imposed upon the operator have to regarded as totally insurable. This may arise in a case where, as permitted under the Conventions, national nuclear law requires the operator to be liable for the consequences of *grave natural disasters.* These may be regarded as unacceptable risks particularly in countries which are prone to the occurrence of severe typhoons or earthquakes, for example. In such cases, with the approval of the authorities, the nuclear liability cover may be permitted to exclude such risks which the State would then regard as being their own responsibility.

Liability for the consequences of *riots and civil commotion,* or acts of *terrorism* may also be legitimate subjects for exclusion.

"Intentional emissions." Liability for the payment of claims arising from damage or injury suffered by third parties (or employees when

393

they are covered under the Pool Liability policy) when this is the consequence of the deliberate release of radioactive matter, whether within permitted safety limits or above, can reasonably be characterised as uninsurable even though the operator would be legally liable. Unless the licensing authorities are prepared to admit a policy which has a specific exclusion of intentional emissions (and they may not, because this would then reduce the cover to below that required by law) insurers will need to cover the *legal* liability but then to negotiate the right to recover from the operator all claims paid to third parties suffering from the consequence from such an event. The need for insurers to protect themselves against paying out claims out of this nature is generally recognised. Possibly a full right of recovery cannot be arranged, in which case it may have to be restricted to payments beyond a certain limit or payments up to a certain limit. It is normally not practicable to deal with this question by applying an excess to the policy, whether this be compulsory or voluntary, because that, too, would mean reducing the cover below that required to comply with the nuclear legislation. It is not permissible under U.K. nuclear legislation.

Where an exclusion of this liability is permitted, however, it may be quite simply worded as "any claim arising from the intentional emission of ionising radiations within the programme of normal operation of the nuclear installation".

Where the matter has to be dealt with by way of a right of recovery this should be merely expressed in straightforward wording which would state that in the event of insurers paying any claims by virtue of the cover afforded under the policy in consequence of the intentional release of ionising radiations from anything on the site in course of normal operation of the installation "the insured shall repay to the insurers on demand all such claims," or "the first .... [amount]" or "all payments made in excess of .... [amount]" whichever option is applicable.

Extensions of nuclear cover

1. Economic Loss, Evacuation Expenses, etc.
The extent of cover, if any, required by the operator in respect of his obligation to meet such expenses will depend primarily upon the legal position. Under some nuclear laws, they would be regarded as a reasonable part of any compensation payable in consequence of a nuclear incident . In some cases, the claim would be admissible only where there is evidence of victims having suffered direct damage due to ionising radiation or contamination by radioactivity. In other cases, they may be able to claim for such expenses in accordance

with their rights under the relevant nuclear law whether or not they or their properties suffer any injury or damage and even in a case where, as a precaution, an evacuation may be ordered in anticipation of an incident which in fact does not eventually take place. When such claims are not included in the amounts payable under the nuclear law, the operator may require additional insurance to protect him against his obligations under common law or possibly some other statute. If such cover is to be given, the extent of it must be carefully defined and it must be subject to a separate limit.

It is important to bear in mind that any claims paid under this heading will be regarded as the consequence of a nuclear occurrence and will have to be brought within the overall limit applying to the policy which, subject to the availability of capacity, may have to be increased to accommodate this additional cover.

2. Costs and Interest

Another extension of cover that may be required is for legal and other expenses including interest payable on claims settlements, which under most nuclear laws cannot be charged against the statutory amount of compensation payable to third parties. Therefore, an additional amount of insurance may be granted to meet these costs. A figure of 10% of the overall nuclear indemnity limit is commonly selected although there is no technical reason for it to be as high particularly in insurance policies providing for the exceptionally high indemnity limits encountered in some countries. On the other hand, where the indemnity limit is relatively low it can and perhaps should be higher than 10%. A wording to cover such additional expenses provided in respect of claims payable under the nuclear section (which may be designated Part I) may be in the following terms:

"The insurers will pay (1) all costs and expenses recoverable by any claimant from the insured (2) all costs and expenses incurred with the written consent of the insurers in respect of claims for damages to which the indemnity provided [by Part I] applies but the aggregate liability of the insurers in respect of all such costs and expenses shall not exceed [amount] irrespective of the number of periods of insurance for which this policy or any previous policies or any policy issued in substitution for this policy may be or have been in force".

In other words, this extension must also be subject to the overall policy limit.

3. Carriage of Nuclear Matter

Any consignments of nuclear matter which is not excepted matter from the installation for which the operator is responsible, or to the installation for which he may accept responsibility, would normally have to be included within the Liability insurance applicable to the operation of the licensed site. It may be, and it is the case in some countries, that such transits would be separable from the operator's site-related liabilities, particularly if the carriage is international in character. Before the policy wording is finalised this aspect must be investigated. If the operator's Transport liabilities have any lower limit in financial terms this must be clarified. The insured's obligations as to notification of such carriage of nuclear matter must be clearly understood by him.

Non-nuclear cover

The policy must cover the whole range of the operator's legal liabilities so it cannot be confined to the specific requirements under nuclear legislation and/or the International Conventions. However, the nuclear liability cover has to be specially worded and to have a separate indemnity limit which cannot be applied to claims falling outside the provisions of nuclear law, so each policy must have a separate section to cover the operator's general or common law liabilities. Because of the possibilities of a certain amount of overlap in relation to various legal liabilities, particularly when there is an occurrence which causes both nuclear and conventional damage at the same time, it is not satisfactory for the non-nuclear liabilities to be insured by way of a conventional policy issued outside the Pool. It is also far more satisfactory for the same insurers to provide cover for all the operator's liabilities and deal with any claims which may arise, under a single policy. The conventional section of the policy, which may be designated as *Part II,* will be very much in line with the sort of cover that would be provided for a conventional industrial risk.

Exclusions in Part II

To avoid a possible duplication of cover, it is necessary to have a full exclusion of the nuclear risk which may be expressed as "any occurrence involving nuclear matter being injury or damage arising out of or resulting from radioactive properties or a combination of those and other toxic explosive or other hazardous properties of that nuclear matter". (In this way any mixed damage which cannot be separated out would fall to be paid for under Part I and this would be in accordance with nuclear legislation). It would also be necessary to exclude "ionising radiations from anything caused or suffered by the insured to be on the site which is not nuclear matter or from any waste discharged (in whatever form) on or from the site". This also reflects the legal position under most laws based upon the Conventions which say that even nuclear matter which may be excluded because of the small quantity or low level of radioactivity from nuclear laws is not so excluded if it is the source of ionising radiation while on a nuclear site. If such matter were away from the nuclear site but were still the legal liability of the operator, it would not be picked up by this exclusion. For the purposes of a separate conventional insurance, Excepted Matter would not be excluded by the terms of the standard Radioactive Contamination Exclusion Clause in the United Kingdom, though the position may be different in other countries.

Otherwise, the conventional Part II would incorporate the usual exclusions in accordance with market practice, notably liability in respect of death or illness of or bodily injury to any person under a contract of service or apprenticeship with or in receipt of a salary from the insured if such death, illness or injury arises out of and in the course of employment or service of such person.

It will be remembered that so far as the rights to compensation under nuclear law are concerned, employees are in the same position as other third parties in many countries, including the United Kingdom and therefore such exclusion is not applied to Part I of a Pool Liability policy.

The reason that the exclusion applies to Part II is that generally speaking insurances written by the Employers' Liability market do not carry a Radioactive Contamination Exclusion Clause although some insurers may decline to cover employees working at nuclear sites even though any claim from them for injury would be payable by the operator under law or recoverable from the operator if for any good reason the insurers initially meet such a claim.

On the other hand, there may be countries in which for various reasons the insurance of employees with respect to injury or damage suffered in consequence of a non-nuclear occurence would be covered by extension of the conventional section of their policy, possibly for a separate limit.

Additional Expenses

National practices may vary but in the United Kingdom and at least some other countries the cover under the Pool policy would give unlimited protection in regard to costs and expenses associated with non-nuclear claims.

Warranties in Liability Policies

As in the case of a Material Damage policy covering a nuclear operator, any form of Third Party policy should carry similar warranties regarding compliance with codes of practice, inspections and the like as are suggested in the section dealing with Material Damage policy wordings. It may be that the term "warranty" is not used in the policies of other countries or that a condition of this degree of stringency which could result in the policy cover being voided if the warranty is not complied with, would not be permissible. In that case, some similar form of policy condition should be incorporated if at all possible.

A further consideration in this connection with Public Liability insurance written in accordance with or related to nuclear legislation, is the need to impose a strict obligation to comply with the terms of the licence or authorisation to operate the nuclear installation issued by the appropriate authorities.

Cancellation conditions

Liability policies covering legal liabilities under nuclear law must comply with the authorised period of cancellation — usually 2 months, sometimes as long as 3. The Licensing authorities must be informed when such notice is given.

CONTINGENT LIABILITY INSURANCES

(a)　**Public Liability Insurance — (other than Operator's Liability)**
Since it is possible under nuclear legislation which follows the International Conventions for a nuclear operator to transfer all or part of his financial obligations (but not his legal liability) to a third party by agreement under which that party must indemnify the operator for any claims payable under the terms of nuclear law, it can arise that persons other than the installation operator may require a third party insurance from the nuclear Pool. Providing capacity is available (because there could be an aggregation between the financial liabilities he assumes and those which are covered in respect of the site if the operator carries insurance) there is no reason why a nuclear pool should not grant to such a party a form of Liability insurance. This will not have to comply with the provisions of nuclear law because the party concerned is not a licensee of a nuclear installation or a licensed carrier of nuclear matter. Therefore, the policy may be drawn up in quite broad terms so as to indemnify the insured against liability at law for damages in respect of any accident happening during the periods of insurance in connection

with his business, also providing cover in respect of costs and expenses recoverable by any claimant from the insured and/or incurred with the written consent of the insurers.

Such policy would exclude employees, damage to property belonging to the insured and according to national practice damage by an explosive nuclear assembly whether this be due to its radioactive, toxic, explosive or other hazardous properties. Such policies should also exclude liability for the consequences of defective workmanship, materials or design, advice or services rendered in a professional capacity by the insured and the supply of products.

If such a Third Party policy is issued in parallel with a Products Liability policy and/or a Professional Indemnity Policy for the interests of the same insured it may be necessary, subject to the capacity available, to impose an overriding limitation clause, specifying each of the policies concerned by number and date, notwithstanding the individual liability limit of each policy.

The period of cancellation will have to be considered in the light of any contractual obligations entered into by the insured. Since this is not an insurance of the legal liabilities of a nuclear operator but only an indemnification of all of or part of his financial responsibilities the period of cancellation under this policy would not necessarily be as long as that required to meet the provisions of nuclear legislation. It is, in effect, an insurance of the contractual liabilities of the party concerned who may be a supplier of goods or services and where he has to accept such legal liabilities as may be set out in his contract it is incumbent upon a nuclear Pool to try to provide the necessary protection. This said, however, it is very desirable that a concern entering into any form of contract with an operator of a licensed nuclear installation should try to avoid a commitment to hold such operator harmless with respect to any part of his financial obligations to compensate third parties for damage or injury suffered in consequence of a nuclear occurrence on the licensed site. Although the International Conventions and legislation based on these allow for such responsibilities to be assumed by others by agreement, such an arrangement really cuts across the whole concept of channelling.

For insurers, it is the financial consequences of such liability rather than the legal liability itself which is the most important consideration. If the operator, as is likely, carries Liability insurance provided by the same or even another nuclear Pool, there is inevitably an element of double insurance and circumstances may arise in which the operator is obliged to pay compensation in addition to any which may be recoverable from a contractor.

399

(b) **Products Liability Insurance**

Even though the supplier of products, whether these be complete
reactors or components which are used or may be used in nuclear
installations, may be able to avoid having to submit to a contractual
obligation to indemnify his principals for any third party claims they
may be obliged to pay under the terms of nuclear legislation, he may
not be able to avoid having to pay for damage to their own property
for which the supplier is legally responsible.

In the section dealing with Material Damage policies, it has been
explained that there is a wide measure of agreement amongst the
Pools that both the insured and the insurers should waive any rights
of recovery against third parties with respect to damage insured under
that policy. However, it is not possible for the Pools to legislate for
the situation applying to the property of a nuclear operator which
does not insure because it is perhaps a Government Department or
a Defence establishment or simply chooses not to purchase
commercial insurance, nor can insurers prohibit their policyholders
from proceeding against third parties for any uninsured risk or for
that part of the insurance which may be excluded by the operation
of an excess or deductible.

In these circumstances, the supplier will need insurance protection
against his obligation to meet possible claims for damage which he
may cause to the property of the nuclear operator or to any other
property on a nuclear site which is used or being constructed in
connection with the operation of the nuclear installation. Furthermore, the manufacturers and suppliers of commonplace components
may not know for certain whether or not their products will go into
a nuclear installation. This could also apply to certain types of
lubricants.

Consequently, the Pools must be prepared to consider granting
Products Liability policies to indemnify such supplier against liability
at law in respect of any accident arising out of the products or the
installing or servicing of products. When such accident causes death,
illness, bodily injury to any person or loss or damage to property
during the period of the insurance, cover will also be needed to extend
to any costs and expenses recoverable by claimants.

The *exclusions* to be applied to such a policy would normally be
in line with market practice as it relates to Products Liability
insurance in the conventional insurance field. It is particularly
important from the point of view of insurers to exclude any claim
arising from faulty, improper or inadequate design or specification
of the product. The consequences of such factors should they cause
a nuclear accident are unpredictable and should not therefore have
to be taken into account in assessing the premium paid. If insurance

cover is needed against any contingent liability associated with faulty design and the like it may be separately insurable under a suitably-drafted policy specially designed to cover the consequences of Errors and Omissions or to provide Professional Indemnity cover.

Since the policy includes liability to pay compensation arising out of nuclear incidents, as well as common law liabilities and possibly contractual liabilities, it is necessary for the indemnity limit under the policy to be reducible by claim payments and not automatically reinstateable, just as in the case of a nuclear operator's nuclear liability insurance.

The Schedule to the policy should set out the actual products supplied to nuclear installations.

As this is not an insurance in accordance with nuclear law, the period of cancellation may be in accordance with what would be customary for ordinary Products Liability policies in the country concerned. Thus, it may be cancellable by the insurers at as little as 15 days' notice. The other conditions again should be in accordance with normal practice including an obligation for immediate notice to be given of any accident or claim or proceedings or any circumstances which may give rise to a claim. The insured should of course be placed under an obligation to take all reasonable precautions to prevent accidents.

Another very important consideration must be the territorial scope of a Products Liability policy. Generally speaking, the Pool would issue a policy which would cover supply of goods to any territory to which the section of the Pool under which the policy is issued would normally apply. It may, however, be necessary to restrict cover to something less than the territorial scope of the Pool, possibly because of undesirable features associated with particular countries. These may include the judgements that a foreign supplier may expect to encounter in the Courts of the country concerned, notably those in certain of the States of the U.S.A.

(c) Errors & Omissions Insurance

This is a somewhat specialised class of contingent Liability insurance which may not be available generally in all countries. The scope of cover to be granted requires careful consideration and the advice of specialised Errors & Omissions underwriters should be sought as to the precise wordings to be used.

Generally speaking, professional concerns and individuals who are accustomed to carrying this class of insurance in relation to their business will be looking to the Pool for cover in respect of the gap in their ordinary insurance policy which would have been created by the application of a nuclear exclusion clause. For this type of cover it is quite reasonable for the Pool policy therefore to be restricted to this area of liability, since the insurance is not specifically concerned with damage or injury suffered by third parties in circumstances where there may be mixed nuclear and non-nuclear damage difficult to distinguish.

Accordingly, the insuring clause may refer to some such description of the cover as indemnification of the insured against liability at law for compensation in respect of claims for breach of professional duty caused by or contributed to by or arising from ionising radiation or contamination by radioactivity from any nuclear fuel or from any nuclear waste from the combustion of nuclear fuel, made against the insured and notified to the insurers during any period of insurance, by reason of any act of negligence, wrongful advice, error or omission occurring or commited in good faith in connection with his business. (It will be noted that this incorporates the terms of the standard British Radioactive Contamination Exclusion Clause applied to conventional policies of certain classes).

Cover may be granted not only to the insured or the predecessors in his business but also to any person presently or previously employed directly or as agent by the insured or his predecessors and any person subsequently to be employed directly or as agent by the insured providing this would be in line with normal market practice in the field of Errors and Omissions insurance.

In order to focus the insurance on the narrow range of liabilities it is intended to cover, it will be necessary to exclude liability for death, bodily injury or damage to property *unless* arising out of wrongful, faulty or inadequate design or advice. (In this way such a policy could be complementary to a Product Liability insurance which specifically excludes wrongful, faulty or inadequate design or advice). Although the policy is specifically designed to cover ionising radiation and radioactive contamination in the terms quoted above it should, nevertheless, carry an exclusion of the consequences of the radioactive, toxic, explosive or other hazardous properties of any explosive nuclear assembly or any nuclear component thereof. The policy should also exclude any claim for loss or expenditure incurred (a) solely in remedying a fault in design (b) by reason of betterment or alteration in design consequent upon death, bodily injury or damage to property arising out of fault in such design.

As in the case of a Product Liability policy, and for similar reasons, the territorial scope of the policy should be carefully defined and, in view of the very heavy damages that tend to be awarded in countries like the United States in consequence of professional negligence, it may be wise not to extend such a policy to that country or its territories or possessions. The usual 10-year limitation on the presentation of claims following the date of a known incident will also apply, and, in accordance with market practice, it would invariably be the case that a policy should be subject to an Excess.

Again, in accordance with usual nuclear liability insurance practice, the limit of indemnity must be an aggregate amount in respect of all compensation costs and expenses and subject to automatic reduction by the amount of every payment made under the particular policy or any policy issued in substitution.

It will also be necessary for the schedule of the policy to set out the contracts to be covered during the particular period of insurance (which would normally be for 12 months), naming the client and the services to be provided, specifying sites where known or, if unspecified, making it clear which contracts apply to unspecified nuclear sites.

As in a Product Liability policy, the period of notice will not need to comply with the provisions of any nuclear law and therefore may be for quite a short period, certainly not exceeding that which would be granted in the case of a conventional Errors & Omissions policy. Other general conditions may have to be brought into line with those applicable to the parallel conventional policy carried by the particular insured.

(d) **Professional Indemnity Insurance**
This is likely to be very similar in form and content to an Errors & Omissions policy but would not be concerned specifically with design work. The insuring clause would be intended to fill the gap created in the professional person's conventional insurance by the application of a nuclear exclusion clause and would aim to indemnify him against any claim or claims arising from nuclear incidents made against him on account of a breach of duty in his professional capacity by reason of any neglect, omission or error commited by the insured or the insured's predecessors in his business, by any person now or previously employed by the insured or his predecessors or by any person thereafter to be employed, or of any business conducted by or on behalf of the insured in his professional capacity as whatever it may be, for example, consulting engineer.

The usual conditions and exclusions would apply and, as in the case of Product Liability and Errors & Omissions insurances, it would be very important to specify the territorial limitations of the intended cover.

It will be appreciated that these forms of contingent Liability insurance may not be available in all countries from the national nuclear Pools. If available from the conventional insurance market they may carry an exclusion of nuclear risks. That, in itself, would not necessarily render them useless, particularly in the case of Errors & Omissions and Professional Indemnity insurances because it may well be that the loss or damage due to a nuclear occurrence which ultimately gives rise to a claim against the policyholder would be too remote from the actual nuclear damage to activate the operation of a nuclear exclusion clause.

Even where a Pool does provide such insurances, the financial limitations on the policy may have to be quite small because of the prior claims of a nuclear operator for Liability insurance required in accordance with nuclear liability legislation and the possibility that claims payable by the Pool under that policy could aggregate with claims arising from the same nuclear incident under the contingent insurances in question.

Demand for such policies seems to be very limited outside the United Kingdom and North America but since the British Pool have received quite a number of enquiries for such insurances it is their practice to reserve a proportion of their Liability capacity out of the margins available above the statutory amounts of cover required in the United Kingdom in order to provide at least a limited amount of insurance for suppliers of goods and services. It has been their experience that a useful amount of reinsurance capacity for such insurances can be obtained from some of the other Pools in accordance with the general objective of the Pools to assist each other with reinsurance when required even if the class of risk in question is not one they would themselves insure in their own countries.

APPENDIX A

MAJOR NUCLEAR ACCIDENTS

Fires, explosions, breakdowns and the release of noxious substances are common enough in most types of industries: nuclear power stations and fuel plants are part of the industrial scene like any other factory and have their share of such events. Because of the mystique and the special hazards of radiation, any mishap in a nuclear installation always attracts close attention and sometimes quite ordinary events are treated by the media and anti-nuclear activists with a degree of anguish and excitement such as is more properly reserved in conventional industrial spheres to real disasters like the terrible explosion in 1974 at the Nypro cyclohexane plant at Flixborough, Scunthorpe, UK which killed 28 and injured 36 others on the site with a blast powerful enough to injure many people in the neighbourhood. Others had far worse effects, involving the release of poisonous fumes from chemical factories: in 1976, a small factory at Seveso in Italy, from which dioxin escaped, killing animals, poisoning hundreds of local inhabitants and forcing local factories to close down; and the worst of all, to date, the leakage of toxic gas in 1984 from the Union Carbide factory at Bhopal in India, causing the death of some 2,800 people and serious illness in many more thousands.

Incidents in nuclear installations are closely monitored in every country and details of many of them (of which the great majority are non-nuclear) are reported to the International Atomic Energy Agency and the OECD's Nuclear Energy Agency who compile lists for distribution on a restricted basis to Governments and others through whom those with a serious interest such as insurance concerns, including BI(AE)C, may receive copies.

So we are not without ample accurate and objective information as to what goes wrong in most of the installations in the WOCA countries. Very few (probably less than 5%) contain even a minor radioactivity element, still less a "catastrophic" nuclear significance, although useful as pointers to potential dangers and possible "near misses".

However, out of all known accidents involving radiation and on a life-threatening scale, only three, which were well-publicised, stand out. All have been written about extensively and in depth and the purpose of this Appendix is to outline the sequence of events and the consequences, with an indication in each case of sources of detailed technical and other information and expert analysis for those requiring it.

1. The Windscale Accident 1957

The accident to No. 1 Pile (one of the two air-cooled graphite-moderated reactors at this UKAEA site) occurred during routine maintenance on 10th October 1957.

The operation being carried out was known as "Wigner release". This required nuclear heating to be applied to the graphite, at intervals, to limit the accumulation of energy in the graphite due to the relatively low operating temperature of this reactor (the procedure is not required in the gas-cooled Magnox reactors and A.G.R.s which have higher operating temperatures). The procedure, which involved shutting down the reactor, switching off the main air blowers and then making the core divergent to produce nuclear heat, began on 7th October. The engineer involved apparently found that the temperature was dropping and the energy release dying away before all the graphite structure was annealed and a second heating was initiated.

It was this that led to an unorthodox boosting of the heat by the physicist in charge and the core diverged again on 8th October with a rapid rise in temperature the extent of which seems not to have been registered because, during Wigner release, the uranium thermocouples were not situated at the position of maximum temperatures. As a precaution, the control rods were inserted but by then fuel damage had occurred due to the over-heating. Consequently the graphite gradually became hotter through the third day, 9th October. This led to failure of other fuel cartridges and by the evening of 10th October, the graphite was burning and the fire was spreading.

Various steps were taken to increase the air-cooling during the 9th but activity on the pile continued to rise. An attempt was made on the 10th to detect the burst cartridges but the scanning gear was jammed. Another instrument, taking out samples, shewed a high reading. Operators in protective clothing then carried out a visual inspection and saw red-hot fuel cartridges. The spread of fire was contained by discharging the fuel from the adjacent channels. The red-hot fuel could not be removed and an attempt to extinguish the fire with CO_2 failed. A high level decision was taken to use water, if necessary, and at midnight the Cumberland police were warned of a possible emergency.

The water hoses were coupled in the early hours of 11th October, the work force ordered to take cover and water was turned on at 08.55. The fire eventually subsided, and after 24 hours the pile was cold.

Air samples taken outside on 10th October gave a reading of 10 times the normal maximum for Beta-emission. On the 11th workers were required to wear protective masks. Readings rose for a few hours but had dropped by the 12th. Some 14 workers received more than the maximum permissible dose over a 13 week period according to ICRP standards and monitoring continued for some time with special checks for radioactive iodine and strontium.

Concerning public health, radiation surveys were made down wind and Gamma ray activity was measured by specially equipped patrol vans. Air measurements were also made and milk samples were collected which shewed the presence of Iodine 131. Analysis shewed some samples contained up to 30k Bq per litre, significantly above what was thought to be a safe level for infants judged by the absorption rate of radio-iodine into the thyroid glands of young children. Therefore milk deliveries were stopped that night and a quantity was destroyed. (Compensation of about £50,000 was paid). Sampling continued on farms at increasing distances from Windscale and along the Lancashire coast, the North Wales coast, Isle of Man, Yorkshire and the South of Scotland. Vegetables, eggs, meat, water supplies and grassland were also examined. Measurements of the radioactive isotopes Strontium 89 and 90 and Caesium disclosed no hazards — from these sources. The reactor had to be written off, sealed and abandoned.

(Reference: "Accident at Windscale No. 1 Pile on 10th October, 1957" Cmnd. 302 HMSO, London)

Subsequent studies have yielded additional information. In addition to the radionuclides mentioned in the Report of the 1957 Committee of Enquiry, a non-fission product, Polonium-210 was also released, having come from bismuth undergoing neutron irradiation in the core. The dose contributed by the Po-210 was about 2mSv, equivalent to the effective dose received annually in the U.K. from natural background radiation. The risk of cancer of the thyroid appearing in the lifetime of those who were infants in 1957 is now thought by the experts to be about 1 in 1,000 for the few individuals receiving thyroid doses of about 100 mSv; for adults the risks are about a factor of 5 less.

The highest annual risk is about 2 per 100,000 years. The risk to the 1957 infants was about 10 times the natural incidence, but very few children were involved at the time of the accident. For the U.K. population as a whole, whose thyroids receive about 1 mSv of background radiation every year, the effect of the Windscale Accident was no more than a few days equivalent of background radiation.

(Reference: — Paper presented by Dr. R.H. Clarke, NRPB, to the British Institute of Radiology, 1987.)

---

2. The Three Mile Island Accident, 1979

Many reports and articles in learned journals and the press, technical or otherwise, have been published since 1979 and still appear from time to time.

This was a very serious and extremely costly nuclear accident, from the worst consequences of which the public were effectively protected by the massive outer containment built around the Reactor No. 2 installation.

This was the second of the 2 Babcock and Wilcox Pressurised Water Reactors comprised in the Three Mile Island (T.M.I.) power station, operated by G.P.U. and located at Harrisburg in Pennsylvania.

In the early hours of 28th March 1979 there was a failure in pumps providing feedwater to the once-through steam generators and the turbine was therefore automatically shut down. This stopped the heat being removed from the primary circuit. In accordance with the safety arrangements, a relief valve in the primary cooling circuit of the reactor was automatically shut down about 10 seconds after the total loss of feedwater signal. Pressure fell, as was intended, but the valve did not reopen as it should have done at this point, although instruments in the reactor control room indicated that it had reopened. Furthermore, a number of relief valves had inadvertently been left closed during previous maintenance, it seems. Because of this, pressure went on falling and the emergency high pressure supply of core-cooling water was automatically injected. Not knowing why, the operators reduced the flow believing the reactor to be too full. The resulting boiling of the water and generation of steam inside the reactor forced out more water. About 2 hours after the start of the accident the core started to overheat with resultant severe damage to the uncooled fuel elements.

This was not all. Because the quantity of water being forced out through the open relief valve was greater than the capacity of the tank provided for it to drain into, it caused sealing discs to be ruptured and 600,000 gallons of coolant water flooded into the reactor sump and the basement of the building. Fission products escaping from the damaged fuel in the water were then released when the water was pumped into a storage tank in the adjoining auxiliary building which overflowed.

At this point radioactive iodine, krypton and xenon began to enter the ventilation system: most of the iodine was trapped in the filters but in the first week 7.5 curies of Iodine 131 and about 2.5 million curies of noble gases were released from the building into the environment. The fission products from the damaged fuel also included radioactive strontium and caesium but little of this was observed to have escaped to the environment. Therefore, although measurable, the radioactive releases were relatively insignificant and the average effective dose to individuals within a 50 mile radius has been estimated at probably 33 man Sv.

Meanwhile within the reactor severe damage to part of the core was taking place because the upper part was uncovered due to the loss of coolant and the temperature had risen (as later estimated) to at least 2,500°C. The chemical reaction between the steam and zirconium fuel cladding produced hydrogen which formed a bubble in the primary circuit. This created fears of an explosion which was probably the decisive factor leading the Governor of Pennsylvania to order the evacuation of children and their mothers and pregnant women within a 5 mile radius. In many cases whole families were moved, amounting in all to about 11,000 individuals.

The large explosion feared (which might have breached the containment building) did not occur and, with hindsight, was agreed to be never likely. However, when entry was eventually gained there was evidence of a lesser explosion having occurred within the reactor hall.

Early estimates of the extent of the damage were excessively over-optimistic, as was the expectation that decontamination and other clean-up operations including the removal of damaged fuel from the core would be completed within 4 years. By 1987, the end of the whole operation was not expected before 1989 — 10 years after the accident occured.

The radioactivity in the reactor building was effectively contained, presenting no serious hazard to the rest of the power station site or the neighbourhood, but the radiation levels were far too high for personnel to enter. However, it was vitally important to make and keep the plant secure. Contractors worked non-stop for the first 2 months to put in alternative safety systems, installing a back-up cooling system and preventing radioactive water leaking into it. The containment had to be purged of radioactive gas. New ventilation was required and extra concrete shielding.

The work required to treat and remove the huge quantity of radioactive water alone involved a massive operation. For example, between November 1979 and December 1980, some 43,000 curies of radioactive material were removed from 565,000 gallons of water from the Auxiliary Building and deposited in 50 resin liners which were subsequently stored in specially designed concrete bunkers.

By June of 1980, after much careful investigation and consideration the Nuclear Regulatory Commission decided that the 57,000 curies of Krypton 85 gas known to be in the atmosphere of the reactor building could be discharged without risk to public health — an operation backed by the National Council on Radiation Protection Measurements; the Environmental Protection Agency; the Department of Energy; and the Union of Concerned Scientists. Controlled purging was then authorised and was complete in early July.

Strictly limited entry of personnel wearing protective clothing became possible soon after and video-recordings of what could be seen were made as well as accurate radiation readings. This allowed for the development of realistic recovery plans.

The events of the following 7 years were far too numerous and complex to enumerate. (There are many good published reports). Suffice to say that in 1982 it was possible to insert a closed circuit TV camera remotely controlled to take a quick look at the core; and by 1983 to examine reactor internals by the same means. This revealed damage to the core far more extensive and difficult to cope with than had at first been expected. However, it was concluded that the reactor head could be removed without flooding the fuel transfer canal.

The preliminary findings (by camera) under the head were of a considerable amount of damage to the fuel in the upper part of the core, much of which had been reduced to rubble which lay at the bottom. Some samples were retrieved by remote control equipment, the core being covered by 10 feet of water during these operations.

The workers have had to wear protective clothing always and a special air-cooled suit was developed to relieve the discomfort. Work can proceed only slowly because of the limited time people can spend in a radioactive environment.

By 1984 this massive clean-up operation was getting into its stride and much was being learned that would be of great value if similar work was ever to be required again. Solutions were found to the extremely difficult problems involved in managing the solid radioactive wastes. A start was made on defuelling the reactor — the most important task of all.

The head lift was successfully completed in July, 1984 opening the way to the removal of the fuel, although this was not to begin until October 1985, being scheduled to take about 18 months and to cost $300 million. Tests on samples shewed that temperatures had exceeded 2,800°C during the accident, evidence that actual melting of fuel had occurred — previously considered unlikely.

The complete recovery operation seems likely to be continued until 1989 — thus extending over 10 years — at a total cost of $1,000 million. The actual damage to the reactor — excluding the decontamination costs — has been assessed at well over $200 million.

Material Damage insurance was provided by the two American Nuclear Pools — ANI and MAERP — and the reinsuring Pools in many other countries — on an "All Risks" basis, the policy being subject to a limit (in 1979) of $300 million. This, including a share of the decontamination costs, was fully expended.

Liability insurance was also written by the 2 Pools who rapidly mounted an extremely efficient and impressive on-the-spot operation to provide immediate hardship payments to evacuee families. Disbursements exceeding $1.3 million were made. Subsequently claims brought to Court under a combined ("class") action, mainly for loss of earnings and interruption of business on account of the evacuation, were settled for $20 million. Additionally, the insurers provided a fund of $5 million to meet the cost of long term medical surveillance for the local inhabitants and, in particular, their children although there has been no evidence of any harmful exposure to radiation of any individual nor of any abnormal levels since the accident. Further claims and costs, exceeding $20 million, have subsequently been advised, mainly for pyschological harm but including expenses incurred by certain Municipalities.

Many other actions are pending so the total claims cost to be met out of Liability insurance may exceed $50 million, even though there was no significant release of radioactivity.

References

Nuclear Engineering International — numerous articles in 1979 issues and every year since.

Comments of U.K. Health and Safety Executive 1979 (I.S.B.N. 0717600416)

American Nuclear Society's Nuclear News (April 1979)

OECD Nuclear Energy Agency Activity Report 1979

Journal of American Society of Safety Engineers, August 1980

New Yorker April 6 and 13, 1981

Atom 313, November 1982 (UKAEA)

New Scientist 13.1.83

Nuclear Safety (USA — Sept/Oct 1980, Jan/Feb 1984)

3. The Chernobyl Accident, 1986

Of the 3 large-scale accidents described, the destruction of Unit 4 at the Chernobyl Power Station near Kiev in the Soviet Repulic of the Ukraine was by far the worst. Not only was there massive and irrecoverable damage to the nuclear plant and the associated buildings, there was also a very serious release of fission products. This was indeed the classic scenario for a nuclear catastrophe foreseen by insurers, although until the morning of 26th April 1986, characterised as so remote a possibility as to be regarded as a tolerable insurance risk. What made it so much worse than the TMI accident were the deaths it caused, and the severe external damage to the local environment from the radioactive fallout, which also affected other countries. This spread considerably further than many experts would have expected: it was the first example of significant transfrontier radioactive pollution. However the first the outside world knew that something serious had occurred was when radiation monitors at the Swedish Forsmark power station gave abnormally high readings 36 hours later. It was then acknowledged by the Russians.

So grave was the accident, and so dramatic, even heroic, the remedies that had to be taken to prevent even worse consequences that it could not be glossed over and the normally reticent Soviet Government soon released details to the IAEA, to other governments, to a specially convened Conference in Vienna and to the media. There was wide coverage in the press and on radio and television of the bold and drastic measures that had to be taken to quench the fire, to neutralise the nuclear reactor, to stop the outpouring of fission products from the damaged core and to seal the shattered reactor unit forever.

The sequence of the complex events started by the tests involving a simulated electricity power failure has been described many times in official reports from the Soviet Government and their experts, and the IAEA, and in the technical journals and other organs of the press. These can be studied by all who wish to make a detailed technical analysis of the disaster. For the purpose of this Appendix, it is sufficient to recall the main steps as follows:

The experiment, undertaken on the occasion of routine maintenance, was to test a voltage regulator which was intended to achieve a better use of power from a running down turbogenerator, in the event of failure of offsite power supplies, until standby diesel generators could be started up. (Similar tests in 1982 and 1984 had not been satisfactory because the voltage fell too quickly for safety). The reactor power was reduced to about 25% as part of the planned operation. Contrary to operating rules this was maintained for about 24 hours. It was a dangerous manoeuvre because the RBMK reactor becomes unstable at low power because of its design. It has a "positive void coefficient" which means that when water in the cooling circuit converts to steam the reactor power tends to increase, converting more water to steam (i.e. more "voids") and producing still higher power. In other designs, if the fuel temperature goes up in this way, it becomes less efficient (i.e., it has a negative void coefficient) and so the power goes down again. At low power (below 20%) the void coefficient of the RBMK may be so large and so positive that power goes up very rapidly. When this happened at Chernobyl the operators should have shut down the reactor immediately. In fact they attempted to bring down the power even more rapidly reaching 30 MW(th) causing an increase in what is known as xenon poisoning (caused by the decay of radioactive iodine) which had been in operation for several hours by then. This "poisoned" the system so it was almost impossible to increase the power to the desired test level even when they violated the rules by withdrawing most of the control and safety rods. The operators over-rode trip signals and disengaged the protection provided to trip the reactor after both turbines had tripped.

At 1.23 hours when the turbines began to run down the main circulating pumps and the coolant flow began to decrease. Cooling was insufficient, the safety shutdown system was turned off and eventually the reactor became "super-critical". Within 4 seconds it achieved 100 times its normal full power releasing an enormous amount of energy. This ruptured the fuel elements and the interaction of coolant and fragmented molten fuel was the probable cause of an explosion of such force that the lid of the reactor vessel was blown off. This destroyed the cooling circuits. Apparently another explosion occurred and burning and molten nuclear fuel fragments (highly radioactive, of course) were blown out to a great height above the reactor building (which by now had been destroyed) some of it falling on and setting fire to the Turbine Hall. (There was no secondary containment shell, such as there was at T.M.I.)

Subsequent reactions set fire to the graphite moderator and radio-active matter (radionuclides) were released continuously for, it is said, the next 10 days. Photographs and films taken from helicopters (which hovered over the reactor, exposing their crews to great danger from radiation) shewed the interior of the reactor to be red hot. It at once became a matter of the utmost urgency to bring the burning reactor under control, to stop the nuclear reaction and to seal the badly damaged building from above and below. This had to be done at any cost — even at the cost of human life. As the world has learned, 31 brave men were soon dead from a massive over-exposure to radiation. 203 were admitted to hospital. All these casualties occurred as a result of on-site operations: the harm to the health of other workers and the local inhabitants cannot be assessed because of the delayed effects of exposure to radiation.

Within a short time, the decision was taken to evacuate the populations of the nearby town of Pripyat and some villages — a total of 135,000 persons who received high doses of radiation. Expert estimates suggest that a small number of these, perhaps rather more than one in a thousand, may suffer fatal cancers over, say, the next 40 years. It has been predicted that over Europe as a whole, the radioactive fallout from Chernobyl may eventually be responsible theoretically, over the next few decades for 2000 thyroid cancers, of which 100 might be fatal. The number of *all thyroid* cancers expected over the next 30-50 years is about 200,000. Fatalities from all types of cancer due to Chernobyl are predicted to be 1,000.

It has to be remembered that the radioactive cloud spread far and wide through the Soviet Union and neighbouring countries, notably Poland, Germany, Italy, France and, perhaps surprisingly, Greece. Among other Common Market countries the United Kingdom did not escape, neither did Belgium, Luxembourg, the Netherlands and Denmark. Ireland, Spain and Portugal were the least affected. The consumption and exportation of food was banned over a wide area. In some countries there was over-reaction but others were ill-prepared.

As for the Soviet Union an impressive programme of decontamination at the power station and surrounding areas was put in hand. A "safe-passage" through the affected areas was provided to enable workers to travel to and from the power station where the other 3 units are still in operation. Unit 4 was sealed with tons of clay, sand, boron, lead and dolomite. Miners put heavy concrete reinforcement into excavations below the site of the damaged reactor which is now entombed in a permanent new building.

For the local people, new settlements were built with impressive speed. The cost of compensating and re-housing the 135,000 alone has been put at the equivalent of £2,000 million. They have been well cared for. Much prolonged decontamination work will have to continue in the environment, involving thousands of Soviet troops. Contaminated vegetation and top soil will have to be stripped out for miles around. It is unsafe to step off the decontaminated roadways. There is a controlled zone 30 km round the scene of the disaster.

The reactor unit and its fuel are obviously a complete write-off. It had been operating only 3 years and would therefore be valued virtually as new. If insured, it would have doubtless been covered on the basis of full replacement value though the policy would certainly have been subject to a limit below that. This can only be speculative because no nuclear insurer has yet been asked to provide nuclear capacity for the USSR. But whatever the limit, it would have been a total insurance loss.

As to Third Party claims: there is no nuclear liability legislation. The USSR is not a party to the Vienna Convention, the power stations are State-owned and uninsured and so the national economy has to bear the heavy financial loss. This will not finally be quantified for decades, but is bound to be much higher than the initial estimate of £2,000 million*. The legal position appears to be that foreign claimants not compensated by their own Governments would have to bring actions under private international Law — an uncertain and complicated process.

As a result, six officials from the Chernobyl power station were charged with criminal negligence and appeared before a local Court in July, 1987. The 3 senior engineers were each sent to prison for 10 years; the others received shorter sentences.

References:

Atom 357, July 1986 (UKAEA)

Nuclear Europe 7-8, 1986 — Article by Dr. H.H. Herries

IAEA Bulletin — Summer 1986

Nuclear Engineering International (various issues from July 1986 onwards)

"Chernobyl" by S.G. Collier and L. Myrddin Davies (CEGB publication September 1986)

The Chernobyl Accident Sequence by T.S. Kress & others (Nuclear Safety, Vol. 28 No. 1 1987)

Numerous reports and articles in The Times, Sunday Times and Financial Times.

---

* Subsequent estimates have put the potential overall cost to the Soviet economy at £8,000 million.

APPENDIX B

Abbreviations

ABI	Association of British Insurers
AEA	Atomic Energy Authority (U.K.)
AIF	Atomic Industrial Forum (U.S.A.)
AGR	Advanced Gas-cooled Reactor
ANI	American Nuclear Insurers
BI(AE)C	British Insurance (Atomic Energy) Committee
BNES	British Nuclear Energy Society
BNF	British Nuclear Forum
BNFL	British Nuclear Fuels Ltd.
BWR	Boiling Water Reactor
CANDU	Canadian Deuterium — Uranium Reactor
CEA	1. Commissariat à l'Energie Atomique (France)
	2. Comité Européen des Assurances
CGARA	Comité Général d'Assurance du Risque Atomique
CMEA	Council for Mutual Economic Assistance
DKVG	Deutsche Kernreaktor Versicherungs-gemeinschaft (Germany)
DoE	Department of Energy (U.K.)
EEC	European Economic Community
EMANI	European Mutual Association for Nuclear Insurance (Belgium)
EPIC	Electricity Producers' Insurance Company (Isle of Man)

EURATOM	European Atomic Energy Community
FAO	Food and Agriculture Organisation
FBR	Fast Breeder Reactor
FPA	Fire Protection Association (U.K.)
GCR	Gas-cooled Reactor
HWR	Heavy Water Reactor
HSE	Health and Safety Executive (U.K.)
IAEA	International Atomic Energy Agency
ICRP	International Commission on Radiological Protection
ICU	International Commission on Radiological Units and Measurements
ILO	International Labour Organisation
ILU	Institute of London Underwriters (U.K.)
IMO	International Maritime Organisation
INLA	International Nuclear Law Association
IUMI	International Union of Marine Insurers
JAEIP	Japan Atomic Energy Insurance Pool
KAEIP	Korean Atomic Energy Insurance Pool
LOCA	Loss of Coolant Accident
LWR	Light Water Reactor
MAERP	Mutual Atomic Energy Reinsurance Pool (U.S.A)
MAFF	Ministry of Agriculture, Fisheries and Food (U.K.)
MOD	Ministry of Defence (U.K.)
NMA	Non-Marine Association (Lloyd's Underwriters — U.K.)
NIAC	Nuclear Insurance Association of Canada
NII	Nuclear Installations Inspectorate (U.K.)

NIREX	Nuclear Industry Radioactive Waste Executive, Ltd.
NNWS	Non-Nuclear Weapons States
NWS	Nuclear Weapons States
NRC	Nuclear Regulatory Commission (U.S.A.)
NRPB	National Radiological Protection Board (U.K.)
NSSS	Nuclear Steam Supply System
OECD	Organisation for Economic Co-operation and Development (formerly OEEC)
OEEC	Organisation for European Economic Co-operation (now OECD)
PNIP	Philippines Nuclear Insurance Pool
PWR	Pressurised Water Reactor
QA	Quality assurance
Rem	"Roentgen equivalent man"
R.O.A.	Reinsurance Offices' Association (U.K.)
SYBAN	Syndicat Belge d'Assurances Nucléaires
SI	Système International d'Unités
TMI	1. Three Mile Island Nuclear Power Station (U.S.A.) 2. the "TMI Accident"
UKAEA	United Kingdom Atomic Energy Authority
UNO	United Nations Organisation
WHO	World Health Organisation
WOCA	World Outside Centrally-planned-economy Area (UNO term)
YNIP	Yugoslav Nuclear Insurance Pool

GLOSSARY

(The meanings given are explanatory only, and do not have any legal authority)

A

Absorbed dose	— quantity of energy taken up by a unit amount of matter from ionising radiation measured in grays (qv)
Accelerator	— machine for increasing the energy of charged particles by accelerating them to very high speeds
Accumulation	— occurs where two or more insurance covers apply to the same risk, exposing Insurers to cumulative losses arising from the same originating cause or a series of events during the period of the insurances
Accidental criticality	— see "Criticality Incident"
Actinides	— a group of elements with atomic numbers (qv) starting with that of actinium and going up to that for lawrencium (15 in all including uranium and plutonium)
Activation	— making material radioactive by bombarding it with neutrons, protons or other nuclear particles
Activity	— the number of atoms in a quantity of radioactive substance which disintegrate in a given unit of time measured in curies or, in the more recent unit, becquerels (qv)
Actual cash value	— the current cost of replacing an article with a similar one in the same condition
Additional costs	— in material damage insurance, expenditure necessarily incurred beyond that required to make good direct damage to property in consequence of the happening of a peril insured by the policy e.g. costs of decontamination, demolition and debris removal

Advanced Gas-cooled Reactor	— developed from the British Magnox reactor but fuelled with slightly enriched uranium oxide clad in stainless steel
Agreed value	— generally means the case where the insured sum specified in a material damage insurance policy which is to be used as the basis for settling losses is fixed by agreement between the parties rather than by way of an objective valuation in accordance with, for example, the cost of replacing damaged property with new
Alpha particle	— a particle consisting of two protons and two neutrons emitted by a radionuclide identical with the nucleus of an atom of helium
Annual aggregate loss limit	— the maximum sum payable under an insurance policy per loss and in the aggregate in any one year of insurance without regard to the total amount of the values stated in the policy. Such limit is reduced by loss payments and can only be reinstated by agreement of the Insurers
Atom	— the smallest part of an element having its chemical properties that can combine chemically with other atoms
Atomic number	— the number of protons in the nucleus of an atom
Automatic reinstatement	— the immediate reinstatement of the original sum insured or policy limit following reduction in the cover as a result of paying a loss
Average	— insurance policy condition which provides that if, at the time of a loss the property damaged is found to have been insured for an amount below its true value according to the intended basis for settling claim payments, the policy holder is regarded as being his own insurer for the amount of such

under-insurance and shall therefore contribute to the loss in the proportion that the insured value falls short of the true value (also known as Proportional Rule)

B

Background radiation — the general level of natural and man-made radiations

Barn — unit of area used in neutron scattering experiments

Becquerel — unit of activity (qv) to replace the curie. It represents 1 disintegration per second or 2.7×10^{-11} (i.e. 2.7 over 10,000 million curies) (Symbol Bq)

Beta particle — an electron (or a positron if the electric charge is positive) emitted by a nucleus of a radionuclide

Binding energy — the energy required, according to theory, to separate a nucleus into neutrons and protons

Biological shield — absorbent material placed around a nuclear reactor or source of radioactivity to reduce the radiation to a safe level for human beings

Blanket — fertile material such as depleted uranium placed round the core of a Fast Reactor to capture neutrons and thus create new fissile material

Blanket policy — a policy of insurance covering a number of items for a single sum without specifying individual insurance values. Such policies should be subject to Average, or a Warranty of full value

Body-burden — the amount of radioactive or toxic substances in a body at any time

Boiling Water Reactor — one in which light water (H_2O) used both as coolant and as moderator, is allowed to boil in the core, the resultant steam being usable directly to drive a turbine

Breeder reactor — one which generates more fissile material that it consumes

Burn-up — the percentage of the fissile material in nuclear fuel "burned" or used up in the nuclear reaction

Burst — describes defect in fuel cladding, which may be no more than a pin-hole or small crack, permitting the escape of fission products into reactor coolant

C

Calandria — closed tank penetrated by pipes arranged in such a way as to prevent liquids or other substances in them from mixing

Can — the sealed container or tube in which nuclear fuel rods or pellets are contained

Canadian Deuterium Uranium Reactor — reactor developed in Canada using heavy water (D_2O) as moderator/coolant and natural uranium oxide fuel in horizontal pressure tubes surrounded by a calandria (qv)

Cartridge — a unit of canned nuclear fuel

Cascade — sequence of operations in, for example, the enrichment of uranium in which the material undergoing processing flows from one stage to the next

Cave — heavily shielded compartment or "hot cell" containing highly radioactive materials which can be remotely handled or examined in safety

Chain reaction — a process which when started is self-sustaining, such as a nuclear reaction in which the neutrons causing fission in uranium or plutonium atoms produce more neutrons which cause further fissioning and so on

Channel — vertical or horizontal channel, through the core of a nuclear reactor in a graphite moderator, into which fuel elements are inserted

Channelling — 1) in nuclear legislation, the imposition on the operator of sole legal liability for nuclear occurrences regardless of who may have been at fault;

2) escape of radiation through, for example, the shielding of a nuclear reactor

Charged particles — nuclear atomic particles having a positive or negative electric charge (i.e. not including neutrons)

Cladding — protective layer covering fuel in a nuclear fuel element

Coinsurance — 1) provision of insurance cover by two or more insurers acting in concert, each usually issuing his own policy and being directly liable to the policyholder for an agreed share of any losses

2) partial "self-insurance" by the policyholder who participates in the insurance for a fixed proportion, thus paying his rateable share of every loss

Collective effective dose equivalent — the quantity produced by multiplying the average "effective dose equivalent" (qv) by the number of persons exposed to a source of radiation ("collective dose").
Measured in "man sievert" (qv)

Common-mode failure — the failure of two or more supposedly independent parts of a system from a common external cause or from interaction between the two parts

Containment — see Reactor containment

Contribution — the sharing of a loss payment when two or more insurers cover the same subject matter against the same peril

424

on behalf of the same interest under separate insurance policies.

Controlled zone — the area within a nuclear power station or other installation where the exposure to radiation of individuals gaining access to it is individually controlled and registered by use of dosimeters

Control rod — a rod of neutron-absorbing material, such as boron or cadmium, which is moved in or out of a reactor core to control the neutrons available for fission and therefore the power of the reactor

Coolant — see Reactor coolant

Cosmic rays — ionising radiations coming from outer space, and the secondary radiation caused by their interaction with constituents of the earth's atmosphere (oxygen & nitrogen)

Coulomb — unit of electric charge (S.I. system) equal to the charge transferred by 1 ampère per second

Critical assembly or mass — minimum mass or volume of a fissile material which, in a particular arrangement, can sustain a chain reaction

Criticality — the state of a nuclear reactor, or nuclear fuel, when undergoing a sustained chain reaction

Criticality incident — the accidental accumulation of fissile material into a critical assembly or mass leading to criticality and the dangerous emission of radiation and heat ("accidental criticality")

Cross-section — measure of probability of collision between a beam of radiation and a particular particle. Measured in "barns" (qv)

Curie — unit of radioactivity — the quantity of radioactive material in which 27,000 million nuclei disintegrate per second (Symbol Ci). Replaced under the SI system by the becquerel (qv)

Cyclotron — an accelerator in which charged particles are accelerated in an outward spiral path in a magnetic field

D

Decay — the spontaneous transformation of a radionuclide through disintegration of the nucleus. The decrease in the activity of a radioactive substance

Decay heat — the heat produced by the decay of radioactive nuclides

Decay product — nuclide or radionuclide resulting from decay of a "parent" radionuclide (also called "daughter product")

Decommissioning — the process by which a nuclear installation is finally taken out of operation and put into a state of safety

Decontamination — the removal of radioactive contaminants from surfaces or equipment

Decontamination costs — insurable costs incurred to remove contamination caused by radioactivity, including the cost of cleaning contaminated property, isolation or shielding of radioactive or irradiated matter, and the treatment, packaging and removal of contaminated solids and liquids

Deductible — the first amount of each and every loss insured, expressed in money or as a percentage of the value, which a policy-holder may choose, or be required, to bear for his own account and which is, therefore, deducted from the amount of the loss otherwise payable by the insurers

Deluge system — fire control or extinguishing system with open sprinkler heads

Depleted uranium	— uranium containing less than the natural content (0.7% by weight) of U235
Design basis	— formal statement of the intended physical performance, limitations and working conditions for a system or component
Direct cycle	— reactor system in which steam is produced in the core, passed directly to a turbine, condensed and returned to the reactor
Dose equivalent	— quantity obtained by multiplying the absorbed dose (qv) by a factor allowing for the differing degrees of harmfulness to human tissue of various ionising radiations (measured in sieverts)
Dosimeter	— instrument measuring doses or dose rates received by individuals exposed to radiation
E	
Effective dose equivalent	— quantity obtained by multiplying the dose equivalents (qv) received by various human tissues or organs by a risk weighting factor (e.g. 0.25 for gonads, 0.12 for the lungs, etc)
Electron	— one of the stable elementary particles contained in all atoms carrying a negative electric charge
Element	— a substance in which the atoms all have the same atomic number
Enriched uranium	— uranium in which the U235 content has been increased to above the natural value of 0.7% by weight
Excess	— sometimes used as a synonym for the insurance term "deductible" but, more correctly, the amount of insurance cover for which a policyholder is liable for his own account, with the insurer being liable only above, or in excess of, that amount

Excursion — rapid increase of reactor power above normal operating level

F

Fail safe — safety design principle whereby the failure of equipment, an individual component or a particular device leads to a safer rather than a more dangerous condition

Fallout — the transfer of radionuclides produced by nuclear explosions or nuclear accidents from the atmosphere to earth; and/or the radioactive matter so transferred

Fast reactor — a reactor system in which most of the fissions are caused by fast neutrons (as distinct from thermal neutrons); contains no moderator (sometimes called a fast breeder reactor)

Fire area — an area, a building or a compartment of a building bounded by a fire resistive enclosure (walls, floors or ceiling) of a defined fire-rating (i.e. minimum fire-resistance rating measured in minutes)

Fire barrier — a structural barrier partially or completely limiting the spread and consequences of a fire

Fire load — calorific potential of combustible materials contained in a space, including the facings of the walls, partitions, floors and ceilings

Fire resistance — ability of an element of building construction to maintain for a stated period of time the required stability, integrity and/or thermal insulation as specified in standard fire-resistance tests

Fire-retardant — the quality of a substance as a means of suppressing, reducing or delaying the combustion of certain materials

First loss limit — agreed limit under a material damage insurance restricting the maximum amount payable in the event of a loss to a figure less than the full value of the property and/or any insured additional costs, calculated in accordance with the probable maximum loss that could be caused by one or more of the insured perils on one occasion

Fission products — fission fragments caused by the fission of heavy elements (uranium or plutonium) plus the nuclides formed by the radioactive decay of these fragments

Flammable — capable of undergoing combustion in the gaseous phase with the emission of light during or after the application of an ignition source

Flask — a heavily shielded container for storing or transporting radioactive material, notably irradiated fuel

G

Gamma rays — high energy electromagnetic radiation, similar to X-rays but more penetrative in human tissues

Gas-cooled reactor — one which is cooled by gas (normally carbon-dioxide) and usually moderated by graphite

Glove box — a protective compartment used when working with alpha-emitting radioactive materials: so-called because gloves are fitted to port holes in the wall of a transparent box to allow operators to manipulate the materials inside without risk of contact or exposure

gray — unit of absorbed dose (qv) according to the SI system (Symbol Gy). Equivalent to 100 rads under earlier units of measurement

H

Half-life
— the time taken for the activity of a radioactive substance to decay to half of its original value — i.e. for half of its atoms to disintegrate. Half lives range from less than a millionth of a second to thousands of millions of years according to the stability of the radionuclide concerned

Heat exchanger
— equipment used to transfer heat from one fluid to another, e.g. from hot gas or liquid metal in a reactor core to water and steam for turbines — without permitting the fluids to be in contact

Heavy water
— deuterium oxide (D_2O) — water in which hydrogen is replaced by heavy hydrogen which makes it a very good moderator because of its low neutron absorption compared with light water (H_2O)

Hertz
— SI unit of frequency (Symbol Hz) = 1 cycle per second

Hot work permit
— authorisation to undertake work in which sparks or locally intense heat are produced increasing the risk of fire

I

Indemnity
— principle whereby a policyholder shall benefit from insurance cover in the event of loss only to the extent that the payment he receives from his insurers shall restore him to the position he enjoyed before his loss, but no more

Indemnity basis of cover
— insurance cover based upon the true asset value (usually written down on account of age) of the property insured as distinct from the cost of replacement as new or reinstatement to its existing condition before the damage occasioning the loss

Indemnity limit	— the limit of the Insurers' liability under a policy of insurance
Indirect cycle	— reactor system in which, after leaving the core, the coolant flows through the primary side of a heat exchanger and thence back to the core
Insurance value	— the value of property as determined by the policyholder or an expert valuer as being the proper amount to be insured for full protection, according to the intended basis of cover and loss settlements
Ionisation	— process of adding electrons to, or removing them from, neutral atoms or molecules, thereby making them positively or negatively charged
Ionising radiation	— radiation of sufficiently high energy to cause ionising in matter — which can be very damaging to the molecular structure of a substance or to biological tissue
Irradiation	— exposure of material to radiation, particularly in penetrating forms such as neutrons or Gamma rays

L

Light water reactor	— one using ordinary water (H_2O) as coolant and moderator
Loss-of-coolant accident	— one in which a substantial part of the reactor coolant is lost from the primary cooling circuit while still being held within the reactor containment

M

Magnox	— an alloy of magnesium with small amounts of beryllium and aluminium used for cladding natural uranium fuel rods
Magnox reactor	— type of gas-cooled graphite-moderated reactor using Magnox-clad fuel

431

Meltdown	— a type of serious reactor accident in which the fuel becomes so overheated that part or all of it melts and collapses into the bottom of the reactor
Mixed oxide fuel	— fuel consisting of mixed dioxides of uranium (probably depleted) and plutonium, used in fast reactors in which the uranium content "breeds" new plutonium
Moderator	— material used in a reactor core to slow down high speed neutrons to increase the likelihood of fission reactions
Molecule	— the smallest portion of a substance that can exist by itself without losing its chemical properties
Monitor	— device used routinely to measure a quantity such as, in the nuclear field, levels of radiation

N

Neutron	— uncharged elementary particle forming part of the atomic nucleus, together with the proton. It occurs in all atomic nuclei except those of normal hydrogen
Nuclear fission	— the splitting of a heavy nucleus (such as uranium), usually into two, nearly equal, fast-moving fragments, accompanied by fast neutrons and Gamma rays
Nuclear island	— the section of a nuclear power station comprising the nuclear steam supply system or the nuclear installations
Nuclear park	— a single site comprising one or more nuclear power stations, with fuel manufacturing and reprocessing facilities
Nuclear wastes	— products of the nuclear energy industry, nuclear research and associated activities of no further value which, being radioactive, are subject to strict controls

Nucleons — the electrons and protons in the nucleus of the atom

Nucleus — central core of an atom bearing the positive electric charge and containing most of its mass around which electrons revolve

O

Off-gas installation — system for treating gaseous effluents, other than normal ventilation prior to release to atmosphere

Order of magnitude — a value or quantity expressed to the nearest power of 10

Outage — total time a power station is out of action and unable to deliver power

P

Photon — a particle containing a quantum (qv) of electromagnetic radiation; also regarded as a unit of energy, travelling at the speed of light

Pile — old name for a nuclear reactor (of the graphite-moderated type)

Pin — type of pencil-thin fuel cartridge (qv)

Poison — in the nuclear context, material in a reactor which reduces the reactivity by strongly absorbing neutrons

Pressure-Tube Reactor — reactor system in which fuel is contained in a large number of separate tubes through which the coolant water flows

Pressure vessel — strong-walled container usually made of thick steel or pre-stressed concrete, capable of withstanding high internal pressures. Houses the core of light-water and gas-cooled reactors and, usually, the moderator, reflector, thermal shield and control rods

Pressurised Water Reactor	— one in which light water in the pressure vessel (kept under high pressure to prevent boiling) transfers the heat from the reactor core to a heat exchanger, steam for the turbines being raised in a separate secondary circuit
Proton	— stable elementary particle forming the whole nucleus of hydrogen atoms and part of all other nuclides

Q

Quality assurance	— planned and systematic actions necessary to assure confidence that an item of equipment will give a satisfactory performance in service
Quality factor	— a figure expressing the biological harmfulness of different kinds of radiation
Quantum	— minimum amount by which properties of a system, such as energy, can change: thus, in radiation electrons are said to be discharged in quanta, not continuously

R

Radiation	— emission of electromagnetic waves or streams of particles from a radioactive source
Radiation damage	— harmful changes in materials and living organisms exposed to radiation (qv)
Radioactive wastes	— see Nuclear wastes
Radioactivity	— spontaneous disintegration of certain atomic nuclei accompanied by the emission of Alpha particles, Beta particles or Gamma radiation
Radiolysis	— decomposition of material by ionising radiation, e.g. water into hydrogen and oxygen
Radwaste	— common abbreviation for radioactive waste

Reactivity — a measure of possible departure from the critical condition where the chain reaction in a nuclear reactor is just self-sustaining (zero reactivity); applied to nuclear fuel, the ability to sustain a chain reaction

Reactor containment — gas- and pressure-tight shell or other enclosure around a reactor installation to confine fission products released in the event of an accident

Reactor coolant — fluid (gas, water or liquid metal) circulated through a reactor core (primary circuit) to carry heat generated in it to boilers or heat exchangers where water (secondary circuit) is turned into steam for the turbines

Redundancy — provision of instrumentation or control measures in duplicate or triplicate accomplishing the same essential function as other equipment to the extent that either may perform the required function. The components of systems may be identical or diverse

Reflector — material outside the core of a reactor (sometimes an extra layer of the moderator) designed to scatter back into the reactor neutrons that would otherwise be lost

Rem — "roentgen equivalent man" — old term for unit of effective radiation dose absorbed. Being replaced by the SI unit the "sievert" (qv)

Residual heat — the sum of the heat originating from radioactive decay and shut-down fission and the heat stored in reactor-related structures

Roentgen — unit of exposure to radiation based on capacity to cause ionisation (see rem)

Runaway	— increase in the power or reactivity in a nuclear reactor if not checked by the control system or stopped by the emergency shutdown system

S

Safe state	— state of plant when it is in all respects within the limits identified and specified for the purpose of limiting the risks due to that plant at any time
Safety assessment	— detailed evaluation of a nuclear installation with respect to its inherent safety, required before a permit to operate will be granted, usually carried out by the official safety authorities of the country where the plant is located
Safety rod	— one of a set of extra control rods specifically for the purpose of achieving an emergency reactor shutdown and for keeping a reactor in a safe state during maintenance
Scram	— the action of bringing about the emergency shutdown of a potentially dangerous nuclear installation
Sealed source	— a radiation source enclosed in a totally shielded capsule from which the radiation cannot leak
Sievert	— the S.I. unit of radiation dose equivalent (Symbol Sv) — the product of absorbed dose measured in grays (qv) and the quality factor (qv); 100 rem (qv)
Somatic effects	— the effects on the body of a person or animal exposed to radiation (as distinct from genetic effects)
Source term	— in the assessment of reactor safety, means the quantity and characteristics of the radioactivity that would be released to the environment in the event of a severe accident in a nuclear power plant

Spent fuel	— nuclear fuel which has been removed from a reactor having reached the end of its useful life as fuel
Sprinkler system	— fire control or extinguishing installation with normally closed sprinkler heads, the glass bulbs in which shatter when exposed to intense heat thus releasing water from the sprinkler head
Steam generator	— boiler or evaporator or heat exchanger in which the heat is used to raise steam
Sub-critical	— having insufficient reactivity to sustain a chain reaction without an additional neutron source

T

Thermal neutrons	— slowed down neutrons with the same average thermal or kinetic energy as the atoms or molecules through which they are passing
Transuranic elements	— artificial elements having heavier and more complex nuclei than uranium
Trip	— rapid automatic shutting down of a reactor when something goes wrong; sometimes spurious when caused by instrument malfunction in the absence of any deviation from normal operation

V

Vitrification	— mixing of liquid radioactive waste with materials such as borax, soda and silica which form glass; heating; and casting into thick stainless steel containers. A method of safe storage of highly radioactive fission product wastes

X

Xenon effect	— Rapid temporary poisoning (qv) of reactor through Xenon-135 building up from the decay of Iodine-131

437

Y

Yellow cake — Crude uranium oxide in concentrated form suitable for transportation

Z

Zircaloy — alloy of zirconium and tin used for cladding nuclear fuel

Appendix C

BIBLIOGRAPHY

Books

Amaldi, Ginestra — The Nature of Matter (trans.) (University of Chicago)

Glasstone, Samuel — Sourcebook on Atomic Energy (D. Van Nostrand Co. Inc; New York)

Isaacs, Alan and others (Editors) — Concise Science Dictionary (Oxford University Press)

Lamm, Vanda — The Utilization of Nuclear Energy and International Law (trans) (Akadémiai Kiadô, Budapest)

Murray, R.L. — Nuclear Energy (Pergamon Press)

Sim, D.F. — Law of Atomic Energy and Radioactive Substances (Reprint from Halsbury's Laws of England) (Butterworths)

Street and Frame — Law Relating to Nuclear Energy (Butterworths)

Tolanski, Samuel — Introduction to Atomic Physics (Longmans Green and Co.)

Yarwood, John — Atomic and Nuclear Physics (University Tutorial Press)

International Atomic Energy Agency
— Legal Series (various)
— Reference Data Series (various)
— Safety Series (various)
— Directory of Nuclear Reactors (Vols I - X)
— International Conventions on Civil Liability for Nuclear Damage

| OECD Nuclear Energy Agency | — Nuclear Legislation — Analytical Studies (various) |
| UK Atomic Energy Authority | — various publications |

"International Guidelines for Fire Protection at Nuclear Installations" (other than power stations)
— British Insurance (Atomic Energy) Committee, London

"International Guidlines for the Fire Protection of Nuclear Power Plants" — Swiss Pool for the Insurance of Nuclear Risks, Zurich

Periodicals

"Atom" (monthly)	— UKAEA
British Nuclear Energy Society Journal	
"Fire Prevention"	— Journal of Fire Protection Association (UK)
IAEA Bulletin (quarterly)	— (Vienna)
"Nuclear Engineering International" (UK) (monthly)	— Reed Business Publishing (UK)
"Nuclear Safety'	— US Department of Energy
"Nucleonics Week"	— McGraw Hill (USA)
"Nuclear Technology International" (annual)	— Sterling Publications (UK)
NEA Newsletter Nuclear Law Bulletins	— OECD Nuclear Energy Agency
Revue Générale Nucléaire (English edition)	— French Nuclear Energy Society
World Nuclear Industry Handbook	— Nuclear Engineering International (UK)

Company, etc. Reports

Amersham International plc (UK)   (Annual)
British Nuclear Fuels, plc (UK)   (Annual)
Central Electricity Generating Board (UK)   (Annual)
Commissariat à l'Energie Atomique (France)   (Annual)
UK Atomic Energy Authority   (Annual)

House of Commons Energy Committee:
— Minutes of Evidence: 14th November 1984
                          20th November 1985
(UK — Her Majesty's Stationery Office)

441

INDEX

A

German Democratic Republic   36, 50, 54, 68, 120, 134, 414.
Germany, Federal Republic of   50, 53, 57, 64, 68, 70,
    84, 94, 95, 96, 100, 102, 112, 116, 119, 120, 166, 281, 414.
Gijn, S.H. van   215.
GLEEP   34, 187.
Gomez del Campo, J.   215.
G.1 Reactor   34, 35.
Governmental Experts, Committee of   95.
Governors, Board of (IAEA)   107.
graphite   10, 39.
Graphite-moderated Reactors   33, 35, 36.
gray   15, 16.
Great Britain   134.
Greece   84, 94, 168, 213, 414.
Greek Atomic Energy Commission   40.
Greenland   241.
Greenwich Naval College   41.
Guatemala   120.
Guatemala Protocol   136.
Gulf Atomics   49.

H
Hague Protocol (1955)   135.
Hague Rules (1924)   132, 133, 138.
Hague-Visby Rules (1968)   133, 134.
Halden   43.
half-life   16, 76.
Halon-1301   316.
Handy-Whitman Index   297.
Harmonie Reactor   53.
Harwell   34, 35, 36, 42, 51.
Hawkins, W.D.   55.
Hazards Analysis   283.
HBWR   43.
Heavy Boiling Water Reactors   43.
heavy water   10, 35, 38, 55, 56.
Heavy Water-moderated Reactors   42, 55, 326.
HECTOR   36, 38.
helium   4, 5, 11, 71.
Hertel, G.E.   215.
Hervey, R.L.   101, 176.
high level waste   74.
High Radioactivity Zone   218, 234, 246, 261, 263, **305-308,**
    339, 349.

uranium trioxide   70, 73.
uranyl nitrate   70, 73.
Urey, H.C.   55.
U.S.A. 39, 40, 42, 44, 53, 55, 57, 60, 69, 70, 71, 72, 74,
   79, 102, 120, 127, 128, 187, 215, 222, 227, 234, 268,
            370, 373, 387, 401.
U.S. Atomic Energy Commission   40, 44, 48.
U.S.S.R. 36, 40, 43, 54, 55, 57, 60, 64, 68, 69, 71, 102,
          119, 120, 126, 274, 415.

V

valuation, bases of   **296-298.**
Venezuela   40.
Vienna Convention 26, 83, **101-107**, 129, 130, 131, 233, 415.
Vietnam   48.
Villard, P.   3.
violence   379.
vitrification   72.
volcanic eruption   164, 276, 291, 311, 379, 381.

W

WAGR   60.
waiting period   354.
Walton, E.T.S.   9.
Waltz Mill   41.
war risks   152, 379, 381.
Warm Zone   303, 304, 332, 333.
Warsaw Convention   135, 136, 138.
water-moderated reactors   39.
Westinghouse Corporation   41, 60.
WHO   77, 142.
Wigner, E.P.   33, 34.
Wigner energy   34, 406.
Williamsburg   223.
Windscale   34, 35, 58, 60, 406, 407.
Windscale AGR   60.
Windscale Piles   34.
windstorm   276, 311.
Winfrith Establishment   36, 45.
Wiser, H.   215.
Workmen's Compensation Insurance 90, 106, 192, 195,
            238, 358.